MILTON STUDIES

VI

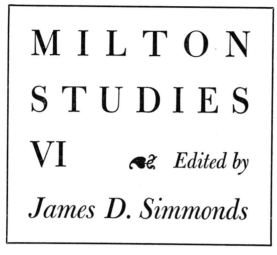

MILTON STUDIES

VI &ε *Edited by*

James D. Simmonds

UNIVERSITY OF PITTSBURGH PRESS

MILTON STUDIES

is published annually by the University of Pittsburgh Press as a forum for Milton scholarship and criticism. Articles submitted for publication may be biographical; they may interpret some aspect of Milton's writings; or they may define literary, intellectual, or historical contexts—by studying the work of his contemporaries, the traditions which affected his thought and art, contemporary political and religious movements, his influence on other writers, or the history of critical response to his work.

Manuscripts should be upwards of 3,000 words in length and should conform to the *MLA Style Sheet*. They will be returned only if sufficient postage is enclosed (overseas contributors enclose international reply coupons). Manuscripts and editorial correspondence should be addressed to James D. Simmonds, Department of English, University of Pittsburgh, Pittsburgh, Pa. 15260.

Milton Studies does not review books.

Within the United States, *Milton Studies* may be ordered from the University of Pittsburgh Press, Pittsburgh, Pa. 15260.

Overseas orders should be addressed to Feffer and Simons, Inc., 31 Union Square West, New York, N.Y. 10003, U.S.A.

Library of Congress Catalog Card Number 69–12335

ISBN 0–8229–3174–5 (Volume I) (out of print)

ISBN 0–8229–3194–x (Volume II)

ISBN 0–8229–3218–0 (Volume III)

ISBN 0–8229–3244–x (Volume IV)

ISBN 0–8229–3272–5 (Volume V)

ISBN 0–8229–3288–1 (Volume VI)

US ISSN 0076–8820

Feffer and Simons, Inc., London

Manufactured in the United States of America

CONTENTS

MILTON STUDIES
VI

MILTON ON WOMEN—YET ONCE MORE

Barbara K. Lewalski

Responding to a feminist study of *Paradise Lost* in terms of sociological role definitions, this article asserts the limitations of such analyses in assessing the true complexity of Milton's literary treatment of women, and the universality of the poem's concerns. Far from being relegated to an exclusively or primarily domestic role, Milton's Eve participates fully in the entire range of prelapsarian human activities—education, working in and sharing responsibility for the human environment (the garden), discussing and analyzing new experience, exercising her powers of symbolization in naming the plants, composing love poetry and divine praises. Milton's portrayal of the first marriage reflects his abiding belief (articulated emphatically in his divorce tracts) that the prime end of marriage as defined in the Genesis story is human companionship, not progeny or the relief of lust. Most important, despite his acceptance of the commonplace of Eve's inferiority to Adam in the natural hierarchy, Milton structured the temptation episode to manifest that she, like the Lady in *Comus*, was "sufficient to have stood." What is profound and enduring in Milton's treatment of the first man and woman is his recognition, on the one hand, of the capacity and responsibility of each to make crucial individual decisions defining his or her life, and on the other, of the depth and intensity of their need for each other to give that life human shape and to make it endurable.

I T W A S bound to happen sooner or later—a feminist analysis of Milton on women. So bad, though, has been Milton's press on the "woman question" that the exercise might have seemed hardly worth the trouble, a merely ritual beating of a very dead horse. However, Marcia Landy's article, recently published in *Milton Studies*,[1] does not merely resurrect the stereotypes of Milton the misogynist importing his own domestic problems into his poems, or Milton the Puritan necessarily echoing and reaffirming the paternalistic ethos and values of the Judeo-Christian tradition. She recognizes at the outset that a great mythopoeic writer reworks and re-creates the myths he inherits, out of "his own consciousness and . . . the consciousness of his time."[2] Nevertheless, her analysis of familial roles and relationships in *Paradise Lost*, culminating in a description of Milton's Eve as a submissive and dependent wife relegated to domestic tasks and valued chiefly for her procreative role, seems to me to miss what is most important in Milton's presentation of the "two great Sexes [which] animate the World" (VII, 151).[3]

Professor Landy begins with a short list of distinguished women Miltonists—which could have been much extended—and then calls attention to the anomaly that none of them has yet attempted a feminist analysis of his work. Of course it may be true, as the article implies, that our consciousnesses have not been raised far enough to permit us to relax the posture of scholarly objectivity imposed by a male-dominated critical climate, so as to be able to treat the poem from the vantage point of female experience. I suspect, though, that it is not so much naiveté about the necessary limits of scholarly objectivity that has deterred us from this enterprise (Miltonists, men and women alike, have always been ready enough to create Milton in their own images) so much as a different set of theoretical and methodological assumptions about how we experience, and what we value in, poems and especially this poem.

My own reservations concerning feminist critiques generally and this article in particular emerge from the following presuppositions. (1) After assenting readily enough to the proposition that our perceptions of art are necessarily affected in important ways by race, class, or sex, I would yet affirm the capacity of great art to transcend these lesser categories of human experience and speak to our common humanity. Which of us, male or female, old or young, black or white, rich or poor, does not understand and respond to King Lear's agony on his heath? On this score, a feminist analysis of *Paradise Lost*, with its nearly exclusive emphasis upon the image and role of woman in the poem, may do real violence to a woman reader's imaginative experience of and response to everything else that the poem contains—Satan's rebellion, Adam's intellectual quest, the idyl of Edenic life, the heroism of Abdiel, the glorious vitality of the Creation scene, and much more. (2) Feminist criticism often seems prone to substitute sociological for literary analysis. Though

the article in question incorporates considerable literary detail, still the
categories imported from sociology and anthropology—the analysis of
family roles—provide a very partial set of terms for approaching the
portrayal of Adam and Eve in the poem. It will not surprise any of us,
surely, to discover that Milton, like everyone else in his era, thought in
terms of hierarchy and of the patriarchal family. But an analysis centered almost exclusively upon the language and postures of family relationship necessarily imposes a conventional and somewhat distorted
framework for examining Milton's re-creation of the myth of the first
man and woman. To see that re-creation clearly requires a sensitive
literary analysis of speech, scene, and action in the poem. (3) Great poets
of necessity mediate their visions of human experience through the categories available to them, but if we read perceptively we will not be
tempted either to condemn them or to condescend to them on that account. We will not, because they are gloriously and supremely right
about the most essential things, presenting us with a vision of the human
condition which astonishes by its profundity even though the categories
through which it is rendered may be outmoded. Homer of course presented the Trojan War against the backdrop of Olympus and all those
now defunct gods, but no one has known or shown more fully the utter
futility, the pointless brutality, the moral deterioration attendant upon
protracted warfare. (The *Iliad* should perhaps be made required reading
for presidents and Pentagon officials.) Dante of course perceived his
universe in Ptolemaic and Thomistic categories, but no one of any age
has shown more vividly or analyzed more trenchantly the modes, varieties, and postures of human evil—particularly those of the intellectual
order. And Milton of course accepted the categories of hierarchy and the
natural inferiority of woman, yet his reworking of the Adam and Eve
myth has explored with remarkable incisiveness and profundity a basic
human predicament. Each character is shown to bear full individual responsibility for his or her own choices, his or her own growth (or lack
of it), his or her own contribution to the preservation and perfecting of
the human environment; but at the same time, each experiences to the
depths of his soul the need for the other, the inescapable bonds of human interdependence. And the truly surprising thing about Milton's
portrayal of Eve is that he has examined this dilemma as carefully in
regard to the woman as to the man. Indeed, I am tempted to say that few
writers of any era—including our own—have taken women so seriously

as Milton does, as multifaceted human beings with impressive intellectual and moral powers and responsibilities.

That apparently outrageous statement will take some proving, and I will begin with a few clarifications regarding Eve's role and activities in Eden. The point here is that, far from being relegated to an exclusively or primarily domestic role, Eve in the ideal (prelapsarian) human marriage is shown to participate fully in the entire range of human activities. That the division of labor along sexual lines is a concomitant of the Fall is more than hinted in Book IX, when Eve's proposal that they undertake separate gardening tasks as a means to greater efficiency is shown to lead directly to the Fall. The Edenic condition is a life of sharing and partnership in almost all activities: for Adam, Eve is "Sole partner and sole part of all these joys" (IV, 411). To be sure, Eve does prepare and serve the noonday meal when Raphael pays his visit (they didn't share the cooking—or rather, the selection, pressing, and setting forth of the fruits from the abundance Edenic Nature provides). But Eve is not off about these tasks while the gentlemen talk about higher things—the dilemma of the modern hostess. It is all accomplished in the moments from Adam's first view of the approaching angel to the time of his arrival in Eden. Nor does Eve withdraw for the washing-up while the gentlemen have their port and cigars: it is curious that many readers (including Professor Landy) seem not to notice that Eve is present throughout almost the whole of the series of lectures Raphael provides to satisfy the first couple's intellectual curiosity about their world. She is thus as fully instructed as Adam is about the substance of the universe —"one first matter all"—and the curiously fluid conception of hierarchy this monism sustains, according to which angels and men are seen to differ in degree only, not in kind, and human beings are encouraged to expect the gradual refinement of their own natures to virtually angelic condition (V, 470–505).[4] (How much more fluid, then, the hierarchical distinctions between man and woman?) Eve is present also for the epic account of the War in Heaven and all the vicarious insights that story provides about the nature of evil, of temptation, of obedience and fidelity. Again, she is present for the account of the Creation—graphically described, as Michael Lieb and others have shown,[5] in terms of the imagery of human sexuality—and therefore is led, as Adam is, to apprehend that sexuality as participation in God's divine creativity. She departs only when Adam poses his astronomical question—and then not because the men wish her gone (her grace "won who saw to wish her stay" [VIII, 43]), nor yet because of any incapacity: "Yet went she not, as not with such discourse / Delighted, or not capable her ear / Of what was high" (VIII, 48–50). In part she leaves for dramatic convenience so that Adam may discuss his marital problem with Raphael, and, as the poet insists, she will receive all the information later, from Adam's account. The prelapsarian educational curriculum, then, is precisely the same for the woman as for the man—ontology, cosmology, metaphysics, moral philosophy, history, epic poetry, divine revelation, physics, and astronomy. And the method is the same except in regard to the last-mentioned topic—though Adam does indeed take the initiative throughout by asking the lecturer leading questions. This identity of educational experiences for the sexes was hardly a conventional concept in the mid-seventeenth century, though it is entirely consonant with Milton's sense of marriage as, in its essence, human companionship and partnership.

Fully shared work in and responsibility for the human world is hardly a seventeenth-century (or even a twentieth-century) commonplace either, yet it is central to Milton's rendering of the Edenic life. As I have argued in more detail elsewhere,[6] both Adam and Eve are images of God "the sovran Planter" in that they must preserve, cultivate, sustain, and raise to higher levels of perfection the world which has been made for them. This labor, though not arduous, is absolutely essential since the highly cultivated garden, made as all things are from the materials of chaos, will revert to wilderness without constant creative ordering. Adam observes in Book IV (623–32) that the couple can barely cope on a day-to-day basis with the "wanton growth" of the garden, to maintain it in a condition of ordered beauty; indeed, at times it is marred by "overgrown" paths and "unsightly" blossoms strewn about. Later Eve makes the same point: the work is "Our pleasant task," yet "what we by day / Lop overgrown, or prune, or prop, or bind, / One night or two with wanton growth derides / Tending to wild" (IX, 207–12). The narrator also testifies to the truth of this description—"much thir work outgrew / The hands' dispatch of two Gard'ning so wide" (IX, 212–13)—though both expect the task to be easier when they have progeny to share it. The point, however, is that Eve, far from being confined to her

bower and her domestic concerns while Adam forges forth in the outside world, is imagined to share fully with her mate in the necessary work
of that world.

   She shares as well in all the other duties and pleasures, all the other
kinds of human self-expression and creativity that the poem records.
Not least among these is the delight of simple human conversation and
dialogue, the constant, ongoing discussion with Adam about the flood
of new observations and experiences that bursts in upon them day by
day—whether the mystery of the stars shining at night, or the sudden
challenge of hospitality for an angelic guest, or the untoward occurrence
of a bad dream, or whatever. Eve participates with Adam also in "naming" the lesser orders of creation, thereby showing her comprehension
of their natures, her rightful dominion over them, and her command
of the human power of symbolization. That Adam named the animals
and she the plants is indicated when she laments the leaving of her beloved flowers, "which I bred up with tender hand / From the first
op'ning bud, and gave ye Names" (XI, 276–77). She names a lesser order
of creation than Adam (hierarchy again), but she shares in the activity,
a point unperceived by many critics, including Professor Landy, who
take Adam's supposedly exclusive naming function as evidence that
poetry and the arts of language are for Milton a masculine prerogative.[7]
But Eve's command of the arts of language is evident throughout the
poem. She is no mean rhetorician, as her graceful, ritualistic addresses
to Adam demonstrate—as does, in another mode, her skillful argumenta-
tion in the marital dispute. She is a poet as well, composing each day
with Adam those divine poems and praises of God which they both in
"various style" and in "fit strains pronounct or sung / Unmeditated."
As the narrator observes, "prompt eloquence / Flow'd from thir lips, in
Prose or numerous Verse, / More tuneable than needed Lute or Harp"
(V, 146–51). Eve is also a poet in her own right: nothing in Milton's
epic is more artful, melodious, and graceful than the love lyric she addresses to Adam (IV, 641–56) which begins, "Sweet is the breath of
morn." To be sure, it is not in the highest genre of poetry according to
the common Renaissance scale or Milton's own, but of its kind it is
superb.

   Enough has perhaps been said to establish the point that Eve,
though perceived as Adam's hierarchical inferior, is not relegated to the
domestic sphere, nor her creativity confined to her maternal role; rather

she—"accomplisht Eve" (IV, 660)—shares and participates in the full range of human activities and achievements. But Professor Landy's further point about Milton's emphasis upon Eve's maternity as that which is somehow necessary to validate her sexual relation to Adam[8] ought to be confronted directly. On this issue, two observations may be made. In the first place, it should be observed that Adam is as constantly and honorifically addressed in terms alluding to his paternity of the human race as Eve is in relation to her maternity: such language is not intended to limit either one to the confines of the familial role (the inadequacies of the sociological analysis become clearest here) but rather to insist upon the honor and dignity shared by both as progenitors of the entire human race. The narrator constantly refers to them in such terms, thereby relating himself and his readers to them as their descendants. They are "our Grand Parents" (I, 29); Eve is "our general Mother" (IV, 492); Adam is "our first Father" (IV, 495) or again "our great Progenitor" (V, 544). Similarly, in his epithalamion to them—"Hail Wedded Love" (IV, 751–75)—the narrator in his emphasis upon their progeny adopts again the perspective of one of their descendants, besides of course conforming to the norms of the genre. Raphael, who addresses Eve in the striking phrase foreshadowing the later *Ave* to the Virgin—"Hail Mother of Mankind" (V, 388)—addresses Adam in similar terms—"Sire of men" (VIII, 218). And while Eve recalls that when she was first presented to Adam she was promised that she would "bear / Multitudes like thyself, and thence be call'd / Mother of human Race," Adam similarly recalls that in his own first moments after creation a divine voice referred to his role as patriarch: "Adam, rise / First Man, of Men innumerable ordain'd / First Father" (IV, 296–98). These terms are not sociological or anthropological role definitions, but praises of the human participation in the superabundant divine creativity.

Second, the text of the poem does not sustain the assertion that the recognition of Eve as mother is prior to and sanction for her roles as lover and spouse. She is certainly not so presented to the reader, who first sees Eve as a young girl on her honeymoon, her hair disheveled in wanton ringlets, engaged in "youthful dalliance" and casual love play with her husband (IV, 304–40).[9] Nor is she so perceived by Adam, who in his long argument with God urges and demonstrates most forcefully his need for a mate—not for progeny but for companionship: "Of fellowship I speak / Such as I seek, fit to participate / All rational delight"

(IV, 289–91). And when he claims her as his wife after she makes a move to turn from him back to her own "wat'ry image," he does so in terms of his desire for her as companion and lover: she was made of his flesh and bone that she might be "Henceforth an individual solace dear; / Part of my Soul . . . My other half" (IV, 486–88). God in establishing their marriage sets forth the same order of priorities: commending Adam for his sound argument and agreeing to his request, God observes, "I, ere thou spak' st, / Knew it not good for Man to be alone," and he promises to bring to Adam "Thy likeness, thy fit help, thy other self" (VIII, 444–50). Also, Eve records that when the divine voice wooed her from the contemplation of her own image in the pool it promised first that she would "enjoy him / Whose image thou art," and only then that she would bear "Multitudes like thyself" and be called "Mother of human Race" (IV, 472–75). And even that last reference, in context, is not so much an emphasis upon her maternity as such as upon her opportunity now to exchange illusory images for true ones, which she can bring into substantial existence.

This emphasis upon marriage as human companionship is precisely what we should expect from the Milton of the divorce tracts, those remarkable documents which argued for divorce on grounds of incompatibility, precisely on the assumption that the prime end of marriage, as defined authoritatively in the Genesis story, is human companionship. The argument seemed both preposterous and scandalous to Milton's contemporaries, who had learned from the Church Fathers, the medieval scholastics, and most of the Protestant theologians that marriage was instituted primarily for progeny and the relief of lust (in recognition of which priorities the various Protestant countries permitted divorce or annulment for impotence, adultery, or desertion) and only secondarily for mutual help and assistance.[10] But Milton insists that the Genesis account bears out his own emphasis upon the companionship of the mind and spirit as the chief end of marriage:

What his [God's] chiefe end was of creating woman to be joyned with man, his own instituting words declare, and are infallible to informe us what is mariage, and what is no mariage . . . "It is not good," saith he, "that man should be alone; I will make him a help meet for him." From which words so plain, lesse cannot be concluded . . . then that in God's intention a meet and happy conversation is the chiefest and the noblest end of mariage; for we find here no expression so necessarily implying carnall knowledg, as this prevention of lonelinesse to the mind and spirit of man. . . . And indeed it is a greater blessing from God, more worthy so excellent a creature as man is, and a higher end to honour and sanctifie the league of mariage, whenas the solace and satisfaction of the mind is regarded and provided for before the sensitive pleasing of the body. And with all generous persons maried thus it is, that where the minde and person pleases aptly, there some unaccomplishment of the bodies delight may be better borne with, then when the mind hangs off in an unclosing disproportion, though the body be as it ought; for there all corporall delight will soon become unsavoury and contemptible.[11]

It is true that Milton sets forth his argument for divorce almost entirely from the standpoint of the needs and rights of the husband. But it is also evident that despite Milton's acceptance of the commonplace of female subordination in the natural hierarchy, he did not make of women either sex objects or mother figures. Indeed, the passage quoted and the entire drift of the divorce tracts show him to be as convinced as even a modern feminist might wish that the dispelling of these particular stereotypes of woman is of the first importance to the happiness of the male sex.

To come now to what is of basic significance in Milton's reworking of the myth of Adam and Eve—his exploration, on the one hand, of each individual's personal responsibility for his own choices, for the direction of his own life; and on the other hand, of the powerful emotional, psychological, and spiritual bonds which make man and woman inextricably interdependent. In the course of this exploration, Milton's treatment of the archetypal woman achieves extraordinary depth and dimension.

Before and after the Fall, both Adam and Eve show some disposition to avoid or lessen the tensions involved in hard choices or the guilt attendant upon wrong choices by appealing to the fact of their interdependence to cast responsibility upon each other. But the poem permits this rationale to neither of them: each is "Sufficient to have stood, though free to fall" (IV, 99), and each must assume responsibility for his own choices. Adam is lightly satirized on several occasions as he pronounces the time-honored male complaints about women as the source of all difficulties and problems and then is roundly rebuked for his foolishness by whatever heavenly visitant is on the scene at the time. In his still unfallen state Adam complains to Raphael (who assumes for the moment the role of the first marriage counselor) that the passion he feels for Eve tends to unsettle his judgment of her qualities and her nature in relation to his own and concludes that the fault is somehow Eve's (or Nature's): she has been made too fair, or Nature has made

him too weak by taking too much from his side in making her. But
Raphael will have none of it: the angel does not assume that the tension
and difficulty Adam is experiencing are out of place in Eden, but rather
"with contracted brow" he places the responsibility for dealing with
them squarely on Adam's shoulders: "Accuse not Nature, she hath done
her part; / Do thou but thine" (VIII, 561–62). This tendency in Adam
is strengthened after the Fall and is expressed in several tirades against
Eve and all womankind. Nothing in Milton's treatment of the first human couple is more sharply perceived than the inevitable transformation—when the pressure of suffering and guilt make the heroic posture
impossible to sustain—of the self-sacrificing romantic hero ready to die
with his lady into a cad ready to denounce that same lady before the bar
of God's judgment in an effort to excuse himself. Eve on that occasion
was "not before her Judge / Bold or loquacious" and her simple confession—"The Serpent me beguil'd, and I did eat" (X, 160–62)—contrasts
impressively with Adam's garrulous complaints against both the woman
and the God who gave him to her:

> This Woman whom thou mad'st to be my help,
> And gav'st me as thy perfet gift, so good,
> So fit, so acceptable, so Divine,
> That from her hand I could suspect no ill,
> And what she did, whatever in itself,
> Her doing seem'd to justify the deed;
> She gave me of the Tree, and I did eat   (X, 137–43)

But he is not indulged in this blame-shifting: the stern judge insists that
he had no business making her his God, nor yet (given her general inferiority to him) his guide in this momentous matter. Later, in the exchange with Michael, Adam shows that he still has not learned his
lesson, as he comments on the daughters of Cain, "But still I see the
tenor of Man's woe / Holds on the same, from Woman to begin" (XI,
632–33). Michael, however, gives such misogynist platitudes short shrift,
retorting sharply, "From Man's effeminate slackness it begins" (XI, 634).

Eve just after the Fall is also ready to shift her guilt to Adam, observing that he should have forbidden her absolutely to go off to work by
herself: "Being as I am, why didst not thou the Head / Command me
absolutely not to go, / Going into such danger as thou said'st" (IX,
1156–58). Many critics who write about the marital dispute take the
same tack, assuming that what was finally required of Adam should all

else fail was a flat command. But this is to miss the point badly: as marriage is conceived in Eden, Adam is Eve's superior and appointed guide, but not her lord and master. Eve is no dependent child-wife: her choices are and must be freely her own, and she bears adult responsibility for them, even as Adam does for his.[12] Adam is accordingly indignant at Eve's words, as a flagrant misrepresentation of the terms of their relationship:

> I warn'd thee, I admonish'd thee, foretold
> The danger, and the lurking Enemy
> That lay in wait; beyond this had been force,
> And force upon free Will hath here no place   (IX, 1171–74)

Indeed, what came to be required of Eve during the marital dispute was not at all childlike dependence but a level of maturity which she (like most of her progeny) could not quite manage in the heat of disputation —the ability to give over an erroneous position without seeking to save face, the grace to admit and be persuaded by the better arguments, and the willingness to eschew too hardy adolescent adventure-seeking in response to counsels of prudence. Adam also needed more maturity than he was master of in the dispute—notably, the capacity to stand up to prolonged emotional pressure without caving in before it.

We are given early on a model of how Adam's leadership should properly function, so as to preserve and enhance Eve's freedom of choice, personal growth, and adult responsibility. This is at the scene of Eve's presentation to Adam when she turns from him back to the fairer image of herself in the water, and Adam proceeds to urge his claim to her firmly and rationally, on the grounds of her origin and nature, and his love. The alternatives thus sharply posed permit Eve to make her choice —to advance from the sterile condition of self-admiration, "pin'd with vain desire" (IV, 466), to human relationship and love, and on the basis of her new experience to adjust her scale of values, recognizing the superiority of wisdom over beauty. In terms of this model we can see what went wrong in the marital dispute. Adam not only ceased to press his own case forcefully and rationally under the pressure of Eve's dismay, but at length he virtually sent her away, supplied with a rationale for going which she had not thought of for herself:

> But if thou think, trial unsought may find
> Us both securer than thus warn'd thou seem'st,

> Go; for thy stay, not free, absents thee more;
> Go in thy native innocence, rely
> On what thou hast of virtue, summon all,
> For God towards thee hath done his part, do thine   (IX, 370–75)

This is a serious abnegation of Adam's proper leadership role: he ought not to command Eve, but neither ought he to argue her case for her. It is as if he had said on that earlier occasion, "If you really want to go back and stare at yourself in that pond, go ahead; it might turn out to be a useful experience." The result is that instead of enhancing Eve's freedom of choice Adam has restricted it, for in the charged emotional climate of their dispute—offered this new reason for going and hearing the reiterated emphatic directive, "Go"—Eve could hardly make another choice if she wanted to. She *is* still responsible for her choice for all that, though Adam has unintentionally made it much harder for her to choose rightly. Her uneasiness about the decision is reflected in the fact that she seeks at once to place responsibility for the decision upon Adam:

> With thy permission then, and thus forewarn'd
> Chiefly by what thy own last reasoning words
> Touch'd only, that our trial. when least sought,
> May find us both perhaps far less prepar'd,
> The willinger I go—   (IX, 378–82)

It must be emphasized, however, that Milton's Eve is not foredoomed to fall before Satan's wiles because her intellectual powers are comparatively weaker than Adam's. Abdiel apparently had no great reputation as an intellectual giant among the angels, but he did very well in his debate with Satan by holding fast to the main point. In Eve's case, Milton has taken some pains to devise the temptation sequence so as to demonstrate that she was intellectually "sufficient to have stood." We see evidence of this sufficiency in her wry comment upon Satan's fulsome flattery: "Serpent, thy overpraising leaves in doubt / The virtue of that Fruit, in thee first prov'd" (IX, 615–16). She is evidently enjoying the flattery, but she is perfectly aware that it *is* flattery, and that the element of falsehood might indeed call into question the "virtue of that Fruit." She does not take the warning from this that she should, but intellectually her perception is quite sound. Later, when she first discovers that the tree the serpent spoke of was indeed the forbidden tree, she shows that she understands clearly the basic principle needed to withstand Satan's subsequent argument—the fact that the tree lies under the special and direct prohibition of God (and hence outside the law of reason), whereas in all other matters Adam and Eve are guided by the law of reason:

> But of this Tree we may not taste nor touch;
> God so commanded, and left that Command
> Sole Daughter of his voice; the rest, we live
> Law to ourselves, our Reason is our Law.   (IX, 651–54)

Satan's entire strategy from this point forward is to confuse the two categories of law which Eve here distinguishes so precisely—to develop, that is, a plethora of reasons and rational arguments demonstrating the probable harmlessness of the tree and the probable benefits to be gained from eating its fruit. But such rational considerations are in this single case quite beside the point, as Eve had perceived clearly enough in the speech cited. In testimony to her soundness at this point in the poem, the narrator uses the epithet "yet sinless" to describe her—for the last time. She is soon brought by Satan's magnificent rhetoric and her own unruly desires to lose her hold on this clear distinction, permitting herself to be bedazzled and deluded by those arguments. But my point is that among the many complex factors involved in Eve's fall, one which is specifically excluded is insufficient intellectual power. Milton has taken great care to present the first woman as having faculties "sufficient" to make free and responsible choices—always for Milton the precondition for any practice of or growth in virtue.

In another genre and in the setting of the fallen world Milton portrays a girl who successfully resists a highly intelligent tempter—and indeed overmatches him in intellectual argument. The Lady in *Comus* is no one's favorite Miltonic character, I suppose, but she certainly displays woman's sufficiency to meet the challenges of life and to make free and responsible choices. At the time of her temptation this Lady is also without her appointed male protectors, her brothers, though quite without her intention or fault. Moreover, this Miltonic Lady has a firmer intellectual grasp of the realities of life in the "blind mazes of this tangl'd Wood" (181) than have her brothers: the Platonizing Elder Brother, serenely confident of the power of Chastity, tends to confuse his sister with Diana the huntress, invulnerable to harm and able for all conquests (420–46); the fearful Younger Brother is convinced that she is helpless alone and certain to be ravished (393–407). The Lady, though, is quite aware that she is not invulnerable, but she knows also that she may rely with confidence upon her own virtue and the aid of heaven to withstand such trials as may present themselves. While lost, she decides her course of action by a rational appraisal of the options available to her: she follows the noises heard in the dark wood though she perceives them to be "the sound / of Riot and ill-manag'd Merriment" (171–72) because she must ask directions of someone; and she accepts the disguised Comus' offer of shelter because she has no grounds for distrusting the supposed shepherd, and because it seems that she could not be "In a Place / Less warranted than this or less secure" (326–27). But she is neither naive nor credulous: she knows that in the dark wood and in the human condition one cannot know all the circumstances bearing upon such decisions, and her prayer as she follows Comus indicates an awareness that there may be difficulties to come: "Eye me blest Providence, and square my trial / To my proportion'd strength" (329–30).

In her long debate with Comus, the Lady claims only to be able to preserve her mind inviolate: "Fool, do not boast, / Thou canst not touch the freedom of my mind / With all thy charms" (662–64). She is not proof against violence, nor against the forces of natural sensuality represented by Comus, which have power to "immanacle" her body "while Heav'n sees good" (665). But to preserve the freedom of her mind in intellectual debate with Comus is no mean feat, especially since many critics of the poem have been so thoroughly bedazzled by his "dear Wit and gay Rhetoric" (790) as to suppose that he wins the debate, or at least finishes in a draw.[13] The Lady's debating strategies differ from those of her opponent, to be sure, but an examination of her speech and of Comus' response to it reveals clearly enough that the victory is hers. She meets the first point, the issue of the nature of Nature, by denouncing with keen logical incisiveness the "false rules prankt in reason's garb" (759) which Comus derives from his eloquent description of a Nature so lavish and excessively abundant in her productivity as to require man's incessant and prodigal rifling of her ever-burgeoning stores of goods and beauties. The Lady did not require the instruction of modern ecologists to perceive that this is an absurd description of the postlapsarian world, that Nature did not intend that "her children should be riotous / With her abundance" (763–64), and that indeed,

> If every just man that now pines with want
> Had but a moderate and beseeming share
> Of that which lewdly-pamper'd Luxury
> Now heaps upon some few with vast excess,
> Nature's full blessings would be well dispens't
> In unsuperfluous even proportion,
> And she no whit encumber'd with her store.   (768–74)

I think we may agree that the Lady wins this point. The other issue, the value and power of Chastity and Virginity, she simply refuses to debate with Comus, for the same reason that Christ counseled against casting pearls before swine, or Socrates remarked the futility of describing to a sensual man the higher joys of the intellectual life[14]—the sheer incapacity of the hearer to understand the argument. But the Lady is stirred by her subject to display something of that "flame of sacred vehemence" (795) which, she asserts, would characterize her praise of "the sage / And serious doctrine of Virginity" (786–87), should she deign to undertake the topic. And however the reader might understand the specific import and the merit of her subject, she makes her point with Comus. He confesses his sense that "some superior power" sets off her words, bathing him in a "cold shudd'ring dew" (801–02), and, conscious of defeat, he gives over the debate and turns to force. Of the strength and sufficiency of this woman's intellect and character, I think we can have no doubt.

Milton does then examine at length the inescapable, individual challenge of responsible choice as it affects women as well as men, insisting that (whatever the mitigating personal or social circumstances) each is sufficient to meet whatever trials may come. But he examines also, with equal care, the strong bonds of human interdependence. Adam and Eve create problems for each other, even in Eden, yet each needs the other to achieve anything resembling a human life, or to experience that life as worth living. Adam makes this point forcefully in his own case: although he is given Eden and all the earth as his domain, he yet finds himself unsatisfied and so pleads with God for a mate. Arguing that he is neither a beast able to find companionship with other beasts, nor yet a God sufficient unto himself, he articulates man's great need of human fellowship—"By conversation with his like to help, / Or solace his defects" (VIII, 418–19). Adam's fall, as we know, is chiefly motivated by his sudden, overwhelming consciousness of loneliness and misery in a world lacking his beloved companion:

> How can I live without thee, how forgo
> Thy sweet Converse and Love so dearly join'd,
> To live again in these wild Woods forlorn?
> Should God create another *Eve,* and I
> Another Rib afford, yet loss of thee
> Would never from my heart.   (IX, 908–13)

Eve has a similar awareness of her need of Adam, for she knows she would still be staring at her image in the pool had not the divine voice brought her to him—"There I had fix't / Mine eyes till now, and pin'd with vain desire" (IV, 465–66). She expresses this awareness also in her beautiful love lyric, which catalogues all the sweet delights in Eden and then culminates in the statement that none of these "without thee is sweet" (IV, 656).

The Fall intensifies their need for companionship and mutual help. Eve, recoiling before Adam's fierce rage—"Out of my sight, thou Serpent" (X, 867)—gives expression to the desolation and aimlessness her life must have without him in these sad new conditions:

> bereave me not,
> Whereon I live, thy gentle looks, thy aid,
> Thy counsel in this uttermost distress,
> My only strength and stay: forlorn of thee,
> Whither should I betake me, where subsist?   (X, 918–22)

Adam's necessity to her (and hers to him) is again evidenced after their reconciliation, as his reasoned critique of her recommendation of sterility or suicide as means for saving their progeny from woe clarifies for them both the divine plan for salvation—penitence, and reliance upon the redeemer to be born of Eve's seed. Indeed, despite Adam's harsh denunciations of Eve and of all womankind under the impetus of his terrible misery, Eve is, if anything, shown to be even more necessary to Adam than he to her. For although their reconciliation with each other and with God is in the final analysis made possible by the removal of the "stony" from their hearts by "prevenient Grace" (XI, 3–4), Eve is the human agent of Adam's salvation, bringing him from the utter hopelessness and immobility of despair to some capacity for thought and action. Without her, he must have remained groveling on the ground, helpless and hopeless, driven into an "Abyss of fears / And horrors . . . out of which / I find no way, from deep to deeper plung'd" (X, 842–44). It is Eve's persistent admissions of guilt, pleas for forgiveness, and expressions of love that revive in Adam those feelings and emotions which bind him to his kind and make life seem again endurable. Eve's behavior breaks through the syndrome of mutual recriminations into which they were heretofore locked, thus making reconciliation possible. Moreover, in her offer to plead with God to transfer upon her the entire sentence of punishment, she echoes the Son's offer to die for man—an inadequate human type of the divine heroism to be sure, but yet the immediate cause of the "redemption" of Adam from his self-destructive anger and despair.[15] Much as he valued intellect, Milton did not forget the superiority of love in the Christian scale of values, and in his reworking of the Adam and Eve myth it is the woman who is made a type of the Messiah's redemptive love.

In that unforgettable final scene, as Adam and Eve "hand in hand with wand'ring steps and slow, / Through *Eden* took thir solitary way" (XII, 648–49), we are again reminded of the depth of our need for each other on this "subjected Plain" as friends, lovers, husbands, and wives. And the verbal paradox of the last lines—"hand in hand," "solitary"—underscores again the basic human dilemma Milton has pointed up with such honesty and clarity in his re-creation of the myth of the first man and woman: on the one hand, the capacity and responsibility of both Adam and Eve for "solitary" choices defining the direction of their own lives, and on the other, their intense need of each other to give that life human shape and to make it endurable. The complexity and profundity of this view of the human condition is matched by few writers, even among those more enlightened about the matter of woman's equality. If our rightful contemporary concern with this equality prevents some readers from perceiving or responding to the Miltonic vision, that is surely unfortunate. Happily, though, great poets have a way of rising like phoenixes from whatever ashes are left in the wake of social and intellectual revolutions, so no doubt it will not be long before we can all again read Milton for what is of enduring importance rather than what is historically conditioned in his conception of man and woman.

Brown University

NOTES

1. "Kinship and the Role of Women in *Paradise Lost*," *Milton Studies*, IV, ed. James D. Simmonds (Pittsburgh, 1972), pp. 3–18.

2. Ibid., p. 5.

3. All quotations from Milton's poetry are from *John Milton: Complete Poems and Major Prose*, ed. Merritt Y. Hughes (New York, 1957).

4. For further development of this point, see Irene Samuel, *Dante and Milton* (Ithaca, N.Y., 1966), pp. 146–62.

5. *The Dialectics of Creation: Patterns of Birth and Regeneration in "Paradise Lost"* (Amherst, Mass., 1970), esp. pp. 56–78; Joseph Summers, *The Muse's Method* (London, 1962), pp. 112–46.

6. "Innocence and Experience in Milton's Eden," in *New Essays on "Paradise Lost,"* ed. Thomas Kranidas (Berkeley, 1969), pp. 86–117.

7. "Kinship and the Role of Women," p. 7.

8. Ibid., pp. 9–11.

9. Professor Landy's argument seems to invest the term "matron" as it appears in Milton's poem with a somewhat misleading sense: "The first human kiss recorded is placed on Eve's 'Matron lip,' and this identification as mother seems to precede that as spouse." Of course the Latin etymology is clear enough, and Milton often played on etymological meanings, but the *OED* indicates that from its first recorded use in English (1375) to Milton's own time the term "matron" meant simply "married woman."

10. See Ernest Sirluck, ed., "Introduction" to *Complete Prose Works of John Milton* (New Haven, 1959), II, 137–58. To be sure, Milton could and did cite notable Protestant Reformers—chiefly Bucer, Calvin, Fagius, Pareus, and Rivetus—as authorities for some parts of his argument, but the total view of marriage and divorce as set forth by Milton was far outside the mainstream of contemporary opinion.

11. *The Doctrine and Discipline of Divorce*, in *Complete Prose Works*, II, 245–46.

12. This point has been argued cogently and persuasively by Stella P. Revard, "Eve and the Doctrine of Responsibility in *Paradise Lost*," *PMLA*, LXXXVIII (1973), 69–78.

13. See, e.g., Don C. Allen, *The Harmonious Vision* (Baltimore, Md., 1954), pp. 24–40; E. M. W. Tillyard, *Studies in Milton* (London, 1960), pp. 87–96; and Cleanth Brooks and J. W. Hardy, eds., *Poems of Mr. John Milton* (New York, 1968), pp. 215–23.

14. Matthew vii, 6; Plato, *Republic*, IX, 581–86.

15. This link between Eve's speech and the Redeemer's is noted by Summers, *Muse's Method*, pp. 176–85. Cf. *PL* III, 236–41 and X, 932–36.

MILTON AND THE RENAISSANCE CIRCE

Leonora Leet Brodwin

Milton's lifelong preoccupation with the Circe myth has not previously been given comprehensive analysis and, where noted, has been misjudged through exclusive reference to the allegorized Circe of Renaissance mythographers, an allegorical approach to brutishness Milton uniquely associates with political and psychological tyranny in his prose and continues to employ similarly in his last three major works. But the Renaissance literary tradition of Ariosto, Tasso, and Spenser went directly to the Homeric source, which depicted not merely the archetypal, swinish metamorphosis but two additional and progressively less embruting temptations, the second temptation of effeminating sex and the third of enervating idleness. Milton's primary use of Circe follows this tradition in distinguishing the three Homeric temptations and focusing upon the higher appeals, which his successive treatments reformulate in increasingly elevated moral terms. *Elegy I* defines the second, sexual temptation, its rural setting reappearing in *L'Allegro, Lycidas, Paradise Lost* (Satan's reaction to Eve), and *Paradise Regained*; the third temptation is defined as festivity and mirthful art in *Elegy VI* and as ignorant happiness in *Prolusion VII*. In *Comus*, these temptations are reformulated to include marriage and a devotional enjoyment of worldly good. Comus' temptation approximates Adam's unfallen condition in *Paradise Lost,* and uxoriousness now constitutes the Circean temptation to needed patience. Finally, in *Samson Agonistes*, the regained patience which redeemed Adam becomes the ultimate temptation of Circe, a figure who has primarily embodied, for Milton, the temptation to renounce higher obligations for the simpler fulfillment of ordinary humanity.

I. Introduction

CASUAL REFERENCE to Milton's use of the Circe myth is scattered throughout Miltonic criticism, and some critics have even given passing notice to its thematic importance in Milton's works. Thus

John M. Patrick suggests that "Circe lurks in Milton's imagination,"[1] and Douglas Bush indicates that "no myth left a deeper or more permanent impress upon him."[2] But there has been no previous attempt to study the precise extent to which Milton employed the Circe figure, whether overtly or by implication, or to assess the meaning of the temptation of Circe in Milton's imagination. There can be no complete understanding of Milton's works, however, without a just appreciation of the central importance of Circean temptation within the Milton corpus.

It should not be surprising that Milton invested the Circe myth with great moral significance, for Circe had become perhaps the most familiar Renaissance symbol of spiritual degradation. Rosemond Tuve considers "the great and famous allegorical figure of Circe" to be "one of the best-known symbolical figures of the Renaissance,"[3] while Bush further asserts that "the moralized myth perhaps most typical of the Renaissance was the story of Circe."[4] In his important study of the Renaissance Circe, Merritt Y. Hughes has shown the general familiarity of the Circe myth, particularly as revealed in the popular emblem books of the time:

We find the impression of familiarity amazingly confirmed. . . . From the voluminous moralization of her myth that is appended earnest readers must have emerged less interested in the Homeric story of Ulysses' adventure with the fairy mistress who turned his followers into swine than they were in its transformation by centuries of pagan and Christian commentary into a kind of scripture on which rested the central article of their psychology and ethics.[5]

This tendency to dismiss the full "Homeric story of Ulysses' adventure" and to focus attention only upon the bestial metamorphosis and its implications is particularly strong in Renaissance mythography. In the most influential work on mythology of its age, Natale Conti's *Mythologiae* (1551), attention to the Homeric source of the Circe myth is limited to the initial circumstance that "Ulysses' companions were changed into beasts, while he himself unconquerable because of his wisdom, which is truly a gift of God, stood firm" ("mutatu fuerunt in beluas Ulyssis socii, cum ipse invictus ob sapientiam, quae vere est Dei munus, perstiterit").[6] It is regrettable that the exclusive attention of Conti and his followers to an allegorization of the archetypal Circe, who transforms intemperate men into beasts but can be resisted by the divine gift of moly (symbolizing right reason or temperance),[7] has led modern scholars to conclude that this represents the Circe of Renaissance writers; for there was another Renaissance tradition which interpreted Circe from the larger perspective of the full Homeric story.

Though much of the easy moralizing of the Circe myth by Renaissance humanists may be credited, as Hughes notes, "to ignorance of Homer, or perhaps to indifference to the primeval Circe,"[8] the literary treatments of the Circe figure in Renaissance epic differ from the mythographic treatments in returning to the full Homeric narrative of Circean temptation. Milton is heir to a Renaissance literary tradition, begun by Ariosto and further developed by Tasso and Spenser, which is grounded in the Homeric text. As the Circe of Renaissance epic has never before been related to the full complexities of the Homeric narrative, it will be necessary, before turning to Milton's treatment of Circe, to analyze this background, beginning with Homer's original presentation of the enchantress who is to become the archetype of degrading temptation in the Western imagination. For the Homeric Circe goes beyond the archetypal sorceress who turns men into swine. Her temptations work on three different levels of intensity, of which the swinish metamorphosis is only the most debased. And as we shall see, the poets of the Renaissance are careful to distinguish these three separate temptations.

A. Homer

The bestial enslavement resulting from the first temptation is the lot of Eurylochos' party. Circe "invited / them in, and all in their innocence entered; only / Eurylochos waited outside, for he suspected treachery" (X, 230–32).[9] For the rest she prepared a dish into which she put "drugs, to make them forgetful of their own country. / When she had given them this and they had drunk it down, next thing / she struck them with her wand and drove them into her pig pens" (X, 236–38). Though they now appeared to be swine, "the minds within them stayed as they had been / before. So crying they went in" (X, 240–41).

Here, then, is the *locus classicus* for the archetypal Circe. The brutish transformation is the result of a drugged condition which enslaves but does not destroy the human mind. The drug causes its victims to forget their native land, but the subsequent brutish enslavement, symbolized by the wand, does not destroy all human remorse over their condition, however powerless their wills may be to effect a return to their native freedom. Though classical and Renaissance mythographers are to

view Circe's drug symbolically, there is nothing in Homer's precise description of the victims' condition to suggest anything beyond the very
real perils of drug addiction. The foolish innocent is the readiest victim
of this first temptation, which produces the most degraded enslavement
of the will. Against such a temptation, the only natural defense is an
initial prudence, as shown by the example of Eurylochos.

Such prudence may save the strong individual from personal degradation, but it can provide no help for the weaker souls of those already degraded. Thus, when Eurylochos suggests to Odysseus that they
quickly escape from Circe's island, Odysseus replies: "you may stay here
eating and drinking . . . I shall go. For there is strong compulsion upon
me" (X, 270, 272). With this evidence of his higher vocation "to set them
free" (X, 284), Odysseus receives the divine aid and instructions of
Hermes, which enable him to meet and conquer both personal temptation and the power of such temptation to brutalize the minds of others.
Hermes gives him the antidote "moly" (X, 305) which will protect
Odysseus from the embruting effects of Circe's drug, and he instructs
him to rush at her with drawn sword when she strikes him with her
wand. She will then invite him to her bed, and he must accept if he
wishes to free his men, but Hermes warns him to protect himself further
against a second form of degrading temptation: "bid her swear the great
oath of the blessed gods, that she / has no other evil hurt that she is
devising against you, / so she will not make you weak and unmanned,
once you are naked" (X, 299–301). It is important to recognize that the
Greek term translated here as "unmanned," ἀνήνορα, signifies that the
vulnerable quality is not humanity but masculinity.

The second temptation of Circe is, then, the degradation of masculinity through sexual enslavement. Forewarned, Odysseus will only
accept Circe into an intimate relationship if it is sanctified by a solemn
oath which will hold her responsible to a higher authority for his welfare while not restricting his own obedience to higher duties, in this case
his obligation to see "his companions set free" (X, 385). Any relationship
with her which does not enshrine an obligation to higher duties—she to
him, he to others—can only destroy his masculine quality of courage. In
the Ovidian version, as translated by Sandys, this relationship, with its
dual obligations and masculine dominance, is termed a marriage: "And
with drawne sword the trembling Goddesse frights. / When vowed

faith with her faire hand shee plights; / And grac't him with her nuptiall bed: who then / Demands in dowrie his transfigur'd men."[10]

Though Odysseus has protected himself against effeminacy or emasculation by insisting that sexual experience be part of a sanctified relationship devoted to higher ends, a final temptation of Circe awaits him upon her invitation that he and his restored men accept her hospitality for the purposes of physical and spiritual recuperation: "come now, eat your food and drink your wine, until / you gather back again into your chests that kind of spirit / you had in you when first you left the land of your fathers" (X, 460–62). But they remain there for a full year, "feasting on unlimited meat and sweet wine" (X, 468), until his men are finally forced to rebuke him: " 'What ails you now? It is time to think about our own country, / if truly it is ordained that you shall survive and come back / to your strong-founded house and to the land of your fathers.' / So they spoke, and the proud heart in me was persuaded" (X, 472–75). And when Odysseus now reminds Circe of "the promise you gave, that you / would see me on my way home" (X, 483–84), the honorable Circe agrees: "you shall no longer stay in my house when none of you wish to" (X, 489).

The third temptation is simply the appeal of carefree happiness. Though it involves no compulsion on Circe's part, such prolonged indulgence can disease the will. This enervation of the will is underscored by Ovid when he says that during that year Odysseus and his men were "Un-nerv'd with slothfull ease."[11] But since such immersion in a life of innocent pleasure does not involve an abdication of the will, a word of reproach is sufficient protection for a proud or manly spirit (συμὸς ἀγήνωρ). Such innocent, carefree pleasure can be virtuously chosen as a restorative vacation from the rigors of higher dedication that a proud heart demands of itself. It only becomes vicious if it becomes habitual and the will grows inattentive to the voice of reproach.

Homer's treatment of Circe involves, then, three levels of temptation, ranging from most brutalized to least degrading, each step of which is provided with its proper mode of protection. Ovid's treatment repeats the three stages of involvement with Circe but omits mention of the defining characteristics of the second and third phases. Ovid notes that Mercury gave Ulysses advice in addition to moly but does not specify the nature of this advice. Similarly, he offers no explanation of why

Ulysses and his men stayed on with Circe for a year. When in the Renaissance we find the danger of sexual involvement with Circe defined as effeminacy rather than bestiality, and Circe's invitation to restful ease defined as a means of recuperation of body and spirit, we may be sure that these Renaissance interpreters have gone directly to the Homeric text.

B. Ariosto

The first major poetic treatment of Circean temptation in the Renaissance is that of Ariosto in *Orlando Furioso*. In this work Ruggiero encounters Ariosto's adaptations of the three temptations of Circe in his progress to, residence at, and retreat from Alcina's realm. The first temptation is represented by Astolfo, whom Alcina has metamorphosed into a myrtle tree. Encountering Astolfo on his way to the "holy" ("*santi*") ' (X, xlv)[12] city of Logistilla, this talking tree tells Ruggiero of his experience with Alcina: "Clasped in her dainty limbs . . . Nor France nor aught beside I thought upon: / In her my every fancy, every hope / Centered and ended as their common scope" (VI, xlvii). His sexual indulgence acts like Circe's drug to make him lose all memory of his native land and its ideals; and he cannot break the captivity of his metamorphosis because, however much pain it has caused him, he still believes his former happiness with Alcina to represent a lost good: "Why thus the good possessed remember still, / Amid the cruel penance I endure?" (VI, xlix).

Despite this warning, Ruggiero soon becomes captivated by Alcina, "And lapt in idleness and pleasure lay; / Nor memory of his lord nor of the dame, / Once loved so well, preserved, nor of his fame" (VII, xl). Though Ruggiero's condition reflects all three temptations of Circe—the oblivion of the first, the sexual pleasure of the second, and the idleness of the third—it is the second temptation which predominates. Alcina's court differs from the gardens of the later Renaissance Circes in that its pleasures include not only sex and idle feasting but such diverse activities as dramatic pageants, balls, literature, tournaments, and hunts (VII, xxxi–xxxii). But seeing how "ingloriously" (VII, xli) Ruggiero is wasting his days, Melissa, Bradamante's adviser, plans with the help of Angelica's magic ring to reclaim him from Alcina's "effeminate, soft realm" ("*regno effeminato e molle*") (VII, xlviii). Here we have clear evidence that Ariosto understood the danger of sexual relations with Circe to be that of which Hermes warned Odysseus, not bestiality but effeminacy. Ruggiero's effeminacy is reflected in his "fine, soft garments" which "ease and wantonness declare" (VII, liii). After berating him, Melissa gives him the ring, of which we are told: "Who with Angelica's, or rather who / Were fortified with Reason's ring, would see / Each countenance, exposed to open view" (VIII, ii). When Ruggiero puts on the ring of reason, "A thousand fathoms deep he fain would lie" (VII, lxv). Ariosto would seem to equate this ring with the Homeric moly, which he interprets as reason, and it provides the "remedy" (VI, liii) Astolfo had hoped Ruggiero would be able to apply in resisting the Circean "drug" of sexual indulgence which had enslaved himself. The restored and protected Ruggiero now flees to the kingdom of Logistilla, leaving Melissa behind to free Alcina's former lovers from their enchanted metamorphoses into trees, rocks, and beasts (VIII, xv). Melissa is able to do this with such ease because Alcina has rushed off in desperate pursuit of Ruggiero, resolved "To risk the ruin of herself and land, / Or repossess the thing she held so dear," impelled equally by "Love" and the sense of "bitter injury received" (X, xlviii).

Alcina's last stratagem is the third temptation in its precise Homeric form. Almost overcome by thirst and fatigue in his journey toward Logistilla, Ruggiero encounters "three ladies of Alcina's court" (X, xxxvi) who "pray, on what he had in hand / He would not show his heart so deeply bent, / But that he in the cool and grateful shade / Would rest [*ristorar*] his weary limbs, beside them laid" (X, xxxviii). The appeal, as in Homer, is simply for recuperative refreshment, rest for his weary body, and "foaming wine" (X, xxxix) to appease his thirst. But Ruggiero rejects this offer because any delay "would time supply / To Alcina to arrive" (X, xxxix).

Thus escaping the final temptation of Alcina, Ruggiero reaches the kingdom of Logistilla, while Alcina, like "Dido" (X, lvi),[13] is reduced to suicidal despair. Logistilla now makes a proper "bit" (X, lxvi) for the Hippogriff which had carried Ruggiero off from his true love Bradamante to the city of Alcina, but as Ariosto recognizes in a comment which reveals his characteristic "mingling of acceptance and regret,"[14] " 'Tis seldom Reason's bit will serve to steer / Desire, or turn him from his furious course" (XI, i). Ruggiero goes off on further adventures rather than returning directly to Bradamante, falls into lust for Angelica, and loses both symbols of reason, the bridled flying horse and the ring.

Though for Ariosto simple refreshment of body and spirit (the third temptation) would allow Alcina to catch Ruggiero again in the effeminacy of love (the second temptation), which would finally lead to her giving him "the chalice dread, / Her lover's final guerdon evermore" (X, xlv), and though the metamorphosis of the first temptation is unlike that of Homer in that the Homeric Circe did not make love to the men she turns into swine, Ariosto does recognize that the temptation of Circe has three carefully distinguished forms, and his depiction of these forms reflects the direct influence of the Homeric original while itself influencing the later depictions in Renaissance epic.

C. Tasso

The Circean motif achieves major thematic and structural significance in the *Gerusalemme Liberata,* with Tasso freely adapting the three Homeric temptations of Circe to a larger analysis of the very nature of love. As in Homer, the victims whom the Circean Armida transforms into beasts—here fish—are not those to whom she has given herself sexually. But unlike the Homeric original, this first temptation does involve a form of love: "She, with sweet words and false enticing smiles, / Infused love among the dainties set, / And with empoison'd cups our souls beguiles, / And made each knight himself and God forget" (X, lxv).[15] "This foolish crew of lovers" (V, lxxi), whom with "jealousy" (V, lxx) and "false hope their longing hearts she fir'd" (IV, lxxxix), would seem to represent the mode of courtly love. Returned to human form, they are cast into a dungeon—"Save false Rambaldo, he became her friend" (X, lxix)—and are finally dispatched in chains on their "way to death" (X, lxxi) when, through "Providence divine" (X, lxxi), they are freed by Rinaldo, "whose high virtue is his guide" (X, lxxi). Rinaldo is the higher Odyssean figure who frees the victims of Circean enslavement and himself converts Armida's hate to love.

In Tasso's version, however, the third temptation precedes the second and partly defines its nature. Rinaldo, bidding his squires to remain on the bank of a stream, takes a waiting boat to a sweet and verdant island. There he beholds a female figure rising from the water who "though no syren . . . seem'd it she had been / One of those sisters false"

(XIV, lxi). Her song bids him to accept natural pleasure and not to strive "For glory vain or virtue's idle ray" (XIV, lxii). Bidden to renounce "thought and care" (XIV, lxiv), he is gradually overcome by the "stealing sleep / (To which her tunes entic'd his heavy eyes)" (XIV, lxv). John M. Steadman has noted "the Horatian conception of the Siren as Idleness (*improba Siren desidia;* Sat. II, iii, 14)—an interpretation echoed by both Conti and Migault,"[16] and this would also seem to be Tasso's conception of the Siren song. But his Siren figure is clearly subservient to his Circe, just as the ladies of Ariosto who offered refreshment to the weary Ruggiero were members of Alcina's court. Ariosto's innovative formulation of the Circean third temptation becomes a standard feature in the Renaissance epic portrayals of Circe, and its persistence indicates that these writers recognized the Ariosto episode and its successors to be not incidental but necessary for a full treatment of their Homeric source.

Armida now comes forth "from her ambush" (XIV, lxv), "Swearing revenge" (XIV, lxv), but one sight of Rinaldo dissolves "the hardness great / Which late congeal'd the heart of that fair dame" (XIV, lxvii). She carries him off to an island distinguished from the former by the mingling of nature and art—yet "No where appear'd the art which all this wrought" (XVI, ix)—and bids him "Gather the rose of love while yet thou mayst" (XVI, xv). Unlike Armida's former slaves of unsatisfied love, Rinaldo's aroused desires are fully satisfied; but the relationship of Armida and Rinaldo still follows the courtly mold: "Her to command, to serve it pleas'd the knight; / He proud of bondage, of her empire she" (XVI, xxi). As with Ruggiero, it is his clothing which reveals his true spiritual condition to be *"troppo lusso effeminato"* (XVI, xxx, 6)[17] and which indicates the specifically Homeric quality, effeminacy, of this second, sexual temptation.

Inspired by the Lord, Godfrey sends two knights to free Rinaldo from "that base and servile love" (XIV, lxxvii). A wizard provides them with a shield in which Rinaldo may view his "wanton soft attire" (XIV, lxxvii) and instructions for avoiding the deadly spring of laughter, "Whose waters pure the thirsty guests entice" (XIV, lxxiv). As this "stream of laughter" (XV, lvii) is soon defined as a place where "these syrens sing" (XV, lvii), the condition of Carlo and Ubaldo as they arrive at the spring is significant: "The passage hard against the mountain steep / These travellers had faint and weary made" (XV, lv). Though

Tasso had not used the recuperative appeal of the Siren in her first appearance to Rinaldo, he now clearly indicates the Homeric character of the third Circean temptation, personified throughout by the Siren sisters. But the knights' ears are protected by "wisdom's rein" (XV, lvii), and they refuse to refresh themselves at the spring or to yield to the Siren song. "Warbled" (XV, lxii) by one of the two naked girls playing in a pond made by the stream of laughter (XV, lvii), the song identifies "this paradise" (XV, lxii) with "the antique golden age" (XV, lxiii) and offers them "endless rest" as "love's champions" in a state freed from "Mars his rage" (XV, lxiii). Though their first sight of "These naked wantons, tender, fair and white, / Moves so far the warriors' stubborn hearts, / That on their shapes they gazed with delight" (XV, lix), "Straight armed reason to his charge upstarts, / And quencheth lust and killeth fond desire" (XV, lxvi).

They now surprise Rinaldo "while the queen her household things survey'd" (XVI, xxvii). Seeing his "wanton habit" (XVI, xxx) in the shield, like Ruggiero "shamed, sad, he would have died" (XVI, xxxi). Now "awak'd" (XVI, xxxi) from the Siren-induced idleness which complemented his effeminate subservience to Armida's desires, his departure is further inspired by Ubaldo's rebuke: "What letharge hath in drowsiness uppend / Thy courage thus?" (XVI, xxxiii). But though Rinaldo is resolved to leave, Armida's pain does arouse his "pity" (XVI, li), and he is forced to admit: "I erred likewise; if I pardon find, / None can condemn you that our trespass hears. / Your dear remembrance will I keep in mind, / . . . Call me your soldier and your knight" (XVI, liii). He is willing to accept her love, but not the abdication of his responsibilities which she desires.

He returns to battle while Armida, like Alcina, suffers the extremes of scorned love, the alternate desire for revenge and suicide, Tasso following Ariosto's conversion of Circe into Dido. When she is on the point of suicide, Rinaldo, having achieved martial victory and followed her to the wood, stays her hand. True to his parting vow, he says: "Madam, appease your grief, your wrath, your fears, / For to be crown'd, not scorn'd, your life I save: / Your foe nay, but your friend, your knight, your slave" (XX, cxxxiv). And she reciprocates: "Behold (she says) your handmaid and your thrall, / My life, my crown, my wealth, use at your pleasure" (XX, cxxxvi). His honor restored and protected by reason, Rinaldo can now accept Armida on a new basis. Their new relationship will be one of mutual subservience, such as Chaucer had earlier suggested in "The Franklin's Tale," fulfilling itself not in a magical but a real kingdom. But Rinaldo can virtuously accept her love on this new basis only because Armida has been willing to, in the words of Congreve's Millamant, "by degrees dwindle into a wife."

In his version of Circean temptation, Tasso has anatomized the nature of love, first rejecting the courtly mode of unsatisfied desire, then the courtly subservience of knight to mistress, and finally affirming a love suggestive of marriage[18] and marked by both equality and social responsibility. In this last he is truest to Homer who, with similar protection, allowed Odysseus to embrace Circe. But Tasso, rejecting the implied male supremacy of the ritualized Homeric relationship of Odysseus and Circe, which Milton will uphold, joins with other Renaissance humanists who projected the ideal of equality between the sexes.[19] Tasso's use of the Circe figure to work out an analysis of contrasting modes of love distinguishes his treatment of Circean temptation; but, like Ariosto, he understood and developed the three temptations of the Homeric text and directly influenced the third great Renaissance treatment of Circe.

D. Spenser

Following the lead of Ariosto and Tasso, Spenser carefully delineates the three separate temptations of Circe in Book II of *The Faerie Queene*. Though we do not meet with actual metamorphosis until Canto XII, the total enslavement of the first temptation is represented by the first of Acrasia's three lovers, Mortdant. Having left his pregnant lady "to seeke adventures wilde" (I, 1),[20] Mortdant, like Ruggiero, soon becomes "thralled to her [Acrasia's] will" in "chaines of lust and lewde desyres" (I, liv). His lady briefly reclaims him; but like Astolfo, he cannot break the influence of Acrasia's "charme" (I, lv). He is incapable of a life of responsible fidelity to his lady and child, "For he was flesh (all flesh doth frayltie breed)" (I, lii), and the attempt at withdrawal from Acrasia's "drugs of fowle intemperaunce" (I, liv) kills him. Mortdant's "feeble nature" (I, lvii), capable only of the irresponsible "pleasure and delight" (I, lii) of sexual adventures, cannot fulfill the demands of either the heroic or the domestic. His "raging passion with fierce tyranny / Robs reason of her dew regalitie" (I, lvii) and subjects him to intemperance.

We next meet the second temptation as it is experienced by Cymocles. Unlike Mortdant, who could live only as the thrall of Acrasia,
Cymocles alternates between the motive forces of sexual indulgence and
heroic wrath, and attends or departs from Acrasia of his own free will.
Though the influence of heroic wrath frees him from dependence upon
Acrasia's "drugs of deare voluptuous receipt" (V, xxxiv), his voluntary
sensual indulgence is a product of a feebleness of nature similar to that
of Mortdant: "for he by kynd / Was given all to lust and loose living, /
When ever his fiers handes he free mote fynd" (V, xxviii). Sent by
Pyrocles to reclaim him, Atin finds Cymocles "sojourning, / To serve
his lemans love," his "ydle mynd" engaged "In daintie delices and lavish
joyes, / Having his warlike weapons cast behynd" (V, xxviii), and thus
admonishes him: "Up, up! thou womanish weake knight, / That here in
ladies lap entombed art, / Unmindfull of thy praise and prowest might"
(V, xxxvi). Spenser is later to define the Genius of the Bower of Bliss in
similarly "effeminate"[21] terms: "His looser garment to the ground did
fall, / And flew about his heeles in wanton wize, / Not fitt for speedy
pace or manly exercize" (XII, xlvi). The identification of Genius as "The
foe of life" (XII, xlviii) further illuminates Atin's reference to Cymocles' present entombment and enables us to understand better the name
Mortdant given to that total feebleness of nature which is enslaved to
intemperate desires, doomed either to a living death of indulgence or,
refraining from this only possible mode of life, to death. Cymocles does
not represent this most vicious form of Circean debasement, but the
lesser debasement of manhood which is "womanish" effeminacy. Like
Ariosto and Tasso, Spenser has defined the second temptation of Circe
in precise Homeric terms.

Spenser reflects Tasso's treatment when "Suddeinly out of his de-
lightfull dreame / The man awoke" (V, xxvii); and like Rinaldo, Cymocles is able to leave Acrasia voluntarily without ill effects. But "The
wrath which Atin kindled in his mind" (VI, ii) is soon allayed by the
watery fluctuations of his nature which his name represents;[22] and he
now encounters the third temptation of the Homeric Circe in the person
of Phaedria. Spenser follows the lead of Ariosto, who figured this temptation by three ladies from Alcina's court, when Phaedria introduces herself to Cymocles as "thine owne fellow servaunt; / For thou to serve
Acrasia thy selfe doest vaunt" (VI, ix). But Spenser bases his own version
of the third temptation largely upon Tasso, recognizing in his Sirenlike

figure, herself subservient to Armida's will, a working out of the Homeric Circe's final temptation of rest similar to that of Ariosto. Phaedria, a figure of "merth" and "laughter vaine" (VI, vi), plies her boat on "The Idle Lake" (VI, x) and brings Cymocles to her island, a "fertile land" (VI, xii) where "Trees, braunches, birds, and songs were framed fitt / For to allure fraile mind to carelesse ease" (VI, xiii). Here she sings her Siren song in which "fruitfull" "Nature" (VI, xv) is contrasted with the "fruitlesse toile" (VI, xvii) of "daunger and adventures vaine" (VI, xvii); and "By this she had him lulled fast a sleepe" (VI, xviii).

By bringing Guyon on the scene at this point, Spenser also synthesizes the ordering of the Homeric temptations as presented by Ariosto and Tasso. Though the reader encounters the three temptations in the natural progression of Homer and Ariosto, Guyon's experience reflects Tasso's reversal of the order of the second and third temptations following the initial introduction to an example of total enslavement: he first hears of Mortdant, then meets Phaedria, and finally enters the Bower of Bliss. But, unlike Rinaldo, Guyon only indulges himself personally in this third temptation. For Spenser, then, this third temptation does not necessarily lead, as in Ariosto and Tasso, to further indulgence in the more debasing forms of Circean temptation, its less vicious and independent nature demonstrated by the fact that it is one which Guyon may permit himself briefly to indulge. When Guyon enters Phaedria's boat, having like Rinaldo left his companion on the shore, "The knight was courteous, and did not forbeare / Her honest merth and pleasaunce to partake" (VI, xxi). Her appeal to Guyon, as in Ariosto and in Tasso's second version of this temptation met by Carlo and Ubaldo, derives from Homer: "here a while ye may in safety rest, / Till season serve new passage to assay: / Better safe port, then be in seas distrest" (VI, xxiii); "And ever bad him stay, till time the tide renewd" (VI, xxvi). Though "halfe discontent" (VI, xxiv), he responds to her portrayal of nature's "happy fruitfulnesse" (VI, xxiv). He succeeds in "fairly tempring fond desire" (VI, xxvi) during his stay on Phaedria's island; but though he "ever her desired to depart" (VI, xxvi), he remains there long enough to receive a wound from Cymocles (VI, xxix) when Cymocles awakes out of the "ydle dreme" of "slouthfull sleepe" (VI, xxvii). Phaedria separates the knights, declaiming like Tasso's Siren against the "deadly harmes" (VI, xxxiv) of battle and offering "lovely peace, and gentle amity" (VI, xxxv). When Guyon now persists in leaving, "She no lesse glad, then he

desirous, was / Of his departure thence; for of her joy / And vaine delight she saw he light did pas" (VI, xxxvii). Closer here to Homer than
either Ariosto or Tasso, Spenser alone recognized that the virtuous can
innocently indulge in the third Circean temptation of recuperative rest
and ease without fear of greater harm. Like Circe, Phaedria permits her
"solemne sad" (VI, xxvii) guest to depart when his will is fully resolved
to this purpose. It is only overindulgence in such idle rest which is spiritually dangerous, as is shown in its effect on the "feeble nature" (VI, i)
of Cymocles: "The whiles Cymocles with that wanton mayd / The hasty
heat of his avowd revenge delayd" (VI, xl). But even Cymocles finally
rouses himself from Phaedria's peaceful island to return to battle and die
at Arthur's hands. Spenser had begun Canto VI with a discussion of the
two forms of incontinence indulged in by one of "feeble nature" like
Cymocles but mastered by Guyon: "joyous pleasure" and "griefe and
wrath," the latter identified as "foes of life" (VI, i). The "wrath" which
inspires his strife against grace is not, then, to be preferred to entombment in Acrasia's love, both equally "foes of life."[23] Though Guyon's
temperance protects him from both excesses—"Yet Vertue vauntes in
both her victories, / And Guyon in them all shewes goodly maysteries"
(VI, i)—Cymocles' "feeble nature" cannot "learne continence" (VI, i)
and the best fulfillment of his lesser nature might well be to rest in the
relatively harmless third form of Circean temptation represented by
Phaedria.[24]

Guyon, however, now proceeds to the final conquest of Acrasia for
which "the palmer him forth drew / From Faery court" (IX, ix). Guyon
and the Palmer, like Tasso's two knights sent to reclaim Rinaldo, finally
arrive at the Bower of Bliss, which like Armida's garden is distinguished
from the natural fertility of the Siren-Phaedria islands by the mingling
of nature and art. As in Tasso, they pass two naked girls sporting in a
fountain, and Guyon's "stubborne brest gan secret pleasaunce to embrace" (XII, lxv), a response not earlier elicited by Phaedria and one
quickly suppressed by the Palmer's rebuke and counsel (XII, lxix). They
now enter the Bower where Acrasia "through languour of her late sweet
toyle" (XII, lxxviii) gazes upon her sleeping lover Verdant while someone sings Armida's song, "Gather the rose of love, whilest yet is time"
(XII, lxxv). Rushing in together, they capture Acrasia and free Verdant.
Guyon next proceeds to destroy the Bower, and the Palmer restores to
human form the beasts, "whylome her lovers" (XII, lxxxv), whom

Acrasia had metamorphosed through "life intemperate" (XII, lxxxv). The destruction of the Bower of Bliss involves an ambiguity similar to that in Medina's earlier counsel to Guyon to "learne from Pleasures poyson to abstaine" (II, xlv); for Spenser leaves it unclear whether all pleasure is poisoned and to be avoided or whether one must abstain only from pleasure's poison, intemperance. Since Acrasia's name signifies such overindulgence, it would seem, however, that not pleasure but intemperate pleasure is to be avoided and that Verdant, his name significantly contrasted with Mortdant, can live fruitfully when protected against overindulgence in sensual pleasure by temperance (Guyon) and reason (the Palmer).

Of the freed lovers, one, like Tasso's Rambaldo (undoubtedly suggested by Homer's Elpenor), prefers his former brutish state of enslavement to "the excellence / Of his creation . . . intelligence" (XII, lxxxvii). The Palmer's response illuminates Spenser's distinctive treatment of Circean temptation: "The donghill kinde / Delightes in filth and fowle incontinence: / Let Gryll be Gryll, and have his hoggish minde; / But let us hence depart, whilest wether serves and winde" (XII, lxxxvii). Since Acrasia had turned her lovers into beasts "According to their mindes like monstruous" (XII, lxxxv), it is the lot of "feeble nature" to be bestial, and only the spiritual elite can resist Circean temptation. The temptation of Circe thus poses a real threat only to that higher nature capable of rising above it to a celebration of his true human excellence. Guyon's brief susceptibility to the sensuality of the naked damsels and actual indulgence in Phaedria's more innocent idle mirth and rest are the most serious instances of Circean temptation in Spenser's account precisely because, temperate by nature and responsive to the counsel of reason, Guyon is shown to be still liable to yield and yet capable of overcoming his moments of temptation.

Spenser's treatment of Gryll, as Hughes has shown,[25] derives from a long tradition originating with Plutarch and represented most significantly in the Renaissance by Gelli's *Circe* (1549). And it is from Gelli that Spenser probably took his elitist conception of Circean temptation. For Gelli, the condition of most men "is little better than that of brutes, and indeed they become very much like the other animals, who have no use at all of reason."[26] To such, Ulysses says: "you are resolved to remain in that despicable condition of a brute rather than be restored to a human shape. And I agree this is best for you and so will allow you to remain a beast."[27] Ulysses can find only one beast willing to "Join with the joy of my spirit, take part in the bursting delight of my mind,"[28] but for Gelli this "one that may properly call himself a man"[29] represents that tiny minority who can truly experience and celebrate "man's excellence."[30] Like Gelli, Spenser, though mourning the lot of "feeble nature," recognizes that "the donghill kinde" are doomed to a living death of bestial enslavement to the senses, that the use of man's highest faculty of reason is limited to an elite, and that the Circean alternative is only a true temptation to those capable of higher spiritual dedication.

E. Sandys

George Sandys is particularly important for a study of the Renaissance Circe because he reflects the two divergent traditions of Circean interpretation, that of the mythographers and that of the epic poets. In the mythographic commentary he added to the 1632 edition of his translation of Ovid's *Metamorphoses*, he follows Conti in focusing only on the bestial metamorphosis and the fact that "*Ulysses* could not loose his shape with the rest, who being fortifyed by an immortall power, was not subject to mutation." He specifically cites Conti for the following virtually translated analysis of "How *Circe* . . . getting the dominion, deformes our soules with all bestial vices; alluring some to inordinate *Venus;* others to anger, cruelty, and every excesse of passion."[31]

In the earlier "The Minde of the Frontispeece," which he prefixed to the 1626 and all later editions of this translation, Sandys, however, does not identify Circe with "all bestial vices" but only with two. The frontispiece contains contrasting emblems of Heroic Virtues and Circe, a contrast which reflects the Aristotelian antithesis of heroic virtue and brutishness in a conventional Renaissance reformulation which equates such Aristotelian brutishness with Circean bestiality.[32] Characterizing those possessed of "*Heroic Vertues*" as aspiring "To *Fame* and *Glorie*" and "well-nigh Deifi'd" by Pallas, Sandys argues:

> But who forsake that faire *Intelligence,*
> To follow *Passion,* and voluptuous *Sense;*
> That shun the Path and Toyles of HERCULES:
> Such, charm'd by CIRCE's luxurie, and ease,
> Themselves deforme: Twixt whom, so great an ods;
> That these are held for Beasts, and those for Gods.[33]

In keeping with the literary tradition of Renaissance epic, Sandys pays primary attention to the higher temptations of the Homeric Circe, the second temptation of *"Passion,* and voluptuous *Sense,"* and the third temptation of "luxurie, and ease," and he uses the bestial transformation only as symbol for this select group of dangers to that superior mentality which strives to follow "the Path and Toyles of HERCULES." It is interesting to note in this context that Sir John Harington, in his allegorical comments to his translation of *Orlando Furioso,* regarded Ruggiero as a *"new Hercules"* for his final ability to reach Logistilla despite the temptations of the Circean Alcina. Following Bononome, Harington interprets this in the twofold manner suggested by Ariosto's treatment: "to this inordinate lusting is joyned idlenesse as an assistant and great furtherer."[34] Whether or not Sandys took the figure of Hercules from Harington, the evidence of these two translators indicates that when allegorical interpretations of Circe are derived from literary treatments rather than mythology they select the specific dangers in the fuller Homeric text which had been given such prominence in the Renaissance epic versions of Circe. Sandys' verses on the Frontispiece, published the same year—1626—as Milton's first important use of the Circe myth,[35] epitomizes this Renaissance poetic tradition and may well have influenced Milton's conception of Circean temptation.

II. MILTON

Milton is the last great Renaissance writer to give central importance to the theme of Circean temptation, and in his lifelong concern with this symbol of degradation, he invested the Circe figure with an ever more subtle quality of moral danger which lifts his treatments far beyond those of Ariosto, Tasso, and Spenser. And yet his many versions of Circean temptation are clearly indebted to this long tradition of Renaissance poetry. Though his only sustained narrative treatment of the three temptations of the Homeric Circe occurs in *Comus,* the higher temptations of Circe inform, to a greater or lesser extent, all of his major poems and many of his minor works. Like Sandys in his prefatory verses, Milton normally evokes the conventional associations of Circe with bestial transformation only as a symbol of the degrading implications of Circean temptation while addressing himself to the dangers of the second and third temptations, either separately or together. And like Spenser, Milton recognizes that there are less embruting forms of Circean temptation which, though regretfully acceptable for those of lesser capacities, pose a unique danger to one imbued with a sense of higher purpose, who would follow, in Sandys' words, "the Path and Toyles of HERCULES."

A. Elegy I

When Milton wrote *Elegy I* at the age of eighteen, the primary temptation to his personal sense of higher vocation was already clear to him and was given the name of Circe. This Latin, autobiographical verse letter to Charles Diodati, written during his term of rustication from Cambridge in 1626, is the most seminal work he ever wrote, and traces of its imagery and meaning are to be found throughout his later works.

Already inspired by bardic ambitions, he begins by comparing his "exile" from Cambridge to the less fortunate exile of Ovid: "Ah! Would that the bard [*vates*] who was a pitiful exile in the land of Tomis had never had to bear anything worse! Then he would have yielded nothing to Ionian Homer and you, O Maro, would have been conquered and stripped of your prime honors" (p. 8).[36] The implication is that Milton will have the opportunity to equal Homer and triumph over Virgil.

He now describes his activities, which consist of alternate periods of inspired study and relaxation from such spiritually exhausting labors. When the reading of Roman comedy and Greek tragedy do not provide sufficient relaxation from the spiritual transports of his studies, he enjoys outings in both the city and country. In the country he responds to the beauty of nature, particularly of "the grove where the elms stand close together" (p. 9). Even more appealing is "the magnificent shade of a place just beyond the city's confines. Here, like stars that breathe out soft flames, you may see groups of maidens go dancing past" (p. 9). Descriptions of these girls and those he observes in London, and of his excited reactions to them, occupy thirty-three of the poem's ninety-two lines. Enticed by their "waving tresses which were golden nets flung by Cupid" and by their "seductive cheeks" (p. 9), he nonetheless never approaches these lovelies, contenting himself with unobserved adoration. As David Daiches so well notes of this aspect of *Elegy I* and other Latin poems on this subject:

This was a side of his nature which he never revealed in his English poetry. And it is not to be thought that it is merely an Ovidian exercise; other Latin poems of Milton's youth show the same excited interest in female beauty and in sex. Paradoxical though it may seem to the modern reader, Milton used Latin to express intimate feelings that he could never bring himself to reveal in English.[37]

But it is precisely the intensity of his sexual yearnings—seen also in *Elegy VII*[38]—which caused him to view female beauty as a temptation to his true life of study, with its promise of bardic triumph. From the first he saw female attractiveness as a temptation of Circe; and, in his later works, it will always retain the symbolic association of this first statement: "But for my part—while the blind boy's indulgence permits it—I am preparing the speediest possible departure from this city of delights—preparing, with the help of divine moly, to secure the safety of distance from the infamous halls of the deceiver, Circe" (p. 10). Milton's first use of Circe, then, identifies her with the second, sexual temptation of the Homeric model. Unable as yet to adopt the proper protection against her power through a sanctified relationship dedicated to higher ends, he avails himself of the first mode of protection exemplified by Eurylochos, prudent withdrawal.

This first "Circe of the Walks," as she might be styled, will remain a permanent feature of Milton's imagination, reappearing, as we shall later see, in such works as *L'Allegro, Paradise Lost,* and *Paradise Regained.* But we can also recognize her appearance in *Lycidas,* when the Swain, disheartened by the apparent futility of continuing to "strictly meditate the thankless Muse" (66) in view of the possibility of premature death, poignantly asks: "Were it not better done as others use, / To sport with *Amaryllis* in the shade" (67–68). To do "as others use," while suggesting no inherent danger to these "others," is a serious temptation only for the person imbued with a sense of higher dedication. From his earliest presentation of this temptation, Milton denounces with the high invective of "the infamous halls of the deceiver, Circe," nothing more vicious than the groups of innocent maidens who stroll past an unseen admirer in his secluded shade. This relatively harmless nature of Circean temptation—which, from the first, defines Milton's conception of Circe—will become still clearer in his next Circean reference.

B. Elegy VI

When Milton addressed a second Latin verse letter to Diodati, three years after the composition of *Elegy I,* his glancing reference to Circe alludes most specifically to the Homeric third temptation of "feasting on unlimited meat and sweet wine." Not only are such pleasures not deemed vicious in themselves, but Milton positively commends them as inspirational to the different character of his friend: "In your case also [in company with Ovid, Anacreon, and Pindar] the sumptuous board with its generous provision gives strength to your mind and fire to your genius. Your Campanian cups foam with creative impulse and you decant the store of your verses out of the wine-jar itself. . . . and through a maiden's eyes and music-making fingers Thalia will glide into full possession of your breast" (p. 51).

But if sumptuous food, drink, and the attentions of ladies are appropriate to Diodati's comic muse, Thalia, they pose a serious threat to Milton's epic aspirations, which, for him, required purity of life:

But he whose theme is wars and heaven under Jupiter in his prime, and pious heroes and chieftains half-divine . . . let him live sparingly, like the Samian teacher; and let herbs furnish his innocent diet. Let the purest water stand beside him. . . . Beyond this, his youth must be innocent of crime and chaste. . . . His character should be like yours, O Priest. . . . For truly, the bard is sacred to the gods and is their priest. (p. 52)

If in *Elegy I* Milton had flirted with the idea of sexual fulfillment, his growing conception of the priestly office of the bard has, in *Elegy VI,* led to his total commitment to chastity. The primary temptation to his higher vocation has now progressed to the more innocent indulgences of carefree festivity, and it is in this context that he introduces the figure of Circe: "So Homer, the spare eater and the water-drinker, carried Ulysses through vast stretches of ocean, through the monster-making palace of the daughter of Phoebus and Perseis" (p. 52). Milton evokes the image of swinish transformation, then, as a symbol for the least vicious of the Homeric Circe's temptations, a pattern he will follow in his next explicit reference to Circe some three years later.

C. Prolusion VII

This Prolusion, on the subject "Learning Makes Men Happier Than Does Ignorance" (p. 621), brings us back to the mood of *Elegy I* in its opening, autobiographical comments, again referring to that special grove of elms:

For my own part I appeal to the groves and streams and the dear village elms under which in the summer now just over I remember that I enjoyed supreme happiness with the Muses. . . . Here also I might have hoped for the same opportunity to retire, if this troublesome nuisance of a speech had not . . . so thwarted and encumbered me in the midst of any peace. I began mournfully to reflect how far away I am from that tranquillity which literary study at first promised me . . . and how much better it would be to give up the arts entirely. (p.622)

As we saw in *Elegy I,* there were two outdoor spots to which Milton would go when in need of mental relaxation, the place at the outskirts of London which was frequented by pretty girls and which he recognized as a haunt of Circe, and the grove of elms. Six years later, he is still drawn to the elm grove, and it soon becomes apparent that it also represents a temptation of Circe. Retiring from the full stresses of high mental labor, it is there that he experiences consummate moments of tranquil communion with the Muses; but the achievement of the tranquility becomes more important than the higher communion and, to ensure such peace, he even speculates that it might be better "to give up the arts entirely." The simple happiness that ordinary people can claim fills him with moments of longing equal in power to the sexual yearning to which he had earlier given expression, and it is similarly crushed by the spectre of Circe it evokes, his final crushing argument against Ignorance giving new perspective to the autobiographical reflections with which he began:

And so at last we may ask what are the joys of Ignorance. Are they to enjoy what one has, to be molested by no one, to be superior to all cares and annoyance, to live a secure and quiet life insofar as possible? Truly, this is the life of any wild beast or bird. . . . Why crave for the heavenly power of the mind in addition to these pleasures? Ergo, let Ignorance throw off her humanity, let her have Circe's cup and betake herself on all fours to the beasts. (p. 628)

His birdlike tranquility in the elms is now recognized and rejected as a temptation of Circe. This marks a progression from the position taken in *Elegy VI,* in which Milton defined the Diodati alternative of a convivial, comic art as a Circean temptation. For Milton the final form of the third temptation of Circe is a life of ignorant happiness, its bestial likeness signifying Circean degradation.

D. *Autobiographical Conclusion: An Apology for Smectymnuus*

From what we have seen, Milton's primary definitions of Circean temptation occur in frankly autobiographical contexts. Indeed, as late as 1642, we still find the figure of Circe intruding upon Milton's autobiographical reflections. Perhaps the most interesting reference to Circe in all of Milton's works occurs in *An Apology,* as he discusses the Platonic sources of his devotion to chastity: "Where if I should tell ye what I learnt, of chastity and love, I meane that which is truly so, whose charming cup is only virtue which she bears in her hand to those who are worthy. The rest are cheated with a thick intoxicating potion which a certaine Sorceresse the abuser of love's name carries about."[39] In this curious reference, Milton would seem to have left the reader far behind as he talks to himself of "a certaine Sorceresse" with whose name he is only too familiar.

This suggestion of personal familiarity with Circean temptation underscores the significance of the earlier autobiographical references to Circe, references which show the temptation of Circe to be inherent in the sexual attractiveness of women and in the carefree happiness of ordinary humanity. In these early references, the personal temptation to forsake his higher vocation for the less demanding happiness of normal society is consistently termed Circean. Since each of his major characters, both before and after 1642, is successively presented with the same temptation, it would seem, at the very least, that this major Miltonic theme had its roots in Milton's own psychic concerns. Milton's personal reflections consistently show that it was not the temptation of glory which haunted his imagination[40] but the opposing temptation to relinquish his bardic vocation for a less demanding happiness. Though Milton's major works ought not to be read simply as veiled autobiography, the persistent reappearance of Circean temptation in forms originally defined in clearly personal terms does suggest that this theme embodies Milton's deepest and most abiding personal agon. But however great the personal power of this temptation may have been, it is never conceived of as inherently vicious. Shortly before the Circean reference in *An Apology,* Milton describes himself as having "a certaine nicenesse of nature," and it is not to be thought that he or the characters he created could have been seriously tempted by the vulgar evil of excessive indulgence. Indeed, with each successive treatment of Circean temptation, whether explicit or implied, the nature of this temptation becomes increasingly rarefied in moral conception until it finally approximates the highest moral potentiality available to ordinary man. If the later works cannot be read as simple transcripts of the author's personal life, the developing theme of Circean temptation in these works can tell us much about the evolution of Milton's moral understanding.

E. *L'Allegro-Il Penseroso*

Of all the works to be considered, the companion poems *L'Allegro-Il Penseroso* are most closely associated with the early autobiographical references to Circe and may be viewed as a culmination, transmuted into enduring poetry, of Milton's more autobiographical grapplings with the temptation of Circe. As Emerson has said, " 'L'Allegro' and 'Il Penseroso' are but a finer autobiography of his youthful fancies."[41]

Written shortly before *Prolusion VII* and responding to the same temptation of ignorant happiness the oration had labeled with the name of Circe, the companion poems cannot be properly understood without also recognizing their imaginative source in *Elegy I*. But it is not the sexual temptation which links the Latin and English poems. Though there are traces of the sexual Circe of *Elegy I*, they are here so distanced from the speaker as to be rendered powerless. In *L'Allegro* the maidens of the country have been reduced to an ambiguous possibility beyond the speaker's immediate field of vision: "Where perhaps some beauty lies, / The Cynosure of neighboring eyes" (79–80). The "store of Ladies" (121) in the city are seen only by the "Knights and Barons bold" (119) at aristocratic festivities, and even here the speaker feels called upon to invoke the sanctification of marriage: "There let *Hymen* oft appear" (125). The companion poems are, then, virtually untroubled by the sexual Circe. But if their content reflects the Circe of *Elegy VI* and *Prolusion VII*, the third temptation, their form and ultimate meaning derive from *Elegy I*.

Despite the lapse of some five years, the close association of activities with those of *Elegy I* reveals the essentially cyclical nature of *L'Allegro-Il Penseroso*, however important the order in which the poems are placed.[42] Separated into the two distinct poems is the deliberate alternation of study and relaxation which Milton describes in *Elegy I* and which also introduces *Prolusion VI*, on the subject "That Sportive Excercises Are Occasionally Not Adverse To Philosophic Studies" (p. 612). Having just returned from the pleasures of London to resume "the scholarly leisure which is the kind of life that I believe that the souls in heaven enjoy," he sees such alternation of activities as necessary to the pursuit of the higher life of dedicated study: "In this way the rotation of work and play can always be relied upon to drive off the tedium of satiety, and interrupted activities are picked up again all the more eagerly" (p. 613).

Il Penseroso describes the experiences of such a "rapt soul" (40) as it contemplates the mysteries of Hermetic and Platonic philosophy, relieved by the reading of Greek tragedy, Chaucer, and Renaissance epic, by "unseen" (65) moonlit walks, and at dawn by "some strange mysterious dream" (147) experienced while sleeping "by some Brook" (139) near the Nymphs' "hallow'd haunt" (138). Since *L'Allegro* also notes "Such sights as youthful Poets dream / On Summer eves by haunted stream" (129–30), the persona is clearly the same as that of *Il Penseroso*. But where, in *Il Penseroso,* there is no trace of personal melancholy (the Saturnian contemplative melancholy being stressed exclusively), *L'Allegro* begins with a violent exorcism of black melancholy and an invocation of "heart-easing Mirth" (13) to bring him a life of "unreproved pleasures free" (40). The solitary life of the mind has not only reached a stage of satiety but has filled him with a sense of "sorrow" (45).

And so, rising with the lark, he goes off for a restorative walk into the countryside. He receives visual delight from the pleasures of the landscape and of the peasants at work, so content in their innocent, simple lives that they merge with their pastoral prototypes in his mind. He observes "many a youth, and many a maid, / Dancing in the Checker'd shade" (95–96), their "secure delight" (91) carrying them through an evening of ale and ghost stories until "to bed they creep" (115). But the speaker has not entered the dance and general festivities, his approach to such simple joys going no further than his negative willingness to remain "not unseen" (57).

When the country folk depart, he returns to the different pleasures of the town. Again he walks "not unseen," surrounded by "the busy hum of men" (118). He observes the Knights and Barons going off to gala evenings which will be graced with "store of Ladies," splendid events of which he has dreamt "on Summer eves by haunted stream." Passing them on his way, he finally reaches his own destination, the theater and an evening presided over by the comic Muse of Jonson or Shakespeare, again surrounded by others and yet alone. Responding most truly to the sweet and complex beauty of the light airs, he invokes the presiding spirit of Mirth to transport him beyond his "eating cares" (135) to that

higher realm of art where his "meeting soul" (138) may be finally engaged, "Untwisting all the chains that tie / The hidden soul of harmony" (143–44).

If he began the day feeling a sense of alienation from the community of men produced by profound exhaustion with the solitary spiritual
life, his day abroad has only confirmed his isolation from the simpler
pleasures enjoyed alike by the thoughtless peasantry and their aristocratic betters, the simple "sorrow" of the morning growing to "eating
cares" by night. He has not joined in their life of "unreproved pleasures
free," however refreshing he found their innocent enjoyment, and it is
finally only the higher pleasure of art that can engage his soul, yet only
such art, transcending even that of Orpheus, that "would have won the
ear / Of *Pluto,* to have quite set free / His half-regain'd *Eurydice*" (148–
50). Since such a divine art, capable of quite vanquishing death, is beyond the power of Mirth to give, he now rejects the earlier attractiveness
of the simple life as "vain deluding joys" (*Il Penseroso,* 1) fit only for
"some idle brain" (5). His mind refreshed by this exposure to the life of
ordinary humanity and reconfirmed, through his unalterable isolation
in the midst of such simple joys, in his dedication to a higher vocation,
he can return to the contemplative life "all the more eagerly" (*Prolusion
VI*) for this brief vacation.

The only true enjoyment he projected in the life of *L'Allegro* was
that solitary pleasure with the Muses which did not expose his alienation
from the ways of simple mankind, and this pleasure more truly belongs
to the sphere of *Il Penseroso,* where Orphic power *can* make "Hell grant
what Love did seek" (108). The music of Orpheus or of "th'unseen Genius of the Wood" (154)—who, in *Arcades,* experiences the music of the
spheres, "which none can hear / Of human mold with gross unpurged
ear" (72–73)—is but a prelude to that highest music, the reward of a life
devoted to the enlargement of the mind, which can "dissolve me into
ecstasies, / And bring all Heav'n before mine eyes" (165–66). But this
culmination of the contemplative life is, itself, only the last necessary
step before the active fulfillment of his ultimate vocation, to "attain /
To something like Prophetic strain" (174).

If we accept the cyclical form of *L'Allegro-Il Penseroso* as narrated
by a unified persona, it becomes clear that to one so imbued with a sense
of higher poetic vocation, the alternative carefree life of *L'Allegro,* even
when raised to the highest level of Thalian art, must ultimately be

viewed as a threat, however attractive it may appear in moments of spiritual exhaustion. It is precisely this threat to a higher dedication which Milton, in *Elegy VI* and *Prolusion VII,* had defined as a Circean temptation. But Homer's own presentation of this third temptation of Circe revealed that it is only vicious if its acceptance by the will goes beyond the needs of spiritual recuperation. Spenser reinforced this meaning by showing that a temporary indulgence in rest is permissible to a nature capable of exercising temperance since such a higher nature would soon find even its relatively harmless pleasures unsatisfying. Like Spenser's Guyon on Phaedria's island, the Miltonic persona avoided permanent immersion in the carefree, undedicated life, his exposed isolation from ordinary convivial society only reconfirming his refreshed spirit in its higher purposes. The innocent life of *L'Allegro,* harmless to its normal participants and refreshing to the solitary visitor, can be recognized as an implied Circean temptation only when viewed in the context of Milton's explicit treatments of Circe, including *Comus.*

F. Comus

An adequate understanding of *Comus,* Milton's major treatment of the myth of Circe, can only be reached by appreciating the essentially nonvicious nature of Circean temptation in Milton's imagination, and this despite the archetypal form given to this temptation in its first presentation. Milton's Comus is a male personification of Circe. The son of Circe and Bacchus, he is "Much like his Father, but his Mother more" (57). His paternal parentage largely reflects Comus' nature as this figure earlier appeared in Jonson's masque *Pleasure Reconciled to Virtue,* and his first introduction in a brief revel, with "a rout of Monsters, headed like sundry sorts of wild Beasts" (prior to 93), carries structural suggestions of the Jonsonian antimasque.[43] This revel is Milton's first specific treatment of the Homeric Circe's initial temptation, and its vicious nature is not a little due to Bacchic influence. Comus invites his bestial followers to joys which are vicious in their excess. The excessive revelry of "Midnight shout" (103) and "Tipsy dance" (104) is soon followed by sexual pleasure in a clearly sinful form: "Come let us our rites begin, / 'Tis only daylight that makes Sin" (125–26). The second Circean temptation of sex and the third of innocent "Joy and Feast" (102) are here given a lurid cast of drunken indulgence which is appropriate to the Homeric first form of bestial enslavement and separates these pleasures from Milton's normal evocations of Circe in her less embruting forms. In Ariosto, Tasso, and Spenser, this first transforming temptation is also compounded of sexual and idle pleasures, but its excessive nature is defined by a total surrender of the will rather than by drunken debauchery. But if Milton has gone further in his depiction of vice than his predecessors, this brief revel has little other than symbolic relevance to the central temptation of the Lady which follows. Though Comus appears with charming rod and glass before the Lady, his temptation will follow the more usual Miltonic practice of focusing upon the less vicious second and third forms.

In the ordering of these temptations, Milton follows the pattern set by Tasso and continued in part by Spenser of inverting the second and third temptations. And his presentation of the third temptation also follows the twofold form of this temptation found in Tasso and Spenser: the pure appeal of idle pleasure offered to Rinaldo and Cymocles, and the more Homeric appeal of restorative refreshment offered to Carlo and Ubaldo and to Guyon. Milton, however, also inverts the order in which these two forms of the third temptation are presented, beginning with the appeal to refreshment and proceeding to his version of the Siren-Phaedria main temptation. The restorative form of this temptation is perhaps closest to the original Renaissance version of Ariosto. Like the three ladies of Alcina's court, Comus asks the Lady, "Why should you be so cruel to yourself" (679) and offers her: "Refreshment after toil, ease after pain, / That have been tir'd all day without repast, / And timely rest have wanted; but, fair Virgin, / This will restore all soon" (687–90).

Of all the Renaissance Circes, Comus most approximates Armida in the special quality of his feeling for the Lady. As Armida's destructive hatred of her victims was changed to love upon her first sight of Rinaldo, a love which finally found its fulfillment in a form suggestive of marriage, so Comus is altered by the first appearance of the Lady, as his private response to her song indicates:

> Can any mortal mixture of Earth's mold
> Breathe such Divine enchanting ravishment?
> Sure something holy lodges in that breast.
>
> .   .   .   .
>
> Such sober certainty of waking bliss,
> I never heard till now. I'll speak to her
> And she shall be my Queen.   (244–46, 263–65)

His usual conviction of "the unexempt condition / By which all mortal
frailty must subsist" (685–86) is displaced by the "Divine" intimations
of her "sober certainty of waking bliss." The "enchanting ravishment"
of her "holy" vision so inspires him that he wishes to reclaim his own
better nature from its profligate indulgence through marriage to her.
Comus' conjugal desire gives a unique character to Milton's versions of
the ensuing third and second temptations of Circe.

Leading her to a palace suited to the aristocratic union he envisions,
he appeals to her first to enjoy the riches normally accruing to her station in life (whether as the fictitious princess of the masque or its aristocratic actress, Alice Egerton). His appeal begins with a celebration of
that highest development of aristocratic society, the cultivation of refined taste: "Wherefore did Nature pour her bounties forth / . . . But all
to please and sate the curious taste?" (710, 714). Though the expression
of this idea may, at first sight, make nature's purposes appear trivial, it
reflects the serious position that the ultimate purpose and value of life
lies not in mere animal survival but in the development of high human
culture.

But his primary argument is that such refinement of appreciation
would enhance her religious devotion:

> If all the world
> Should in a pet of temperance feed on Pulse,
> Drink the clear stream, and nothing wear but Frieze,
> Th'all-giver would be unthank'd, would be unprais'd,
> Not half his riches known, and yet despis'd,
> And we should serve him as a grudging master,
> As a penurious niggard of his wealth,
> And live like Nature's bastards, not her sons.   (720–27)

Though she argues that "swinish gluttony / Ne'er looks to Heav'n
amidst his gorgeous feast" (776–77), this is not what Comus has offered;
rather he has offered a vision of cultivated enjoyment which can accept
the world with true thanksgiving. Against his earlier argument she
affirms the opposing view that the general elimination of "want" (768)
is a higher social objective than the support of "pamper'd Luxury"
(770). These opposing social perspectives may have gained new urgency
in the political conflicts of our own age; but in Milton's time, the communist ideal of distributing wealth "In unsuperfluous even proportion"
(773) could only have been viewed as Utopian, whether seen in the con-

text of More's Renaissance humanism or of the Anabaptist communist communities of "saints" of the radical Reformation.[44] As Milton's other writings give no evidence of his support of Anabaptist social ideals and as these would have been viewed as both distasteful and dangerous by the Egertons, it is more likely that the Lady's social program would have been recognized as a reference to More; but More's Utopian commonwealth was presented as no more than an academic fancy whose actual realization was barred by man's pride.[45] Since the silks, gems, and other luxuries of life which support elite culture cannot be universally distributed, and since they are part of her aristocratic heritage, to refuse the riches of her station can only be a "pet of temperance," a denial which limits her own proper appreciation of nature's bounty without contributing to the good of others; and the thought of such "waste" (729) drives Comus to almost hysterical hyperbole. He would redirect her self-denying devotions into more human channels which, he argues, would enhance rather than negate her capacity for religious worship. Where Tasso had identified this third temptation with a prelapsarian golden age of peace, Milton lifts this Circean temptation still further to include both a higher cultural and religious consciousness. But, like Tasso, he now proceeds to the second temptation with its song of the rose.

In keeping with his privately expressed wish to marry her, Comus now attempts to make her accept the validity of sexual fulfillment:

> List Lady, be not coy, and be not cozen'd
> With that same vaunted name Virginity;
> Beauty is nature's coin, must not be hoarded,
> But must be current, and the good thereof
> Consists in mutual and partak'n bliss,
> Unsavory in th'enjoyment of itself.
> If you let slip time, like a neglected rose
> It withers on the stalk with languish't head.
> Beauty is nature's brag, and must be shown
> In courts, at feasts, and high solemnities.   (737–46)

Though Tasso and Spenser had made the rose song a recognized part of the narrative treatment of Circean temptation, Milton's treatment of the *carpe diem* theme most closely approximates what is probably its most famous example, Herrick's *To the Virgins, to Make Much of Time,* with its beginning "Gather ye rosebuds while ye may," and its closing note on marriage: "Then be not coy, but use your time, / And while ye may, go marry." As Herrick's poems circulated in manuscript within Jonson's circle long before they were published in 1648, and as Henry Lawes, who collaborated with Milton on *Comus,* had written music for Jonson's court masques,[46] Lawes would probably have had access to Herrick's manuscript poems and may well have shown them to Milton at the time of their collaboration. Just as Herrick contrasts virginity not with promiscuous indulgence but with conjugal fulfillment, so Comus hopes to make the Lady his Queen and appeals to her to renounce the lesser good of virginity for "mutual and partak'n bliss." He wishes her to share the normal pleasures of court life, its "feasts, and high solemnities" at which, as *L'Allegro* has shown, Hymen appears. He tempts her to renounce not premarital chastity for promiscuity but the ideal of virginity for that of marriage.[47]

Comus' Circean temptation of the Lady is, then, the appeal of ordinary, if aristocratic, happiness, the happiness of the "store of Ladies" who marry the "Knights and Barons bold" of *L'Allegro* and of which even "youthful Poets dream." It is a degrading temptation to the Lady only because she is devoted to "the sublime notion and high mystery" of "the sage / And serious doctrine of Virginity" (785–87). Hers is not an innocent coyness but a Platonic and Hermetic discipline such as that which absorbed the student of *Il Penseroso,* one which promises an immortalizing spirituality. The Elder Brother had earlier defined this "divine Philosophy" (476):

> So dear to Heav'n is Saintly chastity,
> That when a soul is found sincerely so,
> A thousand liveried Angels lackey her,
> Driving far off each thing of sin and guilt,
> And in clear dream and solemn vision
> Tell her of things that no gross ear can hear
>
> .   .   .   .
>
> Till all be made immortal: but when lust
>
> .   .   .   .
>
> Lets in defilement to the inward parts,
> The soul grows clotted by contagion,
> Imbodies and imbrutes, till she quite lose
> The divine property of her first being.   (453–69)

In this analysis, as in much Renaissance theorizing, Circean bestiality becomes the philosophic enemy which must be overcome if that higher state of spirituality is to be achieved, the state of "clear dream and solemn vision"—"something like Prophetic strain"—"that no gross ear can hear," and which promises final immortality. *Il Penseroso, Arcades,* and *Comus* are all informed by a Renaissance blend of Pythagorean and Neoplatonic thought[48] which made chastity a necessary spiritual preparation for that highest stage of contemplation which can partake even of the music of the spheres.

In *On the Morning of Christ's Nativity,* Milton had invoked this heavenly music—"Ring out ye Crystal spheres" (125)—continuing: "For if such holy Song / Enwrap our fancy long, / . . . leprous sin will melt from earthly mold, / And Hell itself will pass away" (133–34, 138–39). Thus the Lady, though scorning to devote her spiritual energies to the individual salvation of Comus, triumphantly proclaims the ultimate spiritual power of chastity to overcome all worldly evil:

> Thou art not fit to hear thyself convinc't:
> Yet should I try, the uncontrolled worth
> Of this pure cause would kindle my rapt spirits
> To such a flame of sacred vehemence,
> That dumb things would be mov'd to sympathize,
> And the brute Earth would lend her nerves, and shake,
> Till all thy magic structures rear'd so high,
> Were shatter'd into heaps o'er thy false head. (792–99)

In the Jonsonian masque such a triumph of virtue over vice would be visually presented; here the apocalyptic vision provides a philosophic victory, and the poet proceeds with his allegory of individual salvation. Though Comus could be convinced—"She fables not, I feel that I do fear / Her words set off by some superior power" (800–01)—she is content to leave him in his "sensual sty" (77) rather than risk that "defilement to the inward parts" by which, as her elder brother had shown, her own soul might grow "clotted by contagion."

The Lady had begun by invoking Faith, Hope, and Chastity (213–15), and it is clearly charity that she lacks. It has been argued that Milton identified chastity with Augustinian *caritas* and that this is shown by the Lady's desire for a fair and universal distribution of nature's blessings to ensure a fuller praise of the divine giver.[49] But this example of Utopian or millennial charity does not, in itself, prove that Milton's view of chastity is Augustinian rather than Platonic. That the Lady's reference to the "form of Chastity" (215) is Platonic seems well borne out by the behavior of the Lady and of the Attendant Spirit, whose "errand" (15) is only to those "that by due steps aspire / To lay their just hands on that Golden Key / That opes the Palace of Eternity" (12–14).[50] As the Attendant Spirit "would not soil these pure Ambrosial weeds" to aid "low-thoughted" (6) men, so the Lady deems Comus to be "not fit to hear thyself convinc't." Nor is this uncharitable attitude towards sinful man limited to Milton's earlier period. It continues to inform the elitist Christ of *Paradise Regained,* who refuses to devote himself to the conversion and reformation of imperial Rome: "What wise and valiant man would seek to free / These thus degenerate" (IV, 143–44). For Milton, chastity is not to be equated, on the Augustinian model, with charity towards one's neighbor, but is a spiritual discipline leading to personal salvation and to prophetic insight whose message is only to that "fit audience . . . though few" (*PL* VII, 31) who are already virtuous and open to the message of salvation. Milton indicates no criticism of the Lady's substitution of chastity for charity or of her refusal to devote herself to the salvation of Comus precisely because he does not believe the proper mission of the spiritual elite to be to the sinful but, on the model of his later Christ, to regain "lost Paradise" "by vanquishing / Temptation" (*PR* IV, 607–08).

Though there can be no question as to which side of the debate Milton supports, he has presented the temptation to "Saintly chastity" in its most appealing form. William G. Madsen has demonstrated that "for the Italian humanists Comus became the personification of the reconciliation of pleasure and virtue";[51] and such a conception would seem to inform Milton's Comus in his central temptation of the Lady. But it is just because the "mutual and partak'n bliss" of conjugal sex, affirming divine goodness in the midst of courtly festivity and luxury, is such an attractive social ideal that it can threaten the lonely dedication to a higher vocation—at least in the mind of the reader.

Milton has, of course, taken great care to guard the Lady from any such sense of threat. On the dramatic level she is placed immediately on her guard by Comus' inept bungling of the temptation. Satan will convince Eve by the perfection of his disguise; but Comus magically entraps her and reveals his true identity. As only "good men can give good things" (703) and he has revealed himself to be a "false traitor" (690), any argument he could now offer stands convicted of falsehood, and her only concern need be to discover and refute its error. Milton follows the same strategy in the dialectic temptations of *Paradise Regained,* the a priori falsehood of Satan's temptations leading Christ to discover the true meaning of his mission.

On the theoretical level, she is protected by her own chastity "which if Heav'n gave it, may be term'd her own" (419). When she accepts the guidance of the disguised Comus, she prays: "Eye me blest Providence, and square my trial / To my proportion'd strength" (329–30). Since her unaided strength is proportionate to her trial, she has no need of angelic protection to ward off temptation, and she overcomes the temptation to evil through her own spiritual power. Her two brothers, given the Odyssean function of Tasso's Carlo and Ubaldo and Spenser's Guyon and Palmer, are not required to rouse her from temptation and fail either to capture or destroy the tempter. It is not human but divine aid which she still needs to achieve her ultimate salvation, and this is provided by the Hermes–Attendant Spirit figure who brings Sabrina to administer the proper "cure" from her "fountain pure" (912–13). But though she cannot effect her total salvation unaided by grace—"Come Lady, while Heaven lends us grace" (938)—she has earned a special grace through her own devotion to "Saintly chastity." Milton's ideal in *Comus* is not temperance but the "flame of sacred vehemence" which kindles "rapt spirits" to perfect that virtue which can "climb / Higher than the Sphery chime" (1020–21).

The Circean temptation to such virtue has now progressed beyond the form given to it in *Elegy VI* and, by implication, *L'Allegro:* the convivial art and life of mirth which can innocently admit the pleasures of feasting, drink, delight in the opposite sex, and marriage festivities. In *Comus,* these pleasures have been elevated to the refined level of the connoisseur whose pleasure makes him only more fully aware of the divine goodness. A close analogue of Comus' temptation of the Lady is provided in Marvell's *A Dialogue Between the Resolved Soul, and Created Pleasure,* in which *Created* Pleasure thus addresses the Ladylike Resolved Soul:

> Welcome the Creations Guest,
> Lord of Earth, and Heavens Heir.
> Lay aside that Warlike Crest,
> And of Nature's banquet share:
> Where the Souls of fruits and flow'rs
> Stand prepar'd to heighten yours.

The argument is that partaking of nature's banquet will heighten spirituality, that a full knowledge of the world is consistent with heavenly desires: "Try what depth the Centre draws; / And then to Heaven climb." Though the Resolved Soul resists this appeal—"Cease Tempter" —and is celebrated by the Chorus, in *Bermudas, The Garden,* and *Upon Appleton House,* Marvell affirms created pleasure as a superior mode of apprehending and rising to the divine. In similar manner, Milton will move beyond this Circean temptation of created pleasure when, in *Paradise Lost,* the unfallen Adam virtuously accepts marriage and nature's profusion with true thanksgiving. Though the first marriage will be perverted into the image of the Lady's fears in the process of the Fall, it is not through "wilful barrenness" (*PL* X, 1042) that Adam and Eve are to be saved, but through the spiritual recovery of their first condition of "fealty" to God and "Conjugal Love" (*PL* IX, 262–63).

G. Paradise Lost

As we have seen, Circe provided the primary temptation in the corpus of works Milton produced up to 1642. But even as he turns from poetry to political prose, he carries with him a concern with Circean temptation now translated largely into political terms. Thus in *An Apology,* he moves from autobiographical reflections which had evoked the image of Circe to a polemical argument against prelacy in church government in which the Circean image is invested with new political significance. Viewing prelacy as "the second life of tyranny . . . which hath no small power to captivate the minds of men," he argues that "by their sorcerous doctrine of formalities they take the way to transforme them out of Christian men into *Judaizing* beasts."[52] The association of Circe with tyranny, in this case the threat to religious liberty posed by the prelates, reappears in *Eikonoklastes,* where it defines the growing threat to political liberty posed by the royalists. In this later work, Milton compares the royalists who desire the restoration of a king to "men inchanted with the *Circaean* cup of servitude" who "will not be held back from running thir own heads into the Yoke of Bondage," being "now againe intoxicated and moap'd with these royal, and therefore so delicious because royal rudiments of bondage, the Cup of deception, spic'd and temperd to thir bane."[53]

This new political dimension of Circean servitude enters *Paradise*

Lost in an analysis of political servitude philosophically related to the allegorizations of Circe by Conti and his followers:

> Reason in man obscur'd, or not obey'd,
> Immediately inordinate desires
> And upstart Passions catch the Government
> From Reason, and to servitude reduce
> Man till then free. Therefore since hee permits
> Within himself unworthy Powers to reign
> Over free Reason, God in Judgment just
> Subjects him from without to violent Lords.　　　　(XII, 86–93)

Milton's explicit identifications of Circe with similar analyses of tyranny in his prose works indicates that, for him, the inward and outward "Tyranny" (XII, 95) which results when man "permits" "unworthy Powers to reign / Over free Reason" is symbolized by the "*Circæan* cup of servitude." The association of the loss of such true liberty with swinish transformation in *Sonnet XII* is another instance which reinforces the Circean implications of this passage on "Rational Liberty" (XII, 82). This type of analysis was a standard feature of the allegorical interpretation of Circe by Renaissance mythographers. For Conti the bestial metamorphosis of the Circe myth signifies just this loss of rational control. This view of Circean bestiality is also reflected by Gelli, whose *Circe* pervasively portrays the bestial state as entirely subject to natural instinct and devoid of rational choice. It is such Renaissance interpretations of the archetypal Circean temptation which inform Milton's unique treatment of bestial metamorphosis in *Paradise Lost*. Though Milton treats all three forms of Circean temptation in his epic, he breaks with the Renaissance literary tradition in severely dissociating the bestial transformation from the less embruting dangers of sex and idleness and in viewing it exclusively as an allegory of the loss of that "true Liberty . . . which always with right Reason dwells" (XII, 83–84).

Milton represents the archetypal transformation of rational creature into beast of the Circe myth in the bestial metamorphoses of Satan. Consistent with the analysis of "Rational Liberty," it is Satan's permitting "within himself unworthy Powers to reign" which immediately prefaces and serves to explain his first actual metamorphosis into a beast:

And should I at your harmless innocence
Melt, as I do, yet public reason just,
Honor and Empire with revenge enlarg'd,
By conquering this new World, compels me now
To do what else though damned I should abhor.   (IV, 388–92)

His heart melting with compassion, Satan recognizes that the destruction of innocents is an abhorrent condition for achieving his revenge against God and perverts the very "honor" he is seeking to vindicate. Though he chooses to follow the stronger demand of his nature for personal glory, his internal conflict is so great that it causes this perverting need for honor to appear to his conscious mind as a compulsion he cannot withstand. But Milton, associating such compulsion with his concept of tyranny, immediately answers Satan's disclaimer of moral responsibility: "So spake the Fiend, and with necessity, / The Tyrant's plea, excus'd his devilish deeds" (IV, 393–94). Both here and in his discussion of "Rational Liberty," Milton makes clear that such servitude is chosen, permitted by the will, and that the plea of tyrannical compulsion is a psychological alibi of a will too weak to control desires it consciously knows to be devilish. In making this plea, however, Satan is forced to admit the justice of Abdiel's charge: "Thyself not free, but to thyself enthrall'd" (VI, 181). Satan had initially sought to divorce his freedom from God in the belief that submission to God's rule was a "Servility" (VI, 169) which inhibited the development of his true excellence. But he has painfully come to recognize that, rather than freeing his best self to pursue its own conception of good, his continuing refusal to "relent" (IV, 79) in pursuing a vindication he has admitted to be both unjustified and self-defeating "compels" him now to act in violation of his better nature. In refusing to obey the dictates of reason and love which define his true freedom and excellence, his nature has become progressively debased until his best self has become the thrall of an instinctual compulsiveness which most properly defines the bestial state he now assumes: "Down he alights among the sportful Herd / Of those four-footed kinds, himself now one" (IV, 396–97).

Satan recognizes the ironic reversal of his expectations when he is preparing to incarnate himself in the brute form of a serpent: "O foul descent! that I who erst contended / With Gods to sit the highest, am now constrain'd / Into a Beast, and mixt with bestial slime" (IX, 163–65). Again the bestial transformation is associated with the sense of being "constrain'd." When Satan "rebell'd / Against his worthier" (VI, 179–80), he lost the "true Liberty . . . which always with right Reason dwells," since right reason is the capacity to "approve the best, and follow what I approve" (VIII, 611).

The irony of this transformation of "Rational Liberty" into bestial constraint is underscored by the cosmic farce in which the "triumphant" (X, 464) Satan, mocking God to his followers as "worth your laughter" (X, 488) and expecting their "universal shout and high applause" (X, 505), is met instead by a "dismal universal hiss" (X, 508) as first they and then he are "all transform'd / Alike, to Serpents" (X, 520). Though only a temporary "humbling" (X, 576) which dramatically exposes the logical absurdity of Satan's pretensions by demonstrating God's "greater power" (X, 515), this last bestial metamorphosis of Satan also reveals in final symbolic form that not "to rule" (X, 493) but to be "rul'd" (X, 516) is the inevitable "doom" (X, 617) of disobedience to reason.

The Satanic metamorphoses are clearly informed by an allegorical interpretation of the *"Circœan* cup of servitude" which equates such servitude with Aristotelean brutishness, a condition characterized by a total deficiency of reason.[54] But Aristotle had defined such brutishness as the antithesis of heroic virtue, and it is precisely to such heroic virtue as is the salvation of heroes captivated by Circe in the Renaissance literary tradition that Satan aspires. In terms of Sandys' verse representation of this Aristotelian antithesis, Satan should be held a god rather than a beast since he does not "shun the Path and Toyles of HERCULES" for Circe's "passion" and "ease." In fact, it is just this Circean temptation that he resists, as the ensuing analysis will show. For Milton, however, the pursuit of such "Heroic Virtue" (XI, 690) is itself a temptation from "the better fortitude / Of Patience and Heroic Martyrdom" (IX, 31–32). Though opposite in nature from the temptation to the uncommitted life normally associated with Circe, Milton recognized with greater consistency than did Spenser that it was equally "erring, from the path of truth remote" (VI, 173); and to indicate this moral equivalency, he introduced an allegory of the archetypal Circean temptation into the very heart of the opposing temptation of heroic glory. He accomplishes this convergence of opposing temptations to the godly life—and of Aristotelian opposites—by detailing the inexorable steps in which the heroic aspiration to a glory inappropriate to a creature results in the loss of "Rational Liberty" and by symbolizing this loss in bestial metamorphoses with recognizable Circean implications drawn from one of the traditional mythographic interpretations of Circe in the Renaissance. It was shown at the start of this study that for Conti and his followers the bestial transformation signified the loss of either right reason or temperance. While Milton in his normal treatments of the bestial transformation follows the Renaissance literary tradition in viewing such bestiality as symbolic of the intemperance of an idle sensuality, in the formulation of Satan's bestial metamorphoses he adopts the alternative interpretation that it is a brutishness symbolic of the lack of true rationality. But if Milton thus suggests that the heroic and Circean paths will converge at the point of their ultimate doom, he otherwise carefully distinguishes them and, with very few exceptions, views Circe as a temptation to any sense of higher obligation whether to good or evil. Personifying this more usual form of Circean temptation in Eve, his analysis of the associated dangers of sex and idleness reaches a new subtlety.

Eve is most explicitly defined as Circe in her unconscious effect upon Satan and is so labeled when Satan, after his momentary hesitation, finally approaches her:

> shee busied heard the sound
> Of rustling Leaves, but minded not, as us'd
> To such disport before her through the Field,
> From every Beast, more duteous at her call,
> Than at *Circean* call the Herd disguis'd.   (IX, 518–22)

Although an ostensibly innocent reference, Milton never used the name of Circe casually, and the reference comes immediately after Satan momentarily succumbs to the most classic Miltonic form of the temptation of Circe. This is the sexual temptation first defined in *Elegy I* and developed through implicit reference in *Elegy VII, L'Allegro,* and *Lycidas.* It is, in fact, the poetic culmination of this long Miltonic tradition. Satan's reaction to the sight of Eve among the roses, a setting which evokes the allure of the rose song in Tasso and Spenser, is given in a magnificent simile which also recalls Milton's earlier rural settings for Circean temptation:

> Much hee the Place admir'd, the Person more.
> As one who long in populous City pent,
> Where Houses thick and Sewers annoy the Air,
> Forth issuing on a Summer's Morn to breathe
> Among the pleasant Villages and Farms

Adjoin'd, from each thing met conceives delight,
The smell of Grain, or tedded Grass, or Kine,
Or Dairy, each rural sight, each rural sound;
If chance with Nymphlike step fair Virgin pass,
What pleasing seem'd for her now pleases more,
She most, and in her look sums all Delight.   (IX, 444–54)

The rural beauty of *L'Allegro* is here openly heightened, as in *Elegy VII,* by the appearance of feminine beauty: "sometimes the suburban fields offer me their pleasures. Groups of radiant girls with divinely lovely faces come and go along the walks. When they add their glory, the day shines with double splendor" (p. 60). But as *Elegy I* has shown in its original treatment of this theme, this very appeal is the temptation of Circe. And Satan responds fully to this temptation: "That space the Evil one abstracted stood / From his own evil, and for the time remain'd / Stupidly good, of enmity disarm'd, / Of guile, of hate, of envy, of revenge" (IX, 463–66). The phrase "stupidly good" has often been misinterpreted as a reflection of Satan's moral depravity, which equates goodness with stupidity. But the association of this passage with Circean temptation clarifies its meaning. Through sexual allure, the second temptation, the Circean Eve is tempting Satan to renounce his higher commitments, though to evil, for the joys of the ignorant, simple life—to be, quite precisely, "stupidly good"—for him the third Circean temptation of *Prolusion VII*. If such stupid goodness is, for Satan, a moral step above his extreme commitment to evil, it is not good enough for a being of his enormous talents.[55] Anything less than an active witnessing to the Truth, as exemplified by Abdiel and Enoch, is a degraded abuse of his capacities. In *Comus,* the Lady's "enchanting ravishment" had exerted a similar charm, inspiring Comus to a higher social morality; but there it was the Lady who rejected this social ideal as an insufficient form of virtue, as ignorant and embruting.

Milton uses the same reasoning in his much discussed comment on Belial's speech: "Thus *Belial* with words cloth'd in reason's garb / Counsell'd ignoble ease, and peaceful sloth, / Not peace" (II, 226–28). While ignoble ease and peaceful sloth, the Siren-Phaedria temptation to a life uncommitted to a higher good, is morally preferable to active revenge, it is not true peace, which can come only through grateful submission to the will of God. Satan had shown his understanding of the true nature of peace when he said: "Peace is despair'd, / For who can think Submission" (I, 660–61). Such ease and peaceful sloth is not, then, "ignoble" because it fails to respond to the heroic honor code's dictate of revenge, but because it fails to meet the requirements of that "better fortitude / Of Patience and Heroic Martyrdom." The debate of Book II is another instance of the temptation of Circe to which Satan now responds. Peaceful sloth and stupid goodness may be morally preferable to an active opposition to God's will and revenge against His created good, but they are insufficient to ensure that highest state of blessedness which comes from actively fulfilling the will of God. As the Son most perfectly expresses it: "this I my Glory account, / My exaltation, and my whole delight, / That thou in me well pleas'd, declar'st thy will / Fulfill'd, which to fulfil is all my bliss" (VI, 726–29). But even such an inadequate form of goodness is finally rejected in both the public debate of Pandaemonium and Satan's present private debate in favor of the active evil of revenge, just as Cymocles left Phaedria's idle island to fight Arthur and achieve the utterly graceless state of damnation.

Although Milton explicitly associates Eve's momentary influence upon Satan with the temptation of Circe, his major treatment of Eve as Circean temptress is presented more covertly, particularly through such symbolic suggestions as the repeated use of the word "charm." For Eve's major Circean function is none other than to tempt Adam to his fall. But in both her explicit and implicit roles she exerts the same mode of temptation, sexual allure being the means by which higher masculine spirits are led to prefer personal happiness to greater spiritual commitments and so degrade their moral potential. This paradigm of Circean temptation informs Adam's confession to Raphael on his susceptibility to Eve's "charm":

> here only weak
> Against the charm of Beauty's powerful glance.
>
> · · · · · · · ·
>
> when I approach
> Her loveliness, so absolute she seems
> And in herself complete, so well to know
> Her own that what she wills to do or say,
> Seems wisest, virtuousest, discreetest, best;
> All higher knowledge in her presence falls
> Degraded.   (VIII, 532–33, 546–52)

Although he meets Raphael's rebuke at his "subjection" (VIII, 570) by affirming the power of his will to overcome his inner weakness—"I to thee disclose / What inward thence I feel, not therefore foil'd, / . . . Approve the best, and follow what I approve" (VIII, 607–08, 611)—the degrading power of her "charm" over his "higher knowledge" and right reason is soon apparent. He is willing to expose her to temptation, despite his better judgment and clear responsibility, because he cannot endure the loss of her love: "Go; for thy stay, not free, absents thee more" (IX, 372).

This need for love has motivated him from the beginning. Although his first response to life was gratitude to an inferred Maker, "From whom I have that thus I move and live, / And feel that I am happier than I know" (VIII, 281–82), he soon found his solitary existence unbearable: "In solitude / What happiness, who can enjoy alone, / Or all enjoying, what contentment find?" (VIII, 364–66). He asks God for "fellowship" (VIII, 389) and is granted his wish. As he beholds Eve's creation in a trance, his excessive dependence upon her loving presence is again revealed. Her beauty inspires "The spirit of love and amorous delight. / Shee disappear'd, and left me dark, I wak'd / To find her, or for ever to deplore / Her loss, and other pleasures all abjure" (VIII, 477–80). To protect him against such a dangerous indulgence in private despair, which would deny the goodness of creation and Providence, God leads her back to him "guided by his voice, nor uninform'd / Of nuptial Sanctity and marriage Rites" (VIII, 486–87). The protection against the excessive passions of "amorous delight" is marriage, a marriage specially designed to permit Adam to fulfill his higher obligations to God: "Hee for God only, shee for God in him: / His fair large Front and Eye sublime declar'd / Absolute rule" (IV, 299–301).

The conditions of this marriage are similar to those which permitted Homer's Odysseus to embrace his Circe: the woman is bound to serving the man's will and welfare, while he is freed to fulfill higher obligations. Though Milton allowed the Lady of *Comus* her virgin dedication to a higher vocation, he does not permit a wife any higher dedication than the study of her husband's welfare. But he also recognizes that this can only be assured by giving the husband "Absolute rule." For Milton, marriage is instituted to satisfy those masculine needs for "fellowship" and "amorous delight" which would otherwise interfere with man's higher pursuits; but if these delights are not to exercise undue influence over his will, he must preserve masculine domination. The dangers to such a hierarchical institution come not only from the woman's desire to assume equality, "for inferior who is free" (IX, 825), but also from the man's desire to escape the greater demands placed upon him for the easier happiness of personal gratification. This latent masculine desire marks the latest Miltonic reformulation of the second Circean temptation. In *Elegy I*, it was the allure of illicit sex; in *Comus*, of conjugal sex. In *Paradise Lost*, however, Milton's sexual morality has progressed to the point where he can "Hail wedded Love. . . . Whose bed is undefil'd and chaste pronounc't, / Present, or past, as Saints and Patriarchs us'd" (IV, 750, 761–62). It is now not marriage but uxoriousness which is the primary threat. This danger is again shown in the later vision of the "Sons of God" (XI, 622) who fell to the temptation of women "that seem'd / Of Goddesses, so blithe, so smooth, so gay, / Yet empty of all good wherein consists / Woman's domestic honor and chief praise" (XI, 614–17), and wedded them. Like Comus, they are studious "Of Arts that polish Life" (XI, 610), arts which, as the Lady charged, make them "Unmindful of thir Maker" (XI, 611). Adam relates their fall to his own—"But still I see the tenor of Man's woe / Holds on the same, from Woman to begin" (XI, 632–33)—but Michael significantly responds: "From Man's effeminate slackness it begins" (XI, 634). This is Milton's first reference to the specific danger of effeminacy suggested in Homer's account of the second Circean temptation and developed so explicitly in Renaissance epic. In his latest treatment of the Circean second temptation, then, Milton recognizes the danger of uxoriousness to be the "effeminate slackness" of man "who should better hold his place / By wisdom, and superior gifts receiv'd" (XI, 635–36).

Eve is created inferior to Adam, not in intelligence—for her native brilliance equals his—but in character. She has no capacity for that right reason which enables Adam to intuit immediately his proper dependence upon God and to see his creation as a manifestation of unmerited divine goodness: "That rais'd us from the dust and plac't us here / In all this happiness, who at his hand / Have nothing merited" (IV, 416–18). Her immediate response to life is self-absorption in her own perfection, and such self-love continues to inhibit a more just apprehension of her true condition of creaturely limitation and dependence. It is because his reason is "right" and hers operates perversely that her best hope of salvation rests in accepting his wiser spiritual guidance and apprehending "God in him." Similarly, his best hope of salvation depends upon his primary dedication to "God only" and his resistance to that "Female charm" (IX, 999) which is so disconcerting that "All higher knowledge in her presence falls / Degraded." Adam has shown such weakness almost from the moment of his creation, before Eve's personality could have any influence over him; and it is precisely this inborn weakness which makes Eve's emerging personality such a threat to his higher dedication. As their best hope of salvation rests in his maintenance of proper authority, his yielding to personal feeling in allowing her to meet Satan's temptation alone, while it does not exonerate Eve from personal accountability, does involve a great failure of his larger spiritual responsibility.[56]

His inability to endure existence without a loving companion—shown before and immediately after Eve's creation, and in his overwhelming need to preserve her love, whatever the consequences, which permits her solitary departure—becomes fatal in his immediate response, upon her return, to her fallen condition: "And mee with thee hath ruin'd, for with thee / Certain my resolution is to Die" (IX, 906–07). A return to his original loneliness becomes all the more unbearable now that he has experienced the gratifications of love: "How can I live without thee, how forgo / Thy sweet Converse and Love so dearly join'd, / To live again in these wild Woods forlorn?" (IX, 908–10). And his love for Eve's individual personality is so strong that "Should God create another *Eve* ... yet loss of thee / Would never from my heart" (IX, 911–13). So powerful is the personal bond he feels towards her that he prefers death to their separation: "if Death / Consort with thee, Death is to mee as Life; / So forcible within my heart I feel / The Bond of Nature draw me to my own" (IX, 953–56).

His failure is just this preference for the natural over the supernatural bond, for the primacy of personal feelings over his higher obligations. In negating these higher obligations, he moves from the effeminacy of the second Circean temptation into a form of idleness which reflects the final temptation of Circe. For these obligations involve more than the founding of a city, which forced Aeneas to accept the personal pain of separation from Dido that he might fulfill the divine will. They involve no less than the founding of the whole human race and care for its immortal preservation.[57] In "submitting to what seem'd remediless" (IX, 919), he denies not only the power of Providence to remedy his personal grief but the larger role which Providence has assigned him: the founding of a race of creatures in that obedience to the divine will which can preserve life everlasting. In Milton's theology, obedience to spiritual demands that transcend the personal is the path of life, whereas obedience to emotional demands that are purely personal, is a consorting with death, degrading and finally destroying the spirit. What is demanded of Adam in the face of personal tragedy is "the better fortitude / Of Patience," of submitting not "to what seem'd remediless" but to the will of God with enduring faith in Providence.

If such patient fortitude is demanded of Adam for the fulfillment of his larger obligation to found the human race, it is also what is truly demanded of him by his "wedded Love," the antithesis of "Court Amours" (IV, 767). Eve is "much won that he his Love / Had so ennobl'd, as of choice to incur / Divine displeasure for her sake, or Death" (IX, 991–93). But where courtly love celebrates the love-death as the highest voucher of its truth, conjugal love, the "true source / Of human offspring" (IV, 750–51), is united through its progeny to life. In choosing such a death, Adam has inverted not only the hierarchy but the essential meaning of conjugal love for that of courtly love[58] and so violated the divinely sanctioned institution of marriage whose perfection stands as symbol of his "Imparadis't" (IV, 506) state.

But his fall is not simply the result of his willingness "to disturb / Conjugal Love" (IX, 262–63) by exchanging its "bliss" (IX, 263) for the tragic fidelity so celebrated in courtly love: "O glorious trial of exceeding Love" (IX, 961). Its cause, as has already been suggested, rests more significantly in his willingness to give such suicidal expression to his personal grief precedence over his higher obligation to fulfill the will of God despite all personal hardship. In Milton's symbology, this desire for a purely personal fulfillment unrelated to any higher dedication is the temptation of Circe; and Milton points to this temptation when he defines the nature of Adam's fall in the following telling words: "he scrupl'd not to eat / Against his better knowledge, not deceiv'd, / But fondly overcome with Female charm" (IX, 997–99). Critics like E. M. W. Tillyard[59] and A. J. A. Waldock[60] have foundered on this line by not recognizing the moral significance with which Milton's lifelong preoccupation with the temptation of Circe weights the term "Female charm."[61] But Milton immediately points to this significance by showing Adam's ensuing display of "Carnal desire" (IX, 1013), the bestial association of which was earlier drawn by Raphael when he warned Adam not to let himself be "sunk in carnal pleasure, for which cause /

Among the Beasts no Mate for thee was found" (VIII, 593–94). As Adam is soon filled with "shame" (IX, 1079) at the memory of his "foul concupiscence" (IX, 1078), his momentary bestiality cannot be viewed as the inexorable product of his yielding to Circean temptation but only as its symbol. For Milton, this temptation is now seen as the "effeminate slackness" of uxoriousness, and its danger is not that it must lead to a permanent immersion in bestial pleasure but that it can cause a dependence upon human companionship to take precedence over the higher knowledge of dependence upon the divine and the consequent obligation to fulfill the divine will. The fall of Adam is thus not a simple moral failure incommensurate with its enormous consequences. It reflects the failure to withstand the most serious temptation which can afflict the sense of higher vocation in even the most dedicated spirits, the major temptation which, from first to last, informs Milton's works. It is only by seeing Adam's fall in this context, by recognizing its association with Circe and the implications of this symbol in Milton's imagination, that its full significance can be gauged.

H. *Paradise Regained*

If the complete loss of Paradise was due to the temptation of Circe, it can be regained only by one so superior to her "charm" that it would be folly to attempt it on a grand scale. Though Milton does treat all three traditional temptations of Circe in *Paradise Regained*, he does so in a manner which only briefly intrudes on his primary presentation of the three very different Satanic temptations of Christ recorded by Luke.

The subject is first and fittingly raised by Belial, who had earlier provided Circean counsel in Pandaemonium. In the diabolic council Satan now convenes, Belial introduces the possibility of such temptation in words that recall the earliest Miltonic haunt of Circe: "Set women in his eye and in his walk" (II, 153). Belial fully understands the "enchanting" (II, 158) power of women to "Enerve, and with voluptuous hope dissolve, / Draw out with credulous desire, and lead / At will the manliest, resolutest breast" (II, 165–67). As in *Paradise Lost*, such "Female charm" can lead both to the effeminate subjugation of manliness (the second temptation) and to an enervation of higher dedication in idleness (the third temptation). Though Belial's contention that the power of women can affect even "the manliest, resolutest breast" is supported by the weight of other Miltonic evidence, Satan scorns the use of women to tempt one "Made and set wholly on th'accomplishment / Of greatest things" (II, 207–08), preferring the temptation of "glory" (II, 227).

But he does essay the most innocent temptation of Circe in the Homeric formulation so often repeated in Renaissance epic. As Christ now hungers from the effects of his forty-day fast, Satan produces a grove reminiscent of the gardens of Armida and Acrasia: "Nature's own work it seem'd (Nature taught Art)" (II, 295). There the "choicest store" (II, 334) of food and drink is provided on "A Table richly spread, in regal mode" (II, 340), and Satan assures Christ that "Thir taste no knowledge works, at least of evil, / But life preserves, destroys life's enemy, / Hunger, with sweet restorative delight" (II, 371–73). But though Odysseus and Guyon suffered no serious harm from such indulgence, Christ, like the Lady, rejects even such "restorative delight" with a "temperance invincible" (II, 408).

While Milton does not suggest that restorative indulgence taken in the moderation advised in *Sonnet XX* and *Sonnet XXI* would lead to the utter depravity of Circean bestiality, he does give us a vision of the result of total intemperance in his picture of imperial Rome. This den of Circean bestiality, whose fitting symbol is the "brutish monster" (IV, 128) Tiberius, is inhabited by those "once just, / Frugal, and mild, and temperate" (IV, 133–34) who now have become "Luxurious by thir wealth, and greedier still, / And from the daily Scene effeminate" (IV, 141–42). The effeminacy resulting from the second temptation and the indulgence in luxury of the third has, in this instance, transformed Rome into the "brutish" likeness of its emperor, who has "retir'd / To *Capreae* . . . with purpose there / His horrid lusts in private to enjoy" (IV, 91–94). Closer to the drunken revel of Comus' bestial followers than to any other Miltonic reference to brutish transformation, this historical picture of Roman depravity embodies the truly vicious character Milton ascribes to the archetypal first temptation of Circe.

But his purpose is not simply to contrast twin images of total abstinence and total indulgence; for through Christ's rejection of Roman "glory" (IV, 89) as "brutish," Milton once again demonstrates the conversion of heroic aspiration into Circean bestiality. As with Satan's bestial metamorphoses, this conversion depends on the conception of Circean servitude Milton had developed in his prose tracts, a conception at once political and philosophical which associates such servitude with the outward tyranny of those "ambitious grown / Of triumph" (IV,

137–38) and with the psychological compulsions which produce "inward slaves" (IV, 145). Christ had originally made the simple political equation of tyranny and brutishness when he recalled his youthful aspiration "To rescue *Israel* from the *Roman* yoke, / Then to subdue and quell o'er all the earth / Brute violence and proud Tyrannic pow'r" (I, 217–19). Though it was brute tyranny he had then hoped to subdue, when first confronted with the Satanic temptation of glory he begins to perceive the brutish implications of any attempt to "subdue / By Conquest":

> They err who count it glorious to subdue
> By Conquest
>
>   .   .   .   .   .   .
>
> But rob and spoil, burn, slaughter and enslave
>
>   .   .   .   .   .   .
>
> Then swell with pride, and must be titl'd Gods,
>
>   .   .   .   .   .   .
>
> Till Conqueror Death discover them scarce men,
> Rolling in brutish vices, and deform'd,
> Violent or shameful death thir due reward.   (III, 71–87)

This passage is transitional, not only in terms of Christ's emerging conception of his true mission, but in the thematic development of this political-psychological conception of Circean brutishness toward its final convergence with the more conventional view of Circean bestiality which identifies the brutish transformation with intemperate indulgence in sex and idle feasting. While the "brutish vices" by which the glory-seeking conquerors have been "deform'd" need imply nothing beyond the shameful violence to which such conquerors are compelled by their swollen pride, a second sense is suggested by the forms of moral punishment appropriate to these vices, violence and shame. If "shameful" be interpreted in a manner which differentiates it from "violent," the term would seem suggestive of the sensual vices into which the giants fell after their conquests (*PL*, XI, 713–18), and of the "deformities" produced by the "brutish vice" of "Intemperance" in "Meats and Drinks" (*PL*, XI, 472–73, 513, 518), an intimation which is completely fulfilled in the passage on Roman brutishness. In this final passage on brutishness, the association with political and psychological tyranny is fully assimilated to a more conventional view of Circean degeneracy which it now serves to explain; and it is Christ's recognition that both the political and moral forms of Roman brutishness result from a similar self-enslavement that now causes him to renounce his earlier Zealot conception of Messianic deliverance: "What wise and valiant man would seek to free / These thus degenerate, by themselves enslav'd, / Or could of inward slaves make outward free?" (IV, 143–45). Though Satan had preferred the temptation of glory to Belial's Circean suggestion, the major Circean temptation of Christ has proved to be the temptation not to renounce his higher calling but to misinterpret it as a call to earthly conquest with all its implications of brutish transformation. And it is through the political dimension of Circean servitude that Milton effects this convergence of Circean brutishness with the pursuit of "false glory, attributed / To things not glorious" (III, 69–70).

Milton's earlier poetry carefully avoided exploring the temptation of pride that dominates his two epics. But his earlier concern with Circean temptation was to affect this later exploration in an unexpected manner, not directly, but through the intervening metamorphosis of Circe herself into a political symbol. When Milton returned to the composition of his greatest works after the twenty-year hiatus of his political prose writing, he introduced into the essentially opposed temptation of pride the complex new association of Circe with political and psychological tyranny developed in his prose, an association which he also evoked whenever the historical context provided an occasion for the discussion of political tyranny. In the three major works of this later period, the new meanings associated with the symbol of Circean brutishness are extended even to Milton's developing treatment of the more conventionally conceived temptation of Circe, investing it with a new dimension of allegorical implication, but one to which the specific connotations of his literary Circes can never be wholly reduced.

I. Samson Agonistes

Milton's association of brutishness with tyranny continues in *Samson Agonistes,* where it defines the reason for both Samson's and Israel's positions of servitude at the opening of the drama. Israel's servitude is explained on a historical principle commonly cited by Milton: "But what more oft in Nations grown corrupt, / And by thir vices brought to servitude, / Than to love Bondage more than Liberty" (269–70). It is from this "brute and boist'rous force of violent men / Hardy and industrious to support / Tyrannic power" (1273–75) that Samson had failed to deliver Israel in the past when "like a petty God. . . . swoll'n with pride" he "fell" "into the snare" of "venereal trains, / Soft'n'd with pleasure" (529–34). Like that of Israel, his own servitude to Philistine tyranny is a punishment which justly fits and symbolizes his loss of inner freedom: "servile mind / Rewarded well with servile punishment" (412–13). But in a Miltonic reversal of Christ's renunciation as "brutish" of the role of earthly deliverer in *Paradise Regained,* Samson will become the worthy "deliverer" (1270) of Israel and God's "faithful Champion" (1751). This will happen when he is finally able to overcome the very different temptation of Circe which informs the immediate action of the play, not that which enters into pride and converts it into the brutish opposite of the petty godhead to which it aspires, but that which would give over all striving, whether for personal glory or to demonstrate the greater glory of God. If Milton's primary concern in *Paradise Lost* and *Paradise Regained* was with the temptation to substitute personal glory for the glorification of God, in *Samson Agonistes* he once more gives primary attention to his original conception of Circean temptation and transforms the Samson story into the culminating expression of his lifelong creative involvement with this mythic symbol. As in *Paradise Lost,* this temptation to the undedicated life is personified by "Female charm."

Of all the unstated personifications of Circe, Dalila is the most explicit. Milton makes pointed reference to her true Circean identity in Samson's rejection of Dalila's appeal:[62]

> I know thy trains
> Though dearly to my cost, thy gins, and toils;
> Thy fair enchanted cup, and warbling charms
> No more on me have power, thir force is null'd,
> So much of Adder's wisdom I have learn't
> To fence my ear against thy sorceries.   (932–37)

Though any mention of a "fair enchanted cup" is associated in Milton's imagination with "a certaine Sorceresse," Milton would here seem to be combining Tasso's identification of Circe with the Sirens[63] with the Homeric Circe's "warbling charms," the initial impression of Circe conveyed to Eurylochos and his men: "They stood there in the forecourt of the goddess with the glorious / hair, and heard Circe inside singing in a sweet voice" (X, 220–21). But where Homer's Circe imparts to Odysseus the "Adder's wisdom" of how he may protect his crew from the further "warbling charms" of the Sirens (XII, 39–54), Milton's identification of Circe with the Sirens permits Samson to use this knowledge against Circe herself.

Dalila's Circean nature is also suggested in Samson's description of his former yielding to her importunate requests for his secret:

> But foul effeminacy held me yok't
> Her Bondslave; O indignity, O blot.
>
>   .   .   .   .
>
> These rags, this grinding, is not yet so base
> As was my former servitude, ignoble,
> Unmanly, ignominious, infamous,
> True slavery, and that blindness worse than this,
> That saw not how degenerately I serv'd.   (410–19)

Going far beyond the simple "effeminacy" of the second temptation, Samson's degenerate and blind slavery to Dalila evokes a vision of Circe's swine who wallow in the mud and have lost all memory of their native land.

In his descriptive presentation of Dalila, then, Milton has taken care to evoke the archetypal image of Circe, whose enchanted cup can transform men into swine. In his dramatic treatment, however, this first Homeric temptation provides only the moral symbolism for the more crucial, and again joined, second and third temptations, which have always defined Milton's conception of the specific Circean dangers to his highly dedicated characters.

Thus Dalila's primary appeal to Samson, like that of Ariosto's three ladies, Tasso's Siren, and Spenser's Phaedria, is that he relax his moral rigor and partake of the ordinary pleasures of life:

>   though sight be lost,
> Life yet hath many solaces, enjoy'd
> Where other senses want not their delights
> At home in leisure and domestic ease,
>
>   .   .   .   .
>
>   where my redoubl'd love and care
> With nursing diligence, to me glad office,
> May ever tend about thee to old age
> With all things grateful cheer'd.   (914–26)

Dalila's loving desire to attend to him until old age with all the cheerful "solaces" life can provide is the same wish Manoa had earlier expressed,

and it is introduced by a similar argument against willful self-punish-
ment: "what remains past cure / Bear not too sensibly, nor still insist /
To afflict thyself in vain" (912–14).

As Manoa counsels Samson:

> Repent the sin, but if the punishment
> Thou canst avoid, self-preservation bids;
> Or th'execution leave to high disposal
>
> .   .   .   .
>
> Who evermore approves and more accepts
> (Best pleas'd with humble and filial submission)
> Him who imploring mercy sues for life,
> Than who self-rigorous chooses death as due;
> Which argues over-just, and self-displeas'd
> For self-offence, more than for God offended.   (504–15)

Manoa's desire to ransom Samson from the Philistine lords springs from
the same conviction of the enduring worth of life which is to motivate
Dalila's attempt, but it is informed by an even more persuasive moral
argument. Manoa here advises Samson to follow the very path of patient
submission to God's will which would have prevented Adam's fall and
which makes possible Adam's final salvation. By making himself his own
judge, Manoa argues, Samson is usurping the place of God and denying
the power of Providence to derive good from evil.

But in the state of despair produced by his inability to use his great
gifts in a more appropriate service to God, Samson can only view "the
better fortitude / Of Patience" as a degrading temptation:

> Now blind, disheart'n'd, sham'd, dishonor'd, quell'd,
> To what can I be useful, wherein serve
> My Nation, and the work from Heav'n impos'd,
> But to sit idle on the household hearth,
> A burdenous drone, to visitants a gaze,
>
> .   .   .   .
>
>   til length of years
> And sedentary numbness craze my limbs
> To a contemptible old age obscure?
> Here rather let me drudge and earn my bread,
> Till vermin or the draff of servile food
> Consume me, and oft-invocated death
> Hast'n the welcome end of all my pains.   (563–76)

If Samson is "over-just" against himself it is because his superior endowments make patience, the highest form of reverence available to ordinary man, an inadequate form of service to him. To accept patience as his highest possible form of devotion might be morally superior to his present state of spiritual despair; but for him it would constitute a condition of "ignoble ease, and peaceful sloth, / Not peace," which can come only through using his great gifts in a higher service to God. More is demanded of him, as of Satan and his followers, than the "peaceful sloth" of adjusting to a fallen condition. Thus Manoa's suggestion that "perhaps / God will relent, and quit thee all his debt" (508–09) through the simple exercise of patience is shown to be as shallow a conception of the workings of Providence as his belief that God will enable Samson to fulfill his great "work from Heav'n impos'd" by causing "light again within thy eyes to spring" (584).

Manoa stands in the same relationship to Dalila as the Sirens and Phaedria do to Armida and Acrasia, as a separate personification of the more innocent temptation of idleness which the major Circean figure joins with sexual pleasure. But since the main function of Dalila's "Female charm" is to produce masculine idleness, the Manoa-Dalila appeal is ultimately the same.[64] It is just because the appeal of Manoa appears so morally persuasive that Milton must reveal its inadequacy by repeating it through the immediately suspect person of Dalila. Her temptation to enjoy the remaining solaces of life, the third temptation, is prefaced not only by Samson's earlier description of his "former servitude" but also by Dalila's penitent explanation of her treachery, which defines the second temptation:

> I knew that liberty
> Would draw thee forth to perilous enterprises,
> While I at home sat full of cares and fears
> Wailing thy absence in my widow'd bed;
> Here I should still enjoy thee day and night
> Mine and Love's prisoner.   (803–08)

Dalila sees his liberty to fulfill the higher demands of his spirit as the enemy of personal happiness, both her own and his ability to share it fully. She can only build the significance of her own sphere of life by diminishing his, by making him "Love's prisoner," whatever the cost.[65] But where the earlier Renaissance Circes allured their men into preferring a life of indolent sensuality to the rigors of heroic achievement and

thus to imprison themselves in love, Dalila, fulfilling Hermes' warning
to Odysseus about Circe's intentions, takes more forcible means to un-
man Samson and prove her own importance.

Milton recognized that the tragic liability of patriarchal marriage,
whose model he adopted so completely, was that its inherent restriction
of feminine potential could turn loving wives into dominating Circes.
But his only response to this dilemma was an increasing insistence on
male absolutism. If Adam's "absolute rule" was to be exercised "with
gentle sway" (IV, 308), such melioration is now fiercely rejected:

> Therefore God's universal Law
> Gave to the man despotic power
> Over his female in due awe,
>
> . . . .
>
> So shall he least confusion draw
> On his whole life, not sway'd
> By female usurpation, nor dismay'd.   (1053–60)

Eve and Dalila do, of course, act treacherously towards their husbands:
their attempts to raise their own significance by creating circumstances
which will cause their husbands to substitute personal desires for obedience to God draw confusion on all. But though Milton was able to give
imaginative credence to their position in his brilliant development of
their roles, his Pauline conception of marriage could allow them no
moral sanction. It may be better for a man to marry than to burn, but
the institution of marriage must serve man's primary obligation to God
and must be perverted by neither "female usurpation" nor male uxoriousness. Thus Samson answers Dalila's appeal by showing that her former attempt to make him "Love's prisoner" betrays her future course:
"How wouldst thou insult / When I must live uxorious to thy will /
In perfect thraldom" (944–46).

Dalila's vision of life's solaces, of "delights / At home in leisure and
domestic ease," is identical with the vision of life evoked in Samson's
mind by Manoa's offer: "to sit idle on the household hearth. . . . To a
contemptible old age obscure." But where his rejection of Manoa's patient reverence for life betrayed signs of spiritual pride and despair, the
reformulation of this life-affirming alternative by Dalila permits him
more righteous grounds for rejection. The happiness of ordinary mankind offered him by Manoa can now be rejected as no less than "perfect
thraldom" to Circe, his allusion to her "fair enchanted cup, and war-

bling charms" immediately prefacing the delineating of this "thraldom."

But Samson's final argument against reconciliation with Dalila—
"Love-quarrels oft in pleasing concord end, / Not wedlock-treachery en-
dangering life" (1008–09)—does not reflect a general Miltonic principle.
For Eve's decision to offer Adam the fruit only on the assumption that it
would cause death was surely a greater instance of "wedlock-treachery,"
and she was still able to win her final appeal to Adam not to forsake her.
The reason that Adam can accept a solacing relationship with Eve while
Samson must reject a similar relationship with Dalila has nothing, then,
to do with the depth of betrayal but rather with the different spiritual
demands made upon Adam and Samson, demands proportionate to their
spiritual capacities.

As we have seen, two different forms of strength are demanded of
God's servants: "the better fortitude / Of Patience and Heroic Martyrdom." These alternative forms of fortitude are again suggested in the
apocalyptic vision of the Chorus:[66]

> Oh how comely it is and how reviving
> To the Spirits of just men long opprest!
> When God into the hands of thir deliverer
> Puts invincible might
> To quell the mighty of the Earth, th'oppressor,
>   .   .   .   .
> Hee all thir Ammunition
> And feats of War defeats
> With plain Heroic magnitude of mind
> And celestial vigor arm'd.
>   .   .   .   .
>   But patience is more oft the exercise
> Of Saints, the trial of thir fortitude.
>   .   .   .   .
> Either of these is in thy lot,
> *Samson*, with might endu'd
> Above the Sons of men; but sight bereav'd
> May chance to number thee with those
> Whom Patience finally must crown.   (1268–96)

Samson's mortal challenge of Harapha "to decide whose god is God"
(1176) revives the spirits of the Chorus with a vision of the power of
divinely graced deliverers, armed with such "celestial vigor" as Samson

again possesses, to quell the oppressors of the earth. But the Chorus recognizes that his blind condition would seem to make the more ordinary form of sainthood, patience, the only form of virtue to which he can aspire.

It is this very patience, which redeemed Adam and is "oft the exercise / Of Saints," that constitutes, for Samson, the ultimate temptation of Circe.[67] His "plain Heroic magnitude of mind" cannot be satisfied that even such saintly patience can truly justify him. Even Manoa must finally admit that he cannot "sit idle with so great a gift/ Useless, and thence ridiculous about him" (1500–01), though his shallow conception of God convinces him that "God will restore him eyesight to his strength" (1503). But Samson's "rousing motions" (1382) spring from a deeper prophetic insight into the tragic operation of Providence and "presage" (1387) "Heroic Martyrdom" as the true way to redeem his forfeit gift of divine strength. This the Chorus now recognizes:

> O dearly bought revenge, yet glorious!
> Living or dying thou hast fulfill'd
> The work for which thou wast foretold
> To *Israel,* and now li'st victorious
> Among thy slain self-kill'd
> Not willingly, but tangl'd in the fold
> Of dire necessity.   (1660–66)

"Self-kill'd / Not willingly," because the fulfillment of his foretold work would enable him to live in true peace, his fall requires that such restoration now be "dearly bought" with his redeemed life, this tragic paradox "tangl'd in the fold / Of dire necessity." It is in these last lines—not in Manoa's more shallow "Nothing is here for tears, nothing to wail" (1721)—that Milton reveals his deeply tragic conception of the redemptive processes of divine Providence.

Samson's struggle towards this victory marks the final stage in Milton's exploration of Circean temptation, an exploration which has revealed an ever more subtle understanding of the moral danger besetting the sense of higher obligations. The attractions of feminine beauty (in *Elegy I*), of a lesser mirthful art (in *Elegy VI*), and of ignorant happiness (in *Prolusion* VII), combine in varying proportions to define the implied Circean temptation of *L'Allegro,* the innocent happiness of ordinary, thoughtless humanity. In *Comus,* this happiness is raised to include the higher purposes of religious devotion, a devotion which permeates the cultivated apprehension of pleasure and which sanctifies sexual desire with marital intentions. In *Paradise Lost*, the temptation of Comus becomes virtually identified with Adam's "Imparadis't" state, and the Circean danger to his higher obligations has now progressed to the uxorious dependence upon his sanctified personal relationship which can lead him to give it precedence over the need for patient submission to divine Providence. Finally, in *Samson Agonistes*, the temptation of Circe has been elevated to that very saintly patience which redeemed Adam and which Milton's own blindness had earlier urged him to accept as his highest possible service to God, when he affirmed, in what for him is surely the most despairing line he ever wrote: "They also serve who only stand and wait" (*Sonnet XIX*). Absorbing the Renaissance literary tradition which equated Circean temptation not primarily with bestial depravity but with effeminate idleness, Milton lifted the Homeric Circe to new heights of moral subtlety.

Though Milton's first treatments of Circean temptation were in frankly autobiographical contexts, and we have evidence as late as 1642 that this sorceress was such a familiar fixture in his imagination that he felt no need actually to name her, it is not necessary to draw biographical inferences as to Milton's personal consciousness of such temptation to recognize that the temptation of Circe is the most significant thematic thread running through the entire corpus of Milton's works. And yet, given the powerful imprint of Milton's personality upon his works, it is perhaps not an overstatement to say that this theme embodied much of Milton's own moral struggles. Like Samson, Milton finally rejected the counsel of Patience and, through "plain Heroic magnitude of mind," went on to the epic accomplishment of writing his greatest works. Though late, he heroically fulfilled the ambition, confessed in *Elegy I*, of rivaling Ionian Homer, that ambition which was already threatened by the temptation of Circe. He was to reformulate this temptation throughout his creative life, transmuting it into the imaginative forms that fulfill his bardic mission to "justify the ways of God to men" (*PL* I, 26) even as they enshrine his spirit's victory over the primary Circean temptation of simple human happiness and devotion.

St. John's University

NOTES

1. *Milton's Conception of Sin as Developed in "Paradise Lost,"* Monograph Series, vol. VII, no. 5 (Logan, Utah, 1960), p. 45.

2. *Mythology and the Renaissance Tradition in English Poetry,* rev. ed. (New York, 1963), p. 277.

3. *Images and Themes in Five Poems of Milton* (Cambridge, Mass., 1957), p. 130.

4. *Pagan Myth and Christian Tradition in English Poetry* (Philadelphia, 1968), p. 13.

5. "Spenser's Acrasia and the Circe of the Renaissance," *JHI,* IV (1943), 386–87.

6. (Padua, 1616), p. 309. My translation.

7. Conti interprets moly primarily as *"diuina clementia"* (p. 308), though he later augments this, arguing that the protection against Circe's charm is God-given wisdom or right reason and that the wise man will act with *"moderate gubernare"* (p. 309). For a concise lising of allegorical interpretations of moly in the Renaissance, see Robert Martin Adams, *Ikon: John Milton and the Modern Critics* (1955; reprint ed., Westport, Conn., 1972), pp. 14–15.

8. "Spenser's Acrasia," p. 387.

9. *The Odyssey of Homer,* trans. Richard Lattimore, Harper Torchbooks (New York, 1967). All further references within the text are to this edition.

10 *Ovid's Metamorphoses,* trans. George Sandys (Lincoln, Nebraska, 1970), XIV, 299–302, p. 628. This edited reprint of the 1632 edition will be used for all further references to Ovid and Sandys.

11. Ibid., XIV, 436, p. 632.

12. Ludovico Ariosto, *Orlando Furioso,* trans. William Stewart Rose, ed. Stewart A. Baker, with introduction by A. Bartlett Giamatti (Indianapolis, 1968). All translated references are to this edition. All Italian references are to *Opere di Ludovico Ariosto* (Milan, 1966). Canto and verse designations are the same for both.

13. Giamatti, in his introduction to the Rose translation of *Orlando Furioso,* pp. xxxix–xl, points to Ariosto's use of the *Aenead* as the epic model of his work and to the importance of the Alcina-Dido parallel to suggest an identification between Ruggiero and Aeneas.

14. A. Bartlett Giamatti, *The Earthly Paradise and the Renaissance Epic* (Princeton, 1966), p. 139. Giamatti's analysis of Renaissance epic is particularly fine in noting the references to effeminacy in episodes associated with Circe; but by not relating the Renaissance Circes to Homer, he wrongly attributes this association to the invention of Petrarch in the *Trionfo d'Amore,* even though he recognizes that Petrarch's Venus has acquired Circean traits. See pp. 126–27, 142, 157, 205–06.

15. Torquato Tasso, *Jerusalem Delivered,* trans. Edward Fairfax (1600), with introduction by Roberto Weiss (Carbondale, Ill., 1962). All references are to this edition.

16. "Dalila, the Ulysses Myth, and Renaissance Allegorical Tradition," *MLR,* LVII (1962), 562.

17. As Fairfax's normally excellent translation masks Tasso's reference to Rinaldo's effeminate appearance at this point, I quote from the Italian *Gerusalemme Liberata* (Milan, 1923).

18. See John Arthos, *On the Poetry of Spenser and the Form of Romances* (London, 1956), for a discussion, based upon Errico Proto, of Tasso's earlier *Rinaldo* as a

work "devoted to 'the new ideal of marriage, founded on the laws of love'" and its relation to the treatment of love in the *Liberata* (pp. 136–37). Arthos also views this latter treatment as an "analysis of the nature of love" (p. 165), though his interpretation of Tasso's analysis differs from mine.

19. In *Orlando Furioso* (XXXVII, i–xxi), Ariosto offers a mighty encomium to the intellectually emancipated women of his age, represented by Vittoria Colonna, who reveal women's full capacities, hitherto shrouded by domestic tasks or male envy, to be such "As haply ne'er was reached by manly fame" (XXXVII, ii) and which make them all the more worthy as marriage partners: "Worthy of one another are the twain; / Nor better ere were paired in wedlock's chain" (XXXVII, xi). Giovanni Battista Gelli's *Circe* argues this case with equal fervor when the deer, a female victim of Circe, pleads with Odysseus, "Make us your companions instead of slaves" (trans. Thomas Brown, ed. Robert Adams [Ithaca, 1963], p. 90), finally rejecting the possibility of returning to the inferior position of a human female, however much she delights in the exercise of her reason. Rabelais' projection of a condition of equal education and status of the sexes and the appropriateness of this condition to marriage, in the Abbey of Thélème section of *Gargantua*, is too well known to need further rehearsal. For further discussion of this new Renaissance concept of marriage, see the introduction to my book, *Elizabethan Love Tragedy* (New York, 1971).

20. *The Complete Poetical Works of Spenser*, ed. R. E. Neil Dodge (Cambridge, Mass., 1936). As all references to this edition of *The Faerie Queene* are to Book II, I give only canto and verse citations.

21. R. M. Durling, "The Bower of Bliss and Armida's Palace," *CL*, VI (1954), 337.

22. See Harry Berger, Jr., *The Allegorical Temper* (New Haven, 1957), pp. 59–60. Berger gives a most perceptive analysis of the distinction between Guyon's higher character and the "feeble nature" of others (see pp. 12–15 et passim).

23. Ariosto and Tasso had no problem with the conflict between heroic and religious values since, in the tradition of the *Chanson de Roland*, their heroic knights fought for Christianity against paganism. In their treatments, therefore, these knights are reclaimed from the temptations of Circe to pursue their admirable quest for heroic glory. *The Faerie Queene* is, however, permeated with this problem of conflicting values which Spenser is unable finally to resolve (see, for instance, the opposition in Book I between IX, xliii, and XI, ii). In Book II this problem becomes particularly acute, since the Renaissance literary treatments of Circe on which his own treatment is based view Circe as particularly opposed to heroic virtue (see n. 32 below for the Aristotelian basis of this opposition). Thus Guyon is horrified to see Verdant's "warlike armes" left "ydle": "Ne for them, ne for honour, cared hee, / . . . But in lewd loves, and wastfull luxuree, / . . . his bodie he did spend" (XII, lxxx). As this is the same attitude Atin expresses to Cymocles, there is clearly a confusion in Spenser's mind as to the allegorical significance of Circe, whether she is a danger to temperance or to heroic glory (both alternatives derived from Aristotle). Josephine Waters Bennett has traced the source of this confusion in *The Evolution of "The Faerie Queene"* (New York, 1960), showing that Guyon was originally conceived as devoted to the "Idea of pure Glory" (p. 52) "before he became the embodiment of temperance" (p. 94), just as "the quest of Acrasia was begun as an imitation of Ariosto rather than an illustration of Aristotle's idea of temperance" (p. 127). This confusion becomes most critical in the case of Cymocles' reclaimed heroic wrath.

24. M. Pauline Parker, in a comment on Phaedria characteristic of much recent criticism, recognizes that "Phaedria too is a servant of Acrasia, but a comparatively

innocent one." She notes acutely that Guyon's lingering with Phaedria enables Cymocles to wound him, but as the wound is not serious the episode remains for her a "curious incident" (*The Allegory of the Faerie Queene* [Oxford, 1960], p. 128). Even such critics as Giamatti, who associates this "lesser version of the Bower" with Tasso's Siren island, cannot adequately explain its function; for Giamatti it merely represents "Spenser and Tasso's common structural technique of anticipating the final garden" (*The Earthly Paradise*, p. 259). It is only by recognizing the Homeric derivation of this recurring, lesser form of Circean temptation in Renaissance epic that both its true association with Circe and the need to distinguish its more innocuous nature through subservient personifications can be fully appreciated. Paul J. Alpers' comment on Spenser's understanding and use of Ariosto can be equally well applied to the reading of Homer by Renaissance epic poets: "What Spenser chooses to use for his purposes is not what the commentators regard as important for the allegory. . . . he was a superb reader of the poem" (*The Poetry of The Faerie Queene* [Princeton, 1967], pp. 179–80).

25. "Spenser's Acrasia," pp. 381–85, 396.

26. *Circe*, p. 4.

27. Ibid., p. 64.

28. Ibid., p. 177.

29. Ibid., p. 157.

30. Ibid., p. 168.

31. *Ovid's Metamorphoses*, p. 654.

32. Though Hughes points to the Platonic derivation of many of the Renaissance allegorizations of the Circe myth ("Spenser's Acrasia," p. 387), there was also a Renaissance association of the myth with Aristotelian brutishness, as John M. Steadman has demonstrated in *Milton's Epic Characters* (Chapel Hill, N. C., 1959), p. 206 f. Aristotle's few comments on brutishness assumed their Renaissance importance because it was the quality he opposed to heroic virtue: "to brutishness it would be most fitting to oppose superhuman virtue, a heroic and divine kind of nature" (*Nicomachean Ethics*, bk. VII, chap. 1, in *The Basic Works of Aristotle*, ed. Richard McKeon [New York, 1941], p. 1036). I would, however, disagree with Steadman that Aristotle's primary conception of brutishness "entails an excess of vice" (p. 25); rather, Aristotle appears to define it as a form of congenital idiocy. In discussing the "activities belonging to a bad nature," Aristotle distinguishes those "congenital, as in the case of a brute" (bk. VII, chap. 14, p. 1057). The subhuman mentality of the brute is clearly shown in the following analysis: "Now brutishness is a less evil than vice, though more alarming; for it is not that the better part has been perverted, as in man—they *have* no better part. . . . the badness of that which has no originative source of movement is always less hurtful, and reason is an originative source. . . . for a bad man will do ten thousand times as much evil as a brute" (bk. VII, chap. 6, p. 1047). Despite this question of Aristotle's original definitions, Steadman's illustrations (and of these, Sandys' verses are a prime example) of the Renaissance use of this Aristotelian antithesis make clear that Aristotle's brutishness had often been reformulated to approximate a condition of moral degradation similar to the bestiality of Circe's victims.

33. *Ovid's Metamorphoses*, p. 2.

34. *Ludovico Ariosto's "Orlando Furioso,"* trans. Sir John Harington (1591), ed. Robert McNulty (Oxford, 1972), pp. xxxi, 80, 559, 563.

35. This is *Elegy I*. But *On the Death of the Vice-Chancellor*, written in the same year, contains a casual reference to Circe. Milton is never again to use this name so lightly.

36. *John Milton, Complete Poems and Major Prose*, ed. Merritt Y. Hughes (New York, 1957). All further references are to this edition unless otherwise noted. I give page citations for the prose and Latin poetry, and line references for the English poetry.

37. *Milton* (London, 1959), pp. 20–21.

38. Though numbered last of the elegies, *Elegy VII* would seem to have been written a year later than *Elegy I*. Wholly devoted to amorous suffering, this elegy again depicts the favorite sites to which the youthful Milton repaired in the hope of catching a passing sight of maiden beauty. A pertinent quotation will appear in the later discussion of *Paradise Lost*.

39. *An Apology against a Pamphlet call'd a Modest Confutation of the Animadversions of the Remonstrant against Smectymnuus*, ed. Harry Morgan Ayres, in *The Works of John Milton* (New York, 1931), III, pt. I, p. 305. This edition is hereafter cited as CM.

40. As he states in *Prolusion VII:* "to set no value on glory when you have done well, that is beyond all glory." For Milton the earthly glory which attends those who "have lived temperately and dedicated all their time to worthy studies and thereby helped mankind" is honored by Heaven: "Whatever lovely thing we may have done here we shall be present to hear praised there" (p. 628). Having worked out this solution to the honorable pursuit of glory, when the moral problem of such a pursuit did impinge itself upon his consciousness, he could dismiss it with no more than parenthetical comment: "*Fame* is the spur that the clear spirit doth raise / (That last infirmity of Noble Mind)" (*Lycidas*, 70–71); and "These reasonings, together with a certaine nicenesse of nature, an honest haughtinesse, and self-esteem either of what I was, or what I might be, (which let envie call pride)" (*An Apology*, CM, III, pt. I, 304).

41. "John Milton," in *The Early Lectures of Ralph Waldo Emerson*, ed. Stephen E. Whicher and Robert E. Spiller (Cambridge, Mass., 1959), I, 161.

42. This cyclical analysis runs counter to the recent critical stress on a structure of linear ascent in the companion poems: see Jon S. Lawry, *The Shadow of Heaven* (Ithaca, 1968), pp. 41–51; and David M. Miller, "From Delusion to Illumination: A Larger Structure for *L'Allegro-Il Penseroso*," *PMLA*, LXXXVI (1971), 32–39.

43. See John G. Demaray, *Milton and the Masque Tradition* (Cambridge, Mass., 1968), pp. 87–88, 109–10; and pp. 43–44 of my article, "Miltonic Allusion in *Absalom and Achitophel:* Its Function in the Political Satire," *JEGP*, LXVIII (1969), 24–44.

44. See references under index listings for "Communism" in George Huntson Williams, *The Radical Reformation* (Philadelphia, 1962).

45. See St. Thomas More, *Utopia*, ed. Edward Surz (New Haven, 1964), pp. 48, 150. Though Milton venerated the Utopian ideal, viewing More's *Utopia*—in concert with Bacon's *New Atlantis* and Plato's *Critias*—as a "grave and noble invention . . . teaching this our world better and exacter things, then were yet known, or us'd" (*An Apology*, CM, III, pt. I, 294), he would undoubtedly have agreed with More that "it is impossible that all should be well unless all men were good, a situation which I do not expect for a great many years to come!" (*Utopia*, p. 50).

46. See Demaray, *Milton and the Masque Tradition*, pp. 8–9, 49, 84.

47. A. S. P. Woodhouse has ably demonstrated that "Milton's doctrine of chastity culminates in—though even on the religious level it is not co-extensive with—a doctrine of virginity" ("The Argument of Milton's *Comus*," *UTQ*, XI [1941], 59). This analysis of Milton's "sage / And serious doctrine of Virginity" has been challenged by

the influential assertion of E. M. W. Tillyard that "Milton saw that both the Lady and Comus were wrong: that there *was* another meaning in these gifts, but that it was not Comus'. The meaning was marriage" (*Studies in Milton* [New York, 1951], p. 94). While I do not believe that Tillyard's view is supportable, his argument is suggestive in a way he did not intend: "The setting is aristocratic; the Lady, though but young, will one day be a great Lady. She must take her place in society and do what is expected of her. . . . her true part of Amoret" (p. 95). Tillyard correctly associates the aristocratic setting with his perception that the implied "meaning" of Comus' words is marriage, but this is Comus' meaning rather than Milton's. It is just this proper aristocratic role and marriage which Milton is defining, in *Comus*, as the temptation of Circe. Don Cameron Allen may consider Comus' marital intentions to be "as fine a prospect of irrational miscegenation as one is likely to find in the history of marriage" (*The Harmonious Vision* [Baltimore, 1970], pp. 36–37), but he at least recognizes Comus' true intentions. It is not the Lady, but her tempter, who is associated with the ideal of marriage.

48. See Hughes' edition of Milton, p. 602, n. 1.

49. See William G. Madsen, "The Idea of Nature in Milton's Poetry," in *Three Studies in the Renaissance: Sidney, Jonson, Milton* (New Haven, 1958), pp. 207–11.

50. Sears Jayne, in "The Subject of Milton's Ludlow Mask," *PMLA*, LXXIV (1959), 536, argues that the Attendant Spirit "is referred to consistently in the Trinity MS as a 'daemon,' or 'guardian daemon,' and we should think of him in the poem not as an angel from St. Peter's heaven, but as a Platonic airy spirit, carrying out the last stage in the process of emanation from God to the outermost circle of the World Soul." But in *The Occult Sciences in the Renaissance* (Berkeley, 1972), Wayne Shumaker offers materials which suggest an additional derivation from Hermetic sources, a system of thought philosophically related to Platonism. Both systems of thought are associated in *Il Penseroso*, 88–96; and Shumaker suggests that the Miltonic reference to "*Daemons*" (93) at this point may be Hermetic (p. 218). In his discussion of Hermetic philosophy, Shumaker shows the nonmissionary, esoteric quality of its doctrine: "The milieu of the *Hermetica* is not that of temple, court, or city but a retired hermitage—or many hermitages—within which a master and his few disciples meditate" (p. 213); "When Tat achieves regeneration in *CH* XIII, the experience is mystical. Also, it must be borne steadily in mind that there is little (in most documents, no) thought of converting the public. The doctrine is esoteric, and the pious are repeatedly said to be few" (p. 218); "The man who has achieved *gnosis*—the good man—expounds his esoteric doctrine to one, two, or three disciples at a time . . . but he is not seen watering a garden. . . . Neither need he devote much energy to the general service of mankind" (pp. 225–26). If we accept the Attendant Spirit as a Platonic-Hermetic "guardian daemon," we will be better able to appreciate the philosophical sources of both his and the Lady's lack of concern with the conversion of the sinful.

51. Madsen, "The Idea of Nature," p. 185. Despite the evidence he presents for "this general trend of interpretation" (p. 165), Madsen prefers to see Milton's Comus as representing the libertine conception of nature exclusively (see pp. 188–97). Tuve recognizes that "the Circe-Comus myth . . . is elaborated with the greatest originality by Milton, with conceptual refinements and extensions impossible to a lesser genius" (*Images and Themes*, p. 116); but though she grants that Comus' response to the Lady's song represents a sincere "response of the impure to the beauty of the pure" (p. 114), she refuses to see that his temptation of the Lady takes a higher form than that earlier offered to his embruted followers: "the noises are being made by those who

did believe Comus's later-given recommendations for the Forms of Thanksgiving" (p. 145). Milton's "conceptual refinements" of the Circe-Comus myth involve, however, not only a return to the humanist "reconciliation of pleasure and virtue" but the spiritual infusion of this reconciliation with precisely these "later-given recommendations for the Forms of Thanksgiving."

52. CM, III, pt. I, 337, 345.

53. Ed. William Haller, CM, V, 204, 290–91.

54. See n. 32 above for my demonstration that Aristotelian brutishness is characterized by just such a lack of rationality and my disagreement with Steadman's conclusion that it "entails an excess of vice." This disagreement extends as well to our treatments of Satan's last bestial metamorphosis. Seeing this scene as Milton's only exposure of both the evil of Satanic heroism and its bestial form—"Not until divine Providence intervenes and transforms Satan and his companions into serpents . . . does the poet finally expose the heroic idol as bestial vice"—Steadman's analysis of the Aristotelian antithesis of heroic virtue and brutishness causes him to view the final transformation as symbolic not of the quality but only the quantity of Satan's sin: "Satan's final metamorphosis into a serpent. . . . condemns his particular mode of heroism as an extraordinary 'excess of vice'. . . . brutishness" (*Milton and the Renaissance Hero* [Oxford, 1967], pp. 51, 170). Aristotle does note, without further discussion, that in common parlance "we also call by this evil name those men who go beyond all ordinary standards by reason of vice"—the source of Steadman's definition of Aristotelian brutishness as "an excess of vice"—but he everywhere else insists that the state of "a brute is a different kind of state from vice" (*Nicomachean Ethics*, bk. VII, chap. 1). And Milton's treatment of the conversion of Satanic heroism into brutishness, of which the transformation scene is not the only revelation but only the last, in no way associates such brutishness with an "excess of vice" but rather with the punishing psychological compulsion and constraint which Satan experiences when he permits himself to be ruled by internal powers other than reason.

55. See John S. Diekhoff, *Milton's "Paradise Lost": A Commentary on the Argument* (New York, 1963), for a similar interpretation of "stupidly good" which recognizes that "Virtue must be more positive, more active a thing than that" (p. 41).

56. See Joseph H. Summers, *The Muse's Method* (Cambridge, Mass., 1962), for a similar analysis of the emotional cause of Adam's yielding and its seriousness: "he prefers the risk of her destruction to the risk of her momentary resentment" (p. 174). On Eve's personal responsibility, see Stella P. Revard, "Eve and the Doctrine of Responsibility in *Paradise Lost*," *PMLA*, LXXXVIII (1973), 69–78.

57. This special responsibility for the human race is often overlooked in references to Milton's famous definition of Original Sin in *De Doctrina Christiana*: "in the man excessive uxoriousness, in the woman a want of proper regard for her husband, in both an insensibility to the welfare of their offspring, and that offspring the whole human race" (trans. Charles R. Sumner, ed., James Holly Hanford and Waldo Hilary Dunn, CM, XV, 183).

58. Daiches sees in Adam's fall "a cunning parody of the courtly love tradition" (*Milton*, p. 205) and recognizes that for Milton "the knightly code and courtly love . . . are not on the side of Christian good" (p. 165).

59. See *Milton* (New York: Barnes & Noble, 1967), p. 223.

60. See *"Paradise Lost" and its Critics* (Cambridge, Eng., 1962), p. 49.

61. Dennis H. Burden, in *The Logical Epic* (Cambridge, Mass.. 1967), recognizes the moral seriousness of this term but misses its full implications—which go far beyond

"irrationality" (p. 163)—because of his failure to associate it with Circean temptation. Lawry, on the other hand, does recognize the Circean implications of the Fall, by which "Paradise becomes Circe's pigsty" (*Shadow of Heaven*, p. 234); but, for him, this "Circean intoxication" (p. 255) is only the product, not the cause, of Adam's fall. B. Rajan, in *"Paradise Lost" and the Seventeenth-Century Reader* (1947; reprint ed., Ann Arbor, 1967), notes that when Eve "is compared to Circe the implication is that she will reduce Adam from God's image to 'the inglorious likeness of a beast'" (p. 124), but he does not otherwise relate this perception to his analysis of Adam's fall.

62. For critical recognition of the allusion to Circe in this speech and its significance in defining Dalila's Circean nature, see Allen, *Harmonious Vision*, p. 90; Lawry, *Shadow of Heaven*, p. 381; Bush, *Mythology and the Renaissance Tradition in English Poetry*, p. 277; Ralph Nash, "Chivalric Themes in *Samson Agonistes*," in *Studies in Honor of John Wilcox*, ed. A. Dayte Wallace and Woodburn O. Ross (Detroit, 1958), p. 26; and, most importantly, Steadman, "Dalila, the Ulysses Myth, and Renaissance Allegorical Tradition," pp. 560–65.

63. In his "Dalila" article, Steadman traces the association of Circe with the Sirens from Horace to Renaissance mythography, showing the identification of the Sirens with idleness and of both with harlotry. Though Steadman, attending to the "Renaissance Allegorical Tradition" rather than the literary tradition, does not note Tasso's association of the Sirens with the Circean Armida, this has particular importance for Milton's treatment of Circean temptation in *Samson Agonistes*, since, as in Tasso, the full Circean temptation is prefaced by a separate personification of idleness which largely defines its nature.

64. See Allen, *Harmonious Vision*, pp. 85–88, for a similar reading of Manoa's temptation and its relation to the presentation of Dalila.

65. Rejecting the traditional view of Dalila, Daiches sees that her love "may well be sincere and yet represent something evil" (*Milton*, p. 243).

66. See Barbara K. Lewalski. "*Samson Agonistes* and the 'Tragedy' of the Apocalypse," *PMLA*, LXXXV (1970), for an analysis of this apocalyptic vision (p. 1059) which does not bar true tragic effect (p. 1062).

67. William O. Harris, in "Despair and 'Patience as the Truest Fortitude' in *Samson Agonistes*," *ELH*, XXX (1963), asserts that "Victory through patience was to Milton the nobler triumph" (p. 119), a serious misinterpretation which reflects the current critical tendency to read all Renaissance literature as undeviating reflections of what is presumed to have been a common core of Christian and humanist beliefs and modes of interpretation. Poetic meaning in the Renaissance, when the colliding influences of heresy, classical philosophy, and secularism defeated any possible Christian consensus and bred individuality of belief, can only be adequately determined by attending, without critical prejudice, to what the poets say for themselves.

"SHE MAY HAVE MORE SHAPES THAN ONE": MILTON AND THE MODERN IDEA THAT TRUTH CHANGES

Anne B. Long

Recent ideas about how science operates suggest a new approach to the way in which John Milton assimilated the impact of the Copernican Revolution. Thomas Kuhn's theory of scientific paradigms suggests Milton's characterization of God's progressive revelation of truth and the implications Milton depicts in his epic for the individual. Kuhn describes any given scientific framework of thought as an allegory which is "true" only in the sense that it permits creative work. Controversies in science lead to new formulations of truth. When contradiction arises, individuals should wait patiently for the new paradigm. Milton similarly believes that God accommodates truth to man's abilities. *Areopagitica* suggests that truth changes and that conflicts between opposing truths lead to a wider vision. *De Doctrina* details the radically different characteristics of God's dispensations. In *Paradise Lost,* Milton feels free to choose the scientific paradigm which allows him creativity. He depicts conflicts between characters who have explored fully their particular dispensations and who must acknowledge at the moment of conflict the need for a wider truth. Because the creature can never know absolute truth, his patient waiting must be prompted and sustained by a positive and soul-testing allegiance to truth.

MODERN THEORIES of the manner in which science operates suggest a new approach to a problem which continues to puzzle students of Milton. Why is it that Milton remained unconcerned by the seventeenth-century controversy in science which so agonized Donne?[1] Did he lose the excitement about science which animates his early exhortation to his classmates to "follow as companion the wandering sun, and subject time itself to a reckoning and demand the order of its ever-

lasting journey"?[2] If he flatly rejected the change in thought, why does
he allude with admiration to Galileo and give to Raphael descriptions of
the new science beyond the requirements of the epic situation? It seems
to me that it is the conflict itself which interests Milton—the spectacle of
experts disagreeing violently about basic truths, the resistance of many
to a change in a basic scientific framework for explaining phenomena.
Can truth change? Perhaps Milton did appreciate the significance of the
Copernican Revolution but was able to fit the fact of radical change into
his concept of the ways of God with such ease that he could use both the
old and the new as his own creativity required.

In discussing a passage in *Areopagitica,* M. Denis Saurat draws a
surprising conclusion: "Milton hits here upon one of the ideas made
most use of by John Henry Newman . . . truth changes with the ages of
mankind."[3] Saurat must be thinking of Newman's explanation of God's
progressive revelation of truth to men, which Newman deduced from
the writings of Clement and Origen.[4] In *De Doctrina Christiana,* Milton
too details the series of dispensations given to successive ages until the
final revelation of the Covenant of Grace through Christ. Each dispensation provides a new framework for human conduct in response to the
new knowledge of God's ways. The process indeed involves sudden and
radical changes in men's perception of religious truth and in their responsibilities. Perhaps for Milton, changes in scientific truth would simply repeat this pattern of dispensations of religious truth suited to the
historical period.

Saurat's comment is, however, an overstatement of Milton's position. For Milton there is a fundamental continuous truth which God
progressively reveals to men in a way accommodated to human understanding. Truth does not change, only its revelation to men. Saurat has
more accurately described contemporary thinking. For some modern
philosophers, there really is no absolute truth, either scientific or religious, which can be known to men. Men construct systems of thought
which serve their term and are discarded. No one framework is "truer"
than another; there is no progression towards "reality."

Modern theories of the nature of scientific truth are indeed very
suggestive of the traditional concept of religious truth. In fact, Whitehead refers to Newman's belief in the development of doctrine.[5] A review of modern ideas about the history of science calls attention to these
aspects of Milton's thought. Milton's attitude towards apparent changes

in truth has implications which may be helpful to the student of *Paradise Lost.*

Three related aspects of modern theory of the nature of truth are suggestive of Milton's thought: truth for man is really a metaphorical framework which changes from one period of history to another; logical contradictions in human knowledge represent opportunities for a jump to a new framework; the proper attitude towards contradiction is patience.

Whitehead explains the basic idea that any truth exists within a limited context:

We are told by logicians that a proposition must be either true or false, and that there is no middle term. But in practice, we may know that a proposition expresses an important truth, but that it is subject to limitations and qualifications which at present remain undiscovered. It is a general feature of our knowledge, that we are insistently aware of important truth; and yet that the only formulations of these truths which we are able to make presuppose a general standpoint of conceptions which may have to be modified. (p. 164)

Whitehead's idea points towards the currently debated theory of Thomas Kuhn that scientists actually never advance towards any objective or absolute truth since "nothing of that sort can be found."[6] Kuhn believes that "normal" scientists accept a system of thought within which they accumulate solutions to problems until too many anomalies pile up and a new "paradigm of knowledge" is supplied by revolutionary scientists. The paradigm defines the problems and provides models for solutions—it "permits selection, evaluation, and criticism" of phenomena.[7] The paradigm does not represent a "true account of nature"; it is a "myth," an "analogy," a "model," a "metaphysical speculation," a "general epistemological viewpoint."[8] As normal scientists accumulate solutions within the paradigm, they generate conflicting facts which ultimately lead to a crisis which destroys the paradigm. Interestingly, Kuhn stresses that the generation of significant crises is an achievement —not a defeat—for normal science since the conflict is an opportunity for the creation of a new paradigm which renews the possibility of defining and solving problems (chapter 9).

The change from one paradigm to another is a radical jump or revolution; it is "a displacement of the conceptual network through which scientists view the world" (p. 102). Thus successive paradigms are incompatible and often incommensurable (p. 103). Kuhn is almost willing to say that "after a revolution scientists are responding to a different world" (p. 111). Some continuity does exist, however, since many facts are retained in the new framework, though placed into new categories.

I take Kuhn's theory to mean that scientists accept for themselves a giant metaphor or allegory which enables them to explain phenomena for a while but which is not taken as an approximation of some "absolute truth." For some of Kuhn's most important critics this denial of objective truth is the unacceptable aspect of his system. Karl Popper declares that he does believe in absolute truth and that science increasingly approximates it: "The aim is to find theories which, in the light of critical discussion, get nearer to the truth."[9] But Seymour W. Itzkoff summarizes the import of Kuhn's work: "In the end the victory of one set of ideas over another does not necessarily constitute a victory of truth over illusion; it is merely a manifestation of the importance of the new and the innovative to the creative tendencies of each new generation of scientists."[10] Thus new allegories inevitably replace the old, not because they are "truer," but because they suit the needs of the practicing scientist. The change ends the careers of those older men who refuse to accept it, and they soon find their work ignored (p. 19).

Whitehead anticipates Kuhn's stress on the importance to the history of science of apparent inconsistencies or discrepancies which accumulate as normal scientists work within a particular paradigm—they are signals that a wider framework is necessary, that the formulations of truth have to change. This is the second aspect of the theory which seems to me to suggest Milton's thought. As Whitehead asserts, a logical contradiction is an opportunity: "In formal logic, a contradiction is a signal of defeat: but in the evolution of real knowledge it marks the first step in progress towards a victory" (p. 167).

The third similarity to Milton's thought is Whitehead's recommendation of an attitude towards change in science and in religion, especially change which creates an apparent clash between these two kinds of truth: "We should wait: but we should not wait passively, or in despair. The clash is a sign that there are wider truths and finer perspectives within which a reconciliation of a deeper religion and a more subtle science will be found" (p. 165). Kuhn, too, emphasizes the fact that scientists cannot force the appearance of the new, wider paradigm. Their role is to explore their framework by accumulating the facts which are true within it. This process in science is for Kuhn similar to biological evolution and to an individual's mental growth—it is a process in time which cannot be hurried: "As in individual development, so in the scientific group, maturity comes most surely to those who know how to wait."[11]

These aspects of modern theory of truth call attention to characteristic elements of Milton's prose and poetry. Modern critics have repeatedly noted Milton's doctrine of accommodation, which asserts that God does not reveal to men "absolute truth" (God "as he really is"), but a representation "in such a manner as may be within the scope of our comprehension" (p. 453). Nature and the Bible are thus "dispensations" of truth, suited to the senses of men. Furthermore, God changes the dispensation at certain historical moments; there is continuity because God's truth is always the same, but the new dispensation is always a wider revelation which radically rearranges the specific facts of human existence, creating new opportunities and responsibilities.

One obvious difference between Milton's dispensations and Kuhn's paradigms is their origin. For Kuhn, a new paradigm is created by the work of one or more revolutionary scientists at the moment when "normal" scientists have filled in the old paradigm and recorded too many anomalies. For Milton, God reveals the progressive accommodations of his truth to men at the moment of his choice. At first this difference in origin seems so great that any similarity between Kuhn's paradigms and Milton's dispensations may seem besides the point. But the most important implications of both theories are for the situation of the individual "normal" scientist and the individual creature of God. It seems to me that both theories tell the individual that he needs a framework for his thought which is an allegory or accommodation, subject to change beyond his control. For the individual scientist or creature, a conflict which develops as he uses his powers of reason within his dispensation or paradigm is a sign of a radical change which will be for him a tremendous test and a new opportunity.

Both Whitehead and Kuhn ultimately focus upon the attitude of the individual towards conflict and change. Their advice to "know how to wait" makes more understandable that commitment to patience towards which so many of Milton's poems move. It is a vital quality possible only for the individual who understands his role in the fulfillment of his dispensation and has faith in the reward of his effort, which is the wider vision granted by God to give men once again the opportunity to be creative.

In Milton's early pamphlets, and even in *Areopagitica* to a certain extent, the most obvious attitude towards truth is that God gave it in an absolute and pure form to Adam, who shattered it at the moment of his fall. The coming of Christ reintroduced absolute truth, but once again men allowed it to degenerate. The role of the good man is to attempt to rediscover a static, perfect revelation. This attitude underlies the ortho- dox Christian belief that pagan learning was merely a corruption of the perfect knowledge of Adam. As Howard Schultz comments, the preach- ers "liked to measure the distance of the pagans' fall by contrasting un- regenerate learning with Adam's, as they could by supposing that Adam had known everything that frustrated man would like to know."[12] The famous metaphor in *Areopagitica* likening truth to the mangled body of Osiris chiefly suggests that truth was once in the world with Christ "a perfect shape most glorious to look on" and that it need only be redis- covered and repaired through a slow and laborious process. But in *Areopagitica* there is also evidence that Milton is thinking that absolute truth has never been fully revealed to men, that God has more truths to reveal in a progressive manner. Arthur E. Barker describes *Areopagitica* as a significant change in Milton's thinking from reformation to revolu- tion due to this change in his idea about the nature of truth:

He now thinks of the future as a progression from truth to truth which will terminate only when the divine pattern is at length completely imparted to man at Christ's return. He begins to look, not backward with the orthodox Puritans to the express command of God, but forward. To that extent he be- comes less the reformer than the revolutionary, especially since the achieve- ment of the perfect pattern—though finally possible only with divine assistance —requires the human activity of "free reasoning."[13]

Another metaphor for truth in *Areopagitica* suggests both that truth changes and that it is human nature which makes it desirable that truth change—men need the testing that changes of truth provide:

Well knows he who uses to consider that our faith and knowledge thrives by exercise, as well as our limbs and complexion. Truth is compared in scripture to a streaming fountain; if her waters flow not in a perpetual progression, they sicken into a muddy pool of conformity and tradition. A man may be a heretic in the truth. (p. 746)

Interestingly, Milton also defends in this pamphlet the conflicts created by dissenters and sectarians as necessary preludes to the new truth God is preparing to reveal:

Yet these are the men cried out against for schismatics and sectaries, as if, while the temple of the Lord was building, some cutting, some squaring the marble, others hewing the cedars, there should be a sort of irrational men, who could not consider there must be many schisms and many dissections made in the quarry and in the timber ere the house of God can be built. And when every stone is laid artfully together, it cannot be united into a continuity, it can but be contiguous in this world: neither can every piece of the building be of one form; nay, rather the perfection consists in this, that out of many moderate varieties and brotherly dissimilitudes that are not vastly disproportional, arises the goodly and the graceful symmetry that commends the whole pile and structure. (p. 749)

A related idea about truth is evident in this quotation: truth may have a different shape for different men in the same period since the truth is accommodated to the needs of the individual men, to their particular abilities to understand, and to their particular talents. Conflicts are therefore to be expected between opposing truths. This idea is also expressed in a pamphlet two years earlier than *Areopagitica,* the *Apology for Smectymnuus,* in which Milton explains that the disciples and early teachers of Christianity had various personalities in order to appeal to a wide variety of people:

no man being forced wholly to dissolve that groundwork of nature which God created in him . . . but that each radical humor and passion, wrought upon and corrected as it ought, might be made the proper mold and foundation of every man's peculiar gifts and virtues. (pp. 552–53)

Truth appears here to have the same function for Milton as paradigms have for Kuhn—it is a structure which enables any particular man to be creative, an accommodation or allegory which need not be judged separately from the people or person for whom it is intended. God suits his revelation of truth to the abilities of the historical chosen people: "For such is the order of God's enlightening his church, to dispense and deal out by degrees his beam, so as our earthly eyes may best sustain it" (p. 752).

Milton's *De Doctrina Christiana* clearly establishes that Milton believed that God is Truth and that he is immutable. Milton does not bother to define these two attributes beyond citing biblical passages which assert "Jehovah is the true God" (Jeremiah x, 10) and "but thou art the same" (Psalm cii, 27). Having asserted that God exists, Milton lists these attributes automatically. Milton and Popper thus agree that there is an absolute or objective truth independent of man. Nevertheless, Milton considers that God's truth is not available to men: "for to know God as he really is, far transcends the powers of man's thoughts, much more of his perception" (p. 923). The truth which most interests Milton, of course, is God's love for man and his promise of the Covenant of Grace throughout human history. The successive revelations of truth each have an appropriate nature corresponding to stages in an individual's growth towards moral or spiritual perfection. Adam, created perfect, receives the perfect, unwritten law of nature and the command of the tree and the institution of marriage. After the Fall, God declares the covenant directly for the first time as he promises that the seed of woman shall bruise the head of the serpent. The pagans thus live with the dispensation of fallen nature and the vague promise of grace. The Law of Moses is a written manifestation of the truth of God, and the Gospel dispensation "abrogates" and "fulfills" that legal dispensation (pp. 986–87, 1023–28).

Each of these historical dispensations in fact provides a framework within which men exercise their own faculties, including reason; and the frameworks are different, though the object is always the same—men are to love God and follow his truth, which is perhaps goodness or perfect reason. The frameworks are different in very concrete ways. For example, the dispensation which immediately follows the Fall introduces death and woe into the human condition and is very unclear about the existence of a just God, about the promise of regeneration, and about the response demanded of the individual. The Mosaic Law imposes severe rules of conduct and reveals God's justice and man's inability to live according to God's written law. As each new dispensation abrogates the old, however, God's eternal love and man's responsibilities and potentialities are simply more clearly expressed; they have always equally existed. God has always given to the responsive man opportunities to participate in God's creativity. Barker stresses that for the individual who has begun a process of spiritual renewal, the Spirit of God engraves the "divine law" or eternal truth in the heart, providing a basis for true liberty, "and this in turn depends upon what Milton thinks the demonstrable continuity of a providence which makes possible similar responsibilities and opportunities under every dispensation. . . . What God consistently gives his responsive creatures is an opportunity to respond to his providential processes—and to all creatures his own good time." [14] Truth does not change, though the revelation of truth does: "She may have more shapes than one" (p. 751).

From the point of view of the individual man, it seems to me, Milton's system of progressive revelations of accommodated truth means that the framework of one's reasoning may suddenly be changed and that this change is signaled possibly by conflicts of opinion among good men exercising their own best reasoning. The individual faces the same sort of test as the normal scientist in Kuhn's theory of the change of scientific paradigms: he must accept the new framework in order to continue as a creative being. It is a test of one's commitment not to the particular accommodation of truth, the letter of the law, but to the truth itself, though man can never know that truth as it really is.[15] Since God apparently accommodates even to the individual human nature, an individual may be faced with such a change of framework at the appropriate moment of his personal growth as well as at the great moments of historical dispensations. This moment calls for a sort of jump by the individual from one framework to the next, supported by trust in the divine veracity. Because Milton believes that absolute truth does exist, the gap is only an illusion, but it is real enough from the creature's point of view since all he can ever know are the accommodations of truth which change. Both Milton's poetry and prose contain jumps of this nature. A characteristic instance is Milton's assertion in *De Doctrina* that since evil and good are in conflict and since it is "unmeet as it is incredible" that evil should prevail, God exists (p. 923).

In *Paradise Lost,* as in *Areopagitica,* Milton certainly includes the attitude that truth is static. God in Book III predicts all of human and divine history as settled matters of fact, declaring that at the end of history the just shall dwell with "fair Truth" and "God shall be All in All" (III, 335, 341). History as related by Michael seems to involve progressive revelation through the lives of the just men who prefigure Christ but to culminate in a complete revelation of truth in the mission of Christ. Christ leaves truth with the disciples, who in turn leave it recorded in "those written Records pure" (XII, 514). Though these pure records are immediately ignored, perverted, or tainted by wolfish men, Milton implies that good men can understand the written revelation of truth with

the aid of the Spirit. Scripture appears to be a final formulation of truth
in this world. Certainly for bad men there is no progression in truth,
and Michael reports that the world as a whole will go from bad to worse,
"to good malignant, to bad men benign" (XII, 538) until the Last Judgment. Yet Milton's invocations, which ask inspiration from God and
which imply inclusion of himself in the long line of prophets of God's
ways to men, suggest the possibility of new revelations after Christ's
earthly ministry, at least to those individuals who achieve faith. In a
general way even the fact that Milton chose to retell the Bible in poetry
suggests his idea that the framework of truth must change at historical
intervals. Milton is himself receptive to the revelation of a new higher
truth as he restates and explores the sometimes conflicting facts of the
Christian revelation of God's ways.

There are several specific problems for the readers of *Paradise Lost*
which may be clarified by approaching the poem from Milton's idea of
changing revelations of truth. The poem repeatedly poses the problem
of the amount and kind of knowledge appropriate for men. After relating to Adam two conflicting theories of the universe, Raphael advises
Adam to "sollicit not thy thoughts with matters hid" (VIII, 167). Milton
himself includes Galileo in his poem yet chooses a basically Ptolemaic
scheme for his image of the universe. Eve is tempted by Satan's charge
that God does not want her to have the knowledge he has placed in the
tree. Perhaps one of the most puzzling aspects of the poem is its frequent depiction of conflicts of mind in heaven and on earth in situations
where there is no question of either party's being fallen or even mistaken: the Son and God perceive opposite facts, Adam argues with God,
Adam and Raphael disagree politely, and Adam and Eve argue about
whether or not they should work apart. The arguments advanced by all
of these characters are true and yet contradictory. Finally, there is the
problem of Milton's conception of woman. Why is it that Milton's presentation of Eve seems generally acceptable even to the new generation
of aware young women, while paraphrases and elaborations by Milton's
critics arouse outrage?[16] Undoubtedly Milton differentiates between the
abilities of Adam and Eve to draw upon all forms of reason. Adam more
often displays intuitive reasoning, as when he springs to his feet at his
first awakening (VIII, 259–60), or names the animals (VI, 75; VIII, 352–
53). Eve's mode of thinking does seem different from Adam's characteristic logic, and yet somehow one does not feel that she is less able to be

creative than Adam. The attitudes implied by Milton's theory of the changing revelations of truth offer some solutions to these problems.

If God's revelation of truth is an accommodation suited to the perceptive abilities of the creature to whom it is given, then the creature who wishes to be creative can only accept his framework with joy and set to work within it. He needs to know that what he has been given is an accommodation so that he will love absolute truth rather than the accommodation and so that he will understand the possibility for him of growth within his framework until he is ready to be given a new accommodation to suit his new abilities. Raphael explains to Adam that God's creatures are assigned various "active Sphears" appropriate to their degree. Man is characterized by "discursive" reason, which means that he requires process in time in order to perceive and understand (V, 469–505). Raphael instructs Adam that he may change his sphere "improv'd by tract of time." For the moment, the framework within which Adam is to work is Paradise. When Eve listens to Satan's temptation to knowledge, she signals her failure to trust that God is absolute truth and chooses the framework rather than the truth.

Raphael's attitude towards the conflicting astronomical theories of Milton's day calls attention to the fact that man cannot have knowledge beyond the framework for which his abilities suit him. Milton does in a sense take sides, however, since he describes a basically Ptolemaic universe throughout the epic. He has chosen the old scientific paradigm which allows him to be creative, in perfect understanding that it is just a framework and that it is the one suited to his poetic abilities. Raphael confides to Adam that neither theory of the universe is true and that God will laugh at those who mistake their own accommodation for absolute truth (VIII, 78). Similarly, Whitehead discusses this historical scientific conflict from the wider perspective of the modern paradigm of astronomical science and sees that all of the arguments were "true" and yet all were ignorant because they lacked the "more perfect truth" of relative motion. The only reason for preferring Galileo to the Inquisition is that "Galileo's way of stating the facts was, beyond question, the fruitful procedure for the sake of scientific research ' (p. 164). Galileo needed the new paradigm in order to continue to be creative, just as Milton as poet needed the old. Both were right, though they chose what looked like conflicting theories. When Eve listens to Satan's temptation to knowledge of good and evil, she chooses a framework for which she is not ready and in which she cannot be creative. When she is once more ready to accept the accommodation of truth suited to her, God gives her a new dispensation in the Judgment.

Kuhn and Whitehead assert that contradictions and conflicts within a paradigm signal the need for a new and wider truth. In *Areopagitica,* Milton reasons that the presence of conflicting religious sects suggests that "God is decreeing to begin some new and great period in his church" (p. 748). The debates and conflicts in *Paradise Lost* may also be signals that a wider vision or accommodation is needed because the creatures have explored fully the old framework of truth. Irene Samuel explains the debate between the Father and the Son in Book III as a moment when God changes the definition of death. The Son's speech is a true model of trust in God precisely because the Son sees a conflict between God's love and the doom of death and realizes that God will reveal a wider vision to include both apparently conflicting facts.[17] The Son's speech (III, 228) is an example of heroic patience which consists of attaining all the truth a particular accommodation will allow and then waiting in confidence for the wider revelation. The Son "attends the will / Of his great Father" (III, 270–71).

When Adam argues with God in Book VIII, he is similarly demonstrating patience as he articulates accurately the facts of his nature which indicate that he needs a wife. His trust in God's truth is so great that he dares to present facts which contradict the arguments of God against Adam's desire, even though at one point God seems to order him to find companionship among the animals (VIII, 376).

There are several arguments in the poem which leave the reader puzzled because they are not immediately resolved by a wider perspective. When Adam tells Raphael about his passion for Eve, Raphael reminds him to use his judgment because love is reason, not passion. Adam replies that he always does approve what he judges best. Their debate involves Right Reason, which Milton gave definite limits. When the Son accepts death through love of man, he uses his Right Reason up to the limit of his accommodation of truth. Then he waits, and that waiting is prompted not by reason but by trust and love. Adam and Raphael have defined a conflict which signals the need for a wider vision.

The argument between Adam and Eve over their separation in Book IX results from their mutual exploration of their dispensation.

Both are right: Eve should be able to work alone because she is sufficient to withstand temptation, but Adam and Eve are married and should give each other mutual support. Adam sees a conflict between Eve's freedom and her obedience and between his love and his authority. When conflicts are discovered, "we should wait." Upon Eve's return, Adam is confronted with a conflict between his love for her and his obedience to God. The Fall signals his failure to trust in God to reveal a wider vision.

Milton's conception of Eve fits within his conception of all of God's creatures, all of whom are limited in their capacities to perceive truth. The accommodation of truth given to Eve is different from that given to Adam and is suited to her special nature. In *Samson Agonistes*, Samson complains that God gave him great physical strength but only "mean" wisdom. He later understands that what mattered was his choice to keep his vow or not. His framework was adequate for his needs. Eve's responsibility to work within her accommodation is just as great as Adam's, and her opportunities to be creative are just as great. The reader sees Eve as a poet in her expressions of truth such as her first speech (IV, 440–91), in which she creates a parable-like version of her birth and first meeting with Adam to embody her love for Adam. Her mode of expression is more obviously accommodation than Adam's. She shows herself willing in her early speeches to accept the wider visions provided for her by God and by Adam. In Book IX she wants to force a solution to the conflict she suddenly fears between the presence of Satan and their happiness in the garden. She is no longer able to stand and wait but must go out into the garden on her own. After suffering Adam's rejection and discovering that left to herself she can think only of self-destructive escapes, she regains her ability to wait patiently when she resolves in Book X (930–35) to return to the place of judgment to ask God to place the sentence upon her alone.

Milton's idea that the revelation of truth changes may suggest, then, important attitudes for the reader of *Paradise Lost*. Milton himself was engaged in reformulating the truths of the Bible into epic poetry. I believe he would have found compatible the modern insistence upon the choice by the individual of that accommodation of truth which allows him to be creative.

Northern Illinois University

NOTES

1. Merritt Y. Hughes' summary of critical explanations reflects the generally accepted idea that Milton simply subordinated natural science to theology and philosophy (*John Milton: Complete Poems and Major Prose* [New York, 1957], pp. 189–92). Kester Svendsen and others have established that the science used by Milton was largely conventional and obsolete (*Milton and Science* [Cambridge, Mass., 1956]). Marjorie Nicolson suggests that Milton rejected the metaphysics of the new science but felt an aesthetic attraction to some of its aspects (*The Breaking of the Circle* [New York, 1960], p. 182).

2. All citations of Milton's work are to the *Student's Milton*, ed. Frank Allen Patterson (New York, 1930) and will be in the text hereafter. This quotation is on page 1106.

3. *Milton: Man and Thinker* (New York, 1925), p. 184.

4. Saurat does not cite a specific reference in Newman's work, but Cardinal Newman explains progressive revelation in *Apologia pro Vita Sua* (New York, 1931), pp. 42–43:

> I understand these passages to mean that the exterior world, physical and historical, was but the manifestation to our senses of realities greater than itself. Nature was a parable. Scripture was an allegory: pagan literature, philosophy, and mythology, properly understood, were but a preparation for the Gospel. The Greek poets and sages were in a certain sense prophets; for "thoughts beyond their thought to those high bards were given." There had been a directly divine dispensation carried on in favour of the Gentiles. . . . In the fulness of time both Judaism and Paganism had come to nought; the outward framework, which concealed yet suggested the Living Truth, had never been intended to last, and it was dissolving under the beams of the Sun of Justice which shone behind it and through it. The process of change had been slow; it had been done not rashly, but by rule and measure, "at sundry times and in divers manners," first one disclosure and then another, till the whole evangelical doctrine was brought into full manifestation. . . . The visible world still remains without its divine interpretation; Holy Church in her sacraments and her hierarchical appointments, will remain, even to the end of the world, after all but a symbol of those heavenly facts which fill eternity.

5. Whitehead reports that the idea occurs in an early tractate often reissued (*Science and the Modern World* [New York, 1931], p. 163). Further citations of Whitehead's writings are to this edition and will appear in the text.

6. "Reflections on My Critics," in *Criticism and the Growth of Knowledge*, ed. Imre Lakatos (Cambridge, 1970), p. 265.

7. *The Structure of Scientific Revolutions* (Chicago, 1970), p. 17. Further references to this edition will appear in the text.

8. Margaret Masterman in "The Nature of a Paradigm" in Lakatos, *Criticism and the Growth of Knowledge*, states that Kuhn "with that quasi-poetic style of his, makes paradigm-elucidation genuinely difficult for the superficial reader" by giving the word at least twenty-one different senses (p. 61). My synonyms are taken from her list and Kuhn's book.

9. "Normal Science and Its Dangers," in Lakatos, *Criticism and the Growth of Knowledge*, p. 57.

10. *Ernst Cassirer: Scientific Knowledge and the Concept of Man* (Notre Dame, 1971), p. 244.

11. Quoted by Kuhn in Lakatos, *Criticism and the Growth of Knowledge*, p. 245, from his own earlier work.

12. *Milton and Forbidden Knowledge* (New York, 1955), pp. 85–86.

13. *Milton and the Puritan Dilemma* (Toronto, 1942), p. 76.

14. "Structural and Doctrinal Pattern in Milton's Later Poems," in *Essays in English Literature from the Renaissance to the Victorian Age*, ed. Millar MacLure and F. W. Watt (Toronto, 1964), p. 172.

15. Milton's conviction that man cannot know God or absolute truth recalls the classical tradition of scepticism, Pyrrhonism, which received renewed attention and reapplication in the seventeenth century. Schultz has pondered the degree to which Milton may be said to participate in these reformulations of scepticism: "Only a dogmatist would venture to assert categorically that Milton was no sceptic" (p. 166). According to Louis I. Bredvold, in *The Intellectual Milieu of John Dryden* (Ann Arbor, 1934), pp. 18–19, Pyrrhonism as known to the Renaissance taught that human knowledge is impossible since it is all based upon sense impressions which can be shown to be unreliable. The sceptics advised searching for contradictions and conflicting opinions in order to display the futility of human knowledge. The result of such discoveries for the sceptic was resignation to human helplessness and the attainment of a neutral, inactive, mental state. My emphasis upon Milton's belief that man knows only a truth accommodated to his abilities associates Milton with scepticism. The pattern of Milton's thought which I am outlining (the individual receives accommodated truth; he perceives conflicts; he waits) is similar to that of the sceptics; however, Milton's optimistic interpretation of the search for conflicting truths and his final attitude of patient, heroic waiting for a wider vision are quite unlike the spirit of scepticism. It is easy to see why Milton might perceive Pyrrhonism as a parody of the true process of the growth of knowledge. Schultz comments that "consistent skepticism he held to be a piece of pagan folly from first to last, in the seventh Prolusion as in *Paradise Regained*" (*Milton and Forbidden Knowledge*, p. 167).

16. See Saurat, *Milton: Man and Thinker*, for example, pp. 160–63.

17. "The Dialogue in Heaven: A Reconsideration of *Paradise Lost*, III, 1–417," reprinted in *Milton: Modern Essays in Criticism*, ed. Arthur E. Barker (New York, 1965), pp. 233–45.

MILTON'S TECHNIQUE
OF MULTIPLE CHOICE

Virginia R. Mollenkott

Milton presented his readers with two or more possible interpretations of certain situations for the following purposes: to avoid committing himself on issues where he himself was doubtful; to recognize the mysteries of the universe; to make his plot more intriguing; to create a bridge between Hebraic mythological exclusiveness and Hellenic richness; and to provide ironic commentary on the human condition. Always the technique has the effect of drawing the reader into more active participation through choice. Nathaniel Hawthorne used the technique perhaps more frequently than Milton, sometimes more obviously, but always with similar effect.

T HE M OST familiar instance of multiple choice in Milton's poetry is also the most obvious. When Adam asks the angel Raphael about the movement and patterning of the heavenly bodies, he receives an answer sprinkled with invitations either to choose his own theory, or to abandon all theories:

> *Consider* first, that great
> Or bright infers not excellence: the earth,
> Though in comparison of heav'n so small,
> Nor glistering, *may* of solid good contain
> More plenty than the sun that barren shines.
>
> . . . .
>
> *Not that I so affirm.*
>
> . . . .
>
> *What if* the sun
> Be center to the world.
>
> . . . .
>
> and *what if* sev'nth to these

> The planet earth, so steadfast though she seem,
> Insensibly three different motions move?
>
> . . . .
>
> *What if* that light
> Sent from her through the wide transpicuous air,
> To the terrestrial moon be as a star
> Enlight'ning her by day, as she by night
> This earth, reciprocal, *if* land be there,
> Fields and inhabitants?
>
> . . . .
>
> But *whether* thus these things, or *whether not,*
> *Whether* the sun predominant in heav'n
> Rise on the earth *or* earth rise on the sun
>
> . . . .
>
> Solicit not thy thoughts with matters hid.[1]

In other passages Milton similarly sidesteps commitment to either the Ptolemaic or the Copernican system of astronomy by the use of multiple choice, as during Satan's flight to the sun and later Uriel's flight to his command post when Milton finds it "hard to tell" whether the cosmic motion is heliocentric or geocentric (*PL* III, 574–76; IV, 592–97). Elsewhere, Milton pushes the possibility of space conquest of other habitable worlds far past the moon by the single word *perhaps:* "every star *perhaps* a world / Of destined habitation" (*PL* VII, 621–22). And concerning the introduction of the seasons as a result of the Fall, Milton is equally diffident:

> *Some say* he bid his angels turn askance
> The poles of earth twice ten degrees and more
> From the sun's axle; they with labor pushed
> Oblique the centric globe: *some say* the sun
> Was bid turn reins from the equinoctial road.   (*PL* X, 668–72)

Thus Milton has used the technique of multiple choice to gain all the richness, familiarity, regularity, and formal structure of the Ptolemaic system without lending actual credence to it; and he has likewise allowed himself the luxury of speculation concerning the nature of various heavenly bodies and the possibility of their habitation by man.

But Milton also used multiple choice in many other contexts and for other purposes. Often, as in his speculation concerning parallels between heaven and earth, he resorted to multiple choice to avoid committing himself to a theological doctrine or detail for which he could find no concrete support in the Bible. In the words of Raphael,

> what surmounts the reach
> Of human sense I shall delineate so,
> By lik'ning spiritual to corporeal forms,
> As may express them best, *though what if* earth
> Be but the shadow of heav'n, and things therein
> Each to other like, more than on earth is thought?
>
> (*PL* V, 571–76)

What if, indeed? The possibility of earth as heaven's exact shadow is one that Milton cannot positively assert because of his respect for the absolute authority of Scripture, which is silent on the topic; but he cannot exclude it either. "*What if* earth / Be but the shadow of heav'n"? Like inadmissible evidence in the courtroom, Milton's speculation affects the reader's perception even as it is being withdrawn.

Leland Ryken has discussed Milton's deliberate ambiguity concerning the identity of the Creator and the Judge in *Paradise Lost.* In VII, 163–66, the Father sends the *Son* to do the work of creation, and VII, 174–75 and 192–93 identify the creative agent as the Son. But VII, 207–09 refers the work to the entire *Trinity,* while line 219 refers to the Creator's "*Paternal* Glory" and several other passages refer to "the Almightie." Yet VII, 235 credits the "*Spirit* of God." Was the agent of creation the Son alone, the Father alone, the Spirit alone, the Son and Father together (see VII, 516–20), or the entire Trinity? Ryken thinks that Milton creates a dramatic illusion in which "the divine agents and their actions are too remote to yield a clear and definite impression to human view,"[2] and this indeed *is* the aesthetic effect; but no doubt the ambiguity of the Bible necessitated Milton's leaving the identity multiple. Genesis i, 1 identifies *God* as Creator; Genesis i, 2 makes the agent "the *Spirit* of God"; Genesis i, 26 implies a *Trinity* of creators ("Let *us* make man"); while Colossians i, 15 makes an unequivocal claim for *Christ* as creator: "for by him were all things created . . . all things were created by him and for him."

Similarly, in many passages Milton identifies the *Judge* as the Son (X, 56, 71–72, 96, 209, and elsewhere) but elsewhere implies that the Father himself, the "Presence Divine," was the Judge (X, 144, 163, 118–20, and elsewhere).[3] Here again, Milton achieves a sense of remoteness by deferring to biblical ambiguity: Genesis iii, 9 identifies the Judge as "the Lord God," but John v, 22 claims that "the Father judgeth no man, but hath committed all judgment unto the Son."

Milton's inconsistencies concerning the precise identity of the Creator and Judge are neither lapses of memory nor Miltonic innovations to distance the reader from remote actions, though they have that effect. They are deliberate multiple choices presented in such a way as to preserve biblical ambiguity without challenging biblical precision.

After the Fall, when the Judge provides clothing for Adam and Eve, Milton deprives himself of a symbol of the crucifixion by failing to describe the death of a sacrificial animal to provide the covering for them. He is, in fact, *meticulous* about the nature of the apron made for Adam and Eve: "he clad / Their nakedness with skins of beasts, *or* slain, / *Or* as the snake with youthful coat repaid" (X, 216–18). Was the apron made of the skin of a beast which had to die, or of a snakeskin sloughed off in the course of natural growth? This is a curious instance of the multiple choice technique, because Milton is not usually so reticent about providing concrete details where the Scripture has been silent. Milton's reticence concerning the use of the angelic trumpet is also curious—it is blown, he says, to gather the angels to hear about man's Fall, Judgment, and Redemption, and is "heard in Oreb since *perhaps* / When God descended, and *perhaps* once more / To sound at general doom" (*PL* XI, 74–76). Why the double "perhaps"? Exodus xix, 16 makes clear that a trumpet sounded "exceeding loud" at Mount Sinai in Horeb, and Matthew xxiv,31 and 1 Corinthians xv, 52 state that a trumpet will sound at Christ's Second Coming. In the Nativity Ode (155–56; 60–64) Milton had shown no doubt about these two trumpetings. Does the *perhaps* refer only to Milton's inability to decide whether each of these trumpet soundings is to be blown by the same "bright minister"? If so, this use of multiple choice indicates a concern about precise biblical detail which is almost incredible to our theologically careless age.

Milton similarly uses multiple choice to avoid going beyond his source when he describes the potential results should fallen Adam and Eve eat of the Tree of Life before their expulsion from the Garden: they might eat "And live forever, *dream at least* to live / For ever" (XI, 95–96). Would they, fallen, have been able to achieve everlasting life by eating of the Tree of Life? Or would they have enjoyed only an illusion? If only an illusion, why should God be concerned? If a reality, how can God's prophecy of death-for-disobedience be regarded as accurate?

Milton both raises interesting questions and sidesteps the impossible answering of them by his device of multiple choice. His restless, curious mind could not resist asking the questions, but his loyalty to scriptural revelation limited the range of possible speculation. Multiple choice, by which he only mused aloud but did not commit himself to a single answer, provided the necessary safety valve.

The invocation to Light in *Paradise Lost,* Book III utilizes multiple choice for yet another purpose. Like Dante, whose final vision of God in the *Paradiso* moves beyond even the symbol of the Trinity to a flood of divine and wordless light, Milton expresses his awe before the ultimate mystery by refusing to settle upon any single definition of Light. Instead, he presents his reader with four attempts at definition within eight lines, hailing Light as the first-born of God's creation, then allowing for the possibility that Light was actually *un*created, a beam which emanates from the Eternal and is therefore of necessity co-eternal with God. Or perhaps God and Light are one and the same, so that God dwells in a Light which is actually the "Bright effluence" of his own "bright essence," and not really distinguishable from it. Or, finally, he wonders whether Light is to be approached simply as a mystery, a "pure ethereal stream, / Whose fountain who shall tell?" (7–8). Milton cannot tell it. He knows only that *whatever* its ultimate definition, the celestial Light is available even to a blind poet in the form of insight, which will enable him to speak "Of things invisible to mortal sight" (55). Thus he has used multiple choice as a way of expressing respect for the *mysteries* of the Creator and his creation.

In an entirely different vein, Milton sometimes uses multiple choice as an intrinsic part of his narrative or dramatic technique. For instance, Satan offers Eve multiple choice in the climax of her prideful dream. If only she will eat the "fruit divine," she will be able to choose at will whether to live on earth, or in the air, or in heaven itself (V, 78–81). The irony here, of course, is that like Macbeth's kingship, all of these options would legitimately have opened for Adam and Eve if they had resisted the temptation to "catch the nearest way." (Raphael tells them in Book V that if they remain obedient their bodies will work up to spirit so that they will be able to live in Eden or in Heaven at their own choice). Unlike Macbeth, and unlike Adam and Eve, the Son of *Paradise Regained* refuses the temptation to "catch the nearest way" and becomes "king hereafter" in a *legitimate* fashion.

In the last book of *Paradise Lost,* Adam's reaction to Michael's news of redemption is an example of how Milton reveals a character's complex state of mind through multiple choice:

> *Full of doubt I stand,*
> *Whether* I should repent me now of sin
> By me done and occasioned, *or* rejoice
> Much more, that much more good thereof shall spring.
>
> (*PL* XII, 473–76)

It is quite understandable that Adam's mind should boggle at the newly revealed plan of redemption so that he is confused; but it is far less understandable that Milton's *readers* should ignore the many indications that the Fall was not fortunate in the least. *Redemption* is fortunate; sin is not. The doubt expressed is Adam's doubt, not Milton's.[4]

Christ offers Satan multiple choice in *Paradise Regained* to show his disdain for the offer of Athens and the knowledge Athens symbolizes: "Think not but that I know these things, *or* think / I know them not; not therefore am I short / Of knowing what I ought" (IV, 286–88). The careless shrug, the refusal to explain, the tossing of multiple choice into Satan's teeth show the steely strength of the Son, Milton's great hero of nonviolent resistance. Likewise, the reader's mental picture of Samson before he breaks the pillars of the Philistine temple is enhanced by the choice of seeing him *either* "as one who prayed / *Or* some great matter in his mind revolved" (1637–38). Was Samson praying, or thinking? No matter; what matters is that we know how he looked just before the catastrophe, and know that in the catastrophe itself Milton is bringing together the natural (physical) and supernatural (metaphysical) levels of the drama. Samson may be thinking, as the human and fallible man he is; but he may be praying, because once again God's strength is flowing in him. When he acts, he quits himself like Samson—both like a bragging bully and like the hero of God.

Very subtly, Milton offers in *Samson Agonistes* a multiple choice concerning the motives of his characters. Dalila's and Samson's motives are one thing when seen through the eyes of the Israelites, another through those of the Philistines; and too many critics have failed to get the full value of each perspective through an implicit assumption that the chorus and Samson represent the only viable point of view. The description by the Philistine, Harapha, which pictures Samson as "A murtherer, a revolter, and a robber" (1180), is a very precise description of Samson's career from the Philistine point of view; it bears out Dalila's observation that Fame is double-mouthed, so that although she may be vilified in Israel she will be honored in Philistia (971 ff.).[5] Thus, we readers are very naive if we adopt the Israelite point of view as the only one humanly possible. On the human level, Milton has offered us an important choice that enriches the human texture of his drama.

But Milton's most interesting uses of multiple choice occur in relation to mythology. Northrop Frye has pointed out that although both Greek and Hebrew mythologies aimed at "a verbal circumference of human experience," Greek myth developed by accretion, by adding new gods to the pantheon rather than by insisting on the validity of a few original gods; whereas Hebrew myth developed by a rigorous codification and exclusion of unwanted material.[6] Milton gave literal belief to Hebrew mythology as embodied in the Old Testament, yet at the same time he wanted to take advantage of all the riches of the inclusivist Hellenic mythology. To have his cake and eat it also, he utilized the time-honored mythological technique of multiple choice.

Milton's Hebraic exclusiveness is demonstrated in such passages as *Paradise Lost* I, 739–49, where he relates the fallen angel Mammon to the Greek version of the fall of Mulciber, with the following judgment: "Thus they relate, / Erring; for he with this [Satan's] rebellious rout / Fell long before." "Thus they relate, *erring*." Similarly, in X, 578–84 he identifies myths concerning the Titan Ophion ("Serpent") as traditions dispersed among the heathen by the fallen angels themselves. In both cases Milton is able to recount richly poetic Hellenic details while making a Hebraic rejection that excludes them from any semblance of truth, except as a perversion thereof intended to draw mankind away from the one truth embodied in biblical revelation. He uses a similar technique in the roll call of fallen angels as pagan gods in both the Nativity Ode and *Paradise Lost*.

Northrop Frye has commented that people respond to myths either on the level of literal belief, or as allegory, or as archetypes of universal human experience.[7] Milton accorded literal belief only to biblical mythology, which he also used in allegorical and archetypal ways, but sometimes he made an archetypal response to classical mythology, sometimes merely an allegorical one. And sometimes, by means of a multiple choice presentation, he used the connotations of classical or native myth without committing himself one way or the other. An excellent example of

Milton's allegorical response to classical myth, a response which shades over into the archetypal, occurs in *Comus* (513–19):

> 'Tis not vain or fabulous
> (Though so esteemed by shallow ignorance)
> What the sage poets, taught by th'heav'nly Muse,
> Storied of old in high immortal verse
> Of dire Chimeras and enchanted isles,
> And rifted rocks whose entrance leads to hell;
> For such there be, but unbelief is blind.

There really are a Scylla and a Charybdis, Milton asserts: *moral* ones, such as the compulsive cavortings of Comus and his crew. More intrinsic is the structuring of "Lycidas" upon the archetype (or recurrent literary symbol) of the dying god Adonis.[8] Yet so basic is Milton's Hebraism that while he is willing to make archetypal use of Adonis in "Lycidas," in *Paradise Lost* he lists the Babylonian equivalent of Adonis, Thammuz, among the fallen angels (I, 446–57). On the basis of Ezekiel viii, 14, he calls Adonis or Thammuz the instigator of "the dark idolatries / Of alienated Judah." Thus he has structured a major poem upon the archetype of Adonis while rejecting Adonis on the level of literal belief.

Getting directly to multiple choice: the technique is operative when Milton wants certain mythological connotations without granting them literal credence, as when he mythologizes concerning the fate of the fallen angels to become serpents and eat dust: "Yearly enjoined, *some say*, to undergo / This annual humbling certain numbered days, / To dash their pride, and joy for man seduced" (X, 575–77). *Some say*: the reader is invited to take it or leave it, but the aesthetic impact of the suggestion stands free of whatever choice the reader may make. In other words, even if we reject the idea that the fallen angels literally have to become serpents and eat dust once a year, our attitudes have been affected by the suggestion.

Similarly, while describing the entrance of the fallen angels into Pandemonium by means of lessening their stature, Milton achieves his metaphor without admitting anything about his personal beliefs. The demons diminish themselves

> like that Pygmean race
> Beyond the Indian mount, or fairy elves,
> Whose midnight revels by a forest side
> Or fountain some belated peasant sees,

> *Or dreams he sees,* while overhead the moon
> Sits arbitress.   (I, 780–85)

"*Or dreams he sees*": No one can tell from this passage whether Milton believes in fairies; but the fairy metaphor has created a clear picture of the fallen angels crowding into their convention hall.

Anyone familiar with American literature must immediately think of the way Nathaniel Hawthorne used the technique of multiple choice, perhaps more frequently than Milton, sometimes more obviously, but always with similar effect. In "The Minister's Black Veil," there is the testimony of the superstitious old woman who affirmed that the corpse shuddered when Parson Hooper leaned over the casket; the reader can take it or leave it on the conscious level, but he can never free his total perceptions from that suggestive detail. More spectacular is the passage concerning the revelation of Dimmesdale's sin in *The Scarlet Letter:*

Most of the spectators testified to having seen, on the breast of the unhappy minister, a SCARLET LETTER—the very semblance of that worn by Hester Prynne—imprinted on the flesh. . . . *Some affirmed* that the Reverend Mr. Dimmesdale, on the very day when Hester Prynne first wore her ignominious badge had begun a course of penance . . . by inflicting a hideous torture on himself. *Others contended* that the stigma had not been produced until a long time subsequent, when old Roger Chillingworth . . . had caused it to appear, through the agency of magic and poisonous drugs. *Others, again . . . whispered their belief,* that the awful symbol was the effect of the ever active tooth of remorse. . . . *The reader may choose among these theories.*

But no sooner has Hawthorne turned our minds to *this* choice than he adds a choice even more basic:

It is singular, nevertheless, that certain persons, who were spectators of the whole scene, and professed never once to have removed their eyes from the Reverend Mr. Dimmesdale, *denied that there was any mark whatever on his breast,* more than on a new-born infant's.[9]

Was there a mark, or wasn't there? Did Milton's peasant see the fairies, or did he only *dream* he did?

F. O. Matthiessen commented that Hawthorne learned many devices from the seventeenth century;[10] and there can be little doubt that one of those devices was the technique of multiple choice by which he achieved so many brilliant effects throughout his works. Surely this is one of Milton's most concrete bequests to later authors.

Myth-making is involved in Milton's most subtle use of multiple choice. Although the major passage concerning the origin of evil offers no *overt* multiple choice, Milton plays a myth of his own creation (that Sin sprang full-grown from the head of Satan) against the classical knowledge of his readers that Athene, goddess of wisdom, sprang full-grown from the head of Zeus. Says Sin to Satan,

> All on a sudden miserable pain
> Surprised thee; dim thine eyes, and dizzy swum
> In darkness, while thy head flames thick and fast
> Threw forth; till on the left side op'ning wide,
> Likest to thee in shape and count'nance bright,
> Then shining heav'nly fair, a goddess armed
> Out of thy head I sprung.   (*PL* II, 752–58)

Milton derived this myth by combining the mythological birth of Athene with the birth metaphor in James i, 14–15: ". . . every man is tempted, when he is drawn away of his own lust, and enticed. Then when lust hath conceived, it bringeth forth sin; and sin, when it is finished, bringeth forth death." Accordingly, no sooner does Milton's Satan become familiar with his daughter Sin, than he lusts after her; and the "odious offspring" of their incest is Death.

Milton's "fit audience," with its classical background, could not read this passage without seeing behind it the outlines of Athene's origin. The Zeus-Athene myth expresses male envy of the womb, for if the male cannot bring forth babies, behold, he can bring forth something even more important, Wisdom. So Milton's *inversion* of the myth is crucially ironic: a male figure gives birth, certainly; but what he produces is not Wisdom—it is Sin. By superimposing his own myth onto the classical one, Milton has suggested the anguish surrounding many human choices, since so much of what an individual chooses as the best course of action later turns out to be destructive and sinful. If the human brain can give birth to wisdom, it can also (in unawareness) give birth to sin; and which is which can sometimes be most perplexing.

Without overtness, simply by forcing the mind to recognize its inability to separate and choose between the underlying Hellenic myth and the overlay of Hebrao-Christian myth, Milton has embodied the painful tension of the human condition: "There is a way which seemeth right unto a man; but the end thereof are the ways of death. Even in laughter the heart is sorrowful; and the end of that mirth is heaviness" (Proverbs xiv, 12–13).

Milton's technique of multiple choice is an excellent symbol of the transitional age in which he lived, when many things no longer seemed so certain as they once had been. It is also an excellent archetype for the labyrinthine ambiguities of human experience in a fallen world. Sometimes Milton used multiple choice to avoid committing himself on issues where he himself was doubtful; sometimes to recognize the mysteries of the universe; sometimes to make his plot more intriguing; sometimes to create a bridge between Hebraic mythological exclusiveness and Hellenic richness; and sometimes to provide ironic commentary on the human condition. But always the technique has the effect of drawing the reader into more active participation through choice. Does the earth move, or the sun? Did the Father create, or the Son, or the Spirit? Would Adam and Eve have lived forever had they eaten of the Tree of Life before they were expelled from Eden? What, exactly, is the total definition of Light? Do fairies really exist? How do I know whether my decisions are right, or based on various delusions? We have long possessed the answer to the Ptolemaic-Copernican dilemma; but concerning many other Miltonic ambiguities, three centuries later we still label ourselves foolish if we feel too sure.

William Paterson College of New Jersey

NOTES

1. *Paradise Lost* VIII, 90–145; italics mine here and throughout the essay. Quotations from Milton's poems are from Douglas Bush, ed., *The Complete Poetical Works of John Milton* (Boston, 1965).

2. *The Apocalyptic Vision in Paradise Lost* (Ithaca, 1970), p. 171.

3. Ibid., pp. 172–73.

4. See V. R. Mollenkott, "Milton's Rejection of the Fortunate Fall," *Milton Quarterly*, VI (March 1972), 1–5.

5. See V. R. Mollenkott, "Relativism in *Samson Agonistes*," *Studies in Philology*, LXVII (January 1970), 89–102.

6. *Fables of Identity* (New York, 1963), p. 32.

7. "Literature and Myth," in *Relations of Literary Study*, ed. James Thorpe (New York, 1967), p. 34.

8. See Frye, *Fables of Identity*, pp. 119–29.

9. *The Scarlet Letter*, Modern Library ed. (New York, 1950), pp. 293–94. Italics added.

10. *American Renaissance* (New York, 1941), p. 284.

THE MYSTERIES IN MILTON'S *MASQUE*

Alice-Lyle Scoufos

In *Comus,* Milton appears to have used both stock characters and stock plot. Taking his cue from the liturgical text which the *Book of Common Prayer* listed for St. Michael's Day (Revelation xii, 7–13), he turned to the plot of the Woman Wandering in the Wilderness which had been the subject of the Advent plays of medieval drama. The Woman from Revelation, chapter xii, was first dramatized in the twelfth-century *Ludus de Antichristo,* in which she was named Ecclesia (following the tradition of biblical commentaries). Her two companions were Mercy and Justice, two of the Four Daughters of God. Milton appears to have known the work of Reformation playwrights who exploited the older Advent plays. Thomas Kirchmayer re-created the Wandering Woman as Veritas and adapted the Tempter of the medieval drama into a sophisticated villain. John Foxe developed the mystery characters in his *Comoedia Apocalyptica:* Ecclesia reappears, accompanied by two boys. Foxe's heroine resists the Tempter and anticipates her marriage to the Heavenly Bridegroom. The Advent plays had ended with the Archangel Michael winging to the rescue. Milton's Attendant Spirit functions in a similar way to confront Comus, who has inherited the attributes of the seductive Antichrist.

THE JEWISH and Christian literatures of eschatology, and especially Revelation with its abundance of commentary both written and illuminated, provided medieval playwrights with dynamic materials for the apocalyptic dramas which served as terminal plays in the mystery cycles. These plays dealt primarily with the traditional subjects of the *Prophetae* and the Signs of Doom, the Coming of Antichrist, and the Last Judgment. Such themes usually were presented as individual dramas within the cycles, but, as was true in some of the noncyclic plays of the Apocalypse, they at times were combined into one large production.

In the tense sixteenth century, after Reformation polemics had stirred all elements of society, the medieval form of the apocalyptic drama was revived and revitalized as an instrument for the propagation of Protestant doctrine. However, by the time the seventeenth century was well underway, the apocalyptic form had become antique, at least in England. Protestantism there had turned from its external enemies to fight its inward struggles with sects and schisms, and religious drama ceased to be an overt weapon in the Puritan conflict.

To say that John Milton was interested in old literary forms is to use understatement ineffectively. Milton knew the subtle inner structures of older literatures as well as their outer structures, and he adapted both most advantageously in everything he wrote. My own studies in early drama have led me to conclude that Milton was well acquainted with the mystery plays which had been popular in Europe and especially in England in the later Middle Ages. He also seems to have been particularly aware of the apocalyptic dramas with their visionary ideas and of the way the polemic writers of the Reformation adapted those ideas to their own partisan purposes. In his *Masque Presented at Ludlow Castle,* Milton used, I think, both stock characters and stock plot. He depended upon older mystery characters for certain features which we find in the Lady, her two brothers, the Attendant Spirit, and Comus himself. Milton also depended, I believe, upon the plot line of the medieval Advent plays of Antichrist for the basal structure of his masque. I am of the opinion, therefore, that much of the mystery which has boggled twentieth-century critics of *Comus* can be solved by a careful examination of the medieval apocalyptic plays and of the Reformation dramas which revitalized the older form.[1]

We know from Milton's prose writings that he was aware of the dramatic possibilities of the apocalyptic visions. One of his early comments on the subject is to be found in that famous passage at the beginning of Book II in *Reason of Church Government.* At that point Milton allowed himself the liberty of musing upon ideal literary productions "of highest hope and hardest attempting." After considering the works of Homer, Vergil, Tasso, and others, he remarks that "the Apocalyps of Saint *Ihon* is the majestick image of a high and stately Tragedy," and he cites David Paré's *Commentary* concerning the vision of St. John as "a Drammaticall Representation."[2] Milton had also thought upon the literary mode or technique employed in Revelation: "The whole Booke soared to a

Prophetick pitch in types and Allegories," he wrote in his early career.[3] The "types" and "allegories" of Revelation, especially those in the twelfth and thirteenth chapters, offer a salient point at which to begin an analysis of the characters in Milton's masque. In those chapters, St. John describes a Lady Wandering in the Wilderness. Her experiences are dramatic from any point of view, and it is not surprising that medieval playwrights found her story useful to heighten the interest of their Advent plays which predicated the second coming of Christ.[4]

The Lady Wandering in the Wilderness made her theater debut in an august spectacular of the twelfth century called *Ludus de Antichristo*, which originated in the Bavarian monastery of Tegernsee.[5] The production, in Latin, aimed at magnificence: a cast of more than one hundred actors and musicians was required to present the elaborate musical with its seven kings and their combating armies. The date of the *Ludus de Antichristo* is surprisingly early; scholars have identified it as a product of the reign of Frederick Barbarossa, A.D. 1155–89. Even more surprising at this point in space and time is that we find contemporary political ideas controlling the anonymous playwright's dramatic point of view. The author accomplishes a sophisticated manipulation of religious motifs to reinforce a secular, propagandistic point. His play is intentionally slanted not only to flatter the Germanic Barbarossa but to demean the French king and, more subtly, the pope.[6]

The dramatic action of the play, drawn from Revelation, depicts the pseudo-Messiah's meteoric rise to supreme power over the kingdoms of the world. The heroine, Lady Ecclesia, derives her name from the allegorical interpretation of the Lady Wandering in the Wilderness, an interpretation that had been popularized in centuries of biblical commentary which presented the woman of Revelation, chapter xii, as a symbol of the church in the Latter Days.[7] The author of the *Ludus de Antichristo*, therefore, was exploiting a commonplace idea in naming his heroine Ecclesia. But he was original in adding two attendants for his regal queen. In Revelation, the woman goes into the wilderness alone; in the drama, Misericordia and Justitia accompany her. The two ancillary figures, who later were to become popular morality play characters, are "dressed as women" (*utrisque muliebriter indutis*), with Misericordia carrying the oil of mercy and Justitia bearing the sword and scales, ancient signs of their identity.[8] St. John describes the Lady Wandering in the Wilderness as being "clothed with the sun, and the moon under her feet, and upon her head a crown of twelve stars."[9] Cosmic costuming of this order presented some difficulties on the stage, to say the least. In the *Ludus de Antichristo,* Ecclesia wears a feminine costume, but she dons a cuirass or breastplate and wears a crown (*Ecclesia in muliebri habitu procedit induta thoracem et coronata*). That is not, of course, enough protection. She suffers much outrageous abuse and derision (*multis contumeliis et verberibus*) from the conquering Antichrist, who has taken over the Temple of the Lord. The action of the drama continues as Antichrist uses magic and miracles to subjugate the kings of the world; victoriously he stamps the Sign of the Beast upon their foreheads. And finally, the denigrated Ecclesia is driven from the Temple, accompanied by Misericordia, Justitia, and the silent Pope whom the playwright never allows to speak.

In the *Ludus de Antichristo,* the wanderings of the Lady and her attendants are not described.[10] The author was more concerned with his political ideas than with a mystical vision. However, Ecclesia's victory comes at the end of the play, when Antichrist is destroyed and the Lady hails the returning kings with song, "*Laudem dicite Deo nostro.*" We have in this skilfully developed drama an original and imaginative adaptation of the apocalyptic visions for stage presentation. The work, deservedly, was influential for several hundred years, especially upon German and Swiss religious drama.[11]

The legend of Antichrist was popular outside the medieval drama, as readers of the *Cursor Mundi,* the *Pricke of Conscience,* and the *Polychronicon* know.[12] And it remained a popular legend as western Europe moved into the Renaissance period. However, an important shift in point of view in the legend and in its interpretation occurred with the full impact of the Reformation. Thomas Kirchmayer, one of the boldest and most vehement of the new reformers in Germany, inflated the medieval story into a complex polemical artwork for the sixteenth-century stage. He called his play *Pammachius.* Delighted with the breach which the Convocation of Canterbury had caused between England and Rome, Kirchmayer in 1538 boldly dedicated his drama to the archbishop of Canterbury.[13] Kirchmayer's intention is clear: he had created from the old legend a new and elaborate version of the apocalyptic drama. Taking the hint from the medieval playwrights, he devised a violently radical production which aimed its most destructive satire at Rome. The sophisticated Antichrist of the earlier Latin play, with his magic and miracles, moves into Kirchmayer's drama to become even more debonair. But unlike the medieval character who definitely was a devil, Kirchmayer's Antichrist is human and wears the triple crown. He establishes a league with Satan, and the two share Kirchmayer's voluptuous and epicurean lines.[14] Kirchmayer's major ploy is to dramatize the rebels' battle cry, which had echoed through the halls of the dissenters from Wyclif's time to Luther's: "The Pope is Antichrist!" In Kirchmayer's drama the visionary anticipation of the Last Days becomes a concrete historical reality. Pope Pammachius (the All-fighter) has placed the Mark of the Beast upon the foreheads of mankind. Only one fugitive escapes to a place of hiding which Christ has prepared for her in the wilderness (Revelation xii, 6). Her name is Veritas, and she is immortal. Thus Lady Truth replaces Lady Ecclesia because Kirchmayer considered the church to bear the stamp of the Beast under the dominion of Rome. Veritas, hearing of Pammachius' total victory over the forces of good, flies to the gates of heaven, where she makes a tearful plea to Christ for assistance. He assures the poor pariah that a plan has been devised for her on earth in a northern town called Wittenberg. Kirchmayer's *Pammachius* ends abruptly with the news that the Reformation, led by Theophilus (Luther), has started in Germany. The concluding epilogue is filled with the anticipation of Doomsday.

If accurately described, the drama must be classified as an elaborate Protestant mystery play, but Kirchmayer's humanistic training led him to refine the old episodic form of the traditional religious drama. *Pammachius* has a classical structure with clearly defined acts, scenes, and a formal parabasis. The stock characters are drawn from the medieval plays; however, they act as true Terentian characters should, and their witty Latin reflects surprising polish. Moreover, *Pammachius* contains a major doctrinal shift away from the orthodox ideas of the Roman church. In the Catholic morality plays, the allegorical character Good Deeds usually acted a major doctrinal role; but in Kirchmayer's play, faith is stressed as the only mode of salvation for the human soul. Kirchmayer's play is egregiously Protestant.

Pammachius was an instant success in northern Europe, and it was translated into German immediately. John Bale, working in England as a propagandist under Thomas Cromwell, had ideas similar to Kirchmayer's concerning the effectiveness of the stage as a doctrinal weapon. Modern scholars have suggested that Bale "started the Protestant moral-

ity on its way in England."[15] Indeed, Bale supported a group of actors in
his own household, and though we do not know the date of his translation of *Pammachius,* it would appear likely that he was working with
Kirchmayer's play shortly after its publication. Unfortunately, his translation has not survived, but in the three lists of his own works which he
compiled, Bale added the *Pammachius* last after the titles of his own
dramas. Bale was never a compromiser. He boldly attacked what he
called "the lowsie legerdemains" of the older Catholic plays, and his own
dramatic plans appear to have been to develop a new cycle of dramas
which would present the cosmic story of Christ from a rigorously Protestant point of view.[16] His translation of Kirchmayer's *Pammachius* apparently was to have served as the terminal play for this new cycle.

Other readers in England found Kirchmayer's play noteworthy. We
have among the historical records evidence of an unusual performance
of the Latin drama at Cambridge. Early in 1545 some ingenuous or in-
genious (we are not sure which) students of Christ's College presented
Pammachius for the university community. By March 27 of that year,
word of the innovative play with its reflection on "popish ceremonies"
reached the conservative ears of Bishop Gardiner. He was offended, and
as chancellor of the university he deemed it necessary to probe into the
causes which had led the youths of Christ's through "fraylte, lightnes, or
malyce" to abuse their talents. He wrote to Vice-Chancellor Parker to
learn more of the drama "called Pammachius a parte of which tragedie
is soo pestiferous as wer intollerable." Parker, alarmed, replied that the
students had performed the play with the permission of their masters
and that the text of the drama had been carefully sponged to "omyt all
such mattyer wherby offense might justly have rysen." But Gardiner demanded a copy of the text as it was performed, and having studied it
carefully, he admonished the vice-chancellor severely: what had been
deleted was proper, and what had not been deleted was heretical! "Soo
as this boke declarith the parties to have double offended both in denying that is trew and also approving that is false." Moreover, he declared,
the work was so "maliciously weved with truth [and] abhominable and
detestable lies" that no Christian ears "shuld paciently heare it." By
May 16, the Privy Council had entered the conflict. They wrote to Parker
demanding that the culprits be punished and the "poyson eyther in
lernyng or manners be expelled and putt owt."[17] The university was in
for a cleaning.

In the next decade Kirchmayer's play served as both inspiration and model for the imaginative drama of John Foxe, an Englishman most famous for his *Acts and Monuments of the English Church*. Foxe wrote his own apocalyptic drama while he was working in exile as a proof-reader for John Oporinus, a well-known Basle printer of classical works and of Neo-Latin plays. In March 1556, Foxe's dramatic work came from Oporinus' press with the title *Christus Triumphans: Comoedia Apocalyptica*. The martyrologist uses the term *comoedia* in the grand sense, for the work is a true cosmic drama which includes human time from the Fall to Doomsday. Unlike Kirchmayer's play, which has a classical compactness, Foxe's drama sweeps onward in the high style. Nor does Foxe's five-act structure hamper the flow of the action. Moreover, because Foxe's overall plot is that of the medieval cycle plays, the major characters of those older religious dramas reappear in their original splendor. Lady Ecclesia is there with her two attendants, but no longer are the two companions identified with Mercy and Justice. The evangelical Foxe has converted them into Europus and Africus, and they are now the children of Ecclesia, whom Foxe sees as the universal mother church.[18] Ecclesia as tragic heroine becomes the thematic center of the drama. In his prefatory statement Foxe remarks that he is using the story of the Apocalypse, but only "as much of it as bears upon the affairs of the Church." By the third act of the *Comoedia,* Foxe's Antichrist (Pseudamnus, the Pope) has seduced the whole world with his "Circean cups of luxury." With suave confidence, he confronts Ecclesia. Satan has promised him this exquisite woman as his bride. But surprisingly the lady demurs. Indeed, the asperity of her rejection and her emotional insistence that she is the intended spouse of Christ repulse him, and he sends her to Bedlam! At the end of the drama Antichrist is overcome, Africus and Europus are reunited with Ecclesia, and she is clothed in wedding garments by a chorus of virgins who sing an epithalamium which describes her approaching marriage to the Heavenly Bridegroom.

Foxe's drama is much closer to Revelation than Kirchmayer's play; however, both works are filled with polemical doctrine, and both writers exploit the Protestant commentaries upon the Apocalypse of St. John. Each author has attempted to make the scriptural account of the Last Days fit the contemporary sixteenth-century historical setting. The central feminine character in these two plays and in the earlier twelfth-century drama remains virtuous under harassment, and ultimately she is

victorious. In all the plays she is an allegorical representation of the congregation of the faithful who will be rewarded ultimately with marriage
to the Heavenly Bridegroom.

It almost verges upon vulgarity to move Milton's delicate masque
into this vortex of propagandistic art, but that is the matrix from which
Comus sprang. Milton's Lady, analyzed as a descendant of the anagogical heroines of the Latin dramas, becomes a unique stock character, and
within this religious context her dramatic actions lose much of their
mystery. Her name or lack of name is important. We can say without
controversy that Milton knew his biblical commentary; and we can
assume with safety that he was aware of the ubiquity of the "Woman
clothed with the Sun" as a subject for artistic expression. In the illuminated manuscripts of the Apocalypse, which reached their peak of popularity in the thirteenth and fourteenth centuries, there is no ambiguity
concerning the Madonnaic elements in the configuration of the woman
in aureate robes.[19] The medieval artists saw her as a symbol both of "Our
Lady" and of the church. They were using a well-developed tradition.
Early writers from Origen and Methodius to the theologians of the
sixteenth century considered the child in the Woman's arms not only a
representation of Christ but a symbol of Christ "brought foorth . . . in
the harts of the faithful."[20] This Isaianic-Pauline conception of the
Universal Mother and her children is an ecclesiastical symbol which also
includes the conception of the Second Eve and the Spouse of Christ. The
Virgin and Mother figures were early conflated into a symbol for the
church.[21] This was still the accepted interpretation when the editors of
the Rheims New Testament added their marginalia to the text of Revelation xii, 1–2 (the passage in which the Woman is first described): "This
is properly and principally spoken of the Church: & by allusion, of our
B[lessed] Lady also."[22] It was the commonplace Roman Catholic interpretation which John Bale had blasted earlier with his savage attack
upon Romanism in *The Image of Bothe Churches,* one of the first ver-
nacular commentaries upon Revelation printed in England. Bale was
adamant in his insistence that "not Marye Christes mother is this
woman, though many hath so statied in their commentaries. But it is the
true christian Church of whom Mary is a moste notable member."[23] And
the Protestant writers in general followed Bale's leadership. In depicting
his Lady Wandering in the Wilderness, Milton creates, I believe, a pure

symbol of "the visible church of true believers." His Lady is virginal, but she is not the Holy Virgin. Milton works softly but surely through the controverted ideas of the Reformation. His choice is of a pure, virtuous image, yet one which is vulnerable to ruin. His selectivity is more clearly documented by again placing his Lady within the theological context.

The pre-Puritan or Lollard image of the universal church was popularized in England by a famous work called *The Lanterne of Light,* in which the Woman Wandering in the Wilderness was proclaimed a chaste maiden: "þis chirche is clepid a clene chaast maiden. . . . Christ haþ chosun him a gloriouse chirche, neiþir hauyng spott ne bleyne. or ony suche oþir þing but þat þis chirche mai be holi and vndefoulid."[24] However, in Reformation polemics this idea of the undefilable purity of the church was attacked. Kirchmayer changed the name of his heroine to Veritas (the mystical church) because, as noted above, he was convinced that Ecclesia (the visible church) had been seduced by Rome. John Calvin attacked the Roman Catholics for insisting "ever and anon . . . that the Church cannot err," and he insisted that a great universal defection was to come upon the church in the Last Days.[25] In England the question of whether the true church was "spotted or unspotted" ballooned in importance, especially with the early nonconformists. William Tyndale thought the church could "err" because "all men are born into sin."[26] In William Fulke's systematic refutation of the Roman Catholic commentary to the Rheims New Testament, this question of the church's purity appears as a central problem. Fulke quotes first the marginal note to Revelation xii, 6, from the Rhemish translation, which presents the Roman Catholic view of the Woman's flight into the wilderness: "In which time for all that, she shall not want our Lordes protection, nor be so secret, but all faithfull men shall know and follow her: *much lesse shall she decay, erre in faith, or degenerate and folow Antichrist,* as Heretikes doe wickedly faine."[27] By "heretikes" the editors of course meant Luther and Calvin and their followers. Fulke, in reply, quotes a number of the church fathers on this problem of the decay of the church; then he adds: "No, verely, the true Church of Gods elect, shall alwayes continue constant and sound in fayth, in all articles necessary to salvation: neither doe we ever say otherwyse. *But the greatest part of ye visible Church, shal be seduced by Antichrist,* as it is manifest here."[28] This division of the church into visible and invisible was important to Protestants. It afforded them a way of condemning the material church of Rome and of commending the spiritual or mystical church of the reformers.

Milton's writings on the theological definition of the true church in *De Doctrina Christiana* indicate his personal thoughts in this area. He was convinced that the regenerate, through a true fellowship with Christ, formed the "mysticall body called the Invisible Church, whereof Christ is the head." And he quotes at this point the famous verses from 1 Corinthians, chapter xiii on faith, hope, and charity. He adds also the remark on the metaphor of the Bride and Bridegroom: "The love of Christ towards his invisible and spotless Church is described by the appropriate figure of conjugal love." For documentation he quotes the well-known passage from Revelation xix, 7: "The marriage of the Lamb is come, and his wife hath made herself ready."[29] But Milton was aware that the visible church of his day was vulnerable to temptations. He remarks on this vulnerability in *De Doctrina Christiana:* the true body of the regenerate in Christ will "never entirely fall away through any power or malice of the devil or the world, *so long as nothing is wanting on their own parts.*" Milton emphasizes the phrase "so long as nothing is wanting on their own parts" by repetition and concludes that it *is* possible for the real believers to fall into apostasy.[30] The visible or material church cannot achieve perfection in this life, Milton concluded; that perfect happiness is reserved for the church as the Bride of Christ in eternity.[31] Indeed, in his earlier antiprelatical writings, Milton described in passionate terms the lamentable predicament of the visible church: "We have tri'd already, & miserably felt what ambition, worldly glory & immoderat wealth can do, what the boisterous & contradictional hand of a temporall, earthly, and corporeall Spiritualty can availe to the edifying of Christs holy Church." And in a related passage he described the situation in which "Timorous and ingratefull, the Church of God is now again at the foot of her insulting enemies."[32] In other words, Milton idealized the mystical church, but he was quite realistic in his consideration of the worldly state of the Church of England in its early prelatical period.

When Milton gives his female character the anonymous name "Lady," he accomplishes much. She is the stock character, Ecclesia, but she is also further defined by Milton's careful control: her purity is analogous to that of the Holy Virgin, but unlike the mother of Christ (the Roman Catholic view of the church) she is vulnerable to ruin. Her Protestantism, like that of Kirchmayer's Veritas, is stressed through her insistence upon "pure ey'd Faith." The major doctrinal ploy in Kirchmayer's *Pammachius* was, as I have remarked, an emphasized central shift away from the doctrine of good deeds which the Catholic mysteries and morality plays had stressed as orthodox Christian doctrine.[33] Milton clearly places his dramatic emphasis upon the Protestant doctrine of faith ("Heaven it selfe would stoope to her"), and his Lady is an English Puritan! She has the moral stamina to stand rather than fall. Milton's Lady exercises her virtuous will. Her faith, hope, and chastity are the foundations for her disciplined actions, and those actions include intellectual choice. Milton's doctrinal position is clear in this:

We are justified therefore by faith, but by a living, not a dead faith; and that faith alone which acts is counted living. . . . Hence we are justified by faith without the works of the law, but not without the works of faith; inasmuch as a living and true faith cannot consist without works, though these latter may differ from the works of the written law.[34]

The Lady's chaste decisions are the works of faith. Her chastity, however, lends itself harmoniously to the antique apocalyptical plot. With his central character in the masque an allegorical representation of the English Church, and with the overt dramatic action involving "savage hunger or savage heat," Milton needed an idea more explicitly oriented to the ecclesiastical tradition. The ancient metaphor of the relationship between Christ and the church was that of conjugal love. The individual soul, as well as the universal congregation, was to participate in the mystical union with Godhead. Milton's creative adaptation becomes clear, I think, when the Lady's chastity is associated with the Christian doctrine of virginity, which had developed as the end result of an evangelical metaphor. From the fourth century, when Methodius taught that virginity prepared the soul to be the Bride of Christ, the greatest of the patristic teachers echoed the idea—Origen, Jerome, Gregory of Nyssa, Clement of Alexandria, and Ambrose all referred to the spiritual fidelity of the soul in its love for Christ as the essence of all virtues. The idea developed into "the sage doctrine of Virginity."[35] Milton, thinking of the church in metaphoric terms, creates at this point in the masque his own doctrinal propaganda. His ideas differ substantially from those expressed in the old morality plays and in Kirchmayer's mystery play. Milton believed the English church in the 1630s to be pure in doctrine *but unreformed in discipline*. The church had been misled, he felt sure, by Prelatism. The "church-maskers," as he called the prelates, had forced upon the church "an antichristian tyranny."[36] However, in his sanguine idealism Milton believed that the church was strong enough to maintain its spiritual integrity, its "spotless purity." Ingeniously, he employs in the masque "chastity" rather than "charity" (the third theological virtue mentioned by St. Paul) in order to unite the allegory and the dramatic action. In doing so Milton sides with such Puritan thinkers as Thomas Cartwright, who denied that the Lady Wandering in the Wilderness would be seduced and deflowered by Antichrist, but who also admitted that the church might "erre in somethings which are not fundamentall."[37] Milton opposes Calvin, Kirchmayer, Tyndale, and Fulke, who had believed that the universal church would be despoiled in the Last Days.[38] He also opposes Joseph Mede, the professor of Greek at Christ's College during Milton's tenure at Cambridge. Mede continued to insist until his death in 1638 that the prophecies of the Latter Days were being fulfilled in the seventeenth century. He preached bluntly that "the spirituall fornication of the Church and spouse of Christ will be found proper to these times," and he insisted that "the Whoredome of the Church of God is a Spirituall adultery."[39] Within the context of this explosive theological controversy, Milton's Lady obviously becomes highly dramatic. Milton, taking a stock character and a stock action for his poetic device, makes them express his own very individualistic ideas concerning the ecclesiastical problems of his own day. His Lady is enchanted, immovable in Comus' magic seat. We see, however, that her mind is still her own because her will (the source of faith, hope, and chastity) is functioning. But she is in grave danger. She is saved from "the savage heat" of Comus by the return of her brothers, her careless guardians.

The Lady's two brothers are also stock characters who have developed from the same complex line of dramatic progenitors. The Wandering Lady's first attendants, as we have noted, were the allegorical figures of Mercy and Justice. With Truth and Peace they appeared ubiquitously in medieval debates, tractates, allegorical poems, and dramas where they argued endlessly over the ultimate fate of the human soul. When the anonymous author of the *Ludus de Antichristo* gave Ecclesia her two attendants, he was influenced by the mystical writings of Hugo of St. Victor (1097–1141) and Bernard of Clairvaux (1091–1153), writings in which the allegory of the Four Daughters of God was first popularized.[40] In the even more famous feudal romance, *Le Chasteau d'Amour*, Robert Grosseteste, Bishop of Lincoln, transformed the four spiritual figures into secular characters who debated over the punishment of their father's careless servant (mankind).[41] In early Renaissance iconography the eldest of the daughters, Truth (Veritas), is depicted at times as Ecclesia.[42] This commonplace substitution possibly influenced Kirchmayer's decision to name his heroine Veritas rather than Ecclesia because the latter had been defamed in the polemics of the day.

In English literature, the Four Daughters of God became characters in one of the finest of the morality plays, *The Castle of Perseverance* (ca. 1425). In that popular work the four are still females, symbolically dressed: Mercy is clad "in wyth," Justice (Rythwysnesse) in red, "Trewthe in sad grene," and Peace "al in blake." The theme of this morality, as everyone knows, is the eternal struggle between the forces of good and of evil; and throughout the action Humanum Genus, the hero, is accompanied by the competing Bonus Angelus and Malus Angelus. In the final debate over man's soul, Mercy and Peace oppose Truth and Justice before the throne of God in the traditional manner. But in the smaller cast of characters in *Mankind* (ca. 1465), only Mercy is left to defend man, and a radical change has occurred in the presentation of the figure. Mercy becomes in this play a male character dressed as a "semely father." In the action of the drama he functions as a priest to save mankind from destruction.[43] In other words, the ancient allegorical figure had become a representative of the English clergy in the last half of the fifteenth century.

The impact of this shift in meaning from allegorical virtue to flesh-and-blood clergy can be seen in the elaborate masque which John Rightwise, son-in-law of William Lyly and High Master of St. Paul's School (1522–31), prepared for the entertainment of Lord Annas of Montmorenci, Grand Master of France, who came to England in November 1527 to invest King Henry VIII with the honor of the Order of St. Michael. The Michaelesque theme is important. So, too, is the time of presentation, for the masque is filled with topical references to the historical and diplomatic problems of the early Reformation period. The entertainment was presented "in the Latyn tongue in maner of Tragedy," and it contained the characters of Ecclesia, dressed in "garments of sylke, and vayells of lawne and sypers," the Four Daughters of God, and

dozens of other historical and allegorical characters. The Pope is depicted "in captivitie & the churche brought under the foote" of its enemies. The hero of the action is clad in scarlet robes and represents, of
course, Cardinal Wolsey, who is able "to bryng the Pope to his libertie
and to set up the churche againe." In its basic action this masque has the
old morality structure; the Cardinal functions as did Mercy or Justice to
preserve the hero or heroine. The clerical figure from *Mankind* has
evolved into a representation of the highest prelate in the land in this
expensive entertainment. Of even greater interest in John Rightwise's
masque are the two young boys costumed in "cottes of velvet inbraudrid
with gold, and capis of satyn bownd withe velvett." They represent the
French Dauphin and his brother, and in the masque they are held captive by the forces of evil. But they, too, are rescued by the skilled inter-
vention of Cardinal Wolsey in a Michaelesque role. Master Rightwise
had invented an elaborate form of propaganda, using an ancient stock
plot and many of the figures of the medieval religious drama.[44]

We cannot be certain that Rightwise's dramatic work influenced
John Foxe's conception of Latin drama. There is an analogous element
between the masque presented before Henry VIII and Foxe's *Christus
Triumphans;* however, both writers were drawing upon medieval plots
and characters. When Foxe began to write his cosmic mystery play in the
1550s, he turned to the figure of Ecclesia for his tragic heroine, as we
have noted. She is the mother church in his conception, and her attendants are Africus and Europus, two of her three sons, for Asia has not
survived. The two boys are easily seduced by the glib flattery of the
Antichrist figure, whom Foxe calls Pseudamnus. Foxe ironically describes this sophisticated character of evil designs as "Papa, an excellent
man in life, servant of God, and piety itself." With this kind of introduction, Pseudamnus beguiles the boys by promising them that Europus
shall be the "Defender of the Faith" and Africus "shall be called most
Christian."[45] Foxe at this point in the drama indicates how the clergy,
from the point of view of the reformers, was seduced from the true way
of Christ by the papal power of Rome. Africus and Europus represent
the Christian clergies of those two continents. In the play their apostasy
continues until the time of the Reformation, and in the meanwhile
Ecclesia is harassed and persecuted by Satan and Pseudamnus. The boys
at length are reunited with their mother (Act V, scene iv) when the re-
vival of the Gospel spreads the true Word of God. The boys become

militant, as do the two brothers in Milton's masque, and they are prepared to fight the forces of evil, but Ecclesia forestalls their action and warns that only the second coming of Christ can vanquish the monstrous powers of darkness.[46]

Foxe's drama is strongly doctrinaire. The sense of "the end of the world nigh at hand" permeates the play just as it did Kirchmayer's *Pammachius*. Foxe's humanism is pietistic and restrictive. The fusion of classical tropes and structures with the religious fervor of Puritanism creates a hybrid art. It remained for John Milton to turn the ancient plot of the Lady Wandering in the Wilderness with two companions into well-integrated Renaissance form. The seventeenth-century poet extracts the characters from their glutinous contexts of zealous propaganda and recreates them in images of pristine splendor. Utilizing the special occasion of the Ludlow ceremonies, and taking advantage of the tender age of the Earl of Bridgewater's daughter, Milton depicts the Lady in her ancient virginal form. But the two boys, now the brothers rather than the sons of the Lady, are presented in their recent configuration as representatives of the English clergy. We know that Milton thought of the church as being composed of two kinds of members, the ministers and the people.[47] In his masque he carefully suggests that the two brothers, the "near-ushering guides" of their sister, have in Narcissus' fashion neglected their duty to protect the Lady. The dialogue between the two over her welfare comes from the tradition developed in the numerous debates among the Daughters of God over the fate of the human soul. We know that Milton had studied the characters of the Four Daughters because he used them in the first drafts of his ideas for a work on the Fall of man.[48]

Milton also depicts in the two brothers' dialogue the Reformation controversy, described above, which developed over the idea of the church's inviolability. Milton's own position on this point is clear. He felt sure that the community of saints, as he called the church, could never be seduced if faith, hope, and love were in their hearts: "I am persuaded that neither death, nor life, nor angels, nor principalities nor powers, nor things present, nor things to come, nor height, nor depth, nor any other creature, shall be able to separate us from the love of God," he wrote, utilizing Romans viii, 38–39. But if the church fell off from the ideal pattern established by Christ, fell off because of its inner weaknesses, then the church was seriously erring.[49] Analyzed in the light of

these thoughts, the role of the two brothers can be pinned down beyond
that of a mere symbolic representation of the Anglican clergy; the
brothers appear to depict the two major factions of Puritan ministers
in the 1630s. Elder Brother speaks for the more Platonic and liberal
leaders; Younger Brother fetches his precepts from the more conservative Puritan clergy. Such designations omit, of course, the Anglican prelates. However, within the context of the Neo-Latin dramas which developed around the Woman Wandering in the Wilderness, the character
who pursues the Lady is the major representative of the forces of darkness; and in Milton's masque Comus is that figure. The English prelates,
I believe, are furnished forth in the character of that "damn'd wizard hid
in sly disguise," that charming Juggler, Impostor, false Traitor, that
embosser of seductive lies.

The subtle tempter of Milton's antique dramatic device is, I think,
the descendant of the fabulous Antichrist—and who has not heard of
Antichrist, son of Belial? Today we have the literary antiquarian's curious interest in the legend of this mythic figure; we handle it gingerly as
an oddity of belief held seriously only by "sects, eccentric individuals,
and fanatics."[50] But in the seventeen centuries following the birth of
Christ, the legend seized the minds of Christian writers with hypnotic
effects. Scholars today acknowledge that it helped to make history in
the violent struggles between the monarchs of the later Middle Ages and
the papal powers, between the Franciscans and the papacy, the Guelfs
and the Ghibellines, and it was especially useful as a vehicle for propaganda in the early days of the Lutheran revolt.[51]

The Antichrist legend had evolved slowly out of the ancient dragon
myths of the Near East and was turned into allegory in the New Testament writings. In these early redactions Antichrist was bestial. Indeed,
in the Johannine Apocalypse he so appears. This aspect of the legend
survived intact in the pictorial art of the Middle Ages and flourished
again in the illustrated Apocalypse of the Renaissance, especially after
the publication of Albrecht Dürer's splendid woodcuts in 1498. One
medieval scribe insisted that the face of Antichrist was "as a field; his
right eye as of the morning star, and the other one that quaileth not; his
mouth one cubit; his teeth one span; his fingers like unto sickles," and
so on.[52] But in the accounts of the more sophisticated writers, Antichrist
developed into a suave and urbane devil. Some authors insisted he had
been fathered by Belial. However, both Jerome and Chrysostom com-

mented upon the *human* features of Antichrist. Moreover, from the beginnings, the legend had developed political meanings. From the days of Nero to the era of the Reformation, the Beast of Revelation was used to designate human figures responsible for political tyranny. The author of the twelfth-century *Ludus de Antichristo* represents Antichrist as a force of political and moral evil which seduces the minds of kings. In this drama Antichrist is regal and seductive; he uses magic and miracles to beguile the royal leaders and their followers. And to indicate their subjection to him, he places the Mark of the Beast upon their foreheads. But he is a figure of Satanic power, and his magic and miracles are the work of evil spirits. In the sixteenth-century drama *Pammachius*, Antichrist is the human figure of the Pope who has become closely leagued with Satan. He is handsome, vain, elegant, witty, greedy, and superficially wise. His poetic speeches are voluptuous and epicurean. The same is true in Foxe's drama. The sensuous Pseudamnus drools when Satan promises him he shall enjoy the lovely Ecclesia. He will make her his bride and persuade her to drink from his "cup of fornication" which teaches one to revel in sensual delights, for "certainly, voluptuousness teaches men virtue!"[53]

In Milton's masque, Comus is the archetypal tempter. He is polished, persuasive, and elegantly hedonistic. But he is no papal figure; he is immortal. We know from the Bridgewater Manuscript of the *Masque* that Milton depicts Comus as a Neoplatonic daemon. Again, the poet has preferred to use the older tradition and to adapt it to the modern setting by adding a new and sophisticated feature. In this respect Comus is an admirable example of the syncretistic mode. Far from being adventitiously contrived, the character is actually the refined product of that Renaissance urge to amalgamate the analogous elements from all myths and religions in order to create a universal form of art.[54] That Milton's mind rises to true originality in the characterization of Comus can be seen when the figure is examined in detail within the syncretistic mode. By the sixteenth century the tendency had been established to depict Antichrist as a figure which was the inverse of Christ's image. Martin Luther's little volume of woodcuts, *Passional Christi und Antichristi* (1521), is a good example of this procedure. On facing pages the illustrations depict graphically the contrasting actions of Christ and of the pseudo-Christ. The antitheses are elaborately set forth from birth to assumption. Antichrist was to be born of a harlot of the tribe of Dan; he was to become incarnate in man; he would reign first as king of the Jews and would be the false Messiah; he would conquer the rest of the world by false means; he would perform miracles (by magic) and raise the dead (through trickery, of course), and his death would come on Mt. Olivet.[55]

Milton was too sophisticated to believe that the Day of Judgment was at hand, and his definition of Antichrist was an abstract one. In *De Doctrina Christiana,* Milton defines that ancient conception as "the great enemy of the church . . . who according to prediction is to arise from the church itself." This enemy would practice frauds and persecutions; Antichrist could develop, Milton believed, within any congregation. In his early prose Milton argued frequently that the prelates were more antichristian than the Roman Catholics. He indicated the Anglican bishops as "carnal tyrants" who sought "fleshly supportments." He insisted that they tainted the pure Scriptures with "superstitious rites and spurious traditions," and he called them lewd "court masquers" who should be "rooted out as Antichrists."[56]

When Milton insisted that Antichrist was "wallowing in the Church of England," he was using an idea which English reformers had adopted as early as the fourteenth century. One blunt advocate of preaching had said that Antichrist was "þe fals prelates þat don by conseil & þe enticement of hem þat sechen erþelich þinges."[57] And Rudolph Walther, attacking the English clergy in 1557, wrote that "the malignaunt church and congregation the misticall bodie of Antichriste . . . hath not amongest them the true and sincere preaching of the Law and of the Gospel."[58] The idea became a truism with the reformers. In his masque Milton turns the traditional dramatic antagonist of the apocalyptic plays into a syncretistic figure. He overlays the character with forms from classical mythology to create a more universal conception of sensuous evil. Using as a fusing point the Homeric tale of Circe, who turned men into beasts, and the legend of Antichrist, who placed the Mark of the Beast on the foreheads of his subordinates, Milton searched among the pagan myths for other analogous elements which could be exploited. He needed a myth which would amplify the idea of antithesis in the Antichrist legend. And he found what he wanted by uniting the stories of Circe and Bacchus.

The figure of Circe lies behind almost all of the Renaissance images of the enchantress, as everyone knows.[59] But in England it had an especially functional relevance as a vehicle for satire against the mother church. By the sixteenth century enough knowledge had been recovered concerning Old English to indicate that the ancient spelling of church had been *circe*. The reformers were not slow to realize that the pagan enchantress, depicted iconographically with her magic chalice, was a superb analogue for the Roman church and its doctrine of transubstantiation. As everyone knows, the resistance of the reformers from the early days of the Lollard manifestations through the sixteenth century was centered upon the problem of the Sacraments of the Altar and the question of whether the host and the wine actually became the body and blood of Christ or whether they were only symbols of Christ's sacrifice. The Roman church with its doctrinal insistence upon the former seemed to the nonconformists to be an enchantress offering a magic cup which turned men into beasts. The pagan symbol had become a commonplace satiric metaphor when Roger Ascham used it repeatedly in *The Schole-master* to deride Roman Catholicism as an enchantment brought out of Circe's court (Rome) to debauch Englishmen.[60] John Bale used the idea with great vehemence in *The Pageant of Popes* to attack the false "Vicar of Christe" as "ye witch and Circe of the whole worlde . . . having a goulden cuppe full of all filthines & lustes."[61] John Foxe used the term "Circean cups of luxury" in *Christus Triumphans* to describe Antichrist's temptation of the world.[62] And Archbishop Parker wrote of Cardinal Pole as a man "transformed as by a draught of a Circean cup from an Englishman into an Italian, from a Christian into a papist."[63] But Milton needed an image in the 1630s to depict a new evil in the English church, and he created Comus, son of Circe and Bacchus.

Milton's utilization of the Circe myth is thus easily explained, but his adaptation of the Bacchus figure is more abstruse. As every student of classical mythology knows, there was no legend of a union between Circe and Dionysus (Bacchus). This is obviously Milton's imaginative contrivance. I think it is his answer to the problem of finding a classical analogy for the pseudo-Christ of his story. Comus must have a parentage that is both a classical and a modern instrument for Reformation propaganda. The pagan stories of Dionysus served Milton's needs admirably. Like those of Hercules, the ancient legends of Dionysus contained many Christlike elements: all-powerful Zeus fathered Dionysus, but when the lovely mortal Semele, "mysteriously pregnant," demanded to see Zeus in his divine form, she was destroyed. The unborn child was saved by Hermes, who placed it in Zeus' thigh. In three months the child was

delivered and was known as "the twice-born one." He became a savior
figure for mankind because of his benevolence in teaching men to plant
and to use the vine. Having established his cult throughout the world,
he ascended to Olympus to sit at the right hand of his divine father.
Later, with Zeus' permission, he descended into Tartarus to free his
mother, Semele, and bring her to Olympus. This act was known as "the
assumption of the virgin." Semele became a moon goddess, and her
name was changed to Thyone or Cotytto; her orgiastic rites spread from
Thrace throughout northwest Europe.[64] These rituals, combined with
the dithyrambic rites which had been associated with the worship of
Dionysus, provided just the decadent note which Milton needed for the
parentage of his new antagonist. When coupled with the satiric import
of the Circean myth, it provided Milton a perfect background for
Comus. Milton's new character has all the power of his pagan parents,
and at the same time he functions traditionally in the role of the antagonist of the medieval mystery plays. In Milton's creative hands,
the pagan Comus and the Christian Antichrist become one dynamic
tempter.[65]

In addition, by creating both Comus and the Attendant Spirit as
daemons, Milton was able to amalgamate the pagan, the Neoplatonic,
and the Christian elements in his masque even more closely. The famous example of such a daemon from the classical period was the one
which Socrates was reputed to have acknowledged as his spiritual guide.
In the Renaissance period, the Neoplatonic conception of daemon,
based not only upon classical ideas but upon Hermetic and Cabalistic
traditions, included lower forms of spirits both good and bad. The conception was also applied by some theologians and scholars to the Christian idea of angels. Joseph Mede of Cambridge identified the "true" sort
of daemon in this way: "Another kinde of Daemon more high and sublime, which never had been the soules of men, nor ever were linkt to a
mortall body, but were from the beginning, or without beginning, always the same. . . . This sort of Daemons doth fitly answer and parallell
that sort of spirituall powers, which we call Angels."[66] Milton appears to
have had such a conception in mind, for Comus is the Satanic spirit of
evil made manifest in this world. The Attendant Spirit, on the other
hand, comes from Jove's court and is not an inhabitant of this gloomy
"pinfold" here below. The Attendant Spirit undoubtedly represents the
angelic force for good. But more especially, if one considers the Anti-

christ legend, the Attendant Spirit is analogous to the Archangel Michael, who in that legend was the instrument God would use to overcome Antichrist.

Milton's masque was presented at Ludlow Castle on Michaelmas Night. The date is significant, I believe. Milton appears to have utilized several features drawn from the ancient tradition of that militant and protective angel. In the masque, both pagan and Judaic-Christian elements are blended. The Attendant Spirit functions overtly as Mercury or Hermes, the messenger of the gods, in his winged journey from and return to Jove's court, but his journey to lend protection and instruction resembles those angelic journeys described by the Old Testament writers. The same is true when the Spirit functions as Hermes in bringing the magic plant to aid the brothers in their battle with the sorcerer, for the Attendant Spirit also resembles the Archangel Michael, who was considered the orthodox champion of mankind and, especially in the medieval period, the protector against evil spirits.

In Milton's masque, the Spirit does not destroy Comus. A partial victory is achieved, but it comes primarily through the militant actions of the two brothers. This is a surprising turn of affairs if one is following the Antichrist story. However, in the legend there were variations in the ending. In the *Ludus de Antichristo,* the necromancer is destroyed by a "burst" of heavenly thunder. In the sixteenth-century Latin dramas, Antichrist's end is predicted: Kirchmayer's *Pammachius* breaks off at the end of the fourth act with the epilogue warning that the Day of Judgment is near at hand. In Foxe's *Christus Triumphans,* defeat is near for Pseudamnus, but the two boys do not fight the evil power. The play ends with an epithalamium depicting the approach of the Heavenly Bridegroom. Milton has altered the stock ending to some extent, but his dramatic action is sound. It is not necessary to assume that he had read Huon de Mery's *Le Tornoiement de l'Antichrist,* a long poem which also ended surprisingly with the escape of an unscathed Antichrist.[67] Milton's plot is understandable within the ecclesiastical setting of the 1630s. If the figure of Comus represents the prelates of the Anglican Church—as it appears to do when the masque is compared with the apocalyptic dramas—then Milton, being realistic about the contemporary situation and about the impossibility of eradicating the Satanic powers of evil in this world—and also being unwilling to assert that the Day of Doom was at hand—could only allow his symbolic character of

evil an escape from the menace of the two brothers and the Attendant
Spirit. Comus flees with his wand intact. The evil power of Antichrist, as
Milton defined it, was still mesmerizing the minds of men in 1634.

The epilogue of Milton's masque depicts the future of those who
uphold virtue in this life. In these final proleptic lines, Milton continues
the syncretistic mode which had controlled the imagery and ideas of the
masque proper. The poet uses the wedding of Psyche and the god of love
to depict the eternal bliss of the marriage of the Lamb and his Bride.
This is the traditional ending for the apocalyptic dramas. It is based
upon St. John's description (Revelation, chapter xix) of the ineffable
joys of the soul's union with Christ in eternity. John Foxe had used the
story of Psyche in the opening scenes of *Christus Triumphans*. Christ
welcomes Psyche as his bride at the beginning of the play (Act I, scene iv)
to indicate that the love of Christ is a universal thing which encom-
passes all time. At the end of his drama, Foxe presents Ecclesia in wedding veils, surrounded by virgins singing of the Heavenly Bridegroom.
Foxe thus distinguishes between the individual soul (Psyche) and the
community of souls in the church (Ecclesia); he makes them sisters, both
daughters of Eve. But Milton believed that the individual soul *was* the
church, alone or in communion. His Lady represents both Psyche and
Ecclesia in one figure.[68] In his epilogue, Psyche's union with Cupid
(Christ) is foreshadowed in eternity as reward for her fidelity to the
pattern of Christian behavior which Christ had set. In this, Milton was
capitalizing upon a long tradition of the mythographers who saw in the
classical story of Psyche and Cupid an adumbrated account of the human soul's search for God.

The only surviving medieval Antichrist play in the English ver-
nacular is the famous one in the Chester cycle of dramas. That cycle was
performed until the last quarter of the sixteenth century, when the
Elizabethan authorities, in an attempt to stamp out the doctrines of the
old faith, suppressed the antique religious drama with some difficulty.[69]
The Antichrist play of this cycle is very conservative. There is no female
role in it.[70] The wit contest is between Antichrist and the two prophets
Enoch and Elijah. The prophets are defeated, but the Archangel Michael then appears to defeat Antichrist and send him to hell. I believe
that this Chester play was Milton's starting point when he began to draft
the outlines for *Comus*. His masque, as we know, was an occasional
piece. And we know that the Sabrina myth was a part of the regional

folklore of the Ludlow area which Milton seems to have utilized in an attempt to localize the work of art for the contemporary audience at the castle. But the Chester plays belonged to that region also. The people of the western counties had fought to keep their ancient cycle, which was filled with the doctrinal ideas of the older church. It is important to note that the new Lord President who was installed at Ludlow Castle in September 1634 was a Puritan, and the young poet who composed the entertainment for the occasion was also a Puritan. John Milton appears to have supplied the peoples of Shropshire and Cheshire with a new mystery play delicately structured upon the ancient framework of the medieval Antichrist play. Milton's masque contains the old stock characters, but they are so elegantly costumed in "apparel that glisters" that we have difficulty in recognizing them. The same is true of the plot. It is so carefully contrived to represent the contemporary English scene that we fail to note its ancient provenance. Today the apocalyptic drama has so faded from our literary frame of reference that we no longer consider its possibilities as a vehicle for sophisticated art.

The occasion of Milton's masque is important in another aspect. The Michaelmas celebration in the Anglican church has its own liturgical setting with particularized texts for the collect, epistle, and gospel, as William B. Hunter, Jr., has recently pointed out.[71] In 1634 the religious services for St. Michael's Day began with the morning prayer, which was followed later with holy communion. At this latter service, the appointed text for the epistle which the chaplain read to the congregation was Revelation xii, 7–12. This is the description of the Archangel Michael's battle with the Satanic powers and the expulsion of "the great Dragon . . . that old serpent, called the Devill and Satan which deceiveth the whole world," from heaven. This appointed text ends (verse 12) with a warning to mankind: "Woe to the inhabitants of the earth, and of the sea: for the devill is come downe unto you, having great wrath, because hee knoweth that he hath but a short time."[72] Milton would have been familiar with this traditional liturgical setting, and he appears to have used the epistle of the day as prologue for his masque. His audience would have been prepared for a story of the Woman Wandering in the Wilderness, for the readers of Scripture knew that the following verses (13–17) depict the Satanic power of evil in pursuit of the woman and describe her ensuing persecution. This passage ends with a description of the anger of the dragon who is "wroth with the woman" and who

"went to make war with the remnant of her seed, which keep the commandments of God and have the testimony of Jesus Christ." If my analysis of Milton's masque is valid, we can say with a marked degree of confidence that the poet prepared his work of art to be an integral part of
both the civil and religious festivities of St. Michael's Day at Ludlow.[73]

Finally, Milton's use of the old characters from the literature of
eschatology (and the resulting emphasis upon the religious elements of
the masque which an analysis of the anagogical meaning brings) should
not detract from the heavy literary makeup of his *dramatis personae*
or from the complex literary themes of *Comus*. Milton, as a true Renaissance poet, was skilled at employing the syncretistic mode of art. In his
masque the artist uses that unifying mode to accommodate a polysemantic structure of themes: through the Lady and her suave opponent, Milton reaches for a universal statement concerning the eternal contest between the forces of good and evil which takes place within every human
mind. But at the same time he could produce with those symbolic characters an anagogical statement concerning the abrasive contest that was
climaxing in the ecclesiastical setting of his own day.

California State University, Fullerton

NOTES

1. Criticism of Milton's *Masque Presented at Ludlow Castle* has tended to radiate in all directions in the last forty years. Countless critics have noted that the
masque is a cosmic drama based upon the triangle of the old morality-play plot with
the Soul of Mankind centered between a Good Angel and a Bad Angel. However, only
one writer has explored extensively the relationship between the medieval drama and
Comus. See Robert L. Ramsay, "Morality Themes in Milton's Poetry," *SP*, XV (1918),
123–58, especially 147–50.

2. *Of Reformation, The Works of John Milton*, ed. Frank Allen Patterson et al.
(New York, 1931–38), III, 238 (cited subsequently as CM). David Paré's remarks on
Revelation as a "Propheticall Drama" also include the statement that such a dramatic
presentation would reveal "things touching the Church, not past, but to come" (*A
Commentary Upon the Divine Revelation* [Amsterdam, 1644], p. 20).

3. *Of Reformation*, CM, III, 154. The remark was made in *Animadversions* in a
passage concerning dualities in language.

4. The period of Advent celebrates Christ's coming in three eras: (1) the historical birth of Christ; (2) the time when the spirit of Christ enters the soul of each individual; (3) the second coming of Christ in judgment upon mankind. The season of
Advent, the four weeks before Christmas, was the appropriate time for staging the
apocalyptic dramas in the later Middle Ages.

5. *Munich* MS. 19,411 is unique. A modern edition of the play is included in Karl Young's *Drama of the Medieval Church* (Oxford, 1933), II, 369–96. The play has been translated into English by William H. Hulme, "The Mediaeval Religious Plays 'Antichrist' and 'Adam,'" *Western Reserve University Bulletin*, XXVIII (1925), 5–32. For additional commentary on the various problems of date and meaning, see Wilhelm Creizenach, *Geschichte des neueren Dramas* (Halle, 1893–1903), I, 77–79; Sir Edmund K. Chambers, *The Medieval Stage* (Oxford, 1903), II, 62–64; and Hardin Craig, *English Religious Drama* (Oxford, 1955), pp. 75–77.

6. The French king is the only one whom Antichrist kisses. The Pope remains mute throughout the drama. If scholars are correct in dating the play at about A.D. 1160, the drama satirizes Pope Alexander III and King Louis VII, both of whom had caused Frederick Barbarossa serious diplomatic problems.

7. For a survey of the development of this symbol, see Adolph Harnack, *History of Dogma* (London, 1894–99), II, 194–96.

8. Creizenach, *Geschichte des neueren Dramas*, I, 74; Chambers, *Medieval Stage*, II, 64; and Young, *Drama of the Medieval Church*, II, 395, describe this as the first dramatic appearance of these allegorical characters.

9. Revelation xii, 1.

10. In the stage directions between lines 194 and 195, Ecclesia is driven from the Temple of the Lord and *"redibit ad sedem Apostolici"* (returns to the throne of the Popes). This has caused confusion among editors because the Pope has no *sedes* or platform in the play. Young (*Drama of the Medieval Church*, II, 388) suggests that Ecclesia returns to the *sedes* originally occupied by the Holy Roman Emperor which has been vacated by the Rex Theotonicorum. There is no indication that Ecclesia and her attendants wander about the stage as Antichrist subjugates the world.

11. For an account of the extensive influence of the Antichrist legend upon German drama, see Karl Reuschel, *Die deutschen Weltgerichtsspiele des Mittelalters und der Reformationszeit* (Leipzig, 1906), pp. 35–81. Six other German plays on the theme of Antichrist have survived from the medieval period.

The most famous French dramatic treatment of the Antichrist legend occurs in *Le Jour du Jugement*, a fourteenth-century tableau in which an honest pope alone is wise enough to perceive the falseness of the miracles of Antichrist. His bishops are seduced by the glib pseudo-Messiah. See the modern edition by Emile Roy (Paris, 1902). There were other French mystery plays on apocalyptic themes in the fifteenth and sixteenth centuries. See L. Petit de Julleville, *Les Mystères* (Paris, 1880), II, 460–61, 615–18, 629.

The most nearly orthodox Roman Catholic version of the Antichrist legend in Continental drama is the fourteenth-century Italian play, *Lauda Drammatica dell' Antichristo*, in which the female role is given to the Virgin Mary, who intercedes for the souls of those who have been led astray by Antichrist. In this conservative drama there is no Lady Ecclesia; the Holy Virgin performs the function of the church. The drama is included in Alessandro D'Ancona's *Origini del teatro italiano* (Torino, 1891), I, 141–53. For a discussion of the gradual replacement of the Archangel Michael and other angelic intercessors by the Virgin Mary after the ninth century, see Hope Traver, "The Four Daughters of God: A Mirror of Changing Doctrine," *PMLA*, XL (1925), 44–92.

12. *Cursor Mundi*, EETS, LXVI (1877), pp. 1258–82; *Piers the Plowman*, EETS, XXXVIII (1869), pp. 369–76; *Polychronicon* (London, 1871), III, 122–25. For a discussion of other medieval nondramatic works on the theme of Antichrist, see L. E.

Kaster, "Some Old French Poems on the Antichrist," *MLR*, I (1905), 269–82; II (1906), 26–33.

13. The play was printed in the collection of Neo-Latin plays, *Comoediae ac Tragoediae* (Basileae, 1541), pp. 314–449. The Henry E. Huntington Library copy of this early volume has the Bridgewater bookplate in it and what appears to be the first earl's notation on the title page. The modern edition of the play is that edited by Johannes Bolte and Erich Schmidt, *Thomas Naogeorgus' Pammachius* (Berlin, 1891). Naogeorgus was Kirchmayer's pseudonym.

14. A loose translation of one speech will afford the reader some idea of Kirchmayer's voluptuous vulgarity. In Act IV Satan calls for revelry when Pammachius is victorious in conquering the world:

> Hear me great comrades!
> Let there be no more work;
>   I decree an eternal holiday!
> Make instant arrangements, you clerks,
>   for dancing and drinking and play.
> Let none scold the overplied cup;
>   toss it down and empty it swiftly.
> It's jovial when the bottoms are up,
>   and the fumes drape us all in damp mufti.
> And should anyone later repent
>   the result of his generous libations,
> We shall weave him a crown of the vine leaf
>   and adorn his fat head with citations!
> And should this day's end move too quickly
>   upon these delightful festivities,
> Let the revel prolong itself slightly,
>   and add heat to our nightly proclivities.
> Leave nothing undone which pertains
>   to sensual delight and fresh pleasures,
> For aspiring and respiring we must
>   provide our old trunks with new treasures.
> Let the effortless table appear,
>   brimming with delectable delights
> Of the food and the drink and good cheer,
>   you'al choose, let none shove or fight.
> Take it all, there's much more to come,
>   stuff yourselves—it's never too late
> To radiate, congratulate, be satiate,
>   Ad infinitum, ad infinitum, ad nauseam!   (2891 ff.)

15. Honor McCusker, *John Bale, Dramatist and Antiquary* (Bryn Mawr, Pa., 1942), p. 96; E. S. Miller, "The Antiphons in Bale's Cycle of Christ," *SP*, XLVIII (1951), 629–38.

16. J. W. Harris, *John Bale: A Study of the Minor Literature of the Reformation* (Urbana, Ill., 1940), pp. 75–77; Thora B. Blatt, *The Plays of John Bale* (Copenhagen, 1968).

17. The letters among Gardiner, Parker, and the Council are printed at length in C. H. Cooper's *Annals of Cambridge* (Cambridge, 1842), I, 422–27. It is not essential

for my thesis that John Milton, a student at Christ's College some seventy-five years later, had heard of this uproar over *Pammachius,* although I am inclined to think that he knew of the affair.

18. Foxe's own much-corrected manuscript of the play is in the British Museum, *Lansdown* 1073. The new translation of the play by John Hazel Smith has just been published by the Cornell University Press. I regret that this work has come too late for my use in this article. Professor V. Norskov Olsen has allowed me to read his chapter on Foxe's conception of universal time in *Christus Triumphans,* which is part of a longer study he is preparing on Foxe's contributions to ecclesiastical history.

19. For a discussion of the popularity of illuminated manuscripts of the *Apocalypse,* see M. R. James, *The Apocalypse in Art* (London, 1931); and George Henderson, "Studies in English Manuscript Illumination," *JWCI,* XXX (1967), 71–137, especially 104–37, on English Apocalypses.

20. William Fulke, *Praelections Upon the Sacred and Holy Revelations of S. John* (London, 1573), fol. 77; Augustine Marlorate, *A Catholike Exposition upon the Revelation of Sainct John* (London, 1574), fol. 171; Franciscus Junius, *The Apocalyps, or Revelations of S. John* (Cambridge, 1596), p. 146; and Thomas Mason, *A Revelation of the Revelation* (London, 1619), p. 52.

21. For a description of this conflation, see J. C. Plumpe, *Mater Ecclesia* (Washington, D.C., 1943), pp. 35–47; and E. O. James, *The Cult of the Mother Goddess* (New York, 1959), pp. 192–227.

22. *The Text of the New Testament* (London, 1589), fol. 476. This is the edition of the Rheims *NT* edited by William Fulke with the text of the Bishop's Bible printed column by column for comparison and confutation.

23. *The Image of Bothe Churches* [London, 1551?], sigs. Dv–vi.

24. *Þe Lanterne of liȝt, EETS,* CLI (1917), p. 23.

25. *Commentaries on the Catholic Epistles* (Edinburg, 1855), p. 388.

26. *The Whole Workes of W. Tyndall, John Frith, and Doct. Barnes* (London, 1573), p. 257.

27. *The Text of the New Testament,* fol. 477 (italics added).

28. Ibid.

29. CM, XVI, 61, 63, 65. For a modern discussion of this conception of the relationship of the individual conscience to the communal consciousness, see John S. Coolidge, *The Pauline Renaissance in England* (Oxford, 1970).

30. *Of Christian Doctrine,* CM, XVI, 75, 77, 83, 85, 87 (italics added).

31. Ibid., 15, 97, 375–77.

32. *Of Reformation,* CM, III, 75, 232.

33. For a discussion of Kirchmayer's use of Protestant doctrine in his plays, *Pammachius, Pyrgopolinices,* and *Mercator,* see C. H. Herford, *Studies in the Literary Relations of England and Germany in the Sixteenth Century* (Cambridge, 1886), pp. 119–29.

34. *Of Christian Doctrine,* CM, XVI, 37–39.

35. Harnack, *History of Dogma,* III, 129–31. John Calvin, speaking on chastity, gives the traditional interpretation of its meaning: "We know how frequently, in Holy Scripture, is that marriage mentioned which God forms with us. He would have us, then, to be like a chaste virgin, as Paul says (2 *Cor.* XI. 2). This chastity is violated and corrupted by all impure affections towards the world" (*Commentaries on the Catholic Epistles,* p. 331).

36. *Of Reformation,* CM, III, 6, 247; *Eikonoklastes,* CM, V, 158.

37. *A Confutation of the Rhemists Translation, Glosses and Annotations on the*

New Testament ([Leyden,] 1618), p. 731. In this same passage Cartwright continues by admonishing the Roman Catholic writers: "That the Church shall faile or follow Antichrist, are things which you falsly father upon us, and we utterly abhorre."

38. John Calvin, *Institutes of the Christian Religion* (Edinburgh, 1846), III, 54, 152; William Tyndale, *The Whole Workes*, p. 289; and William Fulke, *The Text of the New Testament*, p. 477.

39. *The Apostasy of the Latter Times*, 2nd ed. (London, 1644), pp. 46, 51. Mede's editor notes that this work "was delivered in public some years since." Mede published two editions of *Clavis Apocalyptica*, his commentary upon Revelation, in 1627 and 1632, in which his analysis of the contemporary conditions of the church led him to conclude that the Latter Days had come.

40. For a detailed study of these allegorical figures, see Hope Traver, *The Four Daughters of God* (Bryn Mawr, Pa., 1907). Their ubiquity in medieval and Renaissance art is further explored by Samuel C. Chew, *The Virtues Reconciled* (Toronto, 1947). For a survey of the transformation of Justice from a theological virtue into a secular male figure, see J. Wilson McCutchan, "Justice and Equity in the English Morality Play," *JHI*, XIX (1958), 405–10.

41. For the early English translation of Grosseteste's poem, see the *Castel Off Loue*, ed. R. F. Weymouth (London, 1864).

42. Veritas became a controversial figure in English Renaissance iconography. As Truth, Daughter of Time, she became an ecclesiastical symbol which writers of both the old faith and the new employed for their own purposes. In Mary Tudor's reign, Veritas became the queen's personal device and appeared on coins, royal seals, crests, and other memorabilia. When Elizabeth was crowned queen of England, she adopted the same device with one significant change: the book which Veritas carries became the Bible in English rather than the "Verbum Dei." See the detailed article by Fritz Saxl, "Veritas Filia Temporis," in *Philosophy and History: Essays Presented to Ernst Cassirer*, ed. Raymond Klibansky and H. J. Paton (Oxford, 1936), pp. 197–222; and another perceptive essay on this subject by Donald Gordon, " 'Veritas Filia Temporis,' Hadrianus Junius and Geoffrey Whitney," *JWCI*, III (1939–40), 228–40. Gordon notes the consistent use by Renaissance writers, printers, and painters of the figure of Veritas as a religious symbol, especially of Protestantism.

In English drama, Veritas became an important heroine in Sir David Lindsay's *Satire of the Three Estates*, a nine-hour play first performed at Linlithgow in 1540. In this work, Rex Humanitas, the central character, having been misled by Wantonness and Sensuality, abuses Veritas, who has appeared to chide the wrongdoers "beirand in hir hand the Newtestament." She is banished, of course, and ultimately she is placed in the stocks. Even more interesting, from the point of view of Milton's masque, is that she is accompanied by her attendant, Chastity, who is also placed in the stocks. However, by the end of the play Veritas and Chastity are allowed to make their accusations at the bar, and Rex Humanitas is converted. Lindsay's drama became famous and was published twice before 1634. It would appear highly probable that Milton knew the work.

43. *The Macro Plays*, ed. Mark Eccles, *EETS*, CCLXII (1969).

44. The text of Rightwise's masque is no longer extant, but in the records of the Revels Office there is a thirty-nine-page document of the expenses incurred for costumes and stage props (*Letters and Papers of the Reign of Henry VIII*, IV, part 2, pp. 1604–06). In addition, Edward Hall has left us a detailed description of this production and an account of its plot (*The Union of the Two Noble and Illustre Famelies of Lancastre & Yorke* [London, 1548], fols. CLXV–CLXVI). It should also be

noted that in the preceding July, while traveling on the Continent, Wolsey had been entertained in Bologne-sur-Marne with a pageant in which the allegorical figure of the church was despoiled. Hall remarks that "A pageaunte was presented in which was a Nonne called holy churche, & thre Spaniardes & thre Almaynes had her violated, and a Cardinall her reskued, and set her up of newe agayne" (fol. CLXIv). Poor Ecclesia's experiences were worse than the perils of Pauline.

45. *Christus Triumphans* (Basle, 1556), p. 81.

46. Ibid., pp. 105–06.

47. *Of Christian Doctrine*, CM, XVI, 235.

48. *Common Place Book*, CM, XVIII, 228–32. Milton was not being old-fashioned in his thinking about his early plans for the allegorical daughters. These figures, in their medieval form, remained popular as a subject for seventeenth-century poetry through the first third of the century. They are still allegorical virtues in Giles Fletcher's *Christ's Victory* (1610), in Thomas Peyton's *The Glasse of Time* (1620), in Augustine Taylor's *Divine Epistles* (1623), in Joseph Fletcher's *The History of the Perfect-Cursed-Blessed Man* (1628), and in William Drummond's *Shadow of the Judgment* (1630). In Taylor's epistle to "the Spouse of Christ," the Woman Wandering in the Wilderness appears. She has been so abused that she is unrecognizable: "So foule was thy complection, some did see, / That the whole peece of blacke impurity, / Was all Imploy'd to make thy coatt" (sig. E8v). For a discussion of the survival of the Four Daughters, see Chew, *The Virtues Reconciled*, pp. 49–68. For a discussion of Milton's use of the Four Daughters in *Paradise Lost*, see Merritt Y. Hughes, *Ten Perspectives on Milton* (New Haven, 1965), pp. 108–10, 116.

49. *Of Christian Doctrine*, CM, XVI, 75, 77.

50. James Hastings, *Encyclopaedia of Religion and Ethics* (New York, 1926), I, 581.

51. Ibid.

52. Wilhelm Bousset, *The Antichrist Legend* (London, 1896), p. 156.

53. *Christus Triumphans*, pp. 69–70.

54. Illuminating studies of this syncretistic mode may be found in Frances A. Yates, *The French Academies of the Sixteenth Century* (London, 1947); Jean Seznec, *The Survival of the Pagan Gods* (New York, 1953); and D. P. Walker, "*The Prisca Theologia* in France," *JWCI*, XVII (1954), 204–59.

55. A discussion of the use of antithesis in the Antichrist legend is to be found in M. H. Marchall's "Antichrist in Mediaeval Drama and in the Drama of the Reformation in England" (thesis, Yale University, 1928), pp. 6–10; and in L. U. Lucken's *Antichrist and the Prophets of Antichrist in the Chester Cycle* (Washington, D.C., 1940), pp. 14–17. A detailed discussion of the development of the idea of Antichrist in the seventeenth century may be found in Christopher Hill's *Antichrist in Seventeenth-Century England* (London, 1971). The transition from the idea of the pope as Antichrist to the conception of the bishops as Antichrist is stressed in this work.

56. *Of Reformation*, CM, III, 55; *I Defensio*, CM, VII, 551; *Of Christian Doctrine*, CM, XVI, 315.

57. Elis Fridner, "An English Fourteenth-Century Apocalypse Version with a Prose Commentary," *Lund University Studies in English*, XXIX (1961), 106.

58. *A Short Description of Antichrist Unto the Nobilities of Englande* ([London,] 1557), fol. 7v.

59. See Merritt Y. Hughes, "Spenser's Acrasia and the Circe of the Renaissance," *JHI*, IV (1943), 381–99.

60. *The Scholesmaster* (London, 1570), fols. 24–26, 30ᵣ. Ascham is never ambiguous in the use of the metaphor: "But I am affraide, that over many of our travelers into *Italie,* do not exchewe the way to Circes Court: but go, and ryde, and runne, and flie thether, they make great hast to cum to her: they make great sute to serve her: yea, I could point out some with my finger, that never had gone out of England, but onelie to serve *Circes,* in Italie" (Fol. 26ʳ).

61. *The Pageant of Popes* (London, 1574), sigs. Diᵛ and Eii.

62. Milton used the term "Circean cup" (*"Circaeum poculum"*) in his Seventh Prolusion when he remarked that such a draught should be given to the soul that aspires no higher than the treetops (CM, XII, 281).

63. *De Antiquitate Britannicae Ecclesiae* (Hanoviae, 1605), p. 346.

64. Milton would have known the myth of Dionysus from several classical sources. The modern student will find it in the Loeb Classical Library editions of Euripides, *Bacchae;* Diodorus Siculus, *Library of History,* II, 285–333; Apollodorus, *The Library,* I, 317–33; Pausanias, *Description of Greece,* I, 417.

65. In the woodcuts of Stephen Batman's *A Christall Glasse of Christian Reformation* (London, 1569), Bacchus is depicted as a satiric Reformation figure surrounded by a friar, a "Popishe priest," and a serving man (sig. Fii). Batman's pagan figure represents gluttony, but it also appears to be a symbol for the Roman Catholic clergy. For suggestions of the use of Bacchus and the Dionysian *furor* as a Christianized symbol, see Yates, *The French Academies,* pp. 80–81, 92–93.

66. *The Apostasy of the Latter Times,* p. 19.

67. Reims, 1851.

68. This idea was an old one, of course. Even in the Lollard tract, *The Lantern of Light,* the idea appears commonplace: "þis woman bitokeneþ mannes soule" (p. 28).

69. W. W. Greg, *The Play of Antichrist from the Chester Cycle* (Oxford, 1935). See also Harold C. Gardiner, *Mysteries' End* (New Haven, 1946), pp. 79–83.

70. Henry E. Huntington Library Manuscript, HM 2, was transcribed in 1591 by Edward Gregorie, a "scholler at Bunbury." Near the bottom of folio 41ʳ is the seventeenth-century signature of John Egerton, Esq. This signature is not in the rotund hand of John, first Earl of Bridgewater, who was a collector of literary manuscripts. The provenance of *HM* 2 is unclear. Whether or not Milton had a chance to see this manuscript copy of the Chester plays remains uncertain. The existence of the Peniarth manuscript (ca. 1500) of the Antichrist play from the Chester cycle indicates perhaps that the twenty-fourth play in the cycle was one of the more popular or more significant ones. That other Antichrist plays were produced in the medieval period in England is known from the attack made upon such dramas at the end of the fourteenth century: "So thanne thes men that seyen, pley we a pley of Anti-Crist and of the day of dome, that sum man may be convertid therby, fallen into the heresie of hem that reversyng the aposteyl and seyden, do we yvel thingis that ther comyn gode thingis, of whom, as seith the aposteyl, dampnyng is riʒtwise" (printed by Thomas Wright and J. O. Halliwell, *Reliquiae Antiquae* [London, 1845]. II, 48).

71. "The Liturgical Context of *Comus,*" ELN, X (1972), 11–15. Professor Hunter notes the special relevance of the collect and the gospel text to the subject matter of the masque.

72. *The Book of Common Prayer* (London, 1633), sig. Pppp2ᵛ.

73. For a discussion of the civil traditions of St. Michael's Day and their relevance for *Comus,* see James G. Taaffe, "Michaelmas, the 'Lawless Hour,' and the Occasion of Milton's *Comus,*" ELN, VI (1969), 257–62.

LANDSCAPE IN THE TRANSCENDENT MASQUE

Terry Kidner Kohn

Comus transcends all other masques in its artistry and in the permanence of its moral fable. The treatment of landscape contributes both to Milton's artistic integration of traditional masque elements and to the philosophical content of *Comus*. There are three planes of landscape in Milton's masque. The Wood functions symbolically as a metaphor for earthly existence. Neptune and Sabrina inhabit mythological landscapes possessing both symbolic and realistic qualities. Most complex in function is the natural, realistic landscape, the plane on which the story unfolds. While conventional masque scenery "discovered" the masquers in a purely mechanical way, Milton gives to his natural setting an intensified reality that illuminates theme and discovers identity in a deeper sense. The characters reveal themselves through their reactions to the landscape, and these responses support and clarify the masque's central concerns of temperance, the power of virtue, and the proper attitude toward nature. The "happy climes" of the epilogue transfigure the vistas of earth and climax the movement of physical and mental expansion precipitated by the triumph of virtue in the Wood. In *Comus*, Milton gives to landscape a degree of prominence and a richness of meaning surpassed only by the landscapes of *Paradise Lost*.

THE WORLD which Milton creates in *A Mask Presented at Ludlow Castle* is one of "myth, magic, and metamorphosis."[1] In this respect it resembles its siblings in the masque genre. Unlike most of the best-known masques, however, *Comus* was not written to be performed at Court, but at a castle, now in ruins, which fronted the Welsh Marches, at a time when "rural England . . . was still pastoral, and still unlighted, and still wooded."[2] It is the concreteness of these woods, the reality of the dark where myth, magic, and metamorphosis operate, which in part give to *Comus* the permanence, the enduring relationship to life, in which it transcends all other masques. So potent and pervasive is this sense of realism that Ronald Bayne, writing in the *Cambridge History of English Literature,* attributes its "truer breath of poetry" to the fact that it was an "out-of-door entertainment,"[3] a presumption which *Comus'* stage directions prove untrue.

Bayne's critical faux pas is excusable, for Milton's realization of mutable, flourishing nature in the "wilde Wood" of *Comus* is far different from the static representations of landscapes created from wood, canvas, and the genius of Inigo Jones for the court masques of Ben Jonson and others. In one of their volumes on Jonson, C. H. Herford and Percy Simpson emphasize that "realism was an affection of [the masque's] later years, almost a symptom of its decadence; its characteristic and typical beauty is a beauty of artifice."[4] At times this artifice was employed in relatively representational depictions of natural scenery, as in Ben Jonson's description of a setting for *The Masque of Blacknesse*:

First, for the Scene, was drawne a Landtschap, consisting of small woods, and here and there a void place fill'd with huntings; which falling an artificial sea was seene to shoote forth, as if it flowed to the land, raysed with waues, which seemed to moue, and in some places the billow to breake, as imitating that orderly disorder, which is common to nature.[5]

Here is acceptance of nature for its own sake, joined with a delight in its contrasts, its unity in variety. More characteristic, however, is this design for *The Masque of Beautie:*

On the sides of the Throne, were curious, and elegant Arbors appointed: and behinde, in the backe part of the Ile, a Groue, of growne trees laden with golden fruit, which other litle Cupids plucked, and threw each at other, whilst on the ground Leuerats pick'd vp the bruised apples, and left them halfe eaten. The groundplat of the whole was a subtle indented Maze: And, in the two formost angles, were two Fountaines, that ran continually, the one Hebe's, the other Hedone's.[6]

To the modern reader, at least, this kind of "artifice" seems too often to imply "artificial" in a pejorative sense. One is inclined to mourn, with Jonson, the triumph of Inigo's "ingins" over "the truer breath of poetry," and even Jonson's choice of diction in his famous statement in the preface to *Chlorida*—"Vpon this hinge, the whole Inuention moued"[7]—seems, taken out of context, uncomfortably close to the mechanical truth.

The conventional decorum of the masque is, I think, an acquired taste for the modern reader, conditioned as he is to expect "drama," or anything resembling it, to be a series of events which generates a degree of tension, or suspense, as the action unfolds. The essence of the masque, however, was symbolic presentation, not realistic action. The opposition of masque and antimasque is a static contrast rather than an active conflict; and the masque "expresses, not uncertainty, ended by final success or failure, but expectancy, crowned by sudden revelation."[8] And since the setting was integral to the action of the masque, it follows that the settings should partake of this same nonrealistic character. Partly because of its antecedents in mumming, mystery plays, and tournaments; partly because of its tendency to emphasize the splendid and ritualistic; and partly because the principal purpose of a set was its ability to "discover" the masquers in some novel, and preferably symbolic, way, the masque set tended to avoid the naturalistic in favor of the emblematic. This is not to imply that masque settings were neither functional nor realistic. They were required to be—and were, of course—supremely functional, while many of Inigo Jones' sets are in their own right fine landscapes which show knowledge of Italian theories of perspective and the influence of the distant horizon and open sky of Flemish landscapes.[9]

"So much for the bodily part," as Jonson says.[10] What remains is that whatever the form of the setting, its essence, like the masque's, is presentation. The characters of the conventional masque remain simply *in* their surroundings, rather than *of* them. There are few references within these masques to their settings (except perhaps to a major feature like the labyrinth in Jonson's *Pleasure Reconciled to Virtue*) and certainly small mention of natural landscape, except in stage directions.[11] It is in this respect that *Comus* so clearly differentiates itself. Although Milton's masque has three changes of scene (the Wood, the Palace of Comus, and Ludlow town), their stage description is, at most, minimal. Yet one of the most forceful impressions the masque leaves with us is the reality of the Wood, and this reality is rendered by the verse: it is through the poetry itself that the landscape is realized. Milton's magic transcends the mechanical.

The questions of whether the *Mask Presented at Ludlow Castle* is or is not, in fact, a masque, and if so, in what ways, need not concern us here except as a starting point towards understanding the complex function of the landscape in *Comus*. Since two-thirds of the masque takes place in the Wood, it is defensible to concentrate on Milton's treatment of that particular landscape. On the most fundamental level, the "wilde Wood" does function as a symbolic presentation. The Attendant Spirit tells us immediately what woods these are: this "dim spot" (5) is the "Sin-worn mould" (17) upon which unexempt mortal existence must be enacted.[12]

Its literary and spiritual heritage is one of long standing. The wild Wood follows in the tradition of the murky hollows of Plato's lower earth (in the *Phaedo*), Dante's dark wood, Spenser's Wood of Error. It is also that ageless, primeval, impenetrable forest where numerous children in countless fairy tales have lost their way, where heroes of legend have met adventure along barely discernible paths, where monsters lurk whose reality is not diminished because they may exist only in the imagination. The Wood, on this level, functions as a metaphor for both earthly existence and the darkness of the human mind. In this sense, it is not a wood at all, but a "labyrinth" (77) laced and contorted with "per-plex't paths" (37) where an unwary mortal may easily become "night-founder'd" (83). The Wood is one extreme of a conventional masque contrast which the Attendant Spirit establishes in his opening speech (1–17): "starry threshold" versus "dim spot," calmness and serenity op-posed to smoke and stir, the open-ended vista from the "threshold" con-trasted with the confining "pin-fold." As Daedalus leads the dance which extricates the masquers from the Labyrinth in *Pleasure Reconciled to Virtue*, so the Attendant Spirit, himself an artificer of white magic, con-trols and leads the dance of "divine Philosophy" through the mazes of the Wood, "from darkness up [or out] to light." In a relevant passage of his masque, Jonson says

> Daucing is an exercise
>   not only showes ye mouers wit,
> but maketh ye beholder wise,
>   as he hath powre to rise to it.[13]

In *Comus*, the transcendent masque, the dance is still there, but it is an exercise of "ye mouers wit" to a greater extent than Jonson would have presumed possible. The "masque movement" of *Comus* becomes one with the intellectual movement as patterns of thought counterpoint one another, thematic statements are gracefully interrelated, and an in-direct reference is explained and clarified in a subsequent dialogue. The oppositions which cause the division in the Wood, and of which the Wood is itself one, are resolved in the final, actual "victorious dance" (973) performed on "holier ground" (942).

The Attendant Spirit defines this symbolic landscape for us and by his very presence serves as a reminder of its existence, but it functions primarily as a mental backdrop for the unfolding action; it is present, but not intrusive. Its early introduction is a device to initiate the reader into a particular frame of reference, to inform us that we shall be concerned with worlds within worlds. For landscape, like so many other features of these intricately structured thousand-odd lines, functions at more than one level, and Milton, as always, is careful to make clear exactly which one (or ones) he is implying.

The three principal levels of landscape can be easily—almost schematically—illustrated within the initial thirty lines of the masque. The first, landscape as symbol of the "Sin-worn Mould," has already been touched upon. The second, which I shall call "mythological landscape" (not because it is itself mythic, but because Milton chooses to associate it with mythological figures), is illustrated by the short emblemlike representation of Neptune, surrounded by jeweled isles where tributary gods "wear their Saphire crowns, / And weild their little tridents" (27–28). This type of imagery, reminiscent of Inigo Jones' costume sketches and such splendid devices as the mother-of-pearl shells in *The Masque of Blacknesse,* is deliberately nonrealistic, yet uncomplicated by any great freight of metaphoric meaning. In lines 18–29, the emblematic seascape serves as a bridge between the immensity of space and idea suggested by the first words of the Attendant Spirit and the introduction of the actual Wood. Beginning with "all the Sea-girt Iles . . . ' twixt high and neather Jove" (21, 20), the lines gradually narrow our field of vision and end by focusing our attention on "this Ile" (27) where the action is to take place. Spatially, this type of landscape (which reappears with Sabrina) presents an intermediate realm removed from the center of the Sin-worn mold (the Wood) while still related tangentially, as are Neptune and Sabrina, to the earthly landscape. The simultaneous effect of the "rich and various" gem imagery is to make of these semimythological figures something exotic: they are magic and mysterious creatures removed from everyday actions and artifacts, yet beautiful and beneficent.

As the Attendant Spirit completes his descent, he opens to our mind's eye a vista of natural landscape: "all this tract that fronts the falling Sun" (30). This is the plane on which the story unfolds, and one method of discussing the levels of landscape is to visualize "this tract" on "this Ile" on "this dim spot, / Which men call Earth" (5–6) as the center of a series of circles proceeding inward from the "starry threshold of Jove's Court"(1). There is, however, one more level which must be kept in mind although it is actually glimpsed only in the minds of the characters. This is the underworld, the "hell" whose existence Thyrsis verifies to the Brothers when he speaks of those things.

> Storied of old in high immortal vers
> Of dire Chimeras and inchanted Iles,
> And rifted Rocks whose entrance leads to hell,
> For such there be, but unbelief is blind.   (515–18)

Milton employs the three areas of masque (and standard Elizabethan) staging: heaven, earth, underworld. The Attendant Spirit makes clear that all three areas are equally "real," but it is on "middle earth" that the action must take place. If, to the Spirit, this earth is "dim" and "drear" (37), it is still no mere shadow of heaven. For those who must undergo "this mortal change," it is, indeed, all too real, and this is one of the themes of *Comus*. The Attendant Spirit prepares us for this reality (and mortality) by emphasizing in his prologue his own physical reactions to his descent. The sense of darkness, heat ("Feaverish being" [8]), rankness, confinement, and physical discomfort ("smoak and stirr" [5]) is graphically realized.

In *Comus,* realism is no "affection of [the masque's] declining years" but a tribute to the reality of earthly existence and experience, with both its trials and rewards. Even in the midst of the magic, myth, and metamorphosis of the world of *Comus,* Milton is not about to praise a cloistered virtue. The wild Wood, if magic, is not mythologized into a never-never land. The world of *Comus* is neither nonrealistic nor naturalistic in our modern sense; it is rather a world of intensified reality, where the landscape presents "nature" in both its physical and metaphysical senses.

The principal landscape in *Comus,* then, is the "natural" one. Although it differs from most masque settings, I believe that it is even more integral than usual to the action because it is this landscape which "discovers" the characters in a deeper sense than the ordinary masque scene. The identities and attitudes of the characters must be established before the crisis of the action in Comus' Palace; they must, in other words, "show themselves" by reacting to their situation in a given way, and their situation, in 658 lines of *Comus,* is the Wood. In its passive role, the forest is the background against which the characters move; actively, it is the force against which they realize their identities. Milton's landscape serves "artifice" in a sense which transcends the term as it is commonly applied to the masque.

The initial impression of the Wood is that of a force which itself acts in some maleficent way upon the characters. And so, in part, it does; this is part of the way in which the Wood is symbolically realized. Our first view of the Wood is through the eyes of the Attendant Spirit, who is naturally prejudiced. To him, the darkness, rankness, and confinement of the "mould" are intensified in this "drear Wood" (37). The impression persists throughout the masque in the oppressive connotations of certain adjectives: "ominous" (61), "hideous" (519), "tangl'd" (180), "usurping" (337), "close" (349), "thick" (62). That the Wood may be capable of entrapping, overwhelming, and perhaps even devouring those who wander "forlorn" and "lonely" within it is emphasized by judicious use of personification—"shady brows" of the Wood "nod" and "threat" (38–39), mists "usurp" (336)—as if the Wood not only sheltered evils, but was itself a crouching monster.

Closer reading, however, reveals that the "real" forest differs from the "symbolic" forest in that, of itself, it offers no menace; it exerts no will for or against evil. If its "shady brows" present a "nodding horror" (38), its pines may also provide "spreading favor" (183). If Comus dwells here, so do Sabrina and Echo. If the darkness and confinement of Comus' "inmost bowre" (535) imply imprisonment, the ivy-canopied retreat imagined by Thyrsis liberates the soul to a "pleasing fit of melancholy" (546), and Echo's cave, if deep, is flowery. That the glade is "adventrous" (79) may imply impending danger, but also—in the sense of the Latin *adventura*—that *any* "happening" may occur here. The landscape is therefore neutral, but the characters act upon it: the "wild wood" of the human mind exerts its power over the actual "wilde Wood." The symbolic landscape functions as a metaphor for existence; the natural landscape functions as a reflecting device for each mind which concentrates on it. The mood and the appearance of the Wood vary because the speaker varies, and in so doing they help to reveal the character of the speaker. Milton accomplishes this revelation through two basic elements: content of the speeches (the features of landscape which the character notices) and style (the terms used by the character to describe the landscape).

The contrast between the Attendant Spirit and Comus in this respect serves as a subtle comment on the divergent identities of these two magicians who assume the same disguise to wage their contest. The general antipathy of the Attendant Spirit towards the "mould" has already been discussed. His view of the Wood as a generalized entity ("this drear Wood" [37], "this hideous Wood" [519]) and as the home of Comus is unmitigated and severe. Yet he is not above remarking the small wonders of nature—the "flaunting Honysuckle" (545), the "tender grass" (623), the "verdant leaf" (621); and the two small "landscape miniatures" he paints in his mind's eye for the Brothers—meditating his rural minstrelsy near his sheep and learning of Haemony from the Shepherd Lad—are full of color, light, an unerring eye ("the leaf was darkish and had prickles on it" [630]), and, most important, an undeniable tenderness. And since, even in his disguise as Thyrsis, the Spirit remains the voice of truth, we may believe his statements are sincere.

Comus, in contrast, is a liar. His outward statements and actions, of course, bespeak this plainly. Comparing himself to a serpent (164–65), he aspires to "fair pretence of friendly ends" (160); he lies blatantly to the Lady about his identity, about the actions of her brothers, and about their mutual destination. It would be completely unlike Milton to endow his villain with the physical grossness of Jonson's Comus. Perversions of the mind always interest Milton more than sins of the flesh, and, like Satan, Comus is a sophist whose self-deceit goes hand in glove with his attempts to deceive others.

The Spirit, of course, recognizes these insidious powers, and the Lady as well sees through Comus' specious reasoning. In the speeches before the scene in the Palace, however, the reader has already been given clues to the falsity of Comus' argument: in his references to the Wood, it becomes clear that Comus violates the identity of "most innocent nature" just as he seeks to violate and subvert the identities of mortals. The truth is that although Comus pretends to worship the bounty and plenitude of nature—and his argument hinges on this point—he feels neither zeal nor faith, but only contempt, a contempt mirrored in his attitude towards the landscape in which he dwells. His references to the Wood are filled with death, not life. The Spirit speaks of Comus as "immur'd in cypress shades" (520), echoing Comus' dictum to his crew to "Run to your shrouds, within these Brakes and Trees" (147) ("shroud" is certainly used here in the sense of both "shelter" and "cerement"). Darkness he visualizes as a raven, the bird of death, for the seat of Comus' power lies not in "waking bliss" (262) with all the joys of alert and intelligent observation which the phrase implies, but in maintaining the oppressive sunless atmosphere of "blear illusion" (155) where nothing is seen clearly by either mind or eye. Comus would seek to make the clear "airy shell" of Echo "one blot" (132). He would obscure the "kind [both gracious and natural] hospitable woods" (186) with a "bleak, *un*kindly Fog" (268).

Any positive reference Comus makes to his surroundings is related to either self-deceit or the deceit of others. Thus, as he and his crew can only "Imitate the Starry Quire" (112), so his attempt to identify himself with the Fairies and Elves who merrily trip "By dimpled Brook, and Fountain brim" (119) is false. He is certainly no Peaseblossom, and the mischief of Puck pales beside his evil. Similarly, his description of the Brothers "Plucking ripe clusters from the tender shoots . . . along the side of yon small hill" (295, 294) is a lie formulated to convince the Lady of her brothers' safety and his own good offices. The "tall and prosperous Wood" (269) becomes so only because the Lady is to be flattered into thinking herself safe.

In his argument to the Lady, Comus is of course using "nature" in a much broader context than that of the merely physical plane, but his antipathy, present in previous statements, towards the "merely natural," and his willful introduction of "barbarous dissonance" (449) into the natural order of the Wood certainly prepare one for his ironic advocacy of the uses of plenitude. No one so committed to death-in-life and death-within-nature could, in truth, be capable of the appreciation Comus pretends. There is no such thing as "waste fertility" (728) (not, at least, in Milton's time); and Comus' vision of the "cumber'd earth" (729) is a terrible parody of the overflowing goodness of the Creation, his image of the "forehead of the Deep . . . bestud with Stars" (732–33), an ironic echo of the "rich and various gems" to which the Attendant Spirit likens the sea-girt Iles. He betrays himself, as well, by his inordinate Mammon-like interest in the earth's subterranean riches, rather than the ones which surround him. Comus misuses innocent nature as Bacchus misused the innocent fruit of the purple grape.

Stylistically, Milton differentiates his two "shepherds" by their choice of diction. While this point should not be overemphasized as a major clue to characterization, it does seem relevant to note that the diction of the Attendant Spirit is—while not restrictively so—principally Latinate, while Comus favors words with Old English or Germanic roots. This tendency—in adjectives like "dun," "bleak," "rough," "unkindly," "blabbing," and nouns like "brake" and "blot"—certainly contributes to the bluntness, and possibly to the contemptuousness, of his attitude. The high frequency of such words—"lane," "dingle," "dell," "bosky," "bourn"—in Comus' first encounter with the Lady may be attributed to his attempt to counterfeit a simple shepherd. One effect, however, is to make Comus appear more the "unleter'd Hind" (173) than the true pastor which Thyrsis is. This diction even invades the high rhetoric of Comus' finest, most infamous, hour, the debate with the Lady. The choice of the final term in "Beauty is nature's brag" (744), for instance, subverts, both by its bluntness and its connotation of pejorative superfluity, the attempted profundity and truth of Comus' statement; it reveals, in one more subtle way, his hollow falsity.

The Lady's sincere belief in the goodness and innocence of nature—that belief which triumphs in the cry "Imposter do not charge most innocent nature" (761)—is evident in her reactions to the landscape of the Wood. To her, "dim darkness" (278), not the Wood itself, is villainous; it is "theevish night" (194) which has caused this wood to become a "labyrinth" (298) and a "blind maze" (181). Her distrust of night is one of her most Spenserian characteristics, and her apostrophes to the darkness are reminiscent of Arthur's (*The Faerie Queene*, III, iv, 55–60). When she is not "benighted," as her brother affirms, she is a veritable Britomart (although with softer edges, one would think), secure in her identity (as she continues to be) and strong in purpose. She possesses, in John Arthos' phrase, a "spiritual clarity"[14] which rebels against any kind of darkness and continues to see the Wood as a benevolent entity which is not itself bent on "misleading" her. Therefore, the Wood remains "kind and hospitable," and the pines (she does not see them as mere "Brakes and Trees" as Comus does) confer "spreading favour" (183). The turf is "grassie" (279) for her comfort; the spring her brothers sought would be "cool and friendly" (281). She would, indeed, gladly "drink the clear stream" (721) which Comus denigrates. Her plea to Echo—that life-affirming song which proceeds from her own "enliv'nd spirits" (227) and has such a potent effect on both supernatural listeners

—imagines the "sweetest Nymph" in a beneficent and beautiful land-scape of green banks and violet-embroidered vales. Although the song to Echo was somewhat of a masque staple, this one has special significance, not only structurally, but also in the way it reveals the Lady's love and appreciation of nature even in the face of adversity. I do not believe it is overreading to see the landscape in this song as participating in a kind of gracious and right order which mirrors "Heav'ns Harmonies" (242). The Wood does not threaten the Lady, for she knows her plight as a "prison'd soul" (255) is not permanent; as her brother says, she may be "surpris'd" but not "enthrall'd" (589); her faith in the innocence of the Wood and the goodness of life is one with her faith in her own identity.

The Lady's brothers are, as the perceptive Spirit rightly names them, "good vent'rous youth" (608) who have stumbled, with their sister, upon this "adventrous glade." Their function is partly choric; their dia-logue, which falls approximately mid-masque, is filled with philosophi-cal shadings, mythological comparisons, and theological implications which confirm the substance and extend the scope of the masque as it stands at that point. Yet it is one of Milton's happiest strokes to place these complex speculations in the mouths of two such candid and basi-cally *un*complicated youths. The Brothers are two of Milton's most charming and valid character portrayals; if, like the Wood, they are not "true to life" in a naturalistic sense, they do possess what I have already termed "intensified reality." Their youthful erudition may seem alien to the modern reader (it probably seemed less so to the Egertons' contem-poraries), but this is certainly not true of their youthful bravado. They see themselves as stalwart young knights ready to draw their swords with "courage . . . and bold Emprise" (609) in defense of that fair Diana, that wise Minerva, that quivered Nymph—their own sister. At the same time they are young boys striving to keep up a frail being in what seems to them a woody dungeon, and longing for the familiar sights and sounds of home; they are fairy-tale children lost in the wood who prefer to be-lieve themselves fairy-tale heroes subduing the wilds. In order to do so, they respond to their situation with one of human nature's most pre-dictable reactions: they talk, and talking, weave endless fantasies of possibilities and explanations, some terrifying, some reassuring. In all, they are remarkably successful, and the Elder Brother's final line before Thyrsis speaks is a wonderful example of their combined fear and re-sourcefulness: "Com not too neer, you fall on iron stakes else" (490), while their youthful relief suffuses their next line, "O brother, 'tis my father's Shepherd sure" (493). The beauty of Milton's artifice in this dialogue is that the statements concerning the powers of unarmed Chastity as well as the foulness and inevitable dissolution of evil partake of the Brothers' undoubted sincerity while escaping tendentiousness and pedantry because of the character of the speakers. How charming, indeed, is divine Philosophy!

The Brothers' attitude toward landscape is also consonant with their character. Lacking their sister's "sober certainty" (262), they find it difficult to see beyond (or through) their present situation, and they understandably act uneasy, for they have lost their sister as well as themselves. The Wood, to them, is the dungeon of their own dark "nook" (499) surrounded by "wilde Wast" (402), and they do not like it. It is to them, in one sense, that the Wood is most real, for they are the most unexempt, the most natural of the characters in the masque, with little to protect them except their own good intentions and an unfailing belief in a power beyond their own. They are the ones who recognize that the bank is cold, the dew chill, tree bark rough against young skin, and burrs and thistles abundant. And so, as they imagine their own identities, they imagine the landscape; they minimize the immediate reality by creating a greater one in their heads. Their hyperbolic vision of "unharbour'd Heaths, / Infamous Hills," "sandy perilous wildes," moorish fens, and "grots and caverns shag'd with horrid shades" (422 ff.) both allays their fears by being more terrifying than their own surroundings and comforts themselves (and us) by articulating a basic truth about the power of virtue. That these imaginary constructions are indeed true is proven by Thyrsis' corroboration, couched in the same rhetorical style as the boys' own, that only "unbelief is blind" (518) to the terrors of such places.

While it is true, then, that each character is distinct against the landscape, each is not in equal control of his situation. Control, as it is manifested by mental and spiritual temperance, is of course a central concern of Milton's masque. This is the kind of right reasoned control which espouses neither excess nor abstinence, but dictates external moderation from the disciplined citadel of internal reason. This self-control (in its fullest sense) has as its outward corollary control over the external situation. The implications of this fact are complicated, however, by the relative powers of the characters: two are supernatural, three are merely mortal. The latter, who must depend on their inner security to impose outward order, are pawns in the deadly serious game enacted by the supernatural forces whose incarnations are Thyrsis (or the Attendant Spirit) and Comus. All are faced with the "perplex't paths of this drear Wood" (37). It is the mission of the Attendant Spirit to make the crooked paths straight and guide the mortals to "holier ground"; Comus' intent is to make a labyrinth of matter and mind, to intensify the perplexity until it tightens into a constricting trap, a "deadly snare" (566). Between these two powerful extremes tread the Lady, with "unacquainted feet" (179), and the Brothers, with "wandring steps" (192). And to guide them appear the two shepherds, both of whom claim to "know each lane and every alley green" (Comus, 310) "through paths and turnings often trod by day" (Thyrsis, 568). Although one "pastor" is a false one, both statements here are true. As the Attendant Spirit "knows" these woods, so is Thyrsis his perfect disguise, for it is he "Who with his soft Pipe and smooth-dittied Song / Well knows to still the wilde winds when they roar, / And hush the waving Woods" (86–88). And although Comus is false shepherd and false prophet, his power and his control are very real indeed; the Attendant Spirit himself implies that only fools do not take seriously the power of evil. The reality of this power is the reason for the Spirit's descent, as well as the reason that Comus cannot be permanently vanquished, but only temporarily subdued, and then only by supernatural means.

The kind of evil control which Comus exercises depends for its power on a constriction which is both spatial and mental. As his "haunt" is obscured "Within the navil of . . . this Wood" (519), so he obscures the minds of his victims, robbing them of "reasons mintage" (528). This limiting of mental powers also extends to the sensory aptitudes, of which sight is the most important. Sight, in *Comus,* is a method of revelation, and as such is directly related to the extent of a character's control. Both the depth and insidiousness of Comus' power are emphasized by his hatred of light. Comus fears and loathes light to the same degree that the Lady fears and loathes darkness. He would, if he could, limit the light-bearing natural forces as he limits the landscape; the dawn, in his description, is restricted to a "cabin'd loophole" (140). He fears the sun because with light comes the ability to "discry" (141). His control is marred, however, because it depends for its efficacy on rejection based on deprivation, rather than acceptance based on recognition. His outburst

against the "blabbing" morn (138) is as useless as his tirade against the
Lady, not because the sun will rise in spite of him, but because Comus,
immured in his own restricted and obscured viewpoint, does not understand that "Vertue could see to do what vertue would / By her own
radiant light, though Sun and Moon / Were in the flat Sea sunk" (372–
74). Comus' "unbelief" in this fact is therefore as "blind" as that of those
fools who would ignore the reality of evil. All the other characters of
Comus do recognize the reality of their situation, and by accepting it, see
through or beyond it.

The Attendant Spirit's is naturally the most encompassing vision,
comprehending as it does the earthbound situation while extending far
above and beyond it towards controlling concepts and higher realms.
The Lady's perception of the true and innocent nature of her surroundings has already been noted. In addition, she looks beyond her benighted
state and "sees visibly" (215) the forms of Faith, Hope, and Chastity
coming to her aid. "Eye me, blest Providence" (329), she prays as she sets
forth in Comus' company, and she is confident that "while Heav'n sees
good" (665), Comus himself will be cheated "of power to cheat the eye"
(155) or mind.

Throughout the masque, then, there runs the idea of a counterforce working against the attempt of Comus to "close up" both the landscape and the mind. While recurrent imagery of "pen't flocks" (499) and
sheep in fold (95, 345, 541) serves as a reminder that earth is indeed a
"pin-fold" and mortals poor sheep, it also emphasizes the necessity for a
good shepherd to act as "defence and guard" (42) and eventually to lead
the sheep forth. Nor are the heavens, the welkin above the earth, ever
completely forgotten; each character in some way mentions the stars (1,
93, 196, 330), making it seem that heaven is involved in their actions below whether they wish it or not.

This counterforce also operates in the landscape. Milton enhances
the sense of the "beyond"—a power both visible and invisible which
presides over the Wood while extending its figurative and physical
boundaries—with a corresponding sense of expanding movement within
the landscape itself. In several ways Milton leads the imagination of the
viewer/reader away from the static representation on the stage and towards the realization that there are other landscapes, other worlds, beyond the confines of the Wood. This sense of spatial expansion begins
with a device as simple as the mention of other topographical features

within the Wood itself. The Brothers have "stept . . . to the next Thicket side" seeking berries (184) and moved to "th vally" (281) to find a spring. Comus claims to have seen the youths on the side of "yon small hill" (294); Thyrsis says he ran "down the Lawns" (567) when he heard the Lady's voice. The dingles, dells, bourns, paths, lanes, and alleys which both "shepherds" mention indicate other features of the unseen landscape. It does not matter, in these cases, whether the speaker happens to be telling the truth or not; the resulting expansion of our mind's eye is the same.

A second technique is the inclusion of extended images—miniature tableaux, really—depicting scenes enacted at other places in the Wood. Comus compares his own "tipsie dance" with the nocturnal caperings of fairies, elves, and wood nymphs (117 ff.). The Lady visualizes a more truthful likeness in her imagined wanton revelry of the "loose unleter'd Hinds" (172 ff.). The night-foundered Brothers, wishing for the comforts of civilization, conjure a scene of conventional pastoral peace complete with lighted lodge, sheep pen, and barnyard (342 ff.). The Attendant Spirit, in order to add verisimilitude to his disguise as Thyrsis, pictures himself caring contentedly for his flocks "I' th' hilly crofts / That brow this bottom glade" (530 ff.) or seated "on the tender grass" listening to the Shepherd Lad's praise of Haemony (618 ff.). Even though these short scenic digressions exist only in the minds of the characters, each is realized in detail. Their implication for the theme of the masque is twofold. First, these concrete portrayals of other figures in other landscapes function as a more detailed method of opening up the Wood and directing the eye towards other areas of action. Secondly, these tableaux alert the reader's mind to the realization that not only do other creatures inhabit the Wood, but they have always done so, each going about his particular task, whether it be dancing or sheep tending. Furthermore, the implication that they will continue to do so after this particular night adds to the extended spatial dimension a temporal one, both working to reinforce the expectation of a comic conclusion. For if the major figures are representative men and women, they are still not the only ones, nor is the Wood the whole world, nor is this particular dark night of the soul a prelude to the Apocalypse. Through this artifice, the trials of the masque characters are made part of a cycle of continuing activity—whether for good or evil, natural or supernatural purposes—in this and other landscapes. It is a point which at once deepens the significance of the masque by implying that for those who would "by due steps aspire / To lay their just hands on that Golden Key / That opes the Palace of Eternity" (12–14), this type of trial is not unique, nor is it, perhaps, the only one the Lady and her brothers may have to endure. At the same time, the inclusion of these tableaux in the lines preceding the scene in the Palace helps to convey the sense of an optimistic outcome to the crisis at hand. The ingenuousness of the actions pictured does not diminish the seriousness of the central situation, but makes it seem less appalling. The knowledge that such scenes take place in or near the Wood reduces the forest's oppressiveness and encourages us to glimpse light at its edge.

The flights of fancy indulged in by the Brothers are a third medium which guides the mind's eye "beyond." As self-appointed chroniclers of "The Legend of Chastity," their imaginations conduct a metamorphosed Alice Egerton unscathed through a terrifying symbolic landscape "where very desolation dwels" (427), as well as villains natural and ogres supernatural. The rhetoric is their own, but the sentiment echoes their sister's own fantasy "Of calling shapes and beckning shadows dire . . . On Sands, and Shoars, and desert Wildernesses" (206, 208). As with so many other threads of *Comus*, the Brothers' speeches underline, corroborate, and extend the implications of the Lady's statement. In their imaginary quest the Brothers conjure a world beyond the Wood in which the landscape varies but the threat remains; yet the triumph repeats itself in every exigency, and their conclusion repeats their sister's: "no evil thing . . . hath hurtfull power o're true virginity" (431, 436). Chastity may be startled, but not astounded, "Surpris'd by unjust force, but not enthralled" (589). The breadth of their vision, and its truth, reaffirms on a grander scale the confidence inspired by the other scenes in the Wood. Existence, no matter what its setting, is a trial; this is the price we pay for "this mortal change." One can never be sure what "that power / Which erring men call Chance" (586–87) holds in store; yet Virtue, hopefully with "some good angel" bearing a shield before her, may, and will, triumph. Suddenly, perfectly, the high rhetoric and the high seriousness become a unity; the Wood and every other landscape we have glimpsed expand to encompass the earth and tremble, for if the Brothers' belief is false, "The pillar'd firmament is Rott'nness, / And earths base built on stubble" (598–99). As the confrontation nears, Comus also assumes a breadth of evil commensurate with the power for good represented here by the Brothers and Thyrsis. The mention of Acheron summons to the mind "all the griesly legions" (602) of the underworld landscape, while "all the monstrous forms / Twixt Africa and Inde" (604–05) populate the surface of the earth with equal horrors. In both these cases a broad symbolic landscape is used to extend the confrontation in the Palace to cosmic proportions.

The debate in the Palace is thus a temporal microcosm for the unending contest of good and evil, just as the Wood is a spatial microcosm for the world in which this contest is waged. With the triumph of the Lady and of Virtue—temporary though it may be—comes the release of the "prison'd souls" from their bondage in the Wood, whence they may proceed to "holier ground." Their physical emancipation confirms the feeling of qualified optimism which has been present throughout the masque. Although "Heav'n hath timely tri'd their youth, / Their faith, their patience, and their truth" (969–70), there has always been the sense, in the Elder Brother's words, that the trial this masque presents is a "happy" one which "shall prove most glory" (591). As in any good masque, a definite moral scheme is understood as the basis for the action of *Comus*, and the interest lies in the presentation, illustration, and eventual triumphant revelation of these values. The values themselves are never seriously in question, and although the additional dramatic content of *Comus* emphasizes the reality of the situation to a greater extent than is usual, a happy outcome is expected. Part of this sense of reassurance can be traced to the presence, from the very beginning, of the Attendant Spirit. Part springs from the Circe-Ulysses analogue, with its own positive outcome. And part, as I have tried to illustrate, rests on Milton's treatment of the landscape.

Returning to the Spirit's first speech, for instance, "all this tract that fronts the falling Sun" (30), with its effect of almost boundless length and breadth, may be read as a prediction of the expanding landscape which comes to represent freedom to the characters in the Wood. Such a setting, even an earthly one, whose main characteristic—space without boundary—is reminiscent of the endless expanse of the "starry threshold," cannot be judged completely evil.

In another example, the Lady's song to Echo (229–42) combines myth and masque convention with landscape to reinforce the idea of earth and heaven combined in a harmony which works towards the same end. Milton's Echo is no mere answerer; she is "Queen of Parley," a beneficent power in herself. Her realm extends throughout the entire "airy shell" under the sky. She has also wandered the earth, and Milton particularizes Ovid's description, specifying "Meander's margent green" and the "violet-embroidered vale" in order to emphasize her connection with concrete landscape while retaining her ephemeral ubiquity. The song is, in all, a graceful way of adding breadth to the earthly landscape while approaching, in another way, the theme of heaven's care for earth.

The Sabrina episode, as befits the crowning magic which accomplishes both release and revelation, unites these threads of myth and landscape in a way which permits us to look back and forward to see both a progression and a unity within the masque. As Sabrina's former condition as a mortal maiden threatened by danger parallels that of the Lady, so her "immortal change" (847) to a goddess looks forward to the Lady's final metamorphosis from body back to spirit. Sabrina's metamorphosis differs from Daphne's—"root-bound, that fled Apollo" (661)— in that it renders her active and powerful rather than passive and powerless. This mysterious and beautiful creature is a force for good dwelling not only in *a* landscape, but in *this* landscape, in the River Severn which winds about Ludlow. In one respect she is fully at home in the natural landscape: she dwells "By the rushy-fringed bank, / Where grows the Willow and the Osier dank" (889–90); she plaits her hair with lilies and treads lightly among the cowslips. It is revealed, furthermore, that her good offices are connected with the various pastoral scenes noted throughout the masque: she visits the folded sheep; she alleviates the mischief of the Elves and Fairies; it is she whom the shepherds and hinds celebrate in their festivals and to whom they pay homage with bouquets of pansies, pinks, and daffodils. The reader realizes that her immortal power, if submerged (literally and figuratively), has been present throughout the action, controlling the surroundings and rendering them harmless and innocent. This knowledge, gained at the end of the masque, confers a blessing on these earlier scenes, "unlocking" them from the oppression of the Wood and the influence of Comus as Sabrina blesses the Lady and "unlock[s] / The clasping charm, and thaw[s] the numming spell" (851–82). Sabrina's character and action serve as a climactic affirmation of what has been sensed in all that precedes her entrance: the superior power of virtue and the inherent goodness of the landscape. She is the reverse of Circe and her nymphs, a beneficent Siren,

"sitting / Under the glassie, cool, translucent wave" (860–61), waiting
for the summons to perform good.

If Sabrina "retains / Her maid'n gentleness" (841–42), she is nonetheless the "Goddess of the River" (842), so that the landscape in which
she dwells is both the Severn's realistic one and a jewel-strewn "mythological" setting. She is "Goddess of the silver lake" (864), her hair drops
amber, her bed is paved with coral, the channels of her river run with
turquoise blue and emerald green (893). This imagery carries the reader's mind back to the sapphire-crowned deities who rule the islands
"That like to rich, and various gemms inlay / The unadorned boosom
of the Deep" (22–23), the deities whose names appear as incantations in
the magic summoning of the Attendant Spirit (866–88). Here the effect
once again is to extend the field of vision, for by summoning these deities, the Spirit also summons all the land and water which come under
their benevolent control. And once again we are reminded that "this
Ile / The greatest, and the best of all the main" (27–28) falls under the
special protection and favor of Neptune. It has been, in essence, sanctified from the beginning.

A second consequence of combining the realistic landscape with
nonrealistic imagery is to blur the distinction between the two. Sabrina
is at once the river and the spirit of the river; her dwelling is of the earth,
and yet beyond it. In this respect her landscape is an intermediate one
between earth and the realms beyond, as was Neptune's in the opening
speech. The Sabrina episode (although realized in much greater detail
than Neptune's realm) joins the latter to form the second span, as it
were, of the bridge between the realistic landscape of the masque action
and the framing visions of the Attendant Spirit. The withdrawal from
the earthly plane which culminates in the epilogue is begun in the landscape which surrounds Sabrina. The final speech of the Spirit before the
epilogue is therefore a kind of benediction upon the landscape—"all this
tract that fronts the falling Sun"—as the epilogue is upon what has tran-
spired there. The speech (921–36) emphasizes the favored uniqueness of
the area by mentioning Sabrina's local ancestry. But it also expands the
landscape's connotations by visualizing it first within the temporal
framework of the seasons, thus implying a continual cycle of existence,
then by making of Sabrina a Cybele figure, presiding over a landscape
which, in its "Groves of myrrhe and cinnamon" (936), bears more resem-

blance to an eastern earthly paradise than a rural English river bank. This final allusion, as the masquers leave the Wood, to "other worlds," prepares the reader to turn his eye towards "those happy climes" (975) of the epilogue.

It is not necessary to trace precise sources or decipher each allusion in order to understand the implications of the Spirit's final vision. Like the Garden of Adonis which they resemble, the Gardens of Hesperus unfashionably resist exegesis. Whether its roots are pagan, Neoplatonic, or Christian, this is a metaphysical landscape whose major characteristics are light, peace, and joy. With typical catholicism, Milton has utilized whatever myths and images are appropriate to arouse in the human consciousness the longing for rest after labor, pleasure after pain, heavenly peace after earthly trial. The Lady and her brothers rejoice that their trial is completed; they are at last out of the Wood, and their dance is properly victorious because of the triumph of "Their faith, their patience, and their truth" (970). They are still, however, mortal, and thus their victory remains incomplete, a figure for the immortal change which is to come. The Spirit, too, rejoices in the accomplishment of his mission, but his is the true freedom to leave the earth behind and below: "But now my task is smoothly don, / I can fly, or I can run / Quickly to the green earths end" (1011–13). His is the final triumph which awaits the Lady and the Brothers, the final change from mutable nature to immortality, that metamorphosis which the Brothers have predicted (458–62) and which will be fulfilled, in the phraseology of the *Phaedo*,

when the soul inquires alone by itself, [and] departs into the realm of the pure, the everlasting, the immortal and changeless ... and ... has rest from its wanderings and remains always the same and unchanging with the changeless, since it is in communion therewith.[15]

The boundless, bounteous landscape of the "happy climes" is thus the logical climax of the expanding vision noted throughout *Comus*. The themes of Milton's masque demand, and the epilogue expresses, that feeling which remains unspoken in most masques: "a sense of dilation, of opening vistas, of life regarded *sub specie aeternitatis*. For a moment the world becomes thin as a theatre curtain, a cloudy veil about to be withdrawn."[16]

From the prospect of Paradise, the earth does indeed seem small, thin, and illusory, but for almost a thousand lines we have seen humanity move on it, triumph on it, love and appreciate it. If Milton, in *Comus,* shares Plato's opinion of the soul's imprisonment in the body, I do not believe that he could bring himself to view this as a completely degraded state. Milton is extremely careful to differentiate between the sensual and the sensory, and part of the Lady's triumph over Comus is related to the right use of God-given senses. The proof of this positive view of the human condition is to be found in the final vista, which is no cloudy vacuum populated with ephemeral souls, but a remarkably lovely, remarkably concrete landscape. And it is lovely, in part, because it is so easy to recognize, so full of the natural wonders man associates with "jocond Spring" and wishes for with "eternal Summer." Only in the gardens of Hesperus, their beauty is intensified, as the fruits of Paradise should be. Nor, in this humane heaven, are the senses annihilated, but rather heightened; each one becomes, at last, completely alive to the light, to the songs of the daughters of Hesperus, to the "balmy smels" and "odorous banks," to the "liquid ayr." There is more of everything here, the Spirit implies, but it is never too much, for man, in these happy climes, is become more than man (975–1022).

We know that from the Nativity Ode onward, Milton's concern centers increasingly on the image of God in man, on man as less-than-God rather than man as more-than-man. And after *Comus,* the path of the virtuous man becomes less wayfaring and more warfaring. The broad fields of the sky become more distant, their nature more inscrutable. The Heaven of *Paradise Lost,* if more grandiose and glorious, is less empirical, less familiar, and somehow less comforting than that of *Comus.* In *Samson Agonistes,* nothing outside the circumscribed landscape of Gaza is even glimpsed.

In the landscape of the gardens of Hesperus, and throughout *Comus,* there is revealed a facet of Milton's sensibility which, it might be argued, he chose to exploit fully only once more, in his description of another garden, Eden. This equality is Milton's sincere and deep love of the earth, its plenitude, and its beauty. Perhaps the point is so obvious it need not be made, but it is one which the sheer scope of the later poems makes it easy to overlook. In *Comus,* it cannot be ignored; it pervades the vision of the poem and lends it charm and reality. It is the vistas of earth, of which the gardens of Hesperus are but a transfiguration, which guide us through the poem; they tell us something about Milton and something about man, and we respond to them as much with our senses, rightly used, as with our minds. The surest and best guide to the magic of *A Mask Presented at Ludlow Castle* is still Milton's own: "List, mortals, if your ears be true."

Salem State College

NOTES

1. David P. Young, *Something of Great Constancy* (New Haven, 1966), p. 175. Young is speaking of *A Midsummer Night's Dream,* but the phrase seems equally applicable to *Comus.*

2. Rosemond Tuve, *Images and Themes in Five Poems by Milton* (Cambridge, Mass., 1962), p. 129.

3. Ronald Bayne, "Masque and Pastoral," in *The Cambridge History of English Literature,* ed. A. W. Ward and A. R. Waller (Cambridge, 1910), VI, 380. I am indebted to Enid Welsford, *The Court Masque* (Cambridge, 1927) for directing my attention to this reference.

4. *Ben Jonson* (Oxford, 1925), II, 268.

5. C. H. Herford and Percy and Evelyn Simpson, eds., *Ben Jonson* (Oxford, 1941), VII, 169.

6. Ibid., pp. 188–89.

7. Ibid., p. 750.

8. Welsford, *The Court Masque,* p. 339. I am generally indebted to Miss Welsford's analysis in these conclusions on the nature of the masque.

9. For information on Inigo Jones' set designs, see Percy Simpson and C. F. Bell, eds., *Designs by Inigo Jones for Masques and Plays at Court* (Oxford, 1924).

10. Herford and Simpson, *Jonson,* VII, 169.

11. It is interesting that one of Milton's presumed sources, William Browne's *Inner Temple Masque* (1615), which is usually described as "epicurean" in theme, seems to evoke more of a sense of landscape—that is, of characters in a natural setting —than any of Jonson's productions. See William Browne, *The Masque of the Inner Temple,* ed. R. F. Hill, in *A Book of Masques,* ed. T. J. B. Spencer and Stanley Wells (Cambridge, 1967), pp. 179–206.

12. *The Student's Milton,* ed. Frank Allen Patterson, rev. ed. (New York, 1933), p. 47. All Milton citations are taken from this edition.

13. The lines are from one of Daedalus' songs (Herford and Simpson, *Jonson,* VII, 488).

14. *On A Mask Presented at Ludlow Castle* (Ann Arbor, 1954), p. 27.

15. Harold North Fowler, ed., *Plato,* Loeb Classics Library (London, 1933), I, 79 D, p. 277.

16. Welsford, *The Court Masque,* p. 346.

ON JOHN MILTON'S *A MASK AT LUDLOW*

Thomas O. Calhoun

Considered in the light of its occasion and performance, Milton's *A Mask at Ludlow* is a family drama about conflict among three age groups: children, adolescents, and adults. The adolescents—Lady Alice and "the Spirit of Youth," Comus—are distinguished from children and adults by their immediate concern with the problems of erotic love. For the children, Eros is primarily a subject for fantasy; and for the adults, it is a threat to morality and family unity. Lady Alice, age fifteen, sings to Echo and seeks an escape from the perplexing, sensuous world in which she is lost. But, in confronting Comus, she must face the demands of erotic love directly as a true, wayfaring Christian, and accept the trial which can transform her to adulthood. Milton resolves Alice's trial, however, at the expense of Eros and in favor of family unity, thus meeting the demands of the *Mask*'s occasion. The children and adults combine forces not to resolve, but to suppress the erotic dilemma of adolescence. They overcome Comus, and the Lady is released from her own emotions and the trial of growing up. Nature grants her no liberty, but the kind of apotheosis she had earlier wished for from Echo—a return to father and family. Her victory is qualified as the names of Parthenope and Ligea, figures of erotic frustration and introversion, are invoked.

A YOUNG woman told me once that John Donne says more about "little brethren" in four lines than John Milton can conceive of in the many lines devoted to this topic in his Ludlow *Mask*. The adolescent lover of Donne's fourth elegy portrays his lady's little siblings as fake cupids, sellouts to an adult world which is, at best, voyeuristic.

> Thy little brethren, which like Faiery Sprights
> Oft skipt into our chamber, those sweet nights,
> And kist, and ingled on thy fathers knee,
> Were brib'd next day, to tell what they did see.
> (Elegy IV, "The Perfume," 27–30)

Although Donne's speaker is the victim of his own betrayal, outraged at his own fabrication of a world of miniature spies and colossal authoritarians, he may be right about little brothers. It occurred to me then that Milton confirms the behavior which Donne ironically portrays. Differences between Elegy IV and *Comus* on the subject of little brothers are matters of perspective and tone.

I hope to obtain something interesting from this comparison, but first I want to make a generalization. Most literature is, and has been, written by adults. Whether or not it is written *for* adults, one can hardly say. An unthoughtful answer would be "Yes, it is." But the largest audience for serious literature today is made up of adolescents, and they do not read the same way I do. I have heard, and argued with, student responses to Milton's *Mask* for several years and, with no claims to scientific procedure or even full attention to the matter on my part, I can offer the blunt observation that Milton's college audience is attracted to the *Mask* the way older people are attracted to mortuaries. They don't go to the text willingly; but, once there, they are held by a curious fascination and disrespect. They view the characters of the masque from a position of familiarity and superiority. In places like this, their kind are done away with. By some latent or intuitive morality, or mortality, they know that what happens to Comus and Lady Alice is supposed to happen to them, but they will do what they can to deny, or forestall, the death of sensual life.

There are, indeed, many ways of approaching and understanding the Ludlow *Mask*. I offer this essay as a defensible reading, prompted by the consideration that it may be time to examine the attraction and antipathy shown the work by the contemporary audience which has been created for it. The conclusions I will reach are in some ways unique, but they have been sought before. William Riley Parker, for example, asserts: "What is really important is the fact that *Comus* was a children's entertainment, requested by children and acted by children ... *Comus* was never once intended to be part of the adult masque tradition."[1] R. H. Bowers, advancing the age of the participants somewhat by the terms he uses, suggests that the *Mask* can be read "as a play concerned both directly and obliquely with the emotional life of youth, written by a youthful author largely for youthful performers."[2] I will go one step further to argue that the masque is concerned with three age groups: children, adolescents, and adults. The adolescents, distinguished from children and adults by their immediate concern with problems of erotic love, are the center of attention. The children and adults combine forces not to solve, but to suppress the erotic dilemma of adolescence.

Milton's *Mask* exists in five versions: the autographed "Trinity" manuscript of minor poems; the Bridgewater, or "acting" manuscript; the anonymous publication of 1637; the authorized edition of 1645; and a second edition of minor poems printed in 1673. The prototype for this series of near-replicas does not exist, but since it can be demonstrated that the Trinity manuscript is the copy of an original, it can be assumed that the other versions of the *Mask* are derived from this original as well.[3] The more strongly the hypothetical prototype weighs on one's imagination, the less likely Milton's active involvement in the Ludlow production of the *Mask* becomes. Such a speculator is inclined to believe that Milton wrote the masque by himself, having been commissioned to do so some time before 1634. Then, after he and Henry Lawes reviewed the text and made some changes, Lawes managed the performance at Ludlow, perhaps using the Bridgewater MS as a script. Finally, having consulted with Milton once again, Lawes arranged for the printed edition of the text in 1637. It is not likely that Milton saw the 1634 production, and he probably considered his *Mask* an "act" of the mind, as he was later to think of *Samson Agonistes*. If all this is true, an understanding of the *Mask* through literary and philosophical analogues is entirely in order.

But if we can disregard the literary prototype, or "Ur-*Mask*" as Sears Jayne calls it,[4] if we can pass over the conceptual barrier that copies cannot be copies of themselves, the Ludlow production assumes primary importance. This actualization becomes the aim of Milton's initial drafts, and we must examine the details and characters involved in the formal inauguration of the lord president of Wales in order to understand what the masque is about.

As Milton retains the place and date of the performance in the title of all editions subsequent to 1634, it appears that he wished his readers to regard the masque within the context of its occasion as best they could. If Milton's initial cultured and urbane readers heeded this suggestion, they might well have visualized a small, neatly kept stone castle at Ludlow, surrounded it with images of rural gentry who could have been in attendance at the performance, added images of barbaric Welsh and border-English country folk, and murmured amongst themselves, "Thank God I wasn't sent out there." Politically alert Londoners may have remembered that John Egerton, Earl of Bridgewater, was appointed president of the Grand Council in 1631 but did not assume residence at Ludlow, where the council met, until 1634. "According to Warton, the Lord President of Wales entered upon his official residence at Ludlow Castle with great solemnity,"[5] but one wonders if solemnity is ever a euphemism for reluctance. It is possible that neither Egerton's office nor the priviledge of living at Ludlow was a genuine occasion for celebration. Accordingly, perhaps, Milton's *Mask* is overtly concerned with neither. In spite of the fact that a Shropshire river deity helps to resolve the plot, and regardless of the final scene in Ludlow town where "all the swaynes" are invited to dance, the ostensible occasion for the *Mask* exists as only a periphery for its main concern.

The Earl of Bridgewater and his wife, "Noble Lord and Lady bright," are celebrated at the masque's end as head and head-mistress of their family, and no real effort is made to make family a metaphor for state, or for the counties under the lord president's jurisdiction. At the beginning of the masque, the family is dispersed; at the end, it is unified. The action of the masque is the process by which this family is brought together. Literally speaking, the lord and lady have taken up residence at Ludlow, but three of their children—Lady Alice, John, Jr., the Lord Brackley, and Master Thomas; fifteen, eleven, and nine years of age respectively—have not yet arrived. These three

> are cominge to attend their fathers state
> and newe entrusted scepter, but their waye
> lies through the perplext paths of this dreare wood,
> the noddinge horror of whose shadie browes
> threats the forlorne and wandringe passinger
> and heere their tender age might suffer perill.[6]

Why did the parents not bring their children with them in the first place? Why are the children traveling alone? No literal explanations are available, nor are they necessary. The "real" family is physically intact and presumably has been so all along. The children must then be out of touch with their parents in some other way: emotionally, morally, or spiritually. Their progress through "the perplext paths of this dreare wood" is a process of growing up, of coming into harmony with the world of their parents. The place which Comus inhabits is the interior landscape of youth.

At the end of their ordeal, Henry Lawes presents the children to their mother and father with a song:

> Heav'n hath timely tri'd their youth
> Their faith their patience, and their truth
> and sent them heere through hard assaies
> wth a Crowne of deathlesse praise
> to triumphe in victorious Daunce
> ore sensuall folly and Intemperance.   (891–96)

Milton understands growth, in the *Mask* at least, as determined by a rite of passage, a trial, a test established ultimately by God. Young men and women are placed in emotionally demanding situations to see how they can deal with them. Someone is always watching. If they fail the test, they become like animals, rolling with pleasure in a "sensuall stie" (97). Presumably they become family outcasts, too. If they pass, they can assume an honorable position within the family.

The trial and triumph over sensual folly and intemperance, however, is unequally shared. The Lady Alice has been called upon to defend her very "truth"—which she interprets, rightly in context, as her virginity—while the two boys are tested on the lesser grounds of faith in learned doctrine, patience, and the ability to follow orders. By the time the little brothers face Comus, they have the Demon's instructions and magic haemony. Alice must face Comus on her own. This inequity and pairing are appropriate in one sense, as the masque divides its concern among three discrete age groups. The brothers are portrayed, appropriately for their real ages, as children. Their trials are perhaps suited to their competence. The Demon or Attendant Spirit, played by Henry Lawes, and the Egerton parents are adults. Between these poles stand Lady Alice and Comus. At fifteen years of age, Lady Alice is separated from her brothers in the way we generally understand adolescence apart from youth. Sex and marriage are immediate concerns for her. For the boys, erotic love is primarily a subject for fantasy.

John Diekhoff has said that "Milton emphasizes the players, rather than the parts played" in the *Mask*.[7] Since no one knows who played the part of Comus in the Ludlow production, it is impossible to determine whether Milton conceived the role for an adolescent. But students of the *Mask* understand him as a teen-ager, regardless of the poet's possible intentions, and they do so with some justification. Quite simply, Comus is a god, and therefore he is ageless. But there is textual evidence to support the argument that Comus should be seen as an adolescent, or the spirit of adolescence, running with his gang. First of all, the Attendant Spirit describes Comus as the son of Bacchus and Circe (66–76). We know him first in the relationship of son to parents, and this impression remains. We are told that he is "much like his father, but his mother more" (77). Like Bacchus, he is riotous, an adventurer, a seductively attractive figure blithely youthful in appearance, with "clustringe locks" (74–75). These aspects of his appearance remind me of Caravaggio's *Unnamed Youth*, or *Adolescent Bacchus*. Comus is in the "ripe and frolick of his full growne age" (79), yet he rebels against "strict age, and soure severitie" (129) by staying out late—all night, in fact. Comus is full grown, but not grown up. Like his mother, he is capable of turning the godlike countenance of unsuspecting, weary travelers into "some brutish forme of Wolfe, or Beare, / or ounce, or Tiger, Hogg, or bearded goate" (90–91). Circe has been doing this sort of thing for years, and Comus, proselytized, imitates her in matters of seduction and the transformations that the forces of sensuality can inflict.

Comus operates in the aura of his parents and is never really independent of them until he meets the Lady Alice. He hears the young virgin's "Sweete Echo" song and, enchanted, proclaims her more lovely and affecting than Circe and the Sirens combined. Cocky, he predicts "I'le speake to her / and she shalbe my Qweene" (252). Circe had been his idol up to this point. Now he speaks as a young man in love for the first time. Our initial impressions of Comus suggest his adolescence, and these impressions stand the test of the remaining text, where he operates in conscious disguise, proves falsely courteous, lies, and finally loses his temper over the failure of his arguments.

Early in the *Mask*, Milton sketches the outlines of two families, Bacchus-Circe and the Egertons, which are diametrically opposed to one another. All good stands with the Egertons. The anti-family of Bacchus and Circe is represented as totally evil, and doubly so since they appear attractive to the unwary. Given these ideological trimmings, a liaison between the two families would be calamitous. But each family has a full-grown child who has not yet passed to an independent, mature state, and the scene in which the Lady Alice and Comus meet is in some ways suggestive of just such a liaison. The scene (231–317) dramatizes a mutual attraction which stands opposed to the attitudes displayed by Alice and Comus just prior to their meeting. Comus, who can sense a virgin by vibrations in the ground, hurls his dazzling dust into the air with all the scheming anticipations of a juvenile rapist. But when he sees Lady Alice he falls, if momentarily, under the spell of her beauty. The Lady, too, falls for the moment under the effects of Comus' magic dust. No longer loathing to meet the rude "wassailers" whose noise had irritated her, she is now attracted by the humble appearance and "honest offer'd Curtesie" (309) of her new acquaintance. The courtesy may be inadvertently honest at this point, though Comus tells an elaborate lie about seeing the two brothers, and his main objective is really to find out how alone the Lady is, and then get her to his palace.

The Lady Alice is faced with a sensuous and emotional problem, and her solution is undertaken, at first, by the senses and emotions. Her senses are clearly deceived, and this affects her reasoning. She is high born; Comus is a "gentle Shepheard" (258). From this false information, she derives a youthfully liberal platitude. Honest courtesy "ofte is sooner found in lowly sheds / with smoakie rafters, then in tap'strie halls / and Courts of princes" (310–12). Since she lives in such tapestried halls, these lines could be taken as rebellious. Or they could be a subtle allusion to the rusticity of Ludlow. For the Lady, they are a rationale. She leaves the stage, heading for no "lowe" and "loyall cottage" (306, 307), to spend the night with her newfound friend.

The Lady's emotions are more difficult to assess. Her stated feelings are solely for her little brothers, but she involves the boys in a curious and perhaps ironic confusion of identities in her song to "Sweete Echo." The first six lines of the lyric are an invocation in which Echo's sadness is suggested: "sweetest nymphe that liv'st unseene . . . the love-lorne nightingale / nightly to thee her sad song mourneth well." If the nightingale is Philomela, her particular lovelorn sadness is twofold. She has been violently abused by love, and she has taken violent revenge by murdering a child. Echo, to whom she sings, is grieved because she has been rejected by Narcissus. Nightly, together, these two lament the pathos of love. This is an extremely unusual set of references for a young woman to use in calling for her brothers, but the allusions are fitting and expressive if the young woman has been contemplating, perhaps not even consciously, the problems of erotic love. The literary references are particularly appropriate in that the adolescent, Echo, and Philomela are all unable to talk openly, or even audibly, about the subject. The Lady is admittedly an alien in the dark, sensuous world she has suddenly awakened to. She feels abandoned by her family, her brothers particularly, and wishes to return to that security. But her small-voiced singing gives her courage, perhaps by giving lyric expression to the new feelings and fears which she can speak of only in song. Philomela, victim of Tereus, has no tongue; in her metamorphosed state she can only sing. Echo, victim of Juno, can say nothing except the last thing she hears.

As the song proceeds, the Lady identifies herself with Echo, and her brothers with Narcissus: "Canst thou not tell me of a gentle payre / that likest thy Narcissus are" (223–24). This association is more confused, or ironic, than it is appropriate. Like Echo, Alice has lost what she seeks. But the Lady overlays her relationship with Thomas and Lord Brackley with the frustrated eroticism of Echo and Narcissus. Ovid describes the frustration as follows: "How oft would shee have woo'd him with sweete words! / But, Nature no such liberty affords; / Begin, she could not."[8] The erotic impulse is contrary to Lady Alice's sisterly affection, but it has nowhere else to go. And as this physical embodiment for eroticism is impossible, the Lady seeks a disembodied purity. As a resolution to her problem, and the song, she devises a wish and a promise. If she can reestablish her former, sisterly relationship with her brothers, Echo will be apotheosized—"translated" from her pathetic status, wandering in the "ayrie shell," to a new position "counterpointing" heaven's harmonies (229–30). The promised apotheosis also returns Echo from her sad searchings to her family. She is "daughter to the Spheare," so her translation involves both a release from the problems of erotic life and a return to her father.[9] The Lady Alice wishes to do the same thing, but she does not get her reconstituted nymph for a guide. She gets Comus. That is, she must confront the demands of erotic love directly as a true, wayfaring Christian and accept the trial which can transform her to adulthood.

But Lady Alice's trial is cut short, both as it develops and as it concludes. Her journey with Comus is interrupted as we hear speeches from the "unrazor'd lipps" (277) of the little brothers who will join forces with their music teacher Henry Lawes effectively to truncate the conclusion of the Lady's ordeal. But if the audience is left wondering what is going on with Alice, so are the two boys, and Milton's conception of their fears, sexual fantasies, and ideological safeguards is brilliantly portrayed. Young Master Thomas is worried about "that hapless virgin, our lost sister" (337), but he knows that he and his brothers are also lost, and he is afraid. He envisions his sister's wild amazement and fright, huddled like Proserpine "When the bigg rowling flakes of pitchie clouds / and darkness wound her in" (345–46). That is how he would feel if he were lost, alone in the dark, and it is partly the way he feels now. The older boy chastises his brother for acting like a child, but together they consider the plight of a beautiful young maiden, set upon and ravished.

Our sister is guarded and guided by her virtue, her calm thoughts, and her "nurse contemplacion" (358), the older boy proclaims. The little boy takes this literally. In that, she is a hermit, he says, and who would bother to rob and violate a hermit? But a beautiful maiden is no safer than a treasure heaped outside the den of an outlaw! The elder brother is more aware of the sexual demands of shaggy ruffians, fierce savages, bandits, and "mountaneers," so it is he who makes the point about chastity and its powers of protection. As the little boy had seen himself in his sister's place, so does the elder. Chastity is an armor of complete steel, a quiver of keen arrows, and a bow. Thus imaginatively armed, the boy soon loses himself in a world of fogs and fens, fending off evil hags, horrid monsters, ghosts, and goblins. Visions of unconquered virgins— Diana, Minerva—raise his speech to the heights of heaven from which, companion of the angels, he views foul lasciviousness:

> when lust
> by unchast lookes, loose gesturs, and foule talke
> and most by lewde lascivious act of sin
> letts in defilement to the inward partes,
> the soule growes clotted by contagion,
> imbodies, and imbruts till she quite loose
> the divine propertie of her first beeinge,
> such are those thick, & gloomie shadowes dampe
> oft seene in Charnall vaults, and sepulchers,
> hoveringe and sittinge by a new made grave.   (450–59)

All this is less "divine philosophy," as the little boy's wide-eyed response suggests, than it is a verbal dramatization of youthful imagined fears. The rhetoric thinly veils a terrified view of sex. One drop of carnal sensuality begins to rot the soul, and lovers are soon transformed into shadowy necrophiles. From the boys' point of view, there are two options: black or white, corruption or virginity. This is the way little brothers think about sex when their sister is the object of imagined plunder, and who else can they more naturally imagine as the victim of sexual savagery?

The brothers' moral idealism is the safeguard for fears which result from fantasy. It is powerless without adult supervision, temperance, and understanding. So, as soon as this is realized, the Attendant Spirit enters, disguised as Thyrsis the shepherd. His effect is initially to bring sobriety and reason. The elder brother repeats and confirms his opinions, but this time they are transformed into a reasonable argument. Virtue may be assailed but not hurt, surprised but not enthralled. Goodness will force evil back on itself, if there is any order or justice in the universe, for goodness and virtue are order, and evil is "eternall restless change" (583). But the Demon does not continue this discussion and let the Lady fend for herself. Instead, he confirms the boys' imagined version of Comus, "that damn'd wizard hid in slye disguize" (558) down in the navel of the dark woods. He adds the strength of his conviction to their vigilant zeal. They become "corageous":

> for that damn'd magitian, let him be girt
> with all the grisley legions that troope
> under the sootie flagg of Acheron,
> Harpies, & Hydraes, or all the monstrous buggs
> twixt Africa, and Inde, I'le finde him out
> and force him to restore his purchase back
> or drag him by the Curles, and cleave his scalpe
> downe to the hipps.   (589–96)

Out of hand once more, the older boy dreams death to kidnappers and imagines his display of manly violence before the trapped maiden. The Demon must once more lead him from the juvenile world of "monstrous buggs" and brutality, which is verging on a genuinely cruel conservatism, and this time the lure is magic.

For all the brilliant commentary that has surrounded the healing herb Haemony, this magic-to-counter-magic is seen in context from the perspective of a child's world, or from the perspective of an adult trying to appeal to the sensibilities of children. The genuine ideological threat which Comus represents is reduced immediately to a relatively harmless play of magic wands and oaths repeated backward. By suggesting to the children that this is a game which they can play, the adult gains their allegiance. Together they will exorcise the sensual and intemperate "play" of adolescence.

The scene now shifts to Comus' palace, where the adolescents are engaged in a pantomime of seduction. He advances; she denies his advance. Their speechlessness is broken as they begin to quarrel. Then Comus begins the persuasive seduction speeches (647–63, 675–704) which best represent his role in the masque. These lines tell us at least one interesting thing about Comus: he cannot grow up. As a god, he argues both of and from a world of eternal, youthful, safe, and irresponsible eroticism—an adolescent Eden:

> see heere be all the pleasures
> that fansie can begett on youthful thoughts
> when the fresh blood grows lively, and returnes
> briske as the Aprill budds in primrose season.   (649–52)

By the standards of today's adolescents, Comus' attitude toward erotic love is healthier than that of the Egertons, but it bears the curse of perpetuity (if nothing else), which has bored greater gods to wish for mortal companionship. As a son ripe in the "frolick of his full growne age," Comus can establish his own "crew" distinct from that of his mother, but he can discover no self-image or autonomy outside the role prescribed for him by his parents. He can do nothing creative or original. He can freely assent to nothing, since his decisions and actions are preordained to be "Bacchian" and "Circean." Comus' momentary infatuation with Lady Alice, which could have offered him a chance for some emotional development, is lost almost immediately. He resumes his filial role and adheres to "the Canon lawes of our foundacion" (730) with the zeal of an adolescent who will do nothing that does not conform with the codes of his clique. Comus is an eternal stereotype, but then that is what gods are. In his case, we can revert from the player to the masque role and excuse him on the ground that he is supposed to be a divinity. As the spirit of adolescence, his perpetual immaturity is inevitable and scarcely pitiable.

We can pity Lady Alice, however, who has the advantage of living in the temporal world, where growth is a reality. She has the opportunity to mature, it is cut short, and she does not deserve this fate. She has to remain, in her way, as emotionally retarded as Comus. Her speeches to the tempter (663–74, 705–28) are tonally rigid, and conviction does not follow from her disdainful, petulant integrity. Her lines on the "serious doctrine of Virginity," the canon laws of her foundation, do not appear in the Bridgewater manuscript, but they merely reinforce the fact that sexually she remains the perfect big sister—inviolably virgin. Emotionally she remains what some might consider a prototype daughter. She may have had some things to learn about character judgment, but in a demanding situation she is impervious to intemperance. She is absolutely unsensual. No unwanted suitors have a chance in this house. She is defined, and confined, by her family. The Lady has no identity of her own. But confronting Comus offers her the trial, the opportunity, to think and feel for herself, and test her opinions against someone who forcefully disagrees with them. By the time Comus denounces her "morrall babble" (729) it looks as if her household arguments are about exhausted. And in her second speech she begins to talk directly to Comus, instead of denying his credibility as she had done at first. The real test has just begun. Now she may be capable of saying, with genuine self-awareness, that Comus has no right to demand something of her simply because he wants it, when she does not feel like giving, or that slavery to bodily desires is mere vanity. But she is given no chance to say anything at all.

The brothers rushe in with swords drawne, wrest [Comus'] glasse of liquor out of his hand, and break it against the ground. his rowte make signe of resistance, but are all driven in; the Demon is to come in with the brothers. (between 735 and 736)

Reading audiences of the *Mask* have often considered themselves emotionally and dramatically shortchanged at this point. Traditional responses to the sense of incompletion are of two sorts. Either the genre "masque" is used to explain why things seem to be missing, or Milton is criticized for writing a bad play. Rosemond Tuve's excellent essay on *Comus* uses the first sort of argument: "In a masque psychological refinements are implicit in the meaning of the great images, not interacting before us in complete people. . . . Speakers do not push their personalities into the tone of their lines."[10] We must object to this kind of explanation here. The masque as a form really does not challenge an outstanding poet, even a young one, and Milton is too skilled a portrayer of character to work within its traditional limitations. *Comus* directly resembles no other masque. And we have seen that personalities do intrude on speeches and determine to some extent the nature and tone of the speeches—at least as personality is approximated by age groups. But one need not criticize Milton as an alternative to reading *Comus* within the masque tradition. Milton abbreviates character and dramatic ordeal, especially with regard to Alice Egerton, not because he could not do better, or because this is a particularly limited kind of poetic drama, but because children and adults *do* unite (as John Donne wittily tells us) to "rescue" adolescents from emotional and erotic situations which they might more profitably resolve on their own. The little brothers in the *Mask* idolize their sister and are terrified of sex. The adult Attendant Spirit is willed by Jove to protect his young charge from harm, that is, sensuality. The elder Egertons, we can assume, would have highly approved the protective roles which they witnessed.

The symbolic means by which Lady Alice is saved are extensions of the dramatic collusion between children and adults. Haemony is contributed by information from "a certain shepheard lad" (606), and this magical virtue is administered by the little boys. Sabrina, the second symbolic cure, is remembered from information passed on by the ancient shepherd Millebeus, whose honor is extended as certain others like him—the sheep-hook-carrying informer Proteus, the herald Triton, and old, soothsaying Glaucus—are called upon in the invocation of the Shropshire river goddess. This invocation, verses shared by the two brothers and the Demon, is a catalogue of the victorious forces of the *Mask*. Ancient, pelagic paternalism is invoked by the names of Oceanus, Neptune and his mace, and the hoary, wrinkled old man of the sea, Nereus. Mothers who tried to save their children from mortal fate are called: Leucothea and Thetis. It might be worth noting that their children died anyway. Finally Parthenope, the erotically frustrated Siren who drowned herself because she could not seduce Odysseus, is summoned to mind along with the introverted, narcissistic Ligea.

If these allusions are significant, they suggest a fate that contemporary audiences, especially adolescent audiences, may not want to hear. But who ever said that literature has to be true to our ideal expectations, no matter how good we may consider them? Literature is simply true to the ways things are. This family is reunited at the expense of Eros, and that is the way the conclusion was meant to be. Emotional underdevelopment, erotic sublimations, and introversion are a necessary payment. And in the *Mask*, symbolic gains make up for real losses.

The old and young shepherds, the Demon, and the "little brethren" work in tandem to assure that Lady Alice sees herself as others of her family see her, or would like her to be seen. As the charge of her brothers and her tutor, the Lady silently goes home, thus achieving the fate she had earlier wished for Echo. Nature offers her not liberty, but a kind of apotheosis.[11] The rest of the story is common knowledge, at least to

Milton scholars. Master Thomas Egerton died a bachelor. John Egerton, the Viscount Brackley, married a notoriously virtuous woman and became the next Earl of Bridgewater. The Lady Alice waited until three years after her father's death to marry, at the age of thirty-three, a man whose affection for his first wife constitutes one of England's lesser-known great love stories. The second Lady Carbery, childless, outlived her husband by three years and was buried in Westminster Abbey on July 19, 1689. But the family remained strong and influential for many years.

University of Delaware

NOTES

1. *Milton: A Biography* (Oxford, 1968), I, 132.

2. "The Accent on Youth in *Comus*," in SAMLA *Studies in Milton*, ed. J. M. Patrick (Gainesville, Fla., 1953), p. 72.

3. See John S. Diekhoff, "The Text of *Comus*, 1634–1645," in *A Maske at Ludlow: Essays on Milton's Comus*, ed. J. S. Diekhoff (Cleveland, 1968), pp. 251–75.

4. "The Subject of Milton's Ludlow *Mask*," reprinted in Diekhoff, *A Maske at Ludlow*, p. 168.

5. Quoted by J. G. Demaray, *Milton and the Masque Tradition* (Cambridge, Mass., 1968), p. 99.

6. Lines 55–60 of the Bridgewater Manuscript. This text is available in photographic facsimile in *John Milton's Complete Poetical Works, Reproduced in Photographic Facsimile*, transcription by Harris F. Fletcher, 4 vols. (Urbana, Ill., 1943–48), and as printed by Diekhoff in *A Maske at Ludlow*, pp. 207–40. I have consulted both the facsimile and Diekhoff's version of Fletcher's transcription. Quotations from the *Mask*, which will be noted by line number in the text of the essay, are primarily from Diekhoff's text.

7. *A Maske at Ludlow*, pp. 5–6.

8. *Ovid's Metamorphosis*, Englished, Mythologiz'd and Represented in figures by G. S. [George Sandys] (Oxford, 1632), Bk. III, p. 89.

9. "Echo" songs are quite common in Renaissance masques and entertainments, and the significance of Milton's lyric, in its immediate context, can be diminished by reference to other versions. But, as the Demon explains in his opening speech, Milton's masque and his uses of mythology are in many ways departures from tradition: "I will tell you now / What never yet was heard in tale or songe / from old or moderne bard in hall or bowre" (63–65). So I feel justified in considering the song as an integral dimension of the Lady's character.

10. "Image, Form, and Theme in *A Mask*," in her *Images and Themes in Five Poems by Milton* (Cambridge, Mass., 1962), pp. 154–55.

11. The opposing point of view will be voiced from the disadvantaged position of this footnote. The restrictions placed upon Lady Alice constitute her freedom,

rather than denying it. The desires of the senses, the grip of Eros, constitutes slavery. Flannery O'Connor puts the contrasting points nicely. She herself, as a novelist and a Catholic, "believes that you destroy your freedom by sin; the modern reader believes . . . that you gain it in that way. There is not much possibility of understanding between the two" (*Mystery and Manners* [New York, 1969], p. 116).

"A DEATH LIKE SLEEP":
THE CHRISTOLOGY OF MILTON'S
TWENTY-THIRD SONNET

John J. Colaccio

Milton's "late espoused Saint" appears at the center of two planes of spiritual movement, horizontal and vertical, each culminating in God and corresponding to the traditions of Christian typology and Christian Neoplatonism. On the former, she reveals eschatologically Christ's redemptive self-sacrifice, subtly fulfilling the sacrifice ethos of pagan and Jewish myth and history. On the latter, she, like Dante's Beatrice, descends the Neoplatonic order seeking to "embrace" her beloved through grace. That the sonnet's persona, who represents every Christian, including Milton, fails to recognize the import of the saint is due to the Thomistic-Neoplatonic doctrine of intellectual blindness and man's desiccated will to choose "higher" objects of love. Hence, like Dante in the *Purgatorio,* the persona's unrefined affection casts a veil over his own eyes. His affectional egocentricity ("my . . . Mine") prohibits his understanding that the "late espoused Saint" is now wedded to the true Bridegroom. The vision breaks at the word "delight," as does Adam's dream of Eve (*PL* VIII, 474–80), signifying in the context of the Thomistic idea of dilection (love from rational choice, *electionem*) the persona's archetypical error. The persona's still "fancied sight" causes him to "wake" to the Christian Neoplatonic dream life of mortality.

APPEARING IN 1945, the late W. R. Parker's essay, "Milton's Last Sonnet," engendered years of commentary primarily concerned with the identity of the wife who serves as apparent subject of the poem.[1] However, in view of the fact that the biographical approaches of Parker, Pyle, and later commentators had provided us with closely reasoned—albeit ultimately inconclusive—arguments for or against a particular spouse, Leo Spitzer's judgment seemed well founded: "The poem should . . . be apperceived *half-concretely* as it was intended to be. Such is the tact and discipline required from the reader who should not indulge in unwarranted psychological or historical curiosity, but should abdicate such inquiry when it is nocive to artistic apperception."[2] Spitzer's essay, which was distinguished from earlier studies of Milton's twenty-third sonnet by its concentration on the poem's aesthetic and philosophical qualities and by its avoidance of the temptation to name the wife, in turn encouraged a number of studies chiefly concerned with matters of versification, syntax, tone, and imagery.[3] Ironically, these most recent efforts, much like those of the biographical "school" they superseded, failed to delineate reasonably Milton's achievement or intention.[4] It seems wise, then, to return to Spitzer's seminal remarks as a point of departure for a new attempt at explicating one of Milton's most exquisite poems.

Spitzer noted the sonnet's intellectual foundation in Christian Platonism and pointed out "the tripartite *crescendo* arrangement" of its images: Milton's blindness serves as a metaphor of "our actual world deprived of the Ideal" represented by the veiled wife, who is a glorification of "the intercessory attitude of the Christian woman, which, owing to the cruel separation between the two worlds, is not allowed to come to fruition" (pp. 21, 22). Further, the function of her much discussed veil is one of "foreshadowing, while withholding the perfect heavenly bliss that is to come in the eternal future" (p. 21). The tripartite organization of the sonnet's imagery was outlined by Spitzer as follows:

> I. the ancient pagan tradition represented by Alcestis: Alcestis comes back from the Tartarus "pale and faint" (the souls are shadows in Virgil's *Aeneid*)
>
> II. the ancient Jewish tradition ("the old Law") represented by the physical (ritualistic) purification of women: "mine" (my wife, as opposed to Alcestis) returns purified from the flaw of womanhood as such ("child-bed taint")
>
> III. the Christian tradition represented by the physical and moral purity of the Saints and the hope tendered to man of rebirth and reunion with the latter: the Christian wife returns "pure as her mind," "love, sweetness, goodness in her person shin'd so clear, as in no face with more delight." (p. 21)

Despite the value of Spitzer's essay, a fuller understanding of Milton's last sonnet is possible if we explore more deeply not only its foundation in Christian Platonism (more accurately, Christian Neoplatonism) but also—what Spitzer seemed to imply by "foreshadowing"—its coextensive basis in Christian typology. It is important that we distinguish between the two philosophical attitudes as they work in the sonnet, for, as in *Paradise Lost,* there are two planes of spiritual movement, each leading to union in God: Man ascends to God through an appropriate, well-defined love of Him (vertical or upward movement—Christian Neoplatonism); man progresses to God through his life in history, which through the types of pagan and Jewish myth and history and their fulfillment in Christian antitypes must culminate in Christ and judgment (horizontal or linear movement—Christian typology). Thus Spitzer was not entirely correct in his sole notation of "a continuous *rising* movement" conveyed by Milton's imagery (p. 21; italics added).

The movement of the imagery is also chronological-linear, revolving about and culminating in the wife-saint who is a foreshadowing through grace of the fulfillment in time of the Word, who bears a love for her beloved which is superior to the conjugal love Milton's persona recognizes and which is justly emblematic of Christ's love for man. It is this latter love, or agape, which has the power to draw man upward upon the Neoplatonic Order of Creation to God as supreme good. Further, the unifying image of the sonnet is not so much a "purified" wife or one requiring purification, as Parker, Pyle, Spitzer, Le Comte, Shawcross, and Fabian have concurred, but an eschatological image which fulfills the sacrifice ethos of pagan and Jewish myth and history as made perfect by the redemptive self-sacrifice of Christ. The figure of the "late espoused saint" is, in these respects, much like the figure of Dante's Beatrice in the *Commedia,* allusively Christlike. As one of the saved, not only is she pure (free of original sin—the "child-bed taint" of line 5—bequeathed by Adam to his children), but she shares in the "higher" love of Christ for man, a love which similarly prompted his redemptive mission to man's sin-darkened world.

The critic must not allow speculations into the philosophical-literary context of the twenty-third sonnet to obscure the poem's apparent foundation in an experience of Milton's or the personal value of that experience for Milton. But he is not enjoined from considering Milton's poetic employment of the rich traditions of Christian typology and Christian Neoplatonism which elucidate the sonnet's character as a drama in brief of the salvation continually offered to and lost by man. We may postulate such artificial separation of philosophical modes in the hope that it is the most efficacious approach toward an understanding of the poem's complex and subtle syncretism. As developed in the sonnet and in *Paradise Lost,* these traditions serve didactic and existential purposes. They reveal God's loving grace through Christ as the means of salvation, and history, man's life in time, as the stage upon which man must face the spiritual struggle inherent in his imperative to obey divine will. The reader of the sonnet must perceive the Christology of the dream-vision lest, like the persona, he remain blind to Christ's redemptive message.

Following Spitzer's outline of the pagan, Old Testament, and New Testament components of the sonnet, I shall indicate how the sacrifice ethos—rather than that of purification, which the former subsumes—interpenetrates each; the movement is from type to antitype and, ideally, from blindness to sight.

I

"The ancient pagan tradition represented by Alcestis" which Spitzer considered pertinent to the sonnet is one of blood sacrifice, either of an animal or, more rarely, a human. In the myth, Alcestis, wife of Admetus, is willing to die so that her husband may live. In the sonnet, she is conceived as a type of the sacrificial victim superseded by the antitype of Christ's self-sacrifice; and she possesses, in her pagan aspect, the conjugal love which is the mortal type of Christ's redeeming agape. The willingness of the "saint" to enter her spouse's mortal realm is certainly to be associated with Alcestis' acceptance of death, as well as with Christ's earthly mission. Similarly, the failure of the pagan Admetus to recognize his wife-savior finds its Christian counterpart in the failure of the persona to recognize the true redeemer.

Further, the saint has been "Rescu'd from death by force" (l. 4) through the agency of "*Joves* great Son" (l. 3), Hercules. Some commentators on the sonnet have briefly noted the tradition, dating to the third century and employed by Milton here as elsewhere, of depicting Hercules as a type of Christ. For it is the latter who has brought the saint "from the grave" of sinful mortality, who has rescued her "from death" which is mankind's life apart from God and who, in so doing, has embraced— just as she seeks to "embrace" in line 13—her into the communion of saints, wedding her soul to the true Bridegroom. One of the saved, she seeks to embrace similarly the persona's soul, showing forth the agape of Christ, whose love sacrifice she reflects and whose promised return she indeed foreshadows. Yet, as I shall discuss in connection with Milton's Christian Neoplatonism, the persona is "blind" to the richly Christlike and kerygmatic nature of her presence. However, an instance of this theme may be given in the context of Milton's Christian exposition of the Alcestis myth. As Milton throughout the sonnet has intentionally obscured his syntax and grammar, in consonance with the spiritual blindness of the persona—and reader—so in line 4 he veils reference to the crucifixion. We are given that the saint-as-Alcestis was saved from "death" (sin) "by force," but syntactically we need not understand that the force was used *by* Hercules-Christ. What saved the saint was the "force" which took Christ's life on the cross, the violence of redemptive crucifixion.[5] In *Paradise Lost*, Michael prophesies Christ's atonement: Christ's message of Life will cause him to be *"Seis'd on by force,* judg'd, and to death condemned / A Shameful and accurst, naild to the Cross / By his own Nation, slaine for bringing Life" (XII, 412–14, italics added).

In the second component of the sonnet's tripartite structure, Milton's persona remains "blind" to all but the physical and therefore superficial resemblances between history and the saint. In his outline, Spitzer suggested that lines 5 and 6—"Mine as whom washt from spot of child-bed taint, / Purification in the old Law did save"—allude to "the ancient Jewish tradition ('the old Law') represented by the physical (ritualistic) purification of women." Taken as a whole, the third book of the Pentateuch outlines the ceremonial law administered by Levite priests and is, significantly for the sonnet, an immediate source for the Christian Easter rite. While purification is a central theme, Leviticus is extensively concerned with the rite of sacrifice as the *means* of purification. Coupled with Milton's acceptance of the Christian tradition that "the passover typified the sacrifice of Christ" and that the self-offered blood of Christ replaced Jewish purification ceremonies,[6] the fact that the burden of Leviticus, chapter xii (dealing with the purification of women after childbirth) falls not on the number of days required for purification (which has been emphasized by commentators on the sonnet) but on the sacrifice of a lamb, doves, or pigeons as a part of the purification ritual, bears wide thematic relevance to the sonnet.[7] Milton, who believed that the Levite priesthood was an inferior form, a type of the Christian,[8] again elucidates the sacrifice ethos in history as fulfilled in Christ's perfect, encompassing sacrifice.

It is quite possible to suggest that Milton employs Leviticus in his grammatically clouded lines in a manner which could admit both wives: While only Katherine Woodcock might loosely be said to have been purified from childbirth in the "old Law," *both* she and Mary Powell were spiritually "saved" (purified of sin) through a sacrifice (that of Christ, the antitype of the victim of the Levitical dispensation). Further, in this context of redemption through Christ's sacrifice, which bears so heavily on the total meaning of the sonnet, both Mary Powell and Katherine Woodcock were "washed from spot of child-bed taint" (original sin as transmitted through Adam's progeny and not "the flaw of womanhood as such," as Spitzer believed) through the blood shed by Christ, the antitype of the paschal lamb.[9] For the sonnet, the typological progression of the saint's recapitulation of Christ's history-fulfilling and redemptive sacrifice may be traced as follows: Leviticus xvii, 11: "for it is the blood that maketh an atonement for the soul"; 1 Peter i, 18–19: "ye were not redeemed with corruptible things . . . but with the precious blood of Christ, as of a lamb without blemish and without spot"; Revelation vii, 14: "These are they which came out of great tribulation, and have washed their robes, and made them white in the blood of the Lamb" (the saint is appropriately "vested all in white" in line 9). The oft-noted echo of Revelation, further, leads the reader to the corollary typology of the church as the Bride of Christ—from the Bridegroom's words in the Song of Solomon iv, 7 ("Thou art all fair, my love; there is no spot in thee") to Paul's in Ephesians v, 27 (Christ sacrificed himself for the church "that he might present it to himself a glorious church, not having spot, or wrinkle, or any such thing; but that it should be holy and without blemish"). As I shall show in more detail, the biographical approach many critics have applied to the sonnet, with its single-minded intention of identifying the saint as an individual rather than understanding her as an occasion, thus ignores the richly figurative Christian tradition within which Milton wrote, as well as the sonnet's more precise character as a poem of Christian love.

"The Christian tradition" supporting the final part of Milton's tripartite structure seems to me to be more involved than the one "represented by the physical and moral purity of the Saints and the hope tendered to man of rebirth and reunion with the latter," as Spitzer averred. As I have indicated, Milton's last sonnet evokes the theme of sacrifice as *leading* to purity in pagan, Jewish, and Christian traditions. Christian tradition holds that Christ fulfills as well as surpasses the types of redemptive history through his role as High Priest of his own sacrifice, a culmination of his Messianic interpretation of the concept of the Suffering Servant of God which he derived from Deutero-Isaiah. Milton, like his fellow Protestants, accepted Christ—"our high priest and king"— as surpassing the priests of Aaron and believed that Christ in his "Sacerdotal function" of self-sacrifice "still continues to make intercession for us."[10] The silence of the persona's saint, while deriving in part from the pagan Alcestis myth, also characterizes the Suffering Servant and thus bears typological-eschatological relevance for the sonnet: "He was oppressed, and he was afflicted, yet he opened not his mouth: he is brought as a lamb to the slaughter, and as a sheep before her shearers is dumb, so he openeth not his mouth" (Isaiah liii, 7). In *Paradise Lost*, the Son, after offering himself for man, appears as the antitype of the Judaic sacrificial victim: "his meek aspect / Silent yet spake, and breath'd immortal love / To mortal man" (III, 266–68). With exquisite subtlety Milton thus subsumes the very silence of pagan and Jewish sacrificial types within the eternal Christian antitype.

Milton's persona does not associate the historical figures with which the saint is surrounded with Christian redemptive history; he is "blind" even to the fact that "every metaphor which holds together two disparate aspects of reality in creative tension assumes the character of a prophecy of the final reconciliation of all things in the kingdom of God."[11] The figurative harmony of the vision, stemming from the sacrifice ethos of redemptive history, merely elicits from the "dreamer" a response which is more strongly personal than it is spiritual. As I shall discuss in the next section, the tragedy of Milton's persona, like that of man, lies in his spiritual blindness to love which is *higher* than the conjugal love which the saint can no longer properly bear.

II

Raphael's famous dictum to Adam in *Paradise Lost* that

> love refines
> The thoughts, and heart enlarges, hath his seat
> In Reason, and is judicious, is the scale
> By which to heav'nly Love thou maist ascend,
> Not sunk in carnal pleasure   (VIII, 589–93)

proceeds from Milton's conviction that at the Fall there occurred "the loss of divine grace, and that of innate righteousness, wherein man in the beginning lived unto God," and that this "spiritual death" "consists, first, in the loss, or at least in the obscuration to a great extent of that right reason which enabled man to discern the chief good, and in which consisted as it were the life of the understanding."[12] The "general depravity of the human mind and its propensity to sin" makes such intellectual love necessary and difficult; for the spiritual death bequeathed man by Adam "consists, secondly, in that deprivation of righteousness and liberty to do good, and in that slavish subjection to sin and the devil, which constitutes, as it were, the death of the will."[13] Milton, like Dante, generally follows the Thomistic conception of the intellect as discerning truth and presenting objects to the will, which seeks to attain through love the good thereby presented. It is therefore natural that in his writing, Milton should emphasize the intellective faculty over the volitional, since the former conditions the latter. The traditional metaphor for intellect in this Neoplatonically influenced philosophy is sight, that most spiritually sensitive facility in the Middle Ages and for Dante as well as Milton. In the words of Aquinas: "Intellectual knowledge is more beloved [than sensible knowledge]: for there is no one who would not forfeit his bodily sight rather than his intellectual vision."[14] Proper love indeed depends on proper sight, because sight is the organ of the intellect. Milton's persona, as considered through these traditional assumptions, is profoundly "blind" to the Christian revelation of his vision because of the condition inherent in mortality and summarized by Dante's Peter Damian: *"La mente che qui luce, in terra fuma"* (*Paradiso* XXI, 100)[15] and by Michael's words to Adam: "I perceave / Thy mortal sight to faile; objects divine / Must needs impaire and wearie human sense" (*PL* XII, 8–10).

With the above context in mind, we can better understand Milton's twenty-third sonnet as a universal drama of lost salvation. The first few words—"Methought I saw"—indicate not merely a dream vision but the necessarily fallible character of the persona as intellective observer and lover. He fails to recognize his wife's new identity as a redemptive figure fulfilling Christian eschatology (or showing the way of fulfillment) because his mortal spiritual "sight" cannot pierce the Neoplatonic veil concealing the saint's face in line 10. Simply, the veil represents the barrier between the mortal and heavenly spheres, as Spitzer believed; but mortal sight-intellect, darkened through Adam's transgression, is in itself the barrier or veil. The "veil" of the saint, unlike that of Alcestis in the

Greek myth, may be thought to be over the eyes of the mortal persona. "Her face was vail'd" because his faculties are no sharper than Dante's: "Ma come al sol, che nostra vista grava, / E per soverchio sua figura vela, / Così la mia virtù quivi mancava" (*Purgatorio* XVII, 52–54).[16] And Milton's conviction that "in the Gospel we shall see with open eyes, not under a vaile"[17] testifies to the importance of the revelation afforded by the new dispensation, a revelation symbolized by the saint but unrecognized by the persona, whose faculties, Milton implies, like those of the characters in pagan and Jewish eras, are burdened by the flesh.[18]

But, complementing the Christian Neoplatonic concept of mortal blindness, the saint's veil evokes the Pauline-Neoplatonic symbolism of Christ's flesh as the veil or entranceway to heaven. Since Christ's sacrifice, man enters God's domain "by a new and living way, which he hath consecrated for us, through the veil, that is to say, his flesh" (Hebrews x, 20). As in Hebrews vi, 13–20, Christ-as-veil abrogates, in this concept, the veil of the Jewish tabernacle[19] and is immediately consonant with the typology of Christ as High Priest, discussed in section one of this essay. (Henry Vaughan fuses the Christian Neoplatonic and eschatological implications of Paul in his reference to "That sacred vail drawn o'r thy glorious noon" in the second line of "The Night.")[20] Edward Le Comte's parallel between the saint's veil and the veil placed on Beatrice's face in Dante's dream-portent of Beatrice's death in *Vita Nuova* xxiii[21] is thus especially pertinent within the contexts of the Pauline syncretism of Christian Neoplatonic and typological motifs and Dante's consistent vision of Beatrice as a symbol of Christ's divine love of man. Just as the silence of the saint has parallels in pagan (Alcestis) and Jewish (Suffering Servant of *Isaiah*) literature which Milton subsumes in her Christ-like character, so her veil has significant pagan and Jewish counterparts which Milton utilizes to suggest the Christocentric nature of history and myth through the saint's representation of Christ's redemptive love and sacrifice.

The lines "yet to my fancied sight / Love, sweetness, goodness, in her person shin'd / So clear, as in no face with more delight" contribute further to the theme of the persona's imperfect intellect-vision. Spitzer rightly believed that the persona's "fancied sight" indicates the weakness of his "inner eyes," which "are still unable fully to apperceive a Saint" (p. 21). But more important, "my fancied sight" implies, in addition to the fact of his dream-vision, the persona's intense conjugal love as well, "fancy" denoting the affections as well as the imagination. It is the persona's inability to love on a higher plane than the "fancy" which is at the thematic core of the sonnet, suggesting as it does the burden of the senses imposed on man's intellective powers. This inability causes him to "see" the saint's virtues as shining with unsurpassed "delight," a word significant in its possible etymology and its placement as the concluding word of the third quatrain.

As the persona regards the saint—whom alone, it seems, he wishes to see in heaven—with increasing conjugal affection, it becomes evident that the love each bears for the other is of different kinds and values. From his mortal perspective, the persona sees in the saint the natural love of a wife for her husband, while etymologically "delight," as in the Thomistic conception of love or dilection, can suggest a rational "choice" (*electionem*) of love which is "not in the concupiscible power, but only in the will, and only in the rational nature."[22] While Aquinas maintained that "delight is a movement of the animal appetite arising from an apprehension of sense," he concluded that "a certain delight arises from the apprehension of the reason. Now on the reason apprehending something, not only the sensitive appetite is moved, as regards its application to some particular thing, but also the intellectual appetite, which is called the will. And accordingly, in the intellectual appetite or will there is that delight which is called joy, but not bodily delight."[23] Within this context, Milton's persona commits the error of Adam, who forgets Raphael's injunction not to abandon Wisdom (his obligation to reserve his fullest love for God) "By attributing overmuch to things / Less excellent" (*PL* VIII, 565–66). The notion of the persona that the virtues "Love, sweetness, goodness, in her person shin'd / So clear, as in no face with more delight" is as patently false (if we too regard her conjugally) as Adam's that in Eve's "loveliness, so absolute she seems / And in her self compleat" (*PL* VIII, 547–48); for both women reflect virtue and beauty which perfectly reside in God alone. The use of superlatives by the persona and Adam implies a disproportionate love for created beings and merits the Thomistic warning which Raphael gives Adam: "take heed least Passion sway / Thy Judgement to do aught, which else free Will / Would not admit" (VIII, 635–37), for man's will is free only to love God as the highest good.[24]

The description by Dante's Thomas Aquinas of the marriage of the church to Christ through his love sacrifice illuminates further Milton's traditional use of *diletto:* "Però che andasse ver lo suo Diletto / La sposa di colui, ch'ad alte grida / Disposò lei col sangue benedetto" (*Paradiso* XI, 31–33).[25] Dante derived *diletto* from the Song of Solomon, in which it is generally a referent of the Bride for the Bridegroom.[26] Milton's collateral use of the word is some indication of the saint's future spouse, a subject discussed more fully below. Here it is sufficient to note Paul's injunction in the Vulgate: "Viri, diligite uxores vestras, sicut et Christus dilexit ecclesiam, et seipsum tradidit pro ea" (Ephesians v, 25). The AV rendering is, "Husbands, love your wives, even as Christ also loved the church, and gave himself for it." Clearly, then, it is folly for the persona to believe that the saint's virtues shined "as in *no face with more delight,*" for the very goal of the Christian, as for Dante through the smile of Beatrice, is to see such transcendent joy in the face of God.

The persona of Milton's sonnet, then, much like Dante in Canto XXX of the *Purgatorio,* is guilty of a kind of *Luxuria,* or excessive love of a person, which can cloud a deeper perception of that person's newly achieved spiritual status. The phrase "my late espoused Saint" and especially the syntactically prominent possessive pronoun "Mine" which begins the second quatrain reveal the affectional egocentricity of the mortal husband, his incapacity to perceive that as a "saint" her soul is now espoused to Christ. He is blind to the fact that she is a saint *because* her soul has found union in the one Bridegroom and that in her now transcendent nature she is beyond the application of the essentially prideful possessive pronoun and adjective used by her earthly husband. The love she bears for him is now emblematic of Christ's love of man, a love which prompts her to descend the Neoplatonic ladder in order to uplift her fallen husband, man.

The placement of "delight"at the conclusion of the third quatrain deserves comment. The word defines the persona's spiritual-intellectual blindness and justifies—indeed causes—the conclusion of the poem-vision, beginning with the profound "But O" which ultimately signifies his and man's failure to attain an instinctively desired union with God. Milton uses this psychologically astute device in Adam's account of his dream of Eve's creation. Her countenance

>   infus'd
> Sweetness into my heart, unfelt before,
> And into all things from her Aire inspir'd
> The spirit of love and amorous delight.

> Shee disappeered, and left me dark, I wak'd
> To find her, or for ever to deplore
> Her loss, and other pleasures all abjure.   (*PL* VIII, 474–80)

Spitzer cited line 478 of *Paradise Lost* as an instance of Milton's use of "a poetic pattern familiar to other poets of the Renaissance" whereby a sighted poet may express the "paradoxical inversion of day and night on the part of one bereaved" (p. 19). Yet the context of line 478 bears an unmistakable parallel to our sonnet in vocabulary, syntax, technique, and theme: Adam's dream foreshadows his later immoderate love of Eve as well as his fall into spiritual darkness, the darkness in which dwells Milton's persona, whose correspondingly sensuous nature causes him to repeat the archetypical error of the first man. The parallel misconstructions of "delight" as erotic—eros opposing agape—cause the immediate dissolution of the two love visions, which are inherently Neoplatonic. As I discuss in relation to the last few words of the sonnet, the shattered visions recount the tragic paradox of man, who continually wakes from the dream—which is the reality, to reality—which is the dream.

If the Christocentric nature of the first twelve lines of Milton's sonnet is understood in all the allusiveness which it derives from Christian tradition, lines 13 and 14—"But O as to embrace me she enclin'd / I wak'd, she fled, and day brought back my night"—will suggest meanings richer than those which readers of the sonnet have thus far noted. We have seen how the saint fulfills typologically the sacrifice ethos of pagan and Jewish myth and history, how as an incarnation of Christ's redemptive love for man she descends the Christian Neoplatonic Order of Creation, even unto man's realm of spiritual death, hoping, like Beatrice, to draw her beloved upward to her in Christ. As "delight" conveys the spiritual flaw of the persona which disrupts the vision, so "embrace" in line 13 connotes the mission of the saint as mediator. She, again like Beatrice, incorporates the Pauline-Platonic conception of grace as mediated through Christ and as mystically uniting man with God. Whereas Beatrice succeeds, however, the saint fails in her attempt, central to the concept of grace, to purify the darkened faculties of her beloved. The general irony of the sonnet—only the largest of many—is that, while she reenacts Christ's redemptive mission, the persona reenacts, as we have seen, Adam's "exceeding Love" (*PL* IX, 961).

The assumption of commentators on the twenty-third sonnet that "embrace" is to be taken as the saint's wish to kiss or touch her husband overlooks, as does the persona, her profoundly Christlike character. The words of Paul best summarize the appropriate context in which the saint belongs: "But God, who is rich in mercy, for his great love wherewith he loved us, even when we were dead in sins, hath quickened us together with Christ, (by grace ye are saved;) and hath raised us up together, and made us sit together in heavenly places in Christ Jesus" (Ephesians ii, 4–7). Milton accepted the Christian view that the faculties of man, which were "once indeed naturally free, but now only as they are regenerat and wrought on by divine grace," are permitted a new spiritual understanding of God which is more penetrating than that possessed by "the old man."[27] Man, granted the gift of grace, is "embraced" and uplifted by God through a loving Christ, the mediator. It is unfortunate for Milton's persona, as for man, that he does not apprehend about his saint what the "blind" Dante comes to learn about his: "Quinci su vo per non esser più cieco: / Donna è di sopra che n' acquista grazia" (*Purgatorio* XXVI, 58–59).[28] The persona's failure to recognize her new life in Christ and her Christlike mission of grace causes him to interpret her gesture as she "enclin'd"—the Servant's paradoxical gesture of descending to uplift, of bowing in humility to rise in triumph—on the conjugal level on which he interpreted her "delight." As C. A. Patrides has pointed out, though grace has primacy, man chooses whether to accept or neglect it. Patrides notes the words of the Father in *Paradise Lost:*

> my day of grace
> They who neglect and scorn, shall never taste
> But hard be hard'nd, blind be blinded more,
> That they may stumble on, and deeper fall;
> And none but such from mercy I exclude. (III, 198–202)[29]

Milton believed that "Perfect glorification consists in eternal life and perfect happiness, arising chiefly from the divine vision."[30] Like Beatrice at the end of *Vita Nuova*, Milton's saint sees directly the face of God, and her "love" is thereby a reflection of God's for man. "I will behold thy face in righteousness," Milton quotes from Psalm xvii, 15; "I shall be satisfied, when I awake, with thy likeness."[31] The central paradox of the sonnet is that life apart from God is a dream, and that the real or waking life is not the corporal life of man but life in God. The irony of the last line—"I wak'd, she fled, and day brought back my night"—lies in the persona's direct failure to distinguish between "day" and "night" as they are used metaphorically in Christian tradition. To the persona, "day" is the dawn which wakes him to the fact of his physical blindness, his "night"; yet he "wakes" also to the Christian Neoplatonic dream life of mortality: "And that, knowing the time, that now is high time to awake out of sleep: for now is our salvation nearer than when we believed. The night is far spent, the day is at hand: let us therefore cast off the works of darkness, and let us put on the armor of light" (Romans xiii, 11–12; also Ephesians v, 14; 1 Thessalonians v, 5 ff.). The very sequence "I wak'd, she fled . . ." does not so much contribute "to the sense of hopeless inevitability" of the dream's conclusion, as Stoehr suggests,[32] nor does the ellipsis necessarily "intensify the wounding-healing complexity of the [awakened dreamer's] recaptured experience" as Huntley believes.[33] Rather, the sequence "wak'd . . . fled" momentarily denotes the *reality* of what dreamer and audience had considered an essentially imaginative experience. For an instant, "dream" and "reality" join; what remains in the minds of the persona and audience might be characterized as a fundamental sense of Christian mystery, the reality, awful to comprehend or admit, of divine truth. Indeed, the return in lines 13 and 14 (as the dream concludes) to the regular iambic meter of line 1 (as the dream commences), standing in contrast to the metrical and syntactical confusion of lines 2 through 12, adds to the sonnet's dream-reality paradox. The persona's "dream," as confused as it seemed, revealed divine truth, but its ultimate clarity could in mortal terms only be imperfectly realized and expressed; his days of mortal wakening, divorced from such revelation, offer not spiritual certainty but the confusion which mortals accept as order.

In so failing to recognize the saint as revelatory of man's promised "day of grace," the persona is unmindful that through the efficacy of Christ's loving sacrifice, man's estrangement from God is not eternal; rather it is "a death like sleep" (*PL* XII, 434) from which those "who rightly trust / In this his satisfaction" (418–19) will awake. This Christian aspiration to wake from the death-sleep of mortality is uttered by Henry Vaughan in the morning prayer to *The Mount of Olives*: "yea, with what unmeasurable love hast thou restored unto me the light of the day, and rais'd me from sleep and the shadow of death, to look up to thy holy hill."[34]

Milton's shrewd psychological perceptiveness, in his twenty-third sonnet as elsewhere, derives in part from the philosophical assumptions latent in typology. In his valuable study of typology, A. C. Charity notes that in addition to its function of making history's fulfillment in a Messiah understandable, typology in the Old and New Testaments elicits from man a response which is existential, prompted by the intellect:

> The message of the coming act of God is . . . a question to the present about the present's whole relation to God's action, past and future. For according to the hearer's understanding of the situation he will not only choose to believe or disbelieve the prophet; according to his understanding, also, he will act. Typology in this case can be seen as an encouragement to acting rightly in relation to God's acts by assisting the hearer to hear rightly the message of God's act (or his new act). It is "applied" because it is a means of producing an existential confrontation between man and the action of God.[35]

But the thrust of typology toward "an existential confrontation" stems most profoundly from its application "not only *to* the hearer and his existential understanding, but *in* the actual response of the hearer to God's acts. The hearer's right response means that there is initiated a self-conforming with the act of God, a subfulfilment."[36] The spiritual immediacy of Milton's last sonnet—as well as of much of his major poetry—lies in his subtle use of typological motifs and the call to imperative belief and response implied therein. It is important to note that in its valuation of the intellect as determinant of the will, typology comports with the Thomistic psychology accepted by Dante and Milton. Ultimately, Christian typology and Christian Neoplatonism stress the primacy of man's comprehension in the attainment of personal renewal and immediate conformity to God's will. Thus, the failure of Milton's persona in the sonnet to note and achieve the "subfulfilment" imperative in the Christocentric vision vouchsafed him can be measured by his ultimately ironic recapitulation, previously discussed, of Adam's archetypical neglect of divine will.

For the reader of Milton's twenty-third sonnet who attempts to fathom its theme of offered and lost redemption, a greater understanding of the Christian's mission and responsibility is inescapable. Through a corresponding and necessary self-examination, he becomes once more aware of the central Christian ethic that "we walk by faith, not by sight"; that "In the present moment the sign is comprehended only with eyes of faith"; and that man's "connecting link" to redemptive history is faith in the efficacy of Christ's sacrifice for him as an individual.[37] Perhaps no other poem of Milton's better reveals the skill with which he elucidates the interior drama engendered by the conflict between Christian ethic and man's fallen nature. Certainly in no other poem is Milton a greater Christian humanist.

Rutgers University in Newark

NOTES

1. See *A Variorum Commentary on the Poems of John Milton*, A. S. P. Woodhouse and Douglas Bush, eds. (New York, 1972), II, pt. 2, 486–501, for a thorough summary of biographical and critical approaches.

2. "Understanding Milton," *Hopkins Review*, IV (Summer 1951), 23.

3. Among these are Thomas Wheeler, "Milton's Twenty-third Sonnet," *SP*, LVIII (1961), 510–15; Taylor Stoehr, "Syntax and Poetic Form in Milton's Sonnets," *ES*, XLV (1964), 294–96; Martin Mueller, "The Theme and Imagery of Milton's Last Sonnet," *Archiv*, CCI (1964–65), 267–71; David R. Fabian, "Milton's 'Sonnet 23' and Leviticus xviii.19," *Xavier University Studies*, V (1966), 83–88; and John Huntley, "Milton's 23rd Sonnet," *ELH*, XXXIV (1967), 468–81.

4. A notable exception is Marilyn L. Williamson's "A Reading of Milton's Twenty-Third Sonnet," in *Milton Studies*, IV, ed. James D. Simmonds (Pittsburgh, 1972), pp. 141–49.

5. Cf. Mueller, p. 267.

6. *Christian Doctrine* I, xxviii, in *The Works of John Milton*, ed. Frank A. Patterson et al., 18 vols. (New York, 1931–38), XVI, 169. See also *Christian Doctrine* I, xvi, ibid., XV, 309 and 317. All citations from Milton in this text are from this edition, hereafter cited as CM.

7. Cf. Williamson, "A Reading of Milton's Twenty-Third Sonnet," p. 144.

8. *The Reason of Church-government* I, iii, CM, III, pt. 1, 197; *Colasterion*, CM, IV, 265.

9. "Figuratively . . . the 'spot of child-bed taint' can be as much a way of conveying the postlapsarian condition of all humanity as a specific reference to the cause of the wife's death" (Williamson, "A Reading of Milton's Twenty-Third Sonnet," p. 145).

10. *The Likeliest Means to Remove Hirelings*, CM, VI, 56; *Christian Doctrine* I, xv, CM, XV, 291–95. See *PL* X, 211–14 and XI, 25.

11. F. W. Dillistone, *Christianity and Symbolism* (London, 1955), p. 161.

12. *Christian Doctrine* I, xii, CM, XV, 205, 207.

13. Ibid. I, xi, CM, XV, 195; ibid. I, xii, CM, XV, 207.

14. *The "Summa Theologica" of St. Thomas Aquinas*, tr. Dominican Fathers, 2nd ed. (London, 1927), VI, 364.

15. "The mind, which here [Heaven] is light, on earth is mist." All translations of Dante in this text are mine. All citations are to *La Divina Commedia*, ed. G. A. Scartazzini, 3rd ed. (Milan, 1899).

16. "But as at the sun, which dulls our sight and veils itself with excessive light, my faculties then failed."

17. *The Reason of Church-government* I, ii, CM, III, pt. 1, 191.

18. See Isaiah xxv, 7: "And he will destroy in this mountain the face of the covering cast over all people, and the veil that is spread over all nations." See also 2 Corinthians iii, 14: "but their minds were blinded: for until this day remaineth the same veil untaken away in the reading of the old testament; which veil is done away in Christ." This is also the scriptural-philosophical context of the temporary "blindness" of Milton's epic narrator, whose eyes can "find no dawn; / So thick a drop serene hath quencht thir Orbs, / Or dim suffusion veild" (*PL* III, 24–26).

19. C. H. Dodd, *The Apostolic Preaching and Its Development* (New York, 1964), p. 45; Oscar Cullmann, *The Christology of the New Testament,* tr. Guthrie and Hall, rev. ed. (Philadelphia, 1959), p. 101; and *The Reason of Church-government* II, iii, CM, III, pt. 1, 258.

20. *The Works of Henry Vaughan,* ed. L. C. Martin, 2nd ed. (Oxford, 1957), p. 522; hereafter cited as *Works.*

21. "The Veiled Face of Milton's Wife," *N & Q,* CXCIX (1954), 245–46.

22. *Summa Theologica,* VI, 315–16.

23. Ibid., 358, 362.

24. Dante's Virgil uses *diletto* as reasoned love subject to error by misapplication in his discourse, in *Purgatorio* XVII, 94–102, on the love doctrine inherited by the Christian Renaissance and Milton.

25. "So that the bride of Him who, with loud cries, espoused her with His sacred blood, might go to her Beloved."

26. Johan Chydenius, *The Typological Problem in Dante: A Study in the History of Medieval Ideas* (Helsingfors, 1958), in *Commentationes Humanarum Litterarum* (Societas Scientiarum Fennica), XXV, no. 1 (1960), 142.

27. *Of Civil Power,* CM, VI, 21; *Christian Doctrine* I, xvii, CM, XV, 367.

28. "I go up from here to be no longer blind: A woman is above who purchases grace for me."

29. *Milton and the Christian Tradition* (New York, 1966), p. 210. See *PL* III, 50–55; *Second Defence,* CM, VIII, 73.

30. *Christian Doctrine* I, xxxiii, CM, XVI, 375.

31. Ibid.

32. "Syntax and Poetic Form in Milton's Sonnets," p. 296.

33. "Milton's 23rd Sonnet," p. 478.

34. *Works,* p. 451.

35. *Events and Their Afterlife: The Dialectics of Christian Typology in the Bible and Dante* (Cambridge, Eng., 1966), p. 159.

36. Ibid., p. 160.

37. Seriatim: 2 Corinthians v, 7, cited by Milton in *Christian Doctrine* I, xx, CM, XV, 399; Paul S. Minear, *Eyes of Faith: A Study in the Biblical Point of View,* rev. ed. (St. Louis, 1966), p. 310; Oscar Cullmann, *Christ and Time: The Primitive Christian Conception of Time and History,* tr. F. V. Filson, rev. ed. (London, 1962), p. 219.

THE RULE OF CHARITY
IN MILTON'S DIVORCE TRACTS

Theodore L. Huguelet

To reconcile Christ and Moses on divorce (Matthew, chapter xix and Deuteronomy, chapter xxiv), and to prove that the Scriptures in fact sanction divorce for incompatibility, Milton needed a decisive principle of hermeneutics. He discovered "the Rule of Charity." This rule—the hermeneutical corollary of the Gospel doctrine of charity—became Milton's "loadstarre" of exegesis, enabling him to resolve doctrinal ambiguities by seeking the interpretation most charitable toward mankind. While Milton might have derived the Rule of Charity from Augustine, from Augustinian tradition, or from Erasmus or Hugo Grotius, it is likely that he discovered his key to Scripture in 1641–42, when he applied Ramistic method to exegesis. He observed that doctrinal charity becomes the "supreme axiom" in the *method* of Scripture, or the *art* of divinity. Hence, by the axiom of charity, a literal, merciless interpretation of Christ's words on divorce would invert the Law and the Gospel and violate the divine dialectics of Scripture. Milton's confidence in his divorce argument was bolstered by his perception of divine method behind "the all-interpreting voice of Charity."

WHEN MILTON began his first tract on divorce, he realized that he must overturn a venerable exegetical tradition. He must demonstrate that in Matthew v, 31–32, and Matthew xix, 8–9, contrary to the interpretation sanctioned by canon law, Christ did not, and *logically* could not, uncharitably deny to worthy Christians all hope of a divorce on grounds of mental incompatibility without physical cause, nor deny to either party every prospect of a happier remarriage.

To restore the words of Christ to their pristine truth and clarity, Milton needed a hermeneutical principle so decisive that with it he could expose and sweep away the tradition of errors overburdening Matthew, chapters v and xix, and other texts relating to divorce. When he found the principle he sought, he called it "the Rule of Charity" and proclaimed it on the title page of the first edition (August 1643) of *The Doctrine and Discipline of Divorce: Restor'd to the Good of Both Sexes, From the bondage of Canon Law, and other mistakes, to Christian freedom, guided by the Rule of Charity*. He was confident that by the authority of this rule, he could dispel centuries of scriptural misinterpretation and instigate the liberalization of divorce laws, to the great benefit of Christendom—and all in the space of forty-eight pages quarto. This expectation may appear naive; yet the venture in hermeneutics deserves recognition as one of the high points in Milton's self-appointed profession of public interpreter of Scripture. Whatever the frustration and chagrin of his marital predicament, his intellectual self-assurance and sense of charisma at this moment mounted very high.[1]

What is the Rule of Charity, and where did Milton get it?

So far as I can discover, this question has not been answered. For example, the Yale edition of the *Prose Works*, volume II, does not annotate the Rule of Charity per se or trace its provenance in hermeneutical tradition.[2] Merritt Y. Hughes, in a footnote to the *Doctrine and Discipline of Divorce*, I, iv, states that when referring to "the supreme dictate of charity," Milton "is thinking of Erasmus' Commentary on I Cor. vii"—a fruitful suggestion which, nevertheless, opens only one possibility.[3] C. A. Patrides notes the importance of the general doctrine of love and charity in the divorce argument but does not distinguish Milton's venturous application of charity as the master rule of exegesis.[4] Such brief comments do not establish the credentials of a theological rule which Milton relied upon so confidently in his tracts on divorce. Further investigation seems called for.

To begin with, Milton might have selected the analogy of charity from among the traditional principles of scriptural interpretation handed down from St. Augustine to churchmen through the centuries— in the Reformation era, notably to Erasmus and to Reformed theologians such as Calvin, Bullinger, and Zanchius. One purpose of this paper is to examine some illustrations of the rule of charity in authors who might have conveyed the tradition to Milton. But the primary purpose is to suggest that Milton's Rule of Charity, though traditional, was essentially a concept of his own, the outcome of a discovery. Looking at the Scriptures as containing the perfect *method* of teaching, in accordance with the Ramistic method he knew so well, Milton saw that the doctrine of charity transforms itself into one of the grand axioms of God's scriptural dialectic. Analysis by descending and ascending between general axioms, such as Deuteronomy xxiv, 1 and 1 Corinthians xiii, 1–2, and particular subalterns such as Matthew xix, 8–9, showed the way to convert the scriptural doctrine of charity into the hermeneutical Rule of Charity. By this tactical device Milton felt quite capable of reconciling Matthew xix, 8–9 with other Scriptures which more readily support liberal grounds for divorce.

I

It is necessary to distinguish between the *doctrine of charity,* which is the fulfillment of the Law, and the *rule of charity,* which is charity applied to exegesis. Milton's divorce argument depends upon the hermeneutical rule rather than the general doctrine. Furthermore, the rule of charity has two functions: as the touchstone for understanding every precept of Scripture, and as an irenic principle exhorting the Christian interpreter to forbearance toward other interpreters. The irenic principle has been more commonly invoked. The touchstone principle has a potential use in the dialectics of interpretation, but few theologians have employed it—none more influentially than Erasmus, and none more logically than Milton.

Milton might have learned both functions of the rule of charity from the *loci classici* set forth by St. Augustine in *De Doctrina Christiana* and the *Confessions.* Examining the ambiguities of Genesis i, St. Augustine pleads for charitable latitude:

Let us love the Lord our God with all our heart, with all our soul, and with all our mind: and our neighbour as ourselves. Unless we believe that in regard to these two precepts of charity Moses meant, whatsoever in those books he meant, we shall make God a liar, whenas we imagine otherwise of our fellow servants' mind, than he hath taught us. Behold now, how foolish it is, in such plenty of most true opinions, as may be fetched out of those same words, rashly to affirm which of them Moses principally meant: and thereby, with pernicious contentions to offend charity itself; for whose sake he spake everything, whose words we go about to expound.[5]

This principle prescribes mutual charity among Christian interpreters studying the same hard places of Scripture.

The more technical application of the rule of charity as the touchstone of interpretation is taught by St. Augustine in *De Doctrina Christiana,* I, xxxvi, 40:

Whoever, therefore, thinks that he understands the divine Scriptures or any
part of them so that it does not build the double love of God and of our neighbor does not understand it at all. Whoever finds a lesson there useful to the
building of charity, even though he has not said what the author may be shown
to have intended in that place, has not been deceived, nor is he lying in
any way.[6]

Again, in the conclusion of Book I, xl, 44:

Therefore, when anyone knows the end of the commandments to be charity
"from a pure heart, and a good conscience, and an unfeigned faith" [1 Corinthians xiii, 13], and has related all his understanding of the Divine Scriptures
to these three, he may approach the treatment of these books with security.[7]

That is, the doctrine of charity, latent everywhere in the Scriptures, sets
up its *hermeneutical corollary:* the end of all Scripture being charity,
every precept must be interpreted in the way that promotes charity. Any
doubtful or disputed precept can be clarified, says St. Augustine, by
bringing it into conformity with charity—a procedure which is exactly
what Milton attempts in his divorce argument. Although there is no
evidence that Milton extracted his Rule of Charity from any work by
St. Augustine, his divorce tracts could serve to illustrate the Augustinian
rule applied to a sustained exegetical problem.

The Augustinian rule of charity passed down the centuries as a
familiar irenic principle in hermeneutics.[8] Its sanction of charitableness
in religious controversy no doubt appealed to Erasmus and other exegetes, particularly among members of the Reformed churches, who
witnessed so much unchristian discord during the sixteenth and seventeenth centuries. In *Ratio seu Methodus Compendio Perveniendi ad
Veram Theologiam* (1519), Erasmus names St. Augustine's *De Doctrina
Christiana* among the best guides for "the candidate in theology."[9] He
urges the tyro to keep in mind those two grand principles inculcated by
Christ, faith and charity (*"fidem et caritatem,"* Holborn, p. 237). In a
lengthy discussion of faith and charity, he demonstrates that charity—
the way of peace and concord—is "the scope of theological knowledge in
the four Gospels and the Pauline Epistles" (Holborn, p. 300). As to the
teachings of Christ, "What else does he teach, what does his whole life

inculcate, except supreme charity? This was the one point which he came to teach us."[10] There are in the New Testament no precepts governing food or clothes or ceremonies: "Charity alone he called his precept," Erasmus affirms (Holborn, p. 239). This simplicity of Christ's teaching makes a mockery of philosophical and theological nicety: "Those things are injurious to this same [charity] which are treated wordily and complexly, since Christ wished his doctrine to be most simple and easy and clear even to rustics, as in few and lucid words he explains: *Love the Lord your God with all your heart and your neighbor as yourself.*"[11]

Erasmus makes use of charity in his lengthy annotation (nearly ten thousand words) on 1 Corinthians vii, 42 [AV, vii, 39] in *Novum Testamentum* (1516). He boldly undertakes to show why divorce and remarriage might be permitted even if the death of the husband has not occurred to break the cords of matrimony. He is aware that he is going against received doctrine—against St. Chrysostom, against St. Augustine and the Latin Fathers, and against the Scholastic theologians.[12] He argues from the charitable principle that, as the medicine is altered with the course of the disease, so the divine Scriptures, the law of our life, are not violated when piously and prudently accommodated to the ways of society (*"ad publicos mores accommodare"*).[13] It is not necessary to summarize here the whole array of Erasmus' arguments, textual, legal, historical, and rational, but only to note that in an eloquent peroration, charity is cited as the ultimate authority which persuaded Erasmus, while living in England, to seek a broader interpretation of Christian divorce:

I saw reasons which persuaded Ancients and Neoterics not to be so hasty to inflict so much necessity upon the race of men. Moved by these things, Christian charity demands of those who seem to me more perceptive, if they discern any reason why the word of Gospel and of Paul should be dispensed with which aims at the salvation of many, to which end everything is written for us, and from which end Paul never diverts the Sacred Writings.[14]

It is not surprising that when Milton needed to bolster his divorce argument by enlisting learned authorities, he appealed to the name of Erasmus. In the "Post-Script" to *The Judgement of Martin Bucer, Concerning Divorce* (1644), in *Tetrachordon* (1645), *Colasterion* (1645), and *Defensio Secunda* (1654), Milton refers to Erasmus' *Responsio ad Disputationem cujusdam Phimostomi de Divortio* as well as "his *notes* on

Matthew, and on the first to the *Corinthians*" (*Tetrachordon*, YP, II, 709). When he read Erasmus' "large and eloquent discourse" upon 1 Corinthians vii, 42, Milton noted with approval Erasmus' plea for charitable recognition of the spiritual grounds for divorce ("But the condition of the soul is often more burdensome than the sickness of the body; why is not the remedy of this condition here tacitly understood?") and his plea for a more evangelical interpretation of Christ's sharp words on divorce aimed at the tempting Pharisees in Matthew, chapter v (*Bucer*, YP, II 709). Milton could see how much Erasmus stressed the charitableness of the Gospel as the guiding light of sound Christian exegesis, and in regard to divorce he took special note of Erasmus' concern with England, "for the need he saw this nation had of some charitable redresse herein" (*Bucer*, YP, II, 478). No doubt Milton welcomed the corroboration of so renowned an authority. But there is no evidence that he derived initially from Erasmus that "Rule of Charity" inscribed upon the title page of the first edition of *The Doctrine and Discipline of Divorce*.

Like Erasmus, John Calvin (1509–64) pleads the rule of charity against the contentious spirit prevailing among the churchmen of Europe. He adopts the irenic rather than the exegetic function of charity, stressing the spiritual attitude and public manner proper to the Christian interpreter:

Love *believeth all things*—not that the Christian knowingly and willingly allows himself to be imposed upon—not that he divests himself of prudence and judgment. . . . He requires here [1Corinthians xiii, 7], as I have already said, *simplicity* and *kindness* in judging things; and he declares that these are the invariable accompaniments of love. The consequence will be, that a Christian man will reckon it better to be imposed upon by his own kindness and easy temper, than to wrong his brother by an unfriendly suspicion.[15]

Judging by a remark in *The Doctrine and Discipline*, Milton found little satisfaction in this conciliatory rule of charity: "according to that in the divine hymne of St. *Paul*, 1 Cor. 13. *Charity beleeveth all things:* not as if she were so credulous, which is the exposition hitherto current, for that were a trivial praise, but to teach us that charity is the high governesse of our belief, and that wee cannot safely assent to any precept writt'n in the Bible, but as charity commends it to us" (YP, II, 340).

More direct transmitters of the exegetical rule of charity into Reformed hermeneutics were Hieronymus Zanchius (1516–90) of Strassburg and Heidelburg, and the Swiss reformer Heinrich Bullinger (1504–

75). Zanchius presents a set of thirteen *"Regulae Facientes ad intelligentiam scripturarum"* in the *Prolegomena* to *In Quo SS. Theologiae Loci et Quaestiones Plurimae,* repeated in *De Sacra Scriptura.* He includes the Augustinian rule of charity from *De Doctrina Christiana,* I: "5. One should also keep in mind the aim of every doctrine which the sacred writings teach us. This is twofold: the love of God above all (in which are contained faith and hope), and of our neighbors. Christ teaches this rule in Matthew 22."[16] A *"regula fidei et caritatis"* was also disseminated through Bullinger's influential *Second Helvetic Confession* (1566), where Reformed hermeneutic is compressed into a brief article: "Only that interpretation is orthodox and genuine which we have fetched out of the Scriptures themselves . . . ; which conforms to the rule of faith and charity; and which furthers the glory of God and the salvation of men."[17] The reasoning is Augustinian. Since faith and charity are the twin doctrines of the Gospel, every interpretation of Scripture must promote these virtues. Such a principle is unexceptionable, but perhaps easy to overlook in practical exegesis.

For the immediate source of Milton's Rule of Charity, one must consider a reference to Hugo Grotius (1583–1645) in the foreword "To the Parlament" in *The Judgement of Martin Bucer, Concerning Divorce:*

> When I had almost finisht the first edition [of *The Doctrine and Discipline of Divorce,* 1643] I chanc't to read in the notes of *Hugo Grotius* upon the 5. of Matth. whom I strait understood inclining to reasonable terms in this controversie: and somthing he whisper'd rather then disputed about the law of charity, and the true end of wedlock. Glad therefore of so able an assistant, how ever at much distance, I resolv'd at length to put off into this wild and calumnious world. (YP, II, 433–34)

There is no way to ascertain how much or how little Milton reworked his "almost finisht" manuscript after he encountered Grotius' *Annotationes in Libros Evangeliorum* (1641). The word "whisper'd" suggests that Grotius either corroborated the use Milton had already made of the rule of charity, or else revealed the rule for the first time as the very exegetical principle Milton needed to clinch his argument. Whether Grotius introduced him to the rule or reminded him of it, Milton does not say. Later, in the second edition of *The Doctrine and Discipline,* Milton paraphrases a part of the note on Matthew v, 32 in which Grotius most likely whispered to him:

But it may be objected, saith he [Grotius], that nothing destroys the end of wedlock so much as adultery. To which he answers that mariage was not ordain'd only for copulation, but for mutual help and comfort of life; and if we mark diligently the nature of our Saviours commands, wee shall finde that both their beginning and their end consists in charity.[18]

As for Grotius himself, the influence of "Erasmus, Cajetanus, Catharinus & others" had inclined him toward a charitable interpretation of the Scriptures on divorce. Yet his concluding remark on Matthew v, 32 is cautious: "That belief is strongly to be doubted which aspires to be greater than the sacred and unshakeable faith of matrimony—not lightly we break the ties instituted of God."[19] Milton's contention that Gospel charity indirectly sanctions divorce for incompatibility would probably have seemed unreasonable to Grotius.

II

The above survey of possible sources of Milton's Rule of Charity indicates that his key to Scripture belongs to the Augustinian and Reformed traditions in hermeneutics. Yet it cannot be demonstrated that Milton took his rule from any of the likely sources—St. Augustine, Erasmus, Calvin, Zanchius, Bullinger, or Grotius.[20] It is certainly possible that Grotius' phrase "*& originem & consummationem in charitate consistere*" ("both their beginning and their end to consist in charity") first showed Milton the doctrine of charity in a new hermeneutical light. But internal evidence points to another theory: that some time between 1641 and 1642, the rule of charity—probably familiar to Milton as a commonplace of theology—underwent a transformation and vivification in his mind by reacting with his knowledge of the method of Peter Ramus.[21] This reaction precipitated the triumphant discovery that Gospel charity, in accordance with what he called in 1641 the "right Method" of Scripture, readily converts into the supreme axiom of divinity from which many exegetical inferences may be drawn. Milton saw that charity must be the rule for interpreting those passages of Scripture, as in Matthew, chapters v and xix, and Mark, chapter x, which appear so literal and merciless. This interaction between charity and the presupposition of the harmony, perspicuity, and methodicalness of the Scriptures gave Milton the hermeneutical authority he sought.

The connection between Ramistic method and scriptural exegesis may be conveniently illustrated by Milton's *Artis Logicae Plenior Institutio, ad Petri Rami Methodum concinnata*, particularly the last chapter, "On Method."[22] Milton's chapter opens with Ramus' definition: *"Method is a dianoëtic disposition of various homogeneous axioms arranged one before another according to the clarity of their nature, whence the agreement of all with relation to each other is judged and retained by the memory"* (CM, XI, 471). Axioms are "homogeneous," Milton explains, when they "pertain to the same thing." "Method" is the arrangement of homogeneous axioms "one before another according to the clarity of their nature, as they express arguments that are prior, better known, and clearer." Reduced to simplest terms, Ramus' dialectical method calls for an arrangement of universals before particulars, causes before effects, clear before obscure, known "antecedents" before "unknown consequents" (CM, XI, 475). From this simple and natural hierarchy, Ramus derives the basic rules which give "unity of method" to the various arts and sciences: *"In these all rules should be general and universal, yet their grades are distinguished, and in proportion as any one is more general it will the more take precedence"* (CM, XI, 475–77).

Since this elemental method exists in the nature of things as the essential art of teaching, God would manifest this method infallibly in the Bible, which may be said to contain the art of divinity complete with axioms and subalterns. In other words, Milton posits a divine *art* inherent in the Scriptures, put there by God and grounded upon axioms which are homogeneous, perfectly clear, and methodically arranged. He sees the Bible as the unique repository of the axioms and subalterns of a divine art, written down by men but miraculously disposed for teaching the will of God. The Christian interpreter can expound puzzling texts by comparing them with clearer texts, the particular with the general, and so up the grade to those grand luminary axioms placed as beacons among the lesser precepts of Scripture. Having ascended into the light of an axiom, the interpreter turns and descends to deal with the subaltern text. The *method* of Scripture thus generates its counterpart, the *method* of hermeneutics. God's analytic has provided for man's induction. The simplicity and inevitability of this reciprocal method Milton regarded as divinely fitting: "The very essence of Truth is plainnesse, and brightnes; the darknes and crookednesse is our own" (*Of Reformation*, YP, I, 566).

Milton had noted the connection between Ramistic method and

Scripture by the time he wrote *Animadversions,* between April and July
1641.[23] In this work he appealed to the "Law of Method" as he disputed
with the Remonstrant over 2 Timothy i, 6:

Y'are too quick; this last place is to bee understood by the former, as the Law
of Method, which beares cheife sway in the Art of teaching, requires, that
clearest and plainest expressions bee set formost, to the end they may enlighten
any following obscurity; and wherefore wee should not attribute a right Method to the teachableness of Scripture, there can bee no reason given. (YP, I,
709–10)

Holding firmly to the idea of the "teachablenesse" of Scripture,
Milton transferred the principles of method to exegesis, comparing two
subaltern texts with two axioms of Scripture. The first set is the subaltern in Deuteronomy xxiv, 1, compared with the axiom in Genesis ii, 18.
In the former, Moses declares: "When a man hath taken a wife, and
married her, and it come to pass that she find no favour in his eyes, because he hath found some uncleanness in her: then let him write her a
bill of divorcement, and give it in her hand, and send her out of his
house" (AV). In *The Doctrine and Discipline of Divorce,* Milton produces nine reasons to prove that Deuteronomy xxiv, 1 is a permanent
law, not a dispensation abrogated later by the Gospel. The first reason
of this law is a logical inference from "a prime and principall scope of its
own institution" in Genesis ii, 18: *"It is not good,* saith he, *that man
should be alone; I will make him a help meet for him"* (YP, II, 245–46).
"From words so plaine," Milton argues, "lesse cannot be concluded, nor
is by any learned Interpreter, then that in Gods intention a meet and
happy conversation is the chiefest and the noblest end of mariage; for we
find here no expression so necessarily implying carnall knowledg, as this
prevention of lonelinesse to the mind and spirit of man" (YP, II, 246). If
the essence of marriage is a "meet and happy conversation," it follows
that a marriage does not exist where spiritual affinity is absent or has
died out. Moses is only legalizing divorce in cases where the *reason* of
marriage has already been annulled. In the clear light of the axiom in
Genesis ii, 18, what more is there to say?

There is one additional subaltern text to be reconciled with Deuteronomy xxiv, 1, and this text alone would seem to undo all Milton's
logic. Relying upon God's method and the perfect harmony of the Scriptures, Milton enters the second major stage of his argument with complete assurance. His task is to reconcile "that mercifull decree of God" in

Deuteronomy with the words of Christ to the Pharisees in Matthew xix, 9, the strongest scriptural authority for the canon laws restricting divorce and remarriage: "And I say unto you, Whosoever shall put away his wife, except it be for fornication. and shall marry another, committeth adultery."

Following the method of Scripture, Milton locates collateral texts to clarify Christ's words. In Matthew xii, 1–8 and Mark ii, 24–28, the Pharisees taunt Christ because his disciples have plucked ears of corn on the Sabbath and because he himself has cured the sick on the day of rest. Christ's reply, according to Milton, was intended to rebuff his tempters and to show all believers that "if he preferr'd the slightest occasions of mans good before the observing of highest and severest ordinances, hee gave us much more easie leave to break the intolerable yoake of a never well joyn'd wedlocke for the removing of our heaviest affliction" (*Tetrachordon*, YP, II, 637). With this principle in hand, Milton turns back to the divorce passage in Matthew xix, 9:

And shall we be more severe in paraphrasing the considerat and tender Gospel, then he was in expounding the rigid and peremptory Law? What was ever in all appearance lesse made for man, and more for God alone then the Sabbath? yet when the good of man comes into the scales, we hear that voice of infinite goodnesse and benignity that *Sabbath was made for man, not man for Sabbath* [Mark ii, 27]. What thing ever was more made for man alone and lesse for God then mariage? And shall we load it with a cruel and senceles bondage utterly against both the good of man and the glory of God? (*Doctrine and Discipline*, YP, II, 281)

Milton's confidence in his exegetical method rises to a prophetic strain: "Let who so will now listen, I want neither pall nor mitre, I stay neither for ordination nor induction, but in the firm faith of a knowing Christian, which is the best and truest endowment of the keyes, I pronounce, that the man who shall bind so cruelly a good and gracious ordinance of God [Genesis ii, 18], hath not in that the Spirit of Christ" (YP, II, 281–82). To interpret the strict legality of Deuteronomy xxiv, 1 more charitably than Christ's words on divorce in the "considerat and tender Gospel" would be to violate "the method of religion" (YP, II, 264). The Gospel is the final authority in religion, and its supreme tenet is charity: "But Christ having cancell'd the hand writing of ordinances which was against us, *Coloss.* 2.14. and interpreted the fulfilling of all through charity, hath in that respect set us over law, in the free custody of his love" (*Tetrachordon*, YP, II, 587).

While it ought to be plain that Christians under the Gospel are free of the bondage of the Law, church authorities persist in disturbing the methodical hierarchy of upper and lower commands: "The Canon Law and her adherents, not consulting with charitie, the interpreter and guide of our faith, but resting in the meere element of the Text," have thereby "invaded and disturb'd the dearest and most peaceable estate of houshold society" (*Doctrine and Discipline*, YP, II, 242). Milton's answer to the Canonists is direct. If Christ instructs us to interpret the Scriptures by the sovereign rule of charity, how is it charitable to "cut off all remedy from a good man who finds himself consuming away in a disconsolate and uninjoy'd matrimony?" (YP, II, 283). The supreme axiom of charity clearly instructs us that Christ's words on divorce in Matthew xix, 9 must be interpreted in the light of the whole Gospel.

When the Pharisees depart and the disciples, remembering their master's harsh saying, lament the fate of married men, Christ answers them in Matthew xix, 11: "*All men, said he, cannot receive this saying, save they to whom it is given, he that is able to receive it let him receive it*" (*Doctrine and Discipline*, YP, II, 311). Milton reasons that the ones who cannot "receive this saying" are those who choose not to marry at all. But then, can Christ be so charitable as to give free choice to the single man but be "turn'd on the sudden so rigorous and inexorable to the distresses and extremities of an ill wedded man? Did hee so graciously give leave to change the better single life for the worse maried life? Did he open so to us this hazardous and accidentall doore of mariage to shut upon us like the gate of death without retracting or returning?" (YP, II, 311). Such cruelty, such "hardheartednesse of undivorcing" would be logically as well as spiritually repugnant to the mild yoke of the Gospel. For this reason, the interpreter *must* seek a more charitable exposition, that is, an exposition deducible from and commensurable with the supreme axiom of charity, touchstone of all Scriptures. There is simply no other way, according to the method of Scripture. Hence, Milton concludes that in Matthew xix, 9, Christ rids himself of the tempting Pharisees and at the same time instructs his disciples, and us, to interpret this and all his precepts "first by the institution, then by the generall grounds of religion, not by a particular saying here or there, temper'd and level'd only to an incident occasion, the riddance of a tempting assault" (*Tetrachordon*, YP, II, 679).

Charity being "the generall grounds of religion," the rule of charity becomes the hermeneutical corollary of the doctrine of charity. Guided by this rule, Milton was convinced that he had rediscovered the true Scriptural teaching on divorce. Reasoning from universal method, he had only to appeal to "the all-interpreting voice of Charity," the "load-starre" and "high governesse of our belief," "the supreme decider of all controversie, and supreme resolver of all Scripture," "the summe of all commands."[24] Only by analogy with charity can the precepts of the Gospel or of the Law, Matthew or Deuteronomy, be understood and harmonized. In fact, Milton declares, carrying the method to its logical conclusion, "wee cannot safely assent to any precept writt'n in the Bible, but as charity commends it to us" (*Doctrine and Discipline*, YP, II, 340).

Such accord between logic and divinity appeared to Milton final and indisputable. For us, it is enough to say that Milton's coordination of dialectical method with the doctrine of charity constitutes a note-worthy example of Humanistic learning applied to late Reformation hermeneutics.

III

In the address "To the PARLAMENT" prefacing *Tetrachordon* (1645), Milton admits that the Rule of Charity did not score so effectively as he had hoped when he finished the first edition of *The Doctrine and Discipline of Divorce* in 1643. Hostile readers ignored the dictates of this rule, even of this "loadstarre" of the Scriptures. Friends advised Milton that his argument *"had of reason in it to a sufficiencie; what they requir'd, was that the Scriptures there alleg'd, might be discuss'd more fully"*; others asked for *"more autorities and citations,"* which Milton attempted to supply in the second edition of *The Doctrine and Discipline* (1644) and in *Tetrachordon* (1645) (YP, II, 582). On the title page of the second edition, "to Christian freedom, guided by the Rule of Charity" has been replaced by "to the true meaning of Scripture in the Law and Gospel compar'd" (YP, II, 220–21).

This change of emphasis does not mean that the Rule of Charity had been originally a makeshift which Milton abandoned when it failed to convince. He probably felt that in the Rule of Charity he was invoking a familiar, incontrovertible principle of interpretation as sanctioned by St. Augustine and Erasmus. In this respect, his application of the rule of charity to the divorce argument should be recognized as a lively contribution to the Augustinian and Reformed traditions in exegesis, a contribution not unworthy of mention along with Erasmus' appeal to charity in the annotations upon 1 Corinthians, chapter vii. Furthermore, it is unlikely that Milton was merely grasping at straws when he consulted his Humanistic learning and postulated a "right Method" underlying the Word in Scripture. His most original accomplishment in hermeneutics resulted when he fused dialectical method into the Rule of Charity and forged a sharp tool for cutting an exegetical knot. He remained convinced that, since charity is in logical terms the supreme axiom of the Gospel, it cannot but follow that Christ's words on divorce in Matthew, chapters v and xix, must be interpreted in the way that promotes charity toward mankind, rather than in the crabbed, literal way of traditional canon law. No matter if the narrative details turn out to be debatable, the axiom of charity remains irrefragable. Hence, according to Milton's Ramistic method, a literal interpretation of Matthew, chapters v and xix, stands refuted from the outset. It only remains for the Christian interpreter to seek an explanation in the narrative context for a conclusion logically foregone.

The very ease and celerity with which the methodical Rule of Charity removed the impasse of Matthew, chapters v and xix, assured Milton that the doctrine of divorce had been delivered into his hands.

Western Carolina University

NOTES

1. William Riley Parker, *Milton: A Biography* (Oxford, 1968), I, 240.

2. *Complete Prose Works of John Milton*, ed. Don M. Wolfe et al. (New Haven, 1959), hereafter cited as YP.

3. *John Milton: Complete Poems and Major Prose* (New York, 1957), p. 709.

4. *Milton and the Christian Tradition* (Oxford, 1966), p. 186.

5. *Confessions*, XII, 25, trans. W. Watts, Loeb Classical Library (Cambridge, Mass., 1951), II, 351. See also chaps. 23–24; *Enchiridion*, xxxii, 121.

6. *On Christian Doctrine*, trans. D. D. Robertson, Jr., Library of Liberal Arts (Indianapolis and New York, 1958), p. 30.

7. *On Christian Doctrine*, p. 33.

8. E.g., Peter Lombard, *Sententiarum Libri Quatuor* (ca. 1150), II, 38: "Accordingly, the end of every precept is charity, that is, every precept is referred to charity" (*Patr. Lat.*, CXCII, 743); John Wyclif, *De Veritate Sacrae Scripturae* (ca. 1378), I, 7; William Tyndale, *Prologue to the Book of Genesis* (1530); and William Whitaker, *Disputatio de Sacra Scriptura* (1588), I, V, 13: "And forasmuch as the end of all scripture is, as Augustine observes, the love of God and of our neighbour, he therefore

treats of this in his first book and determines that without any doubt that is no true interpretation which does not serve to build up the edifice of this genuine charity" (trans. William Fitzgerald, The Parker Society [Cambridge, Eng., 1849], p. 493).

9. *Desiderius Erasmus Roterodamus Ausgewählte Werke,* ed. Hajo Holborn and Annemarie Holborn (1933; reprint ed., München, 1964), pp. 177–78, 295, hereafter cited as Holborn. Erasmus' indebtedness to St. Augustine's *De Doctrina Christiana* has been demonstrated by Charles Béné, *Érasme et Saint Augustin, ou Influence de Saint Augustin sur l'Humanisme d'Érasme* (Génève, 1969), pp. 223 ff.

10. Translated from the Latin text in Holborn, p. 238.

11. Holborn, p. 299.

12. *Desiderii Erasmi Roterodami Opera Omnia,* 10 vols. (Leyden, 1703–06; reprint ed., London, 1962), VI, 29.

13. *Opera Omnia,* VI, 692–93.

14. *Opera Omnia,* VI, 703.

15. *Commentary on the Epistles of Paul the Apostle to the Corinthians,* trans. John Pringle (Grand Rapids, 1948), p. 425. John H. Leith has observed that, in contrast with Bullinger, "Calvin's failure to develop either an analogy of faith or an analogy of love led to serious difficulties in his theology" ("John Calvin—Theologian of the Bible," *Interpretation,* xxv [July 1971], 341–42).

16. "5. Tenedus est finis totius doctrinae, quam nobis tradunt sacrae literae. Is est duplex, dilectio Dei nimirum (inque continetur fide, & spes) & proximi. Hanc regulam tradit Christus Matth.22" (*Hier. Zanchii Omnivm Opervm Theologicorvm,* 8 vols. [Geneva, 1619], VI, 16). Zanchius cites St. Augustine's *De Doctrina Christiana,* I, 35–36, as his authority. See also *De Sacra Scriptura, Omnivm Opervm,* VIII, 449.

17. "Cap. II, De Interpretandis Scripturis Sanctis, et de Patribus, Conciliis, et Traditionibus": "sed illam duntaxat Scripturarum interpretationem pro orthodoxa et genuina agnoscimus, quae ex ipsis est petita Scripturis . . . cum regula fidei et caritatis congruit, et ad gloriam Dei hominumque salutem eximie facit" (*Creeds of Christendom,* ed. Philip Schaff, 3 vols. [New York, 1877], II, 239).

18. YP, II, 329–30 (the relevant passage from *Annotationes* is cited in n. 3, 329). See also YP, II, 238, 329, 335: and *Tetrachordon,* ibid., 715. It is significant that for Grotius the appeal to charity in exegesis goes back to Tertullian more directly perhaps than to St. Augustine. It is while paraphrasing Tertullian's *Adversus Marcion,* IV, on Matthew v, 17 that Grotius refers to the "law of Charity" (*Operum Theologicorum* [Amsterdam, 1679], tome II, vol. I, 71–72). Tertullian's answer to the heretic Marcion is a defense of the oneness of the Old and New Testaments, a reconciliation of Christ and Moses, or Christ *in* Moses, since Christ is prefigured in Moses (Exodus xxxii, 32) (*The Five Books of Quintus Flores Tertullianus,* trans. Peter Holmes [Edinburgh, 1863], Bk. II, sec. xxvi, p. viii). One of Tertullian's chief points is that Christ in the Sermon on the Mount teaches the same love of neighbor as was taught under the Law in Leviticus xix, 18, thereby fulfilling the prophecy in Isaiah v, 5 (Bk. IV, xiv–xvi).

19. *Annotationes in Matthaevm,* Cap. 5: "Valeat in dubio ea sententia quae quàm maximè sanctam & inconcussam vult esse matrimonii fidem, ne temere rumpamus vinculum à Deo institutum" (*Operum Theologicorum,* tome II, vol. I, 56). In an earlier work, *De Belli ac Pace* (1625), Grotius showed no inclination toward a charitable view of divorce: "But what God had by the institution joined, Christ forbade man to sunder, taking most worthy matter for a new law from that which is best and most acceptable to God" (trans. Francis W. Kelsey et al. [Oxford, 1925], II, 237; see also 61, 67, 236).

20. I have consulted many other theologians whose works were accessible to

Milton, including Ames, Perkins, Bucer, Beza, Musculus, Wollebius, Melanchthon, Polanus, Keckermann, and Paraeus, without finding any significant example of the rule of charity applied to exegesis.

21. For present purposes it is not necessary to reopen the question of how much Milton owed to Ramus. P. Albert Duhamel ("Milton's Alleged Ramism," *PMLA*, LXVII [1952], 1035–53) has contended that the Aristotelian logic is more deeply ingrained than the Ramist in Milton's thought. Wilbur S. Howell has answered by pointing out that "If Milton, as Duhamel contends, is closer to the Peripatetics than to Ramus, he would obviously have followed these neo-scholastics of the early seventeenth century rather than the *Dialecticae Libri Duo* and Downham's *Commentaries*" (*Logic and Rhetoric in England, 1500–1700* [Princeton, 1956], pp. 216–17). Peter Fisher surveys the "combination of the Aristotelian theory of syllogism and the Ramistic logic of axioms or propositions with which Milton provides us," showing the compatibility of Ramism with Milton's Humanism and Protestantism ("Milton's Logic," *JHI*, XXIII [1962], 37–60). In my study, the term "Ramistic" will be applied to Milton's method to claim a special kinship with Ramus' famous method, while I acknowledge that Milton gathered much of his logic from Aristotle, Plato, Cicero, Downham, Keckermann, and perhaps other authorities.

22. *The Works of John Milton,* ed. Frank A. Patterson et al, 18 vols. (New York, 1931–38), XI, 470–85, hereafter cited as CM. The date of composition of Milton's redaction of Ramus' *Dialecticae* has not been ascertained. David Masson suggested that Milton's textbook of logic "may even have been sketched out in Milton's university days at Cambridge, between his taking his B.A. degree and his passing as M.A." (*The Life of John Milton,* 7 vols. [London, 1896; reprint ed., New York, 1946], VI, 685). G. C. Moore-Smith ("A Note on Milton's *Art of Logic*," *RES*, III [1937], 335) is inclined to agree with Masson but argues that the antitrinitarian remarks in the work must have been written later than *Of Reformation* (1641). Wilbur S. Howell accepts Masson's conjecture of 1629–32 as the probable date of composition (*Logic and Rhetoric,* p. 215). Taking a hint from Edward Phillips, William R. Parker conjectures that *Artis Logicae*, along with the Latin grammar, might have been composed "late in 1642 or early in 1643 (but more probably later, when there was a second 'addition of some scholars')"; but in his note to this passage, Parker demurs: "I assign the work to early 1648 with no great confidence, but it has to be put *somewhere*" (*Milton: A Biography,* I, 259; II, 938, n. 67).

23. For the background of Ramistic method, "the most famous item in the Ramist repertory," consult Walter J. Ong, *Ramus, Method, and the Decay of Dialogue* (Cambridge, Mass., 1958), chap. XI, "The Method of Method." Ong traces Ramus' definition of method from its inception in *Remarks on Aristotle* (1553) through its revisions in the *Dialectics* (1555, 1569, and 1572—the version used by Milton). See also Keith L. Sprunger, "Ames, Ramus, and the Method of Puritan Theology," *Harvard Theological Review,* LIX (1966), 133–51, and Neal W. Gilbert, *Renaissance Concepts of Method* (New York, 1960), pp. 107–15.

24. *Doctrine and Discipline,* YP II, 309, 340; *Tetrachordon,* ibid., 637, 678.

THE SOCRATIC DIALOGUE AND "KNOWLEDGE IN THE MAKING" IN *PARADISE REGAINED*

Elaine B. Safer

An examination of the dialogue form in *Paradise Regained* illuminates Milton's method of educating the reader by involving him as an indirect participant in a Platonic-Socratic dialectic between Christ and Satan. Plato's dialogues use (a) an oblique method of suggesting enigmatic answers that arise from surface contradictions; (b) riddles and questions that make the reader unable to distill a set doctrine from them; (c) myth, allegory, and fable to move toward poetic truths. The overall pattern of the dialogues is from darkness to light. In *Paradise Regained*, the debate between Christ and Satan follows the Platonic pattern. As Christ exposes Satan's definitions, the silent participant in the dialogue (the reader) gradually progresses from ignorance to awareness. That *Paradise Regained* is in dialogue form helps particularly to elucidate Christ's position in refusing Satan's offering of Athenian wisdom. Christ's sharp rebuff of the temptation is a barbed method of cautioning the reader against yearning for codified wisdom, an anathema to the dialectic process itself. The dialectic encourages us to distinguish between knowledge simply taken over and knowledge which is achieved through "much arguing" and "many opinions." Involvement in the dialectic process helps us to separate falsity from truth in order to reach the ultimate joy of the good life: a glimpse of paradise regained for mankind.

CRITICS HAVE extensively examined the form of *Paradise Regained*. They have viewed it as a drama, a morality play, an ecclesiastical allegory, an exemplar of the "triple equation," an inner ritual, a formal meditation, an epic, an anti-epic, and a brief epic like the Book of Job.[1] It may seem superfluous to view the work from still another vantage point, but the Socratic dialogue also should be discussed as a basis for the analysis of *Paradise Regained.*

Miltonists have long recognized that *Paradise Regained* owes much to the Socratic dialogue. Irene Samuel, without discussing the dialogue form of *Paradise Regained,* has emphasized Milton's assimilation of "themes and arguments" from Plato. A. S. P. Woodhouse has called *Paradise Regained* "a dialogue set in a framework of narrative"; Merritt Y. Hughes, "a kind of philosophic dialogue with the climax of a Greek tragedy"; Herbert Agar, "a series of Socratic dialogues." "In spite of the mountains," observes Agar, "or the storms, or the other stage settings, each of the scenes between Jesus and Satan resolves into an argument concerning the wisdom or folly of some particular attitude toward life."[2]

Although the Socratic dialogue as a generic resource for *Paradise Regained* has been clear to many, its form as such has not been a subject of intense study.[3] This may be because the dialogues themselves are not uniform and because a complete parallel between *Paradise Regained* and Plato's dialogues does not exist. However, understanding the pattern of the dialogues helps particularly to illuminate Milton's method of educating the reader as an indirect participant in a dialectic between Christ and Satan. Milton uses the dialogue form to engage the reader in the issues of the philosophical debate.

In order to understand the dialogue form, it is helpful to refer to Aristotle, who groups together the "Socratic Conversation" of Plato and the mimes of Sophron and Xenarchus.[4] This grouping implies that the dialogue[5] and farcical drama are realistic, familiar, and comedic.[6] The dialogue differs from drama in that it presents a mental contest rather than a physical conflict. As Friedrich Gundolf observes, "The dialogue is the appropriate literary form for the discussion of human antagonisms, the drama for their embodiment."[7] The dialogue enacts Socrates' efforts to examine people's values. As a consequence, the reader becomes a silent participant in the combat. "A [Platonic] dialogue has not taken place," notes Jacob Klein, "if we, the listeners or readers, did not actively participate in it; lacking such participation, all that is before us is indeed nothing but a book."[8]

According to Diogenes Laertius, "Aristotle says that the genre of Plato's dialogues lies between poetry and prose."[9] Like poetry, the dialogue uses an oblique method of suggesting truths. It weaves riddles into the context, hinting at enigmatic answers that may arise from surface contradictions. Also, like poetry, the dialogue does not allow the reader to distill a set philosophical doctrine from it. Klein observes: "The dramatic answers may not refer directly to the questions asked but may refer to those implied in, or intimately connected with, them."[10] Similarly, both the Platonic dialogue and poetry often employ myth, allegory, and fable. They move beyond the logical argument and soar upward toward poetic truths that capture the central meaning of the dialogue (for example, the Allegory of the Cave, in the *Republic*, which represents the progression toward truth, "to the light from the darkness";[11] and Aristophanes' story of the origin of human nature, in the *Symposium*, which explores the meaning of love [189c–93d]).

In the Platonic dialogues the characters' moral aspect, or *ethos*, and their reasoning part, or *dianoia*, are clearly exposed: the *ethos* by what they choose and avoid; the *dianoia* by how they prove or disprove arguments.[12] Plato offers no narrative commentary to expand on traits revealed in dialogue. Milton, on the other hand, uses the epic device of evaluative commentary as he adapts the dialogue form to his own purposes.

James Geddes poetically describes the plight of the Sophists who debate with Socrates: "The absurdity of the definition is exposed; a second attempted; and found equally ridiculous; then a third, just as bad as the former. By this time, the antagonist, if modest, withdraws as softly as he can: but, if insolent and proud of his fame for eloquence, he turns in a fury . . . and pours forth all the ill-natured language he is master of."[13] Milton captures the essence of such confusion and fury in Satan: "inly stung with anger and disdain" (*PR* I, 466), "mute confounded what to say" (III, 2), "struck / With guilt of his own sin" (III, 146–47), "swoln with rage" (IV, 499).[14]

Thus, Satan is a caricature of Sophists who have been exposed by Socrates. These include Critias (who tries to conceal his perplexity because he is ashamed to admit that he cannot answer Socrates' challenge [*Charmides*, 169c–d]), Protagoras (who gets involved in multiple contradictions as he tries to rectify the "terrible confusion" of his ideas [*Protagoras*, 349b–51e]), and Euthyphro (who becomes hurt and confounded when Socrates exposes the fallacies in his argument [*Euthyphro*, 15e]). In *Paradise Regained*, Christ, like Socrates, unmasks the "weak arguing and fallacious drift" (III, 4) of the Adversary.

The overall pattern of the Platonic dialectic in *Paradise Regained* is similar to that observed in the Allegory of the Cave (*Republic,* 514a–17a). It is an upward progression from ignorance to awareness, from prejudiced opinion toward the "loftier order of Being" by men "so habituated to their cave-like existence and so fettered to the senses and their insistent clamor that the cognition of superior reality, though implicit, is inhibited and suppressed."[15] It is the pattern of Socrates' quest: "an art of the speediest and most effective shifting or conversion of the soul, not an art of producing vision in it, but . . . an art of bringing this about" (*Republic,* 518d). The dialogue functions to free man from a world dictated by material concerns and accepted conventions. The Socratic need to question the assumptions of mankind parallels Christ's questioning of the worldly values presented by Satan, values which are so close to those of most readers.[16]

At the onset of the First Temptation, Satan tries to turn Christ—and the silent participant, the reader—toward distrust of the good, of God's providence, by stressing material concerns. The fiend observes that Christ is alone "far from path or road of men" (*PR* I, 322) for forty days. He stresses that people live in hardship: "on tough roots and stubs, to thirst inur'd / More than the Camel, and to drink go far" (I, 339–40). Christ's response sets the stage for affirming his value system and questioning our own:

> *Moses* was forty days, nor eat nor drank,
> And forty days *Eliah* without food
> Wander'd this barren waste; the same I now:
> Why dost thou then suggest to me distrust.   (I, 352–55)

In the dialectic of *Paradise Regained,* the movement is from concerns of this world to deeper realizations; from reliance on false opinion, such as Satan's, to trust in the highest order of goodness. Christ, representing the best in man, constantly questions the worldly orientation of Satan. This is most obvious in the Second Temptation, which offers Christ the power and glory of the Kingdoms of the World, as a means to carry out two parts of his mediatorial role: those of King and Prophet.[17]

To aid Christ in his mission as King, Satan offers him empire; for his prophetic function of rendering God's word, Satan offers rhetoric and learning. According to worldly values, the Sophist argues, armies are needed for empire; rhetoric and worldly knowledge for persuasion. The crowd has to be moved: "Great acts require great means of enterprise; / Thou art unknown, unfriended, low of birth" (II, 412–13). Satan advises: "Get Riches first, get Wealth, and Treasure heap." "They whom I favor," continues the fiend, "thrive in wealth amain, / While Virtue, Valor, Wisdom sit in want" (II, 427–31). To this, Jesus "patiently" replies, "Yet Wealth without these three is impotent." He explains: "Extol not Riches then, the toil of Fools, / The wise man's cumbrance if not snare, more apt / To slacken Virtue and abate her edge" (II, 433–55). Jesus' stand resembles that of Socrates to the citizens: "It is my task to tell you that virtue does not spring from wealth, but that wealth and every other good that comes to men in private life or in public proceed from virtue" (*Apology*, 30b).[18] To see Jesus or Socrates as a God here is to misread the point being made. Both are showing their sufficiency as human beings. Both understand that virtue provides its own personal reward. This is a point that Satan cannot understand. It is what the reader gradually begins to appreciate.

Satan's distortions during the debate bring the reader into the struggle: the reader must discern the inconsistencies in the rhetoric of the fiend. Satan argues:

> wherefore deprive
> All Earth her wonder at thy acts, thyself
> The fame and glory, glory the reward
> That sole excites to high attempts.   (III, 23–26)

The Sophist misrepresents the motivation that underlies heroism. Fame and glory do excite mankind, but that is not the sole incentive for virtuous men.[19] In fact, as Jesus asserts, if one acts for glory alone, "The deed becomes unprais'd" (III, 103). The Savior of mankind criticizes Satan's attitude because it represents the distorted value system of the masses, the "herd confus'd, / A miscellaneous rabble" (III, 49–50). Jesus instructs: "For what is glory but the blaze of fame, / The people's praise" (III, 47–48). He explains that the glory of the crowd is far from the "true glory and renown" of "The just man" (III, 60–62). Jesus' statements show that he is criticizing not only Satan, but mankind (the reader) as well. To support his point on false glory, Christ mentions Socrates, his precursor:

> Poor *Socrates* (who next more memorable?)
> By what he taught and suffer'd for so doing,
> For truth's sake suffering death unjust, lives now
> Equal in fame to proudest Conquerors.   (III, 96–99)

As the dialectic between Christ and Satan advances, the Sophist not only becomes tangled in statements that are contradicted by Christ but also contradicts his own conclusions. Salient examples of self-contradiction are Satan's comment "all hope is lost / Of my reception into grace; what worse? / For where no hope is left, *is left no fear*" (III, 204–06, italics added) and his expression of fear of the Father, occurring shortly after: "Whose ire *I dread more* than the fire of Hell" (III, 220, italics added). Milton uses such contrarieties in word and action to expose the moral weakness of the fiend.[20] Satan claims that God the Father "seeks glory. / And for his glory all things made" (III, 110–11). Jesus instructs him that "to show forth his goodness" (III, 124) was God's aim. Then the interlocutor, as in a Socratic dialogue, glimpses his own frailty: that he himself, having no concern for goodness, "Insatiable of glory had lost all" (III, 148). Satan, in his dialectic with Jesus, is in the ironic position of a Platonic Sophister "sweating and turmoyling under the inevitable, and mercilesse dilemma's of Socrates" (*Apology for Smectymnuus*, YP, I, 880). Milton employs these means to ridicule the fiend and the values he upholds.

Mankind's strong inclination for the material values of Satan emerges (to our chagrin) in the Temptation of Athens, where Satan offers Athenian wisdom for Jesus' role as Prophet. The temptation is so potent because it appeals to man's vain desire to *acquire* knowledge, to have it distilled in capsule form. Socrates, recognizing the evils of such codified knowledge, did not write for posterity, and Plato was reluctant to make permanent the Socratic dialogues. In the *Phaedrus*, Socrates states: "He would be a very simple person . . . who should leave in writing or receive in writing any art under the idea that the written word would be intelligible or certain" (275d–e).[21] In *Epistle VII*, Plato asserts that "every serious man in dealing with really serious subjects carefully avoids writing" (344c). Milton, likewise, feared unargued truths. In *Areopagitica* he criticizes his contemporaries for their desire to grasp authoritative tenets "measur'd" by the "bushel" (YP, II, 559). Satan's gift of wisdom is antithetical to "knowledge in the making" (YP, II, 554). It is antithetical to the dialectical process of Socrates, who, as Leonard Nelson explains, would continually cause his interlocutors to examine their premises, "to separate knowledge simply taken over from the truth that slowly attains clarity in us through our own reflection."[22] Milton believed in the growth of knowledge from "much arguing, much writing, many opinions" (YP, II, 554), as did Socrates, who shows such happiness when the slave boy (in the *Meno*) admits ignorance and wants to search for knowledge. Socrates cautions Meno: "I merely ask questions and do not teach him; and be on the watch to see if at any point you find me teaching him or expounding to him, instead of questioning him on his opinions" (84c–d). To attempt to hand knowledge to another vitiates the truth, making it colorless, external, valueless.[23] For the recipient, the "very truth . . . becomes his heresie" (*Areopagitica*, YP, II, 543).

To instruct the reader that presented truths are useless, Milton's Christ responds sharply to Satan as he enigmatically criticizes the offering of Athenian wisdom:

> But these are false, or little else but dreams,
> Conjectures, fancies, built on nothing firm.
> The first and wisest of them all profess'd
> To know this only, that he nothing knew.   (*PR* IV, 291–94)

That Socrates himself declared his wisdom to be "meagre, as disputable as a dream" (*Symposium*, 175e) and that he was recognized as the wisest of men specifically because he confessed his own ignorance (*Apology*, 21a–23b) should help us understand this passage, which has so perplexed readers. Its tone has been described as "tense, vehement, almost savage in places,"[24] unfitting for the Savior of mankind. The passage, however, can best be understood as a barbed method of cautioning an audience against yearning for codified wisdom, an anathema to the educational process of Socrates.

Milton summons the reader to rise to the occasion and see through the "winning words" of the fiend. Miltonists have explained that pagan learning is below Hebrew learning and that Jesus seeks only "Light from above, from the fountain of light" (*PR* IV, 289) for his role as Prophet of his church. But the caustic quality in Christ's denunciation of the Temptation of Athens is not primarily caused, as critics claim, by Milton's sacrifice of pagan knowledge to knowledge of God's ways.[25] Milton uses bitterness to rebuke the reader for being duped, for desiring "things transitory and vain" (*PL* III, 446), the substance of a Paradise of Fools; for not realizing that the offer itself, without comparison to higher truths, is valueless.

The conflict between Christ and Satan, for many critics, appears lacking in "narrative suspense and dramatic sympathy."[26] The perfect heroism of Christ is appreciated on a conceptual, but not a dramatic level. It is possible, observes Northrop Frye, that *Paradise Regained* may be "a magnificent success in its structure and yet often tired and perfunctory in its execution."[27] It seems, however, that it is precisely the execution of the verbal combat between Christ and Satan that does draw us in as silent participants in a Platonic dialogue. The dialectic makes us aware of the inadequacies of a value system based on the power and glory of the Kingdoms of the World. As our awareness grows, we become rather abashed and critical of the misdirection of our daily lives.

It is of interest that modern critics have become caught up in the clash of the disparate value systems of Christ and his tempter as revealed in *Paradise Regained*. For Lawrence Hyman, "Christ's rejection of Satan and of the world that Satan represents is a rejection of us," of "human values and human feelings. . . . We also react as human beings to the *terrible price* that must be paid for our salvation" (italics added). For Stanley Fish, on the other hand, the distance between man and Christ, though apparent early in the poem, diminishes as the reader gradually appreciates the need to deny the self in order to become one with God. The reader progresses toward an epiphany: "To say 'I am nothing' is to be (with God) everything." Northrop Frye's observation parallels that of Fish: "The Christian must learn . . . to perform real acts in God's time and not pseudo-acts in his own."[28] Although these last two observations are implicit in *Paradise Regained,* the poem emphasizes Jesus' humanity, and the instruction is for self-realization, not "selflessness." The progression in *Paradise Regained* is toward man's realization of his potential sufficiency to rise above his fallen condition.

Our reaction to Christ resembles our reaction to Socrates in the *Apology, Crito,* and *Phaedo.* We, like Crito, wish that Socrates would save his life, and at the same time we tremble with joyous appreciation as he affirms man's sufficiency to stand against temptation. As we watch Socrates, our weaknesses are exposed, but our potential to rise is confirmed. So, too, in *Paradise Regained.* We experience a bitter awareness of our fallen condition, but also a desire to change, to perfect ourselves as much as possible in this world. The combat between Christ and Satan educates us to comprehend good through its opposition to evil—in Satan and in ourselves. In this sense we learn by "what is contrary" (*Areopagitica,* YP, II, 515). This does not distance us, but rather involves us in a rebirth in this world, anticipatory to our rebirth in the eternal future. In the *Theaetetus,* Socrates claims to be a midwife for men:

I look after their souls when they are in labour, and not after their bodies: and the triumph of my art is in thoroughly examining whether the thought which the mind of the young man brings forth is a false idol or a noble and true birth. (150b–c)[29]

This is the essence of the dialogue. It effects the reader's reawakening or rebirth; it kindles his "undazl'd eyes at the full midday beam; purging and unscaling . . . [his] long abused sight at the fountain it self of heav'nly radiance" (*Areopagitica*, YP, II, 558).

Milton moves beyond logical argument to myth and allegory, as Plato does in his dialogues. Plato achieves the advance from darkness to light through the use of such myths as Socrates' account of the underworld, the earth on which we live, and the real surface of the whole (*Phaedo*, 110b–14c); his account of the upward motion of the charioteer, depicting true love, in the Myth of the Soul (*Phaedrus*, 246a–54e); and the account of the Allegory of the Cave (*Republic*, 514a–17a). Likewise, Milton uses myth and allegory to evoke the powers of our imagination. He compares the conflict between Christ and Satan to that between Hercules and Antaeus (the spirit and the earth combating), and the fall of Satan to the headlong leap of the Sphinx (amazed that her riddle has been unraveled by man and that her power has ended).

Milton differs from Plato by subordinating pagan myth to Christian theology in order to afford the reader a glimpse of the time when "Earth be chang'd to Heav'n, and Heav'n to Earth" (*PL* VII, 160). Christ's power is revealed at the close of the dialectic when Satan, by adjuring "Cast thyself down" (*PR* IV, 555), unwittingly invokes associations of Christ's offer of himself as supreme sacrifice—the function of his unique High-Priestly role:

Such a high priest does indeed fit our condition—devout, guileless, undefiled, separated from sinners, raised high above the heavens. He has no need to offer sacrifices daily, as the high priests do, first for his own sins and then for those of the people; for this he did once and for all when he offered up himself. (Hebrews vii, 26–27)

Here, also, Satan's ineffectual actions are ridiculed as his desperate attempt of vengeance and despair serves to parody God's design that the Crucifixion—and thus the redemption of mankind—occur.[30] Christ rejects Satan's temptation. He literally and symbolically stands firm while the Adversary, "smitten with amazement," falls: "Also it is written, / Tempt not the Lord thy God; he said and stood. / But Satan smitten with amazement fell" (*PR* IV, 560–62). At the close of the dialectic, Christ "achieves," as Lewalski observes, "a full understanding of and typologically figures forth his sacrificial priestly office."[31] In addition, the silent participant in the dialogue (the reader), by means of Milton's allusions to Christian theology, progresses toward a fuller awareness of Christ's virtue.

Such descriptions of Christ's rise and Satan's fall call to mind multiple theological allusions: the fall of Satan from the Son in Book VI of *Paradise Lost;* the prophecy in Revelation of Satan's inevitable fall "Under his feet" (*PR* IV, 621) in the Second Coming; the final defeat of Satan, predicted in Genesis, when Christ will "bruise / The Serpent's head" (*PL* X, 1031–32); the prediction by Isaiah of the destruction of the sea monster Leviathan or the hooking of the sea serpent at the Last Judgment; and the prophecy in Revelation that the seven-headed dragon will be destroyed.[32]

Like the dialogues of Plato, *Paradise Regained* establishes a mock set of values and a mock ruler (the Prince of Darkness), and by the process of a mental combat enables the reader to choose to reject the values of the Sophist and adopt those of Christ, "Our second Adam," and Socrates, the wisest of pagan men. It encourages us to distinguish between falsity and truth, the shadow and the reality, in order to reach the ultimate joy of the good life: a glimpse of paradise regained for mankind.

University of Delaware

NOTES

1. See, for instance, Arnold Stein, *Heroic Knowledge* (1957; reprint ed., Hamden, Conn., 1965), pp. 3–134; E. M. W. Tillyard, *Milton* (London, 1930), pp. 316–19; Howard Schultz, "Christ and Antichrist in *Paradise Regained*," *PMLA*, LXVII (1952), 790–808; Elizabeth Marie Pope, *Paradise Regained: The Tradition and the Poem* (1947; reprint ed., New York, 1962); Jackson I. Cope, "*Paradise Regained:* Inner Ritual," in *Milton Studies*, I, ed., James D. Simmonds (Pittsburgh, 1969), 51–65; Louis L. Martz, *The Paradise Within* (New Haven, 1964), pp. 171–201; Merritt Y. Hughes, "The Christ of *Paradise Regained* and the Renaissance Heroic Tradition," *SP*, XXXV (1938), 254–77; Ralph Waterbury Condee, "Milton's Dialogue with the Epic: *Paradise Regained* and the Tradition," *YR*, LIX (1970), 357–75; Barbara Kiefer Lewalski, *Milton's Brief Epic* (Providence: Brown University Press, 1966); and Donald L. Guss, "A Brief Epic: *Paradise Regained*," *SP*, LXVIII (1971), 223–43.

2. Samuel, *Plato and Milton* (1947; reprint ed., Ithaca, 1965), p. 21; Woodhouse,

"Theme and Pattern in *Paradise Regained, UTQ,* XXV (1956), 168; Hughes, in his note in *John Milton: Complete Poems and Major Prose* (New York, 1957), p. 480; and Agar, *Milton and Plato* (Princeton, 1928), p. 10.

3. Most critics seem to take a stand similar to Northrop Frye's: *Paradise Regained*'s "closest affinities are with the debate and with the dialectical colloquy of Plato and Boethius." "But," he cautions, "these forms usually either incorporate one argument into another dialectically or build up two different cases rhetorically" ("The Typology of *Paradise Regained,*" MP, LIII [1956], 235). Clifford Davidson ("The Dialectic of Temptation," *Ball State University Forum,* VIII [Summer 1967], 11–16) is the only critic, to my knowledge, to consider seriously the relationship between the Socratic dialogue and *Paradise Regained*. His article, however, focuses primarily on one aspect of the dialectic: the contrarieties observed in Plato and *Paradise Regained*, and their exposition in Milton's *Artis logicae* and Ramist philosophy.

4. Ingram Bywater, trans., *De Poetica,* in *The Works of Aristotle,* ed. W. D. Ross (Oxford, 1924), XI, 1447b.

5. With the exception of the *Apology, Crito,* and *Phaedo,* which tend toward the tragic.

6. See William Chase Greene, "The Spirit of Comedy in Plato," *Harvard Studies in Classical Philology,* XXXI (1920), 63–64. See also Eugene R. Purpus, "The 'Plain, Easy, and Familiar Way': The Dialogue in English Literature, 1660–1725," *ELH,* XVII (1950), 47–58. Purpus does not mention *Paradise Regained*. Milton's appreciation of comedy in the dialogue is excellently shown in *Apology for Smectymnuus:* "Because there is scarce one of them, especially wherein some notable Sophister lies sweating and turmoyling under the inevitable, and mercilesse dilemma's of Socrates, but that hee who reads . . . would be often rob'd of more then a smile" (*An Apology Against a Pamphlet,* in *Complete Prose Works of John Milton,* ed. Don M. Wolfe et al. [New Haven, 1953], I, 880, hereafter cited as YP).

7. *Goethe* (Berlin, 1925), p. 488, as quoted in Paul Friedländer, *Plato,* trans. Hans Meyerhoff (New York, 1958), I, 367.

8. *A Commentary on Plato's Meno* (Chapel Hill, 1965), p. 6.

9. W. D. Ross, trans. and ed., *Select Fragments,* in *The Works of Aristotle* (Oxford, 1952), XII, 74. Most of what Aristotle wrote on the dialogue is no longer extant.

10. *A Commentary on Plato's Meno,* p. 17. See also John Hartland-Swann, "Plato as Poet: A Critical Interpretation," *Philosophy,* XXVI (1951), 12.

11. *The Republic,* 518c, from the translation by Paul Shorey, *Plato: The Republic,* Loeb Classical Library (London, 1935), II. Except where indicated in a note, references are to the translation in the Loeb Classical Library edition.

12. See Aristotle's discussion of these terms (*De Poetica,* 1450b). See also Dorothy Tarrant, "Style and Thought in Plato's Dialogues," *Classical Quarterly,* XLII (1948), 29.

13. James Geddes, *An Essay on the Composition and Manner of Writing of the Antients* (1748; reprint ed., New York, 1970), p. 100.

14. *John Milton: Complete Poems and Major Prose,* ed. Merritt Y. Hughes (New York, 1957). Parenthetic references to Milton's poetry are to this edition.

15. Robert E. Cushman, *Therapeia: Plato's Conception of Philosophy* (Chapel Hill, 1958), p. 143.

16. James Holly Hanford has suggested that Satan comes out to tempt the reader. Satan is "directing his appeal through Christ to humanity at large. Milton slightly masks his purpose by insisting on the human rather than the divine aspect of Christ" ("The Temptation Motive in Milton," *SP,* XV [1918], 181).

17. See Lewalski's discussion of the mediatorial office (*Milton's Brief Epic*, pp. 182–92).

18. Lane Cooper, trans., *Euthyphro, Apology, Crito, Phaedo* (Ithaca, 1941), p. 64.

19. See Samuel's discussion of fame (*Plato and Milton*, pp. 93–95).

20. Milton explains: "Opposites cannot be attributed to the same thing if they are supposed to work with respect to the same thing, under the same relations, and at the same time" (*Artis logicae*, trans. Allan H. Gilbert, in *The Works of John Milton*, ed. Frank Allan Patterson et al. [New York, 1935], XI, 111); see also Davidson, "Dialectic of Temptation," pp. 12–13.

21. From the translation by B. Jowett, *The Dialogues of Plato* (1871; reprint ed., Oxford, 1931), I, 485.

22. *Socratic Method and Critical Philosophy*, trans. Thomas K. Brown (New Haven, 1949), p. 24.

23. Milton asserts: "That vertue therefore which is but a youngling in the contemplation of evill, and knows not the utmost that vice promises to her followers, and rejects it, is but a blank vertue, not a pure; her whitenesse is but an excrementall whitenesse" (*Areopagitica*, YP II, 515–16).

24. Martz, *Paradise Within*, p. 197.

25. Hanford (Temptation Motive," pp. 183–84) explains the rejection in terms of Milton's conviction: "he who receives / Light from above, from the fountain of light, / No other doctrine needs" (*PR* IV, 288–90); Irene Samuel says that Jesus "praises the truth his mind already possesses as superior to the truth he could gain from Greek literature" ("Milton on Learning and Wisdom," *PMLA*, LXIV [1949], 719). See also John Steadman, "*Paradise Regained*: Moral Dialectic and the Pattern of Rejection," *UTQ*, XXXI (1962), 426; Howard Schultz, "A Fairer Paradise? Some Recent Studies of *Paradise Regained*," *ELH*, XXXII (1965), 278; Martz, *Paradise Within*, pp. 198–99; and Frye, "Typology of *Paradise Regained*," p. 235. E. M. W. Tillyard observes, "In Christ's speech there is a tone of anger, for which I fail to make dramatic propriety or historical precedent account. Christ speaks superbly, but somehow he protests too much" ("The Christ of *Paradise Regained* and the Renaissance Heroic Tradition," *SP*, XXXVI [1939], 252). Douglas Bush comments, "It is painful indeed to watch Milton turn and rend some main roots of his being" (*The Renaissance and English Humanism* [Toronto, 1939], p. 125).

26. Frye, "Typology of *Paradise Regained*," p. 234.

27. Ibid., pp. 234–35.

28. Hyman, "The Reader's Attitude in *Paradise Regained*," *PMLA*, LXXXV (1970), 503, 500; Fish, "Inaction and Silence: The Reader in *Paradise Regained*," in *Calm of Mind*, ed. Joseph Anthony Wittreich (Cleveland, 1971), p. 44; Frye, "Typology of *Paradise Regained*," p. 235.

29. From the translation by Jowett, IV, 203.

30. That the Father willed Christ's crucifixion is indicated by Christ's prayer of submission to death in the Garden of Gethsemane: "Father, if it be thy will, take this cup away from me. Yet not my will but thine be done" (Luke xxii, 42). In this light, Satan's command that Christ cast himself from the pinnacle appears as a parody of God's decree that Christ be killed for mankind's redemption.

31. *Milton's Brief Epic*, p. 305.

32. See Frye's excellent elaboration of the value of such typological references ("Typology of *Paradise Regained*," pp. 227–38).

MILTON'S BIBLICAL STYLE
IN *PARADISE REGAINED*

Emory Elliott

In *Paradise Regained*, Milton employs biblical allusions in several significant ways. Through the very words and phrases of Scripture, he draws into the poem essential details of the encircling framework of Christ's total career and teaching, and he thereby puts the particular episode of the temptations into a biblical perspective. Many allusions recall biblical passages which emphasize Christ's humanity—his diligence in the study of the Scripture, his compassion for all men, and his passion and death. Other allusions serve to point up the superior exegetical principles which enable Christ to make Satan appear foolish in his misinterpretations of the Scriptures. Throughout the debates between Christ and Satan, allusions to the epistles of Paul and to the book of Revelation also provide a structural tension between the restraint and self-discipline needed in this world which are stressed in the Pauline allusions in the poem's early books and the eternal reward or punishment of the next world which is stressed in the allusions to Revelation, which increase near the poem's conclusion. Through his manipulations of biblical allusions, Milton alerts his readers to important nuances of Christ's victory and of the poem's meaning.

M OST CRITICS of *Paradise Regained* appear to agree with Professor Balachandra Rajan that it is for modern readers "a poem difficult of access."[1] To be sure, recent studies of this poem have made the poem more accessible by focusing attention upon the identity motif and upon the poem's inner ritual and have thus led to new appreciations of its dramatic qualities. However, as absorbing as such universal themes are, these readings isolate the conflict between Christ and Satan from the background of the cosmic drama of Christ's life and history which is an integral part of Milton's poem. They also tend to slight the complexity of Milton's style. For it is a remarkable feature of Milton's style in *Paradise Regained* that he uses the very words and phrases of Scripture to draw into the poem essential details of the encircling framework of Christ's total career and teachings. Much of the aesthetic pleasure which comes from reading *Paradise Regained* depends, I believe, upon an appreciation of Milton's poetic achievement, and it is therefore primarily through a deeper understanding of Milton's style in *Paradise Regained* that the poem becomes more accessible.[2]

As the narrator points out in the opening lines, the greater drama of Christ's lifelong work of salvation is not external to the dramatic action of the poem. This account of the temptations should not be read apart from the written record of Christ's public life as reported in the Scriptures. Because the narrator views himself as a poet-evangelist, he calls upon the Holy Spirit to inspire his work as He inspired the writers of the Gospels so that he might report, rather than create, the additional details of Christ's encounter with Satan which have been temporarily unrecorded. He asks the Spirit:

> inspire,
> As thou art wont, my prompted Song, else mute,
> And bear through height or depth of nature's bounds
> With prosperous wing full summ'd to tell of deeds
> Above Heroic, though in secret done,
> And unrecorded left through many an Age,
> Worthy t' have not remain'd so long unsung.   (I, 11–17)[3]

Thus, to read this account of the wilderness duel out of its scriptural context would be similar to trying to arrive at a total evaluation of Christ's character after reading only the episode of his expelling the money changers from the temple. Such are the limits of Satan's understanding, but they need not be those of Milton's readers.[4]

Indeed, much of the poem's dramatic power depends upon the reader's awareness of those aspects of Christ's life and character of which Satan is ignorant. For example, in the last lines of Christ's rejection of the temptation of glory which occurs in the very middle of *Paradise Regained*, Milton carefully placed one of the poem's most obvious biblical allusions. In the dispassionate and restrained style characteristic of Milton's young Messiah, Christ declares: "Besides, to give a Kingdom hath been thought / Greater and nobler done, and to lay down / Far more magnanimous than to assume" (II, 481–83). His words echo the familiar passage of John which describes the profound selflessness and human compassion which are the guiding principles of Christ's life and death: "Greater love hath no man than this, that a man lay down his life for his friends" (John xv, 13).[5] The allusion here keeps the reader conscious of this ultimate sacrifice and of the revolutionary nature of the New Testament spirit that the young Christ is in the process of creating. At the same time, Satan knows only that there is a meaning in Christ's words which he cannot grasp: he stands "mute, confounded . . . confuted and convinc't / Of his weak arguing and fallacious drift" (III, 2–4).

In *Paradise Regained,* Milton employs biblical allusions in at least two significant ways. First, many of the scriptural passages to which he alludes emphasize the humanity of the young Christ. Milton's Christ is a young man who is in the process of refining and developing his human nature toward a more mature Christ who will undergo the passion and crucifixion. The allusions call attention to the years of careful preparation preceding his victory over Satan's temptations and his role as an example to all men of the virtues of humility, obedience, and diligence, especially in the study of the Scriptures. Since the central dramatic interest in the poem must be *how* Christ thwarts Satan rather than *that he does,* the poem focuses upon Christ's victory as proof of the power of the Scriptures in providing men not some esoteric knowledge which transcends human experience, but the practical knowledge of the world needed to defeat a Satan who has been educated in the weaker school of worldly experience without the Scriptures.[6] In the wilderness, Christ is forced to endure irrelevant temptations from the subhuman creature which has been the source of all the pain and vileness in the world. This experience calls for particular character traits of controlled severity and calculated indifference and, as a superior young leader, Christ naturally has these traits in his repertory. Through his allusions, Milton puts the particular episode of Christ's life presented in the poem in a greater perspective and keeps before his reader the extraordinary quality of Christ's understanding and compassion which motivated him throughout his ministry and in his final act of charity.

Second, the allusions also bear upon the poem's theme of the right use and interpretation of the Scriptures themselves. Because the young Christ is not perfect until the poem ends, there is always the chance, the risk, that during his debate with Satan he will misinterpret the meaning of the New Covenant and his role in it.[7] He might err in seeing the mission of the Messiah in the "Jewish" way against which the Pauline epistles, especially Romans, warn. In the poem the Scriptures are laid open for both Christ and Satan—as well as Milton's readers—to interpret, and the issue which lies behind the debate is one of critical principles. Christ interprets rightly because he approaches the sacred writings with steadfast faith formed by patient and humble inductive readings of the Bible: he lets the writings themselves and divine inspiration shape his understanding. In contrast, Satan comes to the Scriptures with an arrogance growing out of his preconceived opinions about the irrelevance of the biblical experience to present world events. Thus he twists and tortures the meaning of the Bible to satisfy his own previous notions, and he foolishly misinterprets; he can only understand Christ's kingdom in worldly terms.

Through his use of scriptural allusions to the Old and New Testaments, Milton also keeps before his readers both the continuity of sacred history and the significance of the young Christ's mission as creator of a new world. He stresses the contrast between the old and the new by using biblical allusions to create an imagery of opposites: childhood vs. maturity, death vs. life, lies vs. truth, slavery vs. freedom, and blindness vs. vision. Before the fulfillment men lived in an old world dominated by Satan in which men were as children, blinded to the truth of the sacred writings by their propensity for lies and by their ignorance, which allowed them to be duped by Satan into a life of sin leading to spiritual death. With the New and Final Dispensation men have become mature, and through the grace earned for them by Christ they are capable of using the truth of the Gospel to follow a path of patience, obedience, faith, and good works leading to everlasting life with Christ.

Throughout the debates between Christ and his enemy, Milton's scriptural allusions to the epistles of Paul and to the Book of Revelation provide a structural tension between the restraint and self-discipline needed in this world, which are stressed in the early allusions to Paul, and the extremes of misery or of eternal joy in the next world, which are underlined by the allusions to the book of Revelation which increase near the close of the poem. These biblical allusions heighten the poem's crescendo of emotional intensity, which corresponds to the slow historical process moving toward the Final Judgment and Christ's ultimate victory. In the first book, the allusions refer the reader to passages of Scripture which clarify and emphasize the importance of Christ's mission in establishing the New Dispensation and which identify the role that God expects men to take in his New Covenant. As Book I reaches completion, allusions appear to passages which stress the punishment that awaits those who refuse to participate in the new order and the reward awaiting those who are responsive. In Books II and III, passages which echo Paul's teachings on reward and punishment become more frequent and more emotional and are ironically played off against the debate between Satan and Christ over the values of the earthly and heavenly kingdoms. Book IV presents a series of allusions to verses which envision the final destruction of Satan and his world and the establishment of the kingdom of Christ at the Second Coming. Attention here is also focused upon the role of the individual and the church in bringing about Christ's kingdom on earth. The pattern of frequency of allusions to the book of Revelation indicates this gradual heightening of emotional intensity: three allusions in Book I, one in Book II, six in Book III, and fourteen in Book IV, ten of which appear in the last fifty lines of the poem. Thus, for the alert reader who brings to the poem an acquaintance with the Scriptures, especially of Paul and the book of Revelation, Milton's manipulations of biblical allusions provide another dimension to the poem's aesthetic achievement.

The narrator's opening lines firmly establish both the use of biblical allusions as an integral part of the style of *Paradise Regained* and the importance of Paul's epistles as a source of many of the allusions.[8] The lines contain two unmistakable allusions to passages from the books of Romans and Ephesians, and there are fainter echoes of verses of Hebrews which have thematic relevance to Milton's poem. The epic narrator speaks:

> I who erewhile the happy Garden sung,
> By one man's disobedience lost, now sing
> Recover'd Paradise to all mankind,
> By one man's firm obedience fully tried
> Through all temptation, and the Tempter foil'd
> In all his wiles, defeated and repuls't,
> And *Eden* rais'd in the waste Wilderness.   (I, 1–7)

Behind these lines we hear St. Paul: "For as by one man's disobedience many were made sinners, so by the obedience of one shall many be made righteous" (Romans v, 19). More imporantly, the narrator's phrase, "the Tempter foiled / In all his wiles," recalls Paul's words to the Ephesians to which Milton will allude at least ten times:

Put on the whole armour of God, that ye may be able to stand against the wiles of the devil. For we wrestle not against flesh and blood, but against principalities, against powers, against the rulers of the darkness of this world. . . . Wherefore take unto you the whole armour of God, that ye may be able to withstand in the evil day, and having done all, to stand. Stand therefore, having your loins girt about with truth, . . . wherewith ye shall be able to quench all the fiery darts of the wicked. (Ephesians vi, 11–16)

Each of the Pauline passages bears upon some facet of Christ's human nature by which he will thwart the temptations in the wilderness. The passage from Ephesians also strengthens the structural unity of Milton's poem, for Paul's use of the image of the victorious Christian "standing" against the wiles of Satan underlies the climactic passage of *Paradise Regained* in which Christ "stands" and the Tempter fails. Thus the poem begins and ends with allusions to this crucial biblical passage.

For the reader who remembers Paul's words to the Ephesians as he begins reading *Paradise Regained,* the allusion provides a key to interpreting rightly the severity of Christ's answers to Satan. Paul teaches that neither the flesh nor the things of the world are evil in themselves but that every Christian should guard against their misuse by studying the "sword of the Spirit, which is the word of God" (Ephesians vi, 17) and should ready himself for the time when he will do battle with Satan. The lesson contains a veritable summary of the preparation and attitudes which Christ brings to the temptations in *Paradise Regained.* Even in his most austere statements, Christ never really repudiates the world and the flesh as things corrupt in themselves, but his answers to Satan are carefully designed to demonstrate to other men what their priority of values must be if they are to prepare themselves "to withstand in the evil day."

The narrator's opening speech also points to other passages of Paul which illuminate features of Christ's human nature. In Hebrews ii, 18 Paul explains that God allowed Christ to be tempted so that Christ could learn greater compassion for the failings of other men: "For in that he himself hath suffered being tempted, he is able to succour them that are tempted" (Hebrews ii, 18). Just as any ordinary man learns obedience, Christ learned the obedience needed to overcome temptation and death:

Who can have compassion . . . [unless] he himself also is compassed with infirmity. . . . [Christ] offered up prayers and supplications with strong crying and tears unto him that was able to save him from death . . . yet learned he obedience by the things which he suffered; And being made perfect, he became the author of eternal salvation. (Hebrews v, 2–9)

These passages from Hebrews exemplify Milton's frequent use of biblical allusions to bring into the poem parallels between the temptations and the Passion, the ultimate test of Christ's obedience and the final manifestation of his faith in the Father and his profound love of mankind.[9] Thus these allusions deepen the characterization of Milton's young Jew, alert the reader to the importance of Paul's writings to an understanding of Christ's character, and put Christ's rejections into perspective.

Within Christ's first soliloquy, the biblical allusions, again especially those to Paul, amplify the theme of total world change that Christ's victory represents. Christ tells us that since early childhood he had possessed a sense of his destiny which gave him an early maturity and solemnity:

> When I was yet a child, no childish play
> To me was pleasing, all my mind was set
> Serious to learn and know, and thence to do
> What might be public good.   (I, 201–04)

Milton's words turn upon Paul's analogy for spiritual growth and vision:

When I was a child, I spake as a child, I understood as a child, I thought as a child: but when I became a man, I put away childish things. For now we see through a glass darkly; but then face to face: now I know in part; but then I shall know even as also I am known. (1 Corinthians xiii, 11–12)

Similarly, at the end of Christ's speech Milton placed another allusion to a verse of Paul which touches the same themes and to which Milton alludes several times in *Paradise Regained*. Christ says that at the moment of his baptism by John he finally "knew the time / Now full, that I no more should live obscure" (I, 286–87). His words echo those of Galatians iv, 3–5: "So we, when we were children, were in bondage under the elements of the world: But when the fulness of the time was come, God sent forth his Son . . . that we might receive the adoption of sons." Through these allusions the message of freedom, vision, and responsibility in the Pauline passages reverberates in Milton's lines and undercuts what might otherwise seem an unappealing precocity in the young Christ.[10]

In Christ's opening speech, allusions to the Old Testament heighten the reader's understanding of the character of Christ and forward Milton's theme of the importance of careful interpretation of the sacred writings. Christ reports that he had been a diligent student of the Scriptures since childhood and that time and "again [he] revolv'd / The Law and Prophets, searching what was writ / Concerning the Messiah" (I, 259–61). Even for this quickest of all students, Milton insists, the thorough knowledge of the meaning of the Scriptures needed to prevail against the forces of evil was not attained without unrelenting effort.

Christ's words also contain allusions to passages of the Psalms which underline the importance of the right interpretation and use of the Scriptures. Christ declares that as a youth, "The Law of God I read, and found it sweet" (I, 207), and he thereby recalls the verse "How sweet are thy words unto my taste! *yea, sweeter* than honey to my mouth" (Psalm cxix, 103). Then Christ recounts his visit to the temple, where he "was admir'd by all" for his knowledge which surpassed the "Teachers of our Law" (I, 211–14), alluding to the preceding verses of the same Psalm where the speaker declares the power of Scriptures to make him more learned than his teachers and stronger than his enemies:

O how I love thy law! it *is* my meditation all the day.
Thou through thy commandments hast made me wiser than mine enemies. . . .
I have more understanding than all my teachers. . . .
I understand more than the ancients   (Psalm cxix, 97–100)

Christ's early studies had caused him to think at first of conquering his enemies in the Old Testament way, "to subdue and quell o'er all the earth / Brute violence and proud Tyrannic pow'r" (I, 218–19). As Christ had contemplated the Psalms, certain passages which foretold that the Messiah would "break them with a rod of iron" and "dash them to pieces like a potter's dish" (Psalm ii, 9) must have affected his early concepts of his mission. But Christ chose instead to interpret these passages in his own "more humane" spirit and "first / By winning words to conquer willing hearts" (I, 221–22).[11] The reader's consciousness of the words of the Scriptures which lie behind Christ's decisions deepens his appreciation of the fullness of the humanity of Milton's hero and thus intensifies the ensuing dramatic conflict between Christ and Satan.

At the beginning of Book III, Satan urges Christ to move quickly to attain his worldly kingdom through the kind of valiant action which Christ had once considered in his youth. Christ's answer (III, 43–107) is divided into two distinct parts: the first (43–87) is a preachment upon the blindness, ignorance, and immorality among the people under the Old Dispensation, and the second (87–107) presents the promise that the rewards that under the old law were available to only a few men of great vision, patience, and temperance like Job and Socrates will soon be available to many under the new. In the first part of his answer, Christ describes the ways in which men used to win earthly glory, overrunning countries and destroying all that lay before them, and within his description are echoes of the story from the Book of Joel in which the prophet used the invasion of the locusts which ravaged Juda as a metaphor for the coming of the Lord who will destroy all the wicked of the earth. His words also allude to the New Testament interpretation of the same story in St. Peter in Acts ii, 16–22, where Peter describes the destruction awaiting those who do not heed the new message of Christ. Christ's answer to Satan here, with its tough-minded attack upon the "herd confus'd" and the "miscellaneous rabble" who praise and "admire they know not what" (III, 49–52), has seemed to many to reveal an undue harshness and insensitivity in Christ which make him less appealing. But even within Christ's sharp words, Milton's phrasing points ahead to the profound act of human compassion which Christ will make for men in his entreaty: "Father, forgive them; for they know not what they do" (Luke xxiii, 34). Thus the allusions within this speech emphasize the continuity of the Old and New Testaments and deepen our understanding of Christ.

In the next exchange between Satan and Christ, Milton uses scriptural allusions ironically to point up the folly and ignorance of Satan and by implication the greater stupidity of those followers of Satan who allow weakness or stubbornness to stand between themselves and their everlasting reward.[12] While Satan argues that God is a selfish God to create creatures for the sole purpose of giving him honor and glory, he twists the doctrine that the chief end of man is to give glory to God by exploiting the phrase of the elders in Revelation iv, 11: "Thou art worthy, O Lord, to receive glory and honour." He ignores, of course, the implications for him of the passages of Revelation and of other Scriptures to which he unwittingly also alludes. Satan sneers that God "requires / Glory from men, from all men good or bad, / Wise or unwise, no difference, no exemption" (III, 113–15). But behind his lines are the lessons of Revelation xi, 13, Revelation xiv, 6, and Acts xii, 23, as well as passages of the Old Testament like Malachi ii, 2 and Isaiah xlviii, 7, all of which carry the same warnings of the destruction of those who choose not to interpret God's words correctly and heed his warnings. But Satan remains deaf and blind to these truths.

In answer to this speech and to Satan's next argument that he should be moved to action by "Zeal and Duty . . . Zeal of thy Father's house, Duty to free / Thy Country from her Heathen servitude" (III, 172–76), Christ continues to lecture upon the goodness of God in providing man with the freedom to attain an everlasting heavenly reward. Christ's lesson that God produced all things primarily to "show forth his goodness, and impart / His good communicable to every soul / Freely" (III, 124–26) recalls Paul's epistle to the Romans on God's goodness—words that would be spoken to Satan and his deaf followers in vain:

Despisest thou the riches of his goodness . . . not knowing that the goodness of God leadeth thee to repentance? . . . [God] will render to every man according to his deeds: To them who by patient continuance in well doing seek for glory and honour and immortality, eternal life; But unto them that are contentious, and do not obey the truth . . . indignation and wrath. (Romans ii, 4–8)

Also behind Christ's entire argument that God created men out of his goodness and that men, being unable to repay him for their lives, can find it easiest to give him glory and benediction there stands Paul's discourse at Athens in the midst of the Areopagus where he argued that "God that made the world and all things therein . . . neither is [he] worshiped with men's hands, as though he needed any thing, seeing he giveth to all life, and breath, and all things" (Acts xvii, 24–25). Again, the allusions to the Scriptures carry forward Milton's theme of the right interpretation of the Scriptures themselves as the key to overcoming the forces of evil. Christ comes to the Old Testament history as Paul comes to the Gospels—with a critical method based upon humility, patience, and faith—and therefore God's truth is revealed to both men.

Book IV begins with Satan's presentation of the wonders of the world to Christ. As in the dialogue of Book III, Satan's entire speech is undercut with biblical allusions which make him appear foolish by foreshadowing his own final destruction even in the midst of some of his most imaginative, poetic descriptions. For example, Satan boasts of his power and declares himself "God of this world" and of the "world beneath" (IV, 203). But the title which he so proudly claims is taken from a passage of Paul, where it appears in quite another context: "But if our gospel be hid, it is hid to them that are lost: In whom the god of this world hath blinded the minds of them which believe not" (2 Corinthians iv, 3–4).

In the scriptural allusions within Christ's speeches, however, a change begins to occur. In Book IV his lines no longer allude to passages which tell of the reward of the faithful in mild terms. They now are drawn from passages which vigorously exclaim the glory of the kingdom of heaven and Christ's kingship. In fact, the most intense scriptural passages are woven into those lines which occur after the action of the debates has reached its climax (IV, 561). At the beginning of Book IV, Christ speaks explicitly of his realm in his refusal of the worldly kingdoms:

> Know therefore when my season comes to sit
> On *David's* Throne, it shall be like a tree
> Spreading and overshadowing all the Earth,
> Or as a stone that shall to pieces dash
> All Monarchies besides throughout the world,
> And of my Kingdom there shall be no end.   (IV, 146–51)

Behind this passage are five scriptural verses which foretell the coming of Christ's kingdom. The image of the tree as a symbol of the kingdom occurs in Daniel, when Nebuchadnezzar has the dream of the great tree in the center of the world and of the stone which would smash the earthly kingdoms (iv, 11).[13] Also there are Christ's own words in Matthew that "the kingdom of heaven is like to a grain of mustard seed, which . . . becometh a tree, so that the birds of the air come and lodge in the branches thereof" (xiii, 31–32). Similarly, in Christ's next speech (170–95) his kingship is again underlined by the Scriptures. While he speaks to Satan of his Father's kingdom, the scriptural passages to which his words allude are concerned with praising the kingship of Christ. He refers, for example, to the Father as the "King of Kings" (IV, 185), but in Revelation xvii, 14, Revelation xix, 16, 1 Timothy vi, 15, and Romans ix, 5, it is Christ who is the King of Kings. All these passages continue to point ahead to the poem's conclusion, as well as to both Christ's final victory and the Second Coming, when the angels will declare that Christ has proven himself prepared to establish his kingdom.

Like Christ's early assault upon the "miscellaneous rabble," another crucial passage in Book IV has offended many readers. When Satan tries to entice Christ to act now to free the captive slaves of Rome (IV, 110–53), Christ answers in terms which appear too harsh and uncompassionate to be spoken by the Savior: "I was not sent, nor yet to free / That people victor once, now vile and base, / Deservedly made vassal" (IV, 131–33). But again an awareness of the biblical source of Christ's words mollifies the severity of his answer. Milton here recalls an episode in Matthew in which Jesus displayed the same kind of firmness in his initial refusal to aid the daughter of the Canaanite woman. At first when the woman cried out to him, he ignored her (Matthew xv, 23). As she protested, he answered: "I am not sent but unto the lost sheep of the house of Israel" (Matthew xv, 24). When she continued to display her faith in his power, however, Christ softened and consented to her plea: "O woman, great *is* thy faith: be it unto thee even as thou wilt" (Matthew xv, 28). Her daughter was immediately cured. This example of Christ's human compassion and tendency to be moved by acts of faith lies behind his stern refusal in *Paradise Regained* and suggests again that the sternness which he must display toward Satan should be viewed within the larger context of his ministry.[14]

As we noted earlier, the dominant scriptural allusions in the closing passage of *Paradise Regained* are to the book of Revelations. The substance of all the references gives scriptural emphasis to Christ's final victory over the forces of evil at the Final Judgment. Some of the passages tell of the destruction of Satan: "Fruits fetcht from the tree of life" (IV, 589) recalls "the tree of life, which bare twelve *manner of* fruits, . . . and there shall be no more curse" (Revelation xxii, 2–3); "him long of old / Thou didst debel, and down from Heav'n cast" (IV, 604–5) recalls both "And the great dragon was cast out, that old serpent, called the Devil, and Satan" (Revelation xii, 9) and "the devil that deceived them was cast into the lake of fire and brimstone" (Revelation xx, 10). These are only a few of the allusions which strengthen the apocalyptic theme of the text itself.[15] Milton concludes the passage with the description of the casting of the devils into swine from Matthew viii, 28–32 and Mark v, 7:

> hee all unarm'd
> Shall chase thee with the terror of his voice
> From thy Demoniac holds, possession foul,
> Thee and thy Legions; yelling they shall fly,
> And beg to hide them in a herd of Swine,
> Lest he command them down into the deep,
> Bound, and to torment sent before their time.   (IV, 626–32)

Finally, the allusions of this passage help to culminate the poem's central theme of the ability of every man who lives under the New Dispensation to defeat Satan in his own life through the right use of the Scriptures. In conquering temptation and death himself, Christ transmitted the necessary strength through his disciples to all who follow him. Milton's lines which refer to the "fall" of Satan (IV, 605–20) allude not only to Revelation but to the passage in Luke in which Christ told his disciples: "I beheld Satan as lightning fall from heaven. Behold, I give unto you the power to tread on serpents and scorpions, and over all the power of the enemy" (Luke x, 18–19). And the allusion to the binding of the devils (IV, 632) echoes the passage of Matthew in which Christ gave to Peter and the church his power to bind devils: "whatsoever thou shalt bind on earth shall be bound in heaven" (Matthew xvi, 19).

Without firm belief in the immediate relevance of the events of the Scriptures to the events of our daily lives, without the sense that Satan is still alive and active in the world and that Christ in all his mercy and compassion is still conscious of our trials on earth, and without the knowledge of the Bible which comes from having read, studied, and discussed it daily since childhood, we cannot expect to be engaged in the same intellectual and emotional processes with *Paradise Regained* as the seventeenth-century reader. We cannot expect to react to the character of Milton's young Jew with the same sympathy and admiration, nor can we expect the poem to have the same dramatic interest. However, when we bring to the poem a fuller understanding of Milton's style and of the significance of his manipulation of biblical allusions, *Paradise Regained* may still yield, on its own terms, a rich aesthetic experience.

Princeton University

NOTES

1. *The Lofty Rhyme: A Study of Milton's Major Poetry* (Coral Gables, 1970), p. 122; see also Lawrence W. Hyman, "The Reader's Attitude in *Paradise Regained*," *PMLA*, LXXXV (1970), 496–503.

2. On the theme of identity, see in particular Louis L. Martz, *The Paradise Within: Studies in Vaughan, Traherne, and Milton* (New Haven, 1964), especially p. 180, and Barbara Lewalski, *Milton's Brief Epic* (Providence, 1966). On the inner ritual, see Jackson I. Cope, "*Paradise Regained:* Inner Ritual," in *Milton Studies*, I, ed. James D. Simmonds (Pittsburgh, 1969), pp. 51–65. On Milton's use of the Bible in his poems, see James H. Sims, *The Bible in Milton's Epics* (Gainesville, 1962), especially his index of allusions; and Anne Bowers Long, "The Relations Between Classical and Biblical Allusions in Milton's Later Poems," (doctoral dissertation, University of Illinois, 1967). For valuable commentary on the style of *Paradise Regained*, see Martz, *Paradise Within*, pp. 177–87; David Daiches, *Milton* (New York, 1957), p. 219; Arnold Stein, *Answerable Style* (Minneapolis, 1953); Jon S. Lawry, *The Shadow of Heaven: Matter and Stance in Milton's Poetry* (Ithaca, 1968), in particular pp. 294–300; and Roger H. Sundell, "The Narrator as Interpreter in *Paradise Regained*," in *Milton Studies*, II, ed. James D. Simmonds (Pittsburgh, 1970), pp. 83–101. Sundell stresses the importance of the theme of interpreting rightly in *Paradise Regained*.

3. All citations for *Paradise Regained* are to Merritt Y. Hughes, ed., *John Milton: Complete Poems and Major Prose* (New York, 1957).

4. On the importance of viewing the action of the poem within this larger context, see Rajan, *Lofty Rhyme*, pp. 116–21; and Warner G. Rice, "*Paradise Regained*," in *Milton: Modern Essays in Criticism*, ed. Arthur E. Barker (New York, 1965), p. 419.

5. For similar phrases, see John x, 15 and xiii, 17.

6. For discussions of the roles of biblical and secular knowledge in the poem, see Arnold Stein, *Heroic Knowledge* (Minneapolis, 1957), and Lewalski, *Brief Epic*. Cf. Howard Schultz, *Milton and Forbidden Knowledge* (New York, 1955), pp. 222–27. For an examination of Milton's principles of biblical exegesis, see H. R. MacCallum, "Milton and Figurative Interpretation of the Bible," *UTQ*, XXXI (1961–62), 397–415.

7. This portrait of Christ is in keeping with Milton's view of Christ in *De Doctrina Christiana* (*The Works of John Milton*, ed. F. A. Patterson, et al., 18 vols. [New York, 1931–38], XIV, in particular 231–43, hereafter cited as CM). For commentary on the dramatic problems involved in the characterization of Christ in the poem, see Northrop Frye, "The Typology of *Paradise Regained*," in Barker, *Modern Essays*, pp. 438–40; Arnold Stein, *Heroic Knowledge;* Merritt Y. Hughes, "The Christ of *Paradise Regained*," *SP*, XXXV (1938), 254–77; Elizabeth M. Pope, *Paradise Regained: The Tradition and the Poem* (New York, 1962); and Lewalski, *Brief Epic*, in particular p. 122.

8. In the *De Doctrina*, Milton calls Paul the "interpreter of Christ" (CM, XIV, 201), and he relies heavily upon Paul's writings for his doctrines regarding Christ (e.g., CM, XIV, 19 and 157–67).

9. Other allusions to Hebrews ii, 18 occur in *PR* I, 15–17, 158–67; II, 387–91; III, 193–94, 195–97, 386–97; and IV, 533, 594–96. Other allusions to the Passion include *PR* I, 204 and John xviii, 37; *PR* I, 266–67 and Isaiah liii, 6; *PR* III, 56–57 and Luke vi, 22–26; *PR* III, 188–92 and Luke ix, 22 and xvii, 25; *PR* III, 440 and Romans v, 6–8; *PR* IV, 128–29 and Hebrews ii, 14–15. The most poignant such allusion occurs in *PR* II, 385–86, when Christ declares that he can command "Angels ministrant / Array'd in

Glory on my cup to attend," thus recalling the human agony of an older Christ who prays, "let this cup pass from me" (Matthew xxvi, 39).

10. On Christ's learning in *Paradise Regained*, see Arnold Stein, *Heroic Knowledge;* Albert W. Fields, "Milton and Self-Knowledge," *PMLA*, LXXXIII (1968), 392–99; A. S. P. Woodhouse, "Theme and Pattern in *Paradise Regained*," *UTQ*, XXV (1955–56), 167–82; George F. Sensabaugh, "Milton on Learning," *SP*, XLIII (1946), 258–72; W. W. Robson, "The Better Fortitude," in *The Living Milton*, ed. Frank Kermode (New York, 1961), pp. 124–37.

11. Other allusions which stress the importance of Christ's studies of the Scriptures include the following: *PR* I, 266–67 and Isaiah liii, 6; *PR* I, 346–56 and Deuteronomy viii, 3; *PR* I, 407–08 and John viii, 44; *PR* I, 442–43 and 2 Thessalonians ii, 11–12; *PR* I, 456 and 1 Corinthians xiii, 8; *PR* II, 260–301 and Psalm iv, 4, 1 Kings xvii, 5–6, Daniel i, 8–19; *PR* III, 106–07 and John viii, 14; *PR* III, 182–87 and Ecclesiastes iii, 1, Luke xvii, 14–19; *PR* III, 186–87 and Acts i, 7; *PR* III, 387 and Colossians ii, 18; *PR* III, 387–402 and John vii, 1–20; *PR* IV, 287–89 and James i, 17, Psalm xxxvi, 9; *PR* IV, 310–12 and Acts xvii, 23–30; *PR* IV, 321 and Ecclesiastes xii, 12; *PR* IV, 334–64 and 2 Timothy iii, 10–17; *PR* IV, 341–43 and Jude xvi; *PR* IV, 352 and Romans ii, 14–15; *PR* IV, 571 and 1 Corinthians x, 12; and *PR* IV, 599 and John i, 9.

12. On Satan's biblical ignorance, see Don Cameron Allen, *The Harmonious Vision* (Baltimore, 1954), pp. 110–21; M. M. Mahood, *Poetry and Humanism* (New Haven, 1950), pp. 235–37; Woodhouse, "Paradise Regained," p. 174; Frye, "Typology," p. 436; and Sims, *Bible in Milton's Epics*, pp. 169–86.

13. For discussion of the image of the tree, see John M. Steadman, *Milton's Epic Characters* (Chapel Hill, 1959), pp. 88–89. Other passages are Daniel ii, 35 and 44, and Psalm ii, 9.

14. For example, see Frye, "Typology," p. 439.

15. The allusions to Revelation in the closing lines include the following: *PR* IV, 589 and Revelation xxii, 2; *PR* IV, 590 and Revelation xxi, 6; *PR* IV, 604–05 and Revelation xii, 9; *PR* IV, 616–17 and Revelation xxii, 2–3 and xx, 10; *PR* IV, 624 and Revelation ix, 11; *PR* IV, 628 and Revelation xviii, 2; *PR* IV, 629–32 and Revelation xx, 1–3.

MILTON'S HEBRAIC HERCULEAN HERO

Carole S. Kessner

Samson Agonistes is unique in its treatment of the Herculean hero so prevalent in Renaissance drama (for example, *Tamburlaine, Bussy D'Ambois, Coriolanus*). Milton regarded Samson as a type of Hercules; but neither the biblical nor the Greek hero was adequate as a model for the hero of his drama. Unlike other Renaissance dramatists, whose conception of the Herculean hero derived from traditional versions (for example, Sophocles' *Women of Trachis*) and who portrayed Hercules in all his *areté*, Milton's conception rested on the much more humanized hero of Euripides' *Heracles*. Comparison of *Heracles* with *Samson Agonistes* reveals many similarities in theme, structure, and character. The conflict in both plays is spiritual and internal, and both heroes move from a nadir of despair to insight and gradual accumulation of inner strength. A persistent image in both plays is the movement from darkness to light, in each case reflecting the thematic movement from physical blindness to spiritual vision. Furthermore, the Amphitryon-Heracles relationship is very much like that of Manoa and Samson; Theseus functions in much the same way as does the Chorus in *Samson;* Hera's role is similar to Dalila's; and Lycus has much in common with Harapha. Finally, both plays end with emphasis on the hero's fame in history and his continuing influence on society; and both plays ignore traditional reference to the hero's deification or immortality.

M OST ANTHOLOGISTS of seventeenth-century drama exclude Milton's *Samson Agonistes,* no doubt because Milton himself says in his preface to the drama that the work was never intended for the stage. Yet I suspect that many anthologists also may be inclined to omit *Samson* because they regard the work as *sui generis*—that is, totally unrelated to the drama of its time. It is quite true, of course, that *Samson Agonistes* is unique in its combination of classical structure with Old Testament subject, but it seems to me that it nevertheless is in the mainstream of that seventeenth-century drama which flows from Marlowe through Chapman to Dryden. This certainly is not to imply that Milton's *Samson* is any the less unique, but rather to suggest that its uniqueness lies in part in its singular treatment of an established tradition—that of the Herculean hero.

The career of this special kind of hero, Eugene Waith informs us, consists of great physical exploits which "are strange mixtures of beneficence and crime, fabulous quests and shameful betrayals, of triumphs over wicked enemies and insensate slaughter of the innocent."[1] Moreover, this hero has the largeness of a man who is almost a god; his morality or virtue is comprised of a ferocity and physical force which render him capable of bounding over ordinary human perimeters—a quality the Greeks called *areté* and the Romans, *virtus*. The quintessence of such a hero is the mythological Hercules, that fabulous incarnation and exaltation of man's most powerful drives and instincts, whose spectacular life is recorded first in Greek folklore and epic and later in Greek drama. And it is this figure who inspired such fascination in the Renaissance and in the seventeenth century that he became, as Waith demonstrates, the model for the protagonists of the plays *Tamburlaine, Bussy D'Ambois, Antony and Cleopatra, Coriolanus, Conquest of Granada, Aureng Zebe,* and *All For Love.*

For the most part, the Renaissance and seventeenth-century plays that Waith analyzes rest on a conception of Hercules that is found in Sophocles' *Women of Trachis.* This play, which focuses on Heracles in the throes of extreme pain and physical suffering, is nevertheless a conventional portrait which glorifies the hero in all his *areté.* Sophocles' Heracles is fierce, proud, and self-absorbed; he reveals little or nothing that today we would regard as humane; and nowhere does he exhibit the slightest trace of ability to learn, grow, or feel remorse. But Sophocles does not mean his hero to be indicted for immorality, for Heracles' actions are excused by virtue of his *areté*; he is meant to be admired, to inspire love and admiration. Furthermore, his death, which he faces with the same superhuman fortitude and strength that he displayed throughout his life, is to be regarded as nothing less than a great loss to mankind.

Euripides' *Heracles* also focuses on the hero in his suffering, although this time it is the mental suffering that Heracles endures after he has, in his madness, murdered his wife and children. But there is a more fundamental difference between the two Greek representations of the mythological demigod—a difference which reveals itself in two totally disparate conceptions of the nature of the hero—for in the Euripidean drama we see the hero, as William Arrowsmith puts it, "reduced to his humanity."[2] In a conflict that is spiritual and internal, not physical and external as in the Sophocles play, we are shown a Heracles capable of tender and warm human relationships, and perhaps more importantly, capable of despair, learning, and remorse.

Thus the real distinction between the two Greek dramas lies in their dissimilar conceptions and treatments of heroic behavior. For Sophocles, heroic behavior consists entirely in superhuman energy and physical courage. For Euripides, the first fact is the condition of being human, and heroic strength and courage are circumscribed by the limitations and the possibilities of this fact.

It is fairly easy to establish the fact that Milton thought of Samson as a Herculean figure.[3] In addition to the fact that the chorus in *Samson Agonistes* hints at the similarity, "Like whom the Gentile's feign to bear up Heav'n" (150), Milton makes the identification unequivocally in Book IX of *Paradise Lost:*

> So rose the *Danite* strong
> *Herculean Samson* from the Harlot-lap
> Of Philistean Dalilah, and waked
> Shorn of his strength. (1059–62)

Moreover, the myth of Samson as recorded in the Book of Judges outlines a career and personality very much like those of the mythical Hercules. Both Hercules and Samson have a mark of divinity attending their births. Hercules, we remember, is the product of the union of Zeus, in the guise of Amphitryon, and Alcmene. Samson's birth, too, is divinely inspired, for the biblical hero's birth was twice foretold to his long barren mother by an angel of God. Furthermore, both heroes are aggressive, libidinal supermen whose chief virtue is physical strength, and whose chief weakness is inordinate sexual desire. Samson and Hercules' careers consist of great and fabulous exploits. Hercules, we remember, clad only in his lion skin, with but the simplest of weapons, battles monsters and giants, penetrates Hades, carries off the three-headed dog Cerberus, and successfully completes twelve impossible labors. And the biblical Samson, Milton reminds us, is

> That Heroic, that Renown'd
> Irresistable *Samson?* whom unarm'd
> No strength of man, or fiercest wild beast could withstand;
> Who tore the Lion, as the Lion tears the Kid,
> Ran on embattled Armies clad in Iron,
> And weaponless himself,
> Made Arms ridiculous.   (125–31)

As for amorous adventures, Hercules has inspired an almost un-
countable number of legends, including the story of the fifty daughters of
Thespius, whom he is reputed to have enjoyed in one night.[4] In the case
of Samson, we can only account for the Timnian woman, the harlot of
Gaza, and Dalilah—but these three should suffice to establish his reputation. Both heroes, in addition, are brought low at the height of their
careers by women.

The two are also subject to great fits of rage. When Samson succumbs to the pleas of the woman of Timna and reveals the answer to the
riddle of the lion, he meets the demands of the bargain he has made and
gives the Philistines their promised change of garments, but not before
he has killed thirty of them and has taken their spoil. The biblical account tersely remarks, "And his anger was kindled" (Judges xiv, 19).
Hercules' innumerable great rages are epitomized in Hyllus' report of
the murder of Lichas in *The Women of Trachis*. Heracles caught
"Lichas by the foot where the ankle turns / and threw him against a
wave-beaten rock that juts from the sea. / It pressed the pale brains out
through his hair, / and, split full on, skull and blood mixed and spread"
(779–82). Yet despite these ignoble actions, both heroes are regarded as
benefactors of mankind. As Amphitryon tells us at the beginning of the
Euripides play, Heracles' promise to Eurystheus for the return of his
father is "to civilize the world" (26). As for Samson, the case is sufficiently
clear: the biblical account says, "And he shall begin to deliver Israel
out of the hands of the Philistines" (Judges xiii, 5). And that Milton
regarded Samson as a savior is made quite clear in his famous identification in *Areopagitica* of Samson with the British nation, which he
regarded as a world savior: "Methinks I see in my mind a noble and
puissant nation rousing herself like a strong man after sleep, and shak-
ing her invincible locks."[5]

It is apparent, then, that Milton regarded Samson as a type of Hercules. But the traditional Hercules never could have provided Milton

with the model for the Samson of his individual imagination—nor, for that matter, could he follow the outlines of the primitive biblical Samson, for from the biblical account Milton could see that Samson acted in many cases out of personal considerations. The climactic verse 28 of Judges xvi renders the biblical Samson absolutely antithetical to Milton's imagined Samson: "And Samson called unto the Lord, and said, O Lord God, remember me, I pray thee, and strengthen me, I pray thee, only this once, O God, That *I may be avenged of the Philistines for my two eyes*" (italics added).

Furthermore, as Samuel Stollman points out, Milton was quite aware that post-biblical rabbinical tradition did not place Samson at the top of its list of heroes.[6] The rabbis of the Babylonian and Jerusalem Talmuds regarded Samson as a mixed figure—on the one hand, admirable in respect of his virility, his faithfulness as a judge, and his selflessness in his deliverance of Israel, but on the other hand, weak in respect of his fleshly appetite—more a type of Esau, brawny, but lacking in the ethical virtues and wisdom of a Moses, a Joseph, or a Solomon. Moreover, Milton was undoubtedly familiar with the legends of the rabbis in the Aggadic Midrash,[7] in which Samson is often represented as far from an ethical and moral paradigm. For example, one of the rabbinical legends reads as follows:

When Samson told Delilah that he was a Nazarite unto God, she was certain that he had divulged the true secret of his strength. She knew his character too well to entertain the idea that he would couple the name of God with an untruth. There was a weak side to his character too. He allowed sensual pleasures to dominate him. The consequence was that "he who went astray after his eyes, lost his eyes." *Even this severe punishment produced no change of heart.* He continued to lead his old life of profligacy in prison, and he was encouraged thereto by the Philistines, who set aside all considerations of family purity in the hope of descendants who should be the equals of Samson in giant strength and stature. (italics added)[8]

Thus Milton's Samson was the fruit of a most unusual cross-fertilization; for whereas Milton found the outlines for his hero in the primitive myth of the Hebrew Bible, he turned to another tradition for the substance and spirit. For these, he drew on the Euripidean conception of Heracles, which itself was a mutation of the Greek hero of received tradition.[9] The product of such a union, then, was the true expression of Milton's personal conception of the nature of human heroic behavior.[10]

Milton draws attention to the Euripidean tragedy at the very outset of *Samson Agonistes*. Samson, in his blindness, says, "A little onward lend thy guiding hand" (1), and although Merritt Hughes, in a footnote to this line, suggests resemblances to Euripides' *Phoenissae*, Sidney's *Arcadia*, and Shakespeare's *King Lear*, he fails to mention what seems to be an even clearer allusion. Milton himself, in the *Second Defense*, in a tribute to the kindness of his true friends since his blindness, quotes the lines of Theseus to Heracles: "Lend your hand to your devoted friend, / Throw your arm round my neck and I will guide you on the way."[11] Moreover, this quotation follows the section in the *Second Defense* in which Milton articulates one of the major themes of the play. Again, speaking of his blindness, he says:

And indeed, in my blindness, I enjoy, in no inconsiderable degree the favor of the Deity, who regards me with more tenderness and compassion in proportion as I am able to behold nothing but himself. Alas! for him who insults me: who maligns me, merits public execration! For the divine law not only shields me from injury, but almost renders me too sacred to attack; not indeed so much from the privation of my sight, as from the overshadowing of those heavenly wings which seem to have occasioned this obscurity; and which, when occasioned, he is wont to illuminate with an interior light, more precious and more pure.[12]

With this allusion in mind, I suggest that further investigation of the relationship of *Samson Agonistes* to *Heracles* will reveal a number of most convincing similarities and parallels. Firstly, both plays focus on the hero in his sufferings, and both emphasize his gradual accumulation of inner strength. And, of course, whereas it is true that unlike *Samson*, which opens at the moment of the hero's reduction, *Heracles* begins with a long dramatic representation of the conventional material or received tradition about Heracles, it is also true that *Samson* incorporates this kind of material within the dialogue. *Samson*, we know, begins in good epic fasion, in *medias res*; but as Merritt Hughes points out, during the course of the action we have flashbacks of the earlier episodes, or received tradition, of Samson's life. In fact, Hughes suggestively remarks that "familiarity with the entire biblical account would have been assumed, just as the familiarity with the myth behind a tragedy like the *Mad Hercules* of Euripides would have been assumed in an Athenian audience."[13] Moreover, even though *Heracles* presents the conventional material as the first action of the play, it, too, includes reminiscences of the hero's life in speeches made by other characters in the play.

There are, then, certain structural resemblances between the two plays. But, in addition, there are quite obvious image parallels. As everyone knows, one of the most pervasive image patterns in *Samson Agonistes* is the movement from darkness to light, metaphoric of the thematic movement from physical blindness to spiritual vision. In *Samson* we find this pattern present from the opening monologue, "For yonder bank hath choice of sun or shade" (3), through the end, when the semichorus intones:

> he though blind of sight,
> Despis'd and thought extinguish't quite,
> With inward eyes illuminated
> His fiery virtue rous'd
> From under ashes into sudden flame.   (1687–91)

In *Heracles* the same pattern is to be found. Heracles, in his horror, cries out, "O black night of grief that covers me" (1140) and "let my garments hide my head in darkness" (1159). But Amphitryon encourages him: "My son, drop your robe from your eyes / Show your forehead to the sun" (1204). And Theseus implores him to "lift up your head and show your face to your friends. / There is no cloud whose utter blackness / Could conceal in night a sorrow like yours" (1215–17).

Thus, in both plays the physical condition of the hero mirrors the spiritual or inner state, and both are rendered metaphorically in images of darkness and light. Furthermore, Milton surely must have perceived the analogy between Samson's blindness and Heracles' madness, for it is quite explicit in *Heracles* that in his madness Heracles, too, was unable to see. The chorus says, "Darkness lies upon his eyes" (1071). In describing the murder, the messenger reports, "Suddenly he changed: / his eyes rolled and bulged from their sockets, / and the veins stood out, gorged with blood." (931–33). And when his son pleads for his life, the messenger says that Heracles merely "stared from stony gorgon eyes" (990).

In addition to structural and imagistic echoes from *Heracles* to *Samson*, there are reverberations from one to the other in the very characters of the two plays. First of all, since there is no biblical prededent for the tender father-son relationship of Manoa to Samson, just such a relationship may have been inspired by the Amphitryon-Heracles model. In *Heracles*, the fact of filial devotion and parental pride is established in the opening speech, when Amphitryon explains Heracles' absence:

> Then my son left home, left Megara and kin,
> hoping to recover the plain of Argos
> and those gigantic walls from which I fled
> to Thebes, because I killed Electryon.
> He hoped to win me back my native land
> and so alleviate my grief. And therefore,
> mastered by Hera or by necessity,
> he promised to Eurystheus a vast price
> for our return: to civilize the world.   (12–20)

This theme continues throughout both parts of *Heracles*, later revealing its intensity as Heracles, calling for death, is begged by his father to give up his self-destructive thought:

> O my son, I implore you,
> by your beard, your knees, your hand,
> by an old man's tears:
> tame that lion of your rage
> that roars you on to death,
> yoking grief to grief.   (1208–13)

Is this not faintly reminiscent of Manoa's "act not in thy own affliction, Son; / Repent the sin, but if the punishment / Thou canst avoid, self-preservation bids" (503–05).

A further similarity in characterization is that between Theseus in *Heracles* and the Chorus in *Samson*. Both function as loyal friends who seek "to comfort him as they can," as Milton puts it in the Argument. They offer counsel and consolation, and both, despite their love, fall short of total understanding. Theseus proves himself finally unequal to the regenerated Heracles at the close of the play, when he chides the hero for his continuing grief and tears. He says, "If someone sees your weakness, he will not praise you . . . where now is famous Heracles?" (1412, 1414). By this question, Theseus reveals his conventionality and lack of understanding, for he continues to measure Heracles in terms of the outworn concept of *areté*. As William Arrowsmith puts it, "Having claimed the dignity of his new courage, Heracles can without weakness or loss of tragic stature make plain the wreck of his life and his own dependent helplessness: strong but also weak, in need and in love, a hero at every point."[14] Similarly, the Chorus in *Samson* reveals its total conventionality, for it can hope for Samson's regeneration only in terms of a miracle—the restoration of his eyesight. And when Samson makes that great speech heralding the return of his spiritual strength, despite his continuing physical weakness—"I begin to feel / Some rousing motions in me which dispose / To something extraordinary my thoughts" (1381–83)—the Chorus flatly responds, "In time thou has resolv'd. The man returns" (1390). The Chorus fears only that Samson may cause more disturbance that he already has. He should not add "fuel to the flame" (1351).

For consolation, both Theseus and the Chorus assure their respective heroes of their love; and for counsel they offer words which are remarkably alike. Both offer the counsel of patience and fortitude. Theseus says, "My advice is this: be patient, suffer / what you must, and do not yield to grief" (1313–14). The Chorus advises Samson, "Many are the sayings of the wise / In ancient and in modern books enroll'd / Extolling Patience as the truest fortitude" (652–54).

Furthermore, it is in the mouths of Theseus and the Chorus that both poets put speculations about cosmic order and the justice of God's ways, though of course their conclusions are not at all the same. When Heracles complains that Hera is to blame for his misfortune, Theseus tells him that

> Fate exempts no man; all men are flawed,
> and so the gods, unless the poets lie.
> Do not the gods commit adultery?
> Have they not cast their fathers into chains,
> in pursuit of power? Yet all the same,
> despite their crimes, they live upon Olympus.
> How dare you then, mortal that you are,
> to protest your fate, when the gods do not?   (1314–21)

When Samson complains that God too often raises men to great heights and then deserts them, the Chorus answers:

> Just are the Ways of God,
> And justifiable to Men;
> Unless there be he who think not God at all:
> If any be, they walk obscure;
> For of such Doctrine never was there School,
> But the heart of the Fool,
> And no man therein Doctor but himself.   (293–99)

The Chorus then proceeds to show the errors of all who doubt God's justice, for "with his own Laws he can best dispense" (314). It seems, then, that the characterization of the Chorus in *Samson* is a transformation of the characterization of Theseus in *Heracles*.

Before I move on to a consideration of the two main characters, I should like to mention a few further similarities between the two plays —ones which are not quite as easy to substantiate, but which nevertheless suggest themselves. For example, one might equate Hera with Dalila, for both are agents of false gods and both are the efficient cause of the protagonists' downfall. Heracles rails against Hera:

> Let the noble wife of Zeus begin the dance,
> pounding with her feet Olympus' gleaming floors!
> For she accomplished what her heart desired,
> and hurled the greatest man of Hellas down
> in utter ruin.   (1303–07)

And Samson cries out against Dalila,

> Out, out Hyaena.
>
> .   .   .   .
>
> That wisest and best men full oft beguil'd
> With goodness principl'd not to reject
> The penitent, but ever to forgive,
> Are drawn to wear out miserable days,
> Entangl'd with a pois'nous bosom snake,
> If not by quick destruction soon cut off
> As I by thee, to Ages an example.   (748, 759–65)

Moreover, Samson accuses Dalila of being an agent of false gods:

> To please thy gods thou didst it: gods unable
> To acquit themselves and prosecute their foes
> But by ungodly deeds, the contradiction
> Of their own deity, Gods cannot be.   (896–99)

How very reminiscent this is of Heracles' repudiation of the Olympian gods. In an assertion of utter disbelief in the power of these traditional deities, Heracles declaims:

> I do not believe the gods commit
> adultery, or bind each other in chains.
> I never did believe it; I never shall;
> nor that one god is tyrant of the rest.
> If god is truly god, he is perfect,
> lacking nothing. These are poets' wretched lies.   (1341–46)

One further prefiguration before I move on to the heart of the comparison. There is an interesting exchange between Lycus and Amphitryon which summons up remembrances of the Harapha-Samson exchange. Lycus, the tyrant who conquered Thebes in Heracles' absence, appears only in the first half of the play and is thus a representative of the world of conventional heroism. In his apparent triumph over the absent Heracles, he exults over the beaten Amphitryon and Megara and ridicules Heracles' reputation. He says to Megara:

> What was so prodigious in you husband's deeds?
> Because he killed a hydra in the marsh?
> Or the Nemean lion? They were trapped in nets,
> not strangled as he claims, with his bare hands.
> Are these your arguments? Because of this,
> you say, the sons of Heracles should live—
> a man who coward in everything else,
> made his reputation fighting beasts,
> who never buckled shield upon his arm,
> never came near a spear, but held a bow,
> the coward's weapon, handy to run away?
> The bow is no proof of manly courage;
> no, your real man stands firm in the ranks
> and dares to face the gash the spear may make.   (151–64)

Does this not recall Harapha of the outworn chivalry, who taunts Samson?

> Much have I heard
> Of thy prodigious might and feat perform'd
> Incredible to me, in this displeas'd,
> That I was never present on the place
> Of those encounters, where we might have tried
> Each other's force in camp or listed field;
>
> . . . .
>
> O that fortune
> Had brought me to the field where thou art fam'd
> To have wrought such wonders with an Ass's Jaw;
> I should have forc'd thee soon wish other arms,
> Or left thy carcase where the Ass lay thrown.
>   (1082–87, 1093–97)

Finally, Harapha accuses Samson of trickery:

> Thou durst not thus disparage glorious arms
> Which greatest Heroes have in battle worn,

> Thir ornament and safety, had not spells,
> And black enchantments some Magicians Art
> Arm'd thee or charm'd thee strong, which thou from Heaven
> Feign'dst at thy birth was giv'n in thy hair.   (1130–35)

If all of the above analogies, echoes, and similarities suggest a relationship between *Heracles* and *Samson Agonistes,* the case becomes even more convincing when one examines the two heroes and defines the two poets' concepts of heroism. For Euripides, it is clear that heroism does not lie in the outworn concept of *areté.* The direction of the action is from mere physical strength, to suffering and reduction to humanity, to despair, and to a new inner strength and courage. The low point of *Heracles* is that moment when the hero succumbs to desperation, when he can think only of death—when he moans, "to death, to go back whence I came, beneath the earth" (1247). But from this moment on, Heracles "rises and keeps on rising to his sufferings with an enormous range of spirit,"[15] until, demonstrating his greatest nobility, he rejects death and chooses life. He has confronted and recognized necessity which he now shares with all mankind, for lost is his great physical prowess which before seemed to exempt him from necessity. But if he now is no longer exempt, he at least has come to understand the power of the one thing that can help him endure the inevitable—the power of love. "Love," Arrowsmith puts it, "is the hope . . . which permits him to endure, and his discovery of that hope keeps step with his knowledge of anguish. He survives by virtue of love, for love lies close to, if it does not usurp, the instinct for survival."[16] Thus, Heracles' last words in the play are, "The man who would prefer great wealth or strength more than love, more than friends, is diseased of soul" (1425–27). And so the Greek demigod has been humanized.

The fact that Euripides chose to ignore any reference to Hercules' later death and deification (Sophocles hints at it) emphasizes his intention to humanize his hero. Nowhere in the play is there the slightest suggestion of everlasting life or union with the gods. To the contrary, Theseus clearly says to Heracles that when he dies "Athens shall raise you up a monument / of stone and honor you with sacrifice. / And so my city, helping a noble man, / shall win from Hellas, a lovely crown of fame" (1332–35). Thus Heracles will achieve immortality through the survival of his memory, and by the continuation of his fame in history as an influence upon society.

In this Euripidean Heracles there are surely adumbrations of Milton's Samson, for Samson too moves steadily upward in a mounting progression from a nadir of despair and yearning for death after acknowledgment of his own guilt, through a progression of insights and self-discoveries until, like Heracles, he can choose life—that is, he chooses to act rather than to succumb.

At the moment before Samson resolves to go to the Philistine temple, he has no knowledge of what his necessity will be; but in choosing to act he freely exercises his will in the direction of faith in God and moral responsibility. After initially refusing to accompany the officer to the idolatrous rites, Samson engages in an internal struggle to justify his own decision to demur. He offers four excuses which alternate between obedience to ritual law and assertion of human pride. He does not wish to go (1) because he is an "Ebrew" and his Law forbids his presence at their religious rites; (2) he does not want them to "make a game" of his calamities; (3) he is not so broken and debased that his mind "will ever condescend to such absurd commands," and (4) he will not abuse his "consecrated gift of strength" (1319–62). But finally Samson's argument turns from the excuses of ritual law and pride to freely chosen acceptance of what he understands to be God's will. He admits that no one "constrains" him to the temple of Dagon. He has been commanded by the Philistine lords, but he has not been forced physically. Hence, he reasons:

> Commands are no constraints. If I obey them,
> I do it freely; venturing to displease
> God for the fear of Man, and Man prefer,
> Set God behind: which in his jealousy
> Shall never, unrepented, find forgiveness.
> Yet that he may dispense with me or thee
> Present in Temples at Idolotrous Rites
> For some important cause, thou needest not doubt.   (1372–79)

Thus, in Samson's gradually accumulating wisdom he comes to understand, like Heracles, the power of love. But the human love that was learned in *Heracles* is, in *Samson*, transformed into love of God. Moreover, Samson learns that God has not deserted him as he feared, and that love of God will provide him with the strength to face his necessity, whatever it may be.

It is at this moment, just after he has freely turned his will to the

will of God, that Samson says, "Be of good courage. I begin to feel /
Some rousing motions in me which dispose / To something extraordinary my thoughts." These words are crucial, for it is only after Samson,
of his own free will, has announced the *possibility* of attending the rites
that he feels "some rousing motions"—words which are to be understood
as divine inspiration suddenly operating in him.[17] These "rousing motions" are not an ever-present sanctifying grace, but rather a divine impulse which has prompted Samson to great actions "from time to
time."[18]

The "something extraordinary" which Samson senses is, of course,
his cataclysmic actions at the temple of Dagon. But Milton makes it absolutely clear that Samson has not committed suicide. Like all mortal
men, he has succumbed to his necessity, but he has demonstrated his
truly humanly heroic nature by first choosing to act purposefully that he
might fulfill his potential or destiny. The Chorus says:

> thou hast fulfill'd
> The work for which thou wast foretold
> To *Israel,* and now li'st victorious
> Among thy slain self'kill'd
> *Not willingly,* but tangl'd in the fold
> Of dire necessity, whose law in death conjoin'd
> Thee with thy slaughter'd foes in number more
> Than all thy life had slain before. 　　(1661–68, italics added)

Thus, Samson is dead, "conjoin'd" inevitably with all of humanity.
But here it is important to emphasize the fact that Milton nowhere suggests for Samson everlasting life in Heaven. Despite the reference to the
Phoenix (it is the Phoenix's *fame* that survives, not its body or soul), we
are to understand that Samson's immortality is, like Heracles', fame in
history.

Furthermore, it should be noted that Milton consciously eliminates
the biblical reference to personal revenge. The account in Judges reads:
"I pray thee, only this once, O God, that I may be at once avenged of the
Philistines for my two eyes" (xvi, 28). But by eliminating the motive of
revenge, which would be absolutely antithetical to Samson's moral
progress in the drama, Milton raises Samson to the highest level of heroism. Samson dies a true Hebrew martyr, not with words of vengeance on
his lips, but in a selfless triumphant act of atonement and completion

which bears witness to God's promise and providence—an action which inevitably brings about Samson's death, but which nevertheless fulfills his individual destiny and temporarily secures the life of his nation. Consequently, Samson's name will not only survive in history, but it will also be a force and inspiration upon those who come after him. Thus, in words which ring familiar from *Heracles,* Manoa says that he will bring Samson's body home and

> there will I build him
> A Monument, and plant it round with shade
> Of Laurel ever green, and branching Palm,
> With all his Trophies hung, and Acts enroll'd
> In copious Legend, or sweet Lyric Song.
> Thither shall all the valiant youth resort,
> And from his memory inflame thir breasts
> To matchless valor, and adventure high. (1734–41)

State University of New York, Stony Brook

NOTES

1. *The Herculean Hero* (London, 1962), p. 16.

2. Introduction to *Heracles,* in *The Complete Greek Tragedies: Euripides II,* ed. David Greene and Richmond Lattimore (New York, 1968), p. 57.

3. F. Michael Krouse, in *Milton's Samson and the Christian Tradition* (Princeton, 1949), p. 44, points out that the similarity between Samson and Hercules was recognized as early as the time of Julius Caesar by Diodorus Siculus and that the comparison became a commonplace of homiletics and poetics during the patristic period.

4. Waith, *Herculean Hero,* p. 19.

5. *John Milton: Complete Poems and Major Prose,* ed. Merritt Y. Hughes (New York, 1957), p. 745.

6. "Milton's Samson and the Jewish Tradition," *Milton Studies,* III, ed. James D. Simmonds (Pittsburgh, 1971), pp. 195–200.

7. Aggadic Midrash is a body of rabbinical legends and allegories which embellish and reinterpret the text of the Bible. Harris Fletcher, in *Milton's Rabbinical Readings* (Urbana, 1930) demonstrates that Milton knew the Buxtorf Rabbinical Bible of 1618, which includes Midrashic material.

8. Louis Ginzberg, *Legends of the Jews* (Philadelphia, 1913), IV, 48–49.

9. P. W. Timberlake, in his essay, "Milton and Euripides" (*The Parrott Presentation Volume,* ed. Hardin Craig [New York, 1935]), describes in great detail Milton's lifelong admiration for and indebtedness to Euripides. Timberlake points out Euripidean influences and echoes in much of the poetry and prose, but of *Samson Agonistes* he says: "One would expect to find in the only completed classical tragedy of Milton

the fullest illustration of his liking for that poet who was himself a Greek dramatist; and one does find it there, even though Euripides did not supply a model for Samson" (p. 338). Timberlake mentions *Heracles* only once, and then only with reference to choric meter.

10. This reading makes it difficult to accept F. Michael Krouse's thesis that Samson is a type of Christ, a martyr-saint in the Christian understanding of the word (*Milton's Samson and the Christian Tradition*).

11. *Second Defense of the English People,* in Hughes, p. 827.

12. Hughes, pp. 826–27.

13. Ibid., p. 531.

14. Introduction to *Heracles,* p. 57.

15. Ibid., p. 58.

16. Ibid., p. 57.

17. Here "motions" are to be understood as divine inspiration. The *OED* gives as one meaning of the word "A working of God in the soul," and it quotes the 1549 *Book of Common Prayer, Coll. 1st Sunday in Lent,* "That . . . wee may ever obeye thy Godlye motions."

18. The biblical account of Samson in Judges xiii, 24–25, reads, "And the woman bare a son, and called his name Samson: and the child grew, and the Lord blessed him. And the Spirit of the Lord began to move him at times in the camp of Dan between Zorah and Eshtaol." Rashi, the twelfth-century rabbinical commentator, glosses the phrase "to move him" as "to great and powerful actions from time to time."

MILTON'S EVENING

Dustin H. Griffin

Eighteenth-century poets and critics admired Milton's "evening ear," giving particular praise to the arrival of evening in Eden (*PL* IV, 598–609). They praised Milton for his powers of natural description and evocation of mood but did not remark how this passage seems to contain the poem in miniature. Evening there and elsewhere is an epitome of Eden, leisurely, harmonious, creative, self-renewing, interanimate, sustained by divine presence. By contrast, evenings in Virgil and Renaissance pastoral are often brief, damp, and threatening. Milton focuses on evening as a calm, quiet time, as a gradual process rather than the hurried end of day. In contrast to noon and midnight, times of crisis and decisive action, evening is a time of relaxation, contemplation, and restoration. Although Satan flatters Eve by suggesting that she is the evening cynosure, the narrative voice denies this anthropocentric view and presents evening as an instance of the interanimate unity of all creation. Not so much a precarious balance between day and night, evening is a moving moment, a "grateful vicissitude," just as Eden itself is marked not by physical and moral stasis, but by ceaseless change. After the Fall, as a measure of all that is lost, evenings become Virgilian—cold, damp, and perilous.

I

WHEN WILLIAM Collins, in his "Ode on the Poetical Character," spoke of Milton's "evening ear," he may have been paying tribute to the greatest English poet of the evening and the model for many eighteenth-century evening poems. As everyone has noticed, many of the details of Collins' own "Ode to Evening"—the beetle's sullen horn, the calm vot'ress, the upland fallows gray—find their prototypes in *Lycidas*, *Comus*, and the paired *L'Allegro* and *Il Penseroso*. What is more, as a recent editor has pointed out, the last two of these poems provide much of the furniture for many poems in two popular and related eighteenth-century genres, the landscape poem and the night poem.[1] That mid-eighteenth-century English poets looked back to Milton for inspiration has indeed long been a commonplace of criticism. But very little has been made of evening in Milton's own poems—of what evening meant to *Milton*—particularly in that poem where it figures by far most often, *Paradise Lost*.

Eighteenth-century poets and editors knew of the evening pieces in *Paradise Lost* and gave particular praise to the description of the arrival of evening in Eden:

> Now came still evening on, and twilight grey
> Had in her sober livery all things clad;
> Silence accompanied, for beast and bird,
> They to their grassy couch, these to their nests
> Were slunk, all but the wakeful nightingale;
> She all night long her amorous descant sung;
> Silence was pleased: now glowed the firmament
> With living sapphires: Hesperus that led
> The starry host, rode brightest, till the moon
> Rising in clouded majesty, at length
> Apparent queen unveiled her peerless light,
> And o'er the dark her silver mantle threw.   (IV, 598–609)[2]

"Surely there never was a finer evening; words cannot furnish out a more lovely description. The greatest poets in all ages have as it were vied with one another, in their descriptions of evening and night; but for the variety of numbers and pleasing images, I know of nothing parallel or comparable to this to be found among all the treasures of ancient or modern poetry." So wrote Thomas Newton in 1749 in his influential edition of *Paradise Lost*.[3] And numerous poets—including Pope, Thomson, Collins, and Cowper—shone in the borrowed light of imitation.[4] But for the most part, all the eighteenth century saw in Milton's passage was natural description for its own sake: "An exact and curious Description of a Moon-Light Night," says Patrick Hume, in his *Annotations on Milton's Paradise Lost* (1695).[5] The many descriptions in eighteenth-century poetry of the arrival of evening, and of the moon in a cloudy or cloudless sky, are usually designed as description or atmosphere. Even when Joseph Warton writes semiallegorically of "cloudless nights, / When silent Cynthia in her silver car / Through the blue concave slides,"[6] he means nothing more than that the silvery moon slid silently through the blue sky. What is gone from Warton's poem, and from

Collins' "Ode to Evening," is the mythological element, the implication of supernatural agencies whose actions may reveal something of divine purpose and order. By the end of Collins' evening poem, the supernatural is thoroughly naturalized—it does not exist apart from the natural setting; evening is evening. In Milton's evening pieces, natural description and evocation of a mood—what the eighteenth century saw and imitated—is only part of what is going on. In some respects "Now came still evening on" is a calm center around which the entire poem moves. Like many passages in *Paradise Lost*, it seems to contain the poem in miniature. Milton not only describes a moonlit evening, but creates in brief the very essence of Eden—its harmony, its order, its creativeness and self-renewal as sustained by the powers of heavenly beings.

To describe the qualities of the Edenic evening will require not only close attention to the most elaborate evening passage, but also comparison with other evenings in the poem. Thereafter, it will be possible to define some of the ways in which the moonlit evening functions symbolically to suggest the divine presence in the world. The first step, however, is to review the materials Milton inherited. Evening had long been a subject for poetry, and Milton had to modify or reinvent much of the material for his own purposes.

II

In a famous essay, Erwin Panofsky spoke of "that vespertinal mixture of sadness and tranquillity which is perhaps Virgil's most personal contribution to poetry. With only slight exaggeration," he goes on, "one might say that he 'discovered' the evening."[7] Panofsky has in mind the quiet close of Eclogues 1, 6, and 10:

> et iam summa procul villarum culmina fumant
> maioresque cadunt altis de montibus umbrae.
>
> cogere donec ovis stabulis numerumque referre
> iussit et invito processit Vesper Olympo.
>
> surgamus: solet esse gravis cantantibus umbra,
> iuniperi gravis umbra, nocent et frugibus umbrae.
> ite domum saturae, venit Hesperus, ite capellae.[8]

"At the end of Virgil's Eclogues we feel evening silently settle over the world."[9] It is true that Hesperus appears, and shadows fall from the hills in these three eclogues, but both the stately softness of Virgil's *maiores umbrae* and Panofsky's "he 'discovered' the evening" have assumed a disproportionate place in the minds of readers. Evening occupies but eight lines in ten poems. In the Eclogues it is a time of cold shadows and dangerous mists. It comes rapidly; goats must be hurried into shelter. Shepherds too seek shelter, where Tityrus promises Meliboeus food and companionship. Evening is not so much sadness and tranquility as the sudden end of a Mediterranean day, lasting but a moment before the hostile night takes control. This may be seen more clearly yet in the *Aeneid*, where evening hardly exists at all. There is no twilight, no gradual transition from day to night. When night falls while Aeneas visits Evander's house, Virgil says simply, *"nox ruit et fuscis tellurem amplectitur alis"* ("night rushes down and clasps the earth with dusky wings") (VIII, 369). As Turnus and Aeneas arrive together before Laurentum,

> continoque ineant pugnas et proelia temptent,
> ni roseus fessos iam gurgite Phoebus Hibero
> tinguat equos noctemque die labente reducat.
> considunt castris ante urbem et moenia vallant
>
> (XI, 912–15)[10]

This is by far the longest description of dusk (or dawn) in the poem. Ordinarily dawn arrives in a single line—"et interea revoluta ruebat / matura iam luce dies noctemque fugarat" ("meanwhile the returning day was rushing on with fulness of light, and had chased away the night") (X, 256–57).[11] Half-lights are either not present in Virgil's Mediterranean world or of no interest to him. Day is the time for light and labor, night for food and sleep.[12]

English Renaissance pastoralists do not, for the most part, make much advance on Virgil's evening scenes. They are largely content to repeat his formulaic eclogue endings. Thus Spenser:

> Hye thee home shepheard, the day is nigh wasted.   ("February")

> But see the Welkin thicks apace,
> And stouping Phebus steepes his face:
> Yts time to hast us homeward.   ("March")

> But let us homeward: for night draweth on,
> And twincling starres the daylight hence chase.   ("April")

> But now is time, I gesse, homeward to goe:
> Then ryse ye blessed flocks, and home apace,
> Least night with stealing steppes doe you forsloe,
> And wett your tender Lambes, that by you trace.   ("June")[13]

In Spenser, the day abruptly ends. "Night nigheth fast" ("August"), and brings cold dews and dangers.[14] There is no time called "evening."

For another poet working in the Spenserian pastoral tradition, the coming on of night, though described at greater length, is still Virgilian. Phineas Fletcher has night bringing wreaths of smoke, dusky shades in the eastern sky, threatening dampness. But we can detect some greater interest in the *process* of evening, in its quietness and softness, and in the night's own lights, "Vesper, fair Cynthia, and her train":

> But see, the smoak mounting in village nigh,
> With folded wreathes steals through the quiet aire;
> And mixt with duskie shades in eastern skie,
> Begins the night, and warns us home repair:
> Bright Vesper now hath chang'd his name and place,
> And twinkles in the heav'n with doubtfull face:
> Home then my full-fed lambes; the night comes, home apace.

Evening occupies a period of *time*—it steals and creeps through the air—though what it brings is, as with Virgil and Spenser, essentially hostile:

> But see, the stealing night with softly pace,
> To flie the western sunne, creeps up the east;
> Cold Hesper 'gins unmask his evening face,
> And calls the winking starres from drouzie rest:
> Home then my lambes; the falling drops eschew.[15]

It is the process of evening that chiefly interests Milton. Evening is not abrupt, but still, gray, sober, and silent—all terms suggesting a gradual easy fading away. "Now came still evening on." The "now" is a continuous present.[16] Evening is both "quiet" ("still") and "always" ("still") com*ing*. *Night* never actually begins at a particular point (contrast Fletcher's "Begins the night"), as indeed it does not in our experience of a northern evening. Yet by line 603 it *is* night ("She all night long"). The gradualness and indistinctness of the transition from day to night is increased by the doubling of personified presences. In reading the first line—"Now came still evening on, and twilight gray"—we are unsure of the relation between the two figures. Is twilight a companion, a subordinate, or merely an aspect of evening? Are two figures coming, or one? With the next line ("Had in her sober livery") these questions remain unanswered. Is it evening's livery, or twilight's? Does the possessive indicate that twilight is wearer (and hence evening's servant) or owner (and hence someone's master)? The uncertainty and indistinctness seem appropriate for a time when all distinctions are fading. The relation of twilight to "all things" is likewise vague. "Livery" now suggests that they are her servants; the (presumably) gray vestments suggest religious pilgrims.[17] By line 600 yet another figure appears: "Silence accompanied."[18] The noun is barely personified, the verb is suitably vague in import. Accompanied by what, when? Is the verb a simple past tense, or a past participle? Is accompaniment associative or musical (the latter sense supported by the nightingale in line 602)? Such disruption of verb tenses, too, makes evening indeterminate, something that *happens*, though not in the way that determinate events happen. "Now came" is both present and past, and as we saw earlier, continuous. The next verb is pluperfect: twilight had clad, not simply "twilight clad." The detail is right. The event—the act of clothing—took place imperceptibly. We cannot say when the event took place, only that it *had* by now happened. In the course of three lines Milton has made evening, in all its indistinctness, happen before our eyes. His dependence for this effect on poetic resources (syntactical misdirections and uncertainties) rather than the logic of prose may be demonstrated by quoting from an eighteenth-century paraphrase of the lines: "Now came on the still evening, and the gray twilight had begun to cover all on earth with darkness."[19] Relationships of persons and tenses have here been cleaned up, and the result is merely flat and prosaic.

Milton's evening, also unlike the Virgilian-Spenserian evening, is utterly without peril. It is not cold, wet, and threatening, but benign, full of protective presences, song, and light. Milton here draws on another tradition—night as the time for love, a stock feature of epithalamia from Theocritus to Spenser, and eminently suitable in describing a night in which the world's first wedded pair will go to their bridal bower and make love. Prominent in his description is the wakeful nightingale, who all night long "her amorous descant sung," and Hesperus, the evening star (Venus), the traditional "glorious lamp of love." Yet Hesperus plays a rather different role in Milton than in the epithalamic tradition. In Catullus, for example, Vesper is the sign under which the marriage bond is sealed: "Hespere, qui caelo lucet incundior ignis? / qui desponsa tua firmes conubia flamma"[20] (carm. 62). In Spenser, it not only "leads the starry host" but also guides lovers:

> the bright evening star with golden creast
> Appeare[s] out of the east.
> Fayre childe of beauty, glorious lampe of love
> That all the host of heaven in rankes doost lead,
> And guydest lovers through the nightes dread,
> How chearefully thou lookest from above,
> And seemst to laugh atweene thy twinkling light
> As joying in the sight
> Of these glad many which for joy doe sing.
>
> ("Epithalamion," 286–94)

But in Milton, as in Fletcher, Hesperus simply ushers in the moon and stars. Milton then plays down the epithalamic association of Hesperus.[21] This *is* a night of love, but not simply for two human lovers. The nightingale sings to Adam and Eve, but just as much to the birds and beasts, slunk to their couch and nest. The anthropocentric view of evening is in fact satanic. In tempting Eve in her sleep, Satan describes this same evening in quite lover-centered terms:

> Now is the pleasant time,
> The cool, the silent, save where silence yields
> To the night-warbling bird, that now awake
> Tunes sweetest his love-labored song; now reigns
> Full-orbed the moon, and with more pleasing light
> Shadowy sets off the face of things; in vain,
> If none regard, heaven wakes with all his eyes,
> Whom to behold but thee, nature's desire.   (V, 38–45)

Satan's evening is simply not the same as the one Milton had described earlier. Though all the details are the same (silence is broken only by the amorous nightingale, full moon reigns, stars shine), the scene has been sexualized.[22] Satan's language is that of shallow cavalier flattery.[23] His evening focuses quite literally not on the moon but on Eve. For Satan, Eve is the cynosure; the setting exists simply to please her and regard her. For Milton, the moon is heaven's "apparent queen." Her shining is far more than stage effects.

Satan in fact seriously misinterprets the function of the moon and stars, as well as the proper role of man in God's universe—an error to which both Eve and Adam (and the reader) are liable. They hold a narcissistic view of the universe that is at once innocent because true (they *are* lords of creation), and potentially threatening (should they forget the Lord of Creation). Eve's magnificent love song, "With thee conversing I forget all time / All seasons and their change, all please alike" (639–56) is one of the human highlights of the poem. Though the description of evening and night recalls the narrator's description earlier in Book IV, the sentiments she expresses (and we find beautiful) are potentially dangerous to her. The world is sweet, she sings in amorous descant, but not without you:

> sweet the coming on
> Of grateful evening mild, then silent night
> With this her solemn bird and this fair moon,
> And these the gems of heaven, her starry train.
> But neither breath of morn when she ascends
>
> .   .   .   .
>
> Nor grateful evening mild, nor silent night
> With this her solemn bird, nor walk by moon,
> Or glittering starlight without thee is sweet.
>
> (IV, 646–50, 654–56)

She says here what both she and Adam say after Eve's fall in Book IX: I cannot live without you. There we see their error; they should live to praise God. Here we do not perhaps sense the potential danger, though her opening words ("With thee . . . I forget") should alert us. Eve, still innocently narcissistic, then abruptly asks Adam at the conclusion to her song, "But wherefore all night long shine these, for whom / This glorious sight, when sleep hath shut all eyes?" (IV, 657–58). It is on this theme, as we have seen, that Satan played while tempting her that night. Adam's answer left her still wondering. But his words are important and ought to make the reader now fully understand that evening in Eden is not designed for human lovers. He tells Eve that the moon and stars have the duty of

> Ministring light prepared . . .
> Lest total darkness should by night regain
> Her old possession, and extinguish life
> In nature and all things, which these soft fires
> Not only enlighten, but with kindly heat
> Of various influence foment and warm,
> Temper or nourish, or in part shed down

Their stellar virtue on all kinds that grow
On earth, made hereby apter to receive
Perfection from the sun's more potent rays.
These then, though unbeheld in deep of night,
Shine not in vain, nor think, though men were none,
That heaven would want spectators, God want praise;
Millions of spiritual creatures walk the earth
Unseen, both when we wake, and when we sleep:
All these with ceaseless praise his works behold
Both day and night. (IV, 664–80)

The moon and stars, it is now clear, are not present in Eden merely to guide lovers, to look on them, or be seen by them only. Rather they serve as protective presences for all creation. keeping night and chaos back (and hence, in a way, continuously re-creating), nourishing, or tempering (and hence restoring, renovating). These lights are observed by spiritual creatures, whom we are perhaps free to associate with figures already described—evening, twilight, silence. It is because of such presences and figures (rather than the certain return of morning) that night in Eden is not perilous, except of course for the perils within, the liability of man to moral error. But the benignity of evening and night is not that of the traditional human love-night presided over by the evening star. It is rather a night in which "all things" share in the peace and harmony of Eden.

Evening in Eden is, then, not simply a time for love; nor is it merely, to adapt Herrick's witty words in denying twilight as a subject for poetry, "the last part of day, and first of night."[24] The night is meant by God for rest (IV, 613), but the evening is a special time, and separate. It is mild (IV, 647, 654), still (IV, 598), dewy (I, 743), brown (IX, 1088), cool (X, 95), and especially grateful (IV, 647, 654; V, 645)[25]—that is, pleasing. It is a time to pen flocks, milk goats, and tend flowers. It is when the sun sups with the ocean, when the angels in heaven enjoy their sweet repast, when the fields revive and birds their notes renew.[26] Its approach is "sweet," Hume explains, because the evening is the time fittest for "retirement and diversion," citing the proper translation of Psalm lxv, 9, "God makes the outgoings of the morning and evening to sing."[27]

Milton seems to have taken some care to contrast evening with other times of day, particularly noon and midnight (often seen in Christian tradition as symbolically identical).[28] Noon is a time of great heat and light, evening a time of cool and shadows; noon a critical time for human and divine judgment,[29] evening a time of relaxation. Noon is an hour of stillness, a timeless moment or turning point; evening, a time of gradual process and transition. Traditionally, as Cirillo has shown, noon was thought to be morally the most dangerous time of day, the hour of extreme sexual temptation.[30] Evening is rather an hour of quiet contemplation and restoration, preparation for love and sleep. Critical events happen at noon or midnight: Satan's rebellion in Heaven (V), Christ's triumph over Satan in the war in Heaven (VI), Satan's first view of the universe (III), Satan's address to the sun and his first entry into the garden (IV), Satan's reentry into the garden (IX), the Fall of man (IX), and the expulsion from the garden (XII). Though several evenings are described in the poem, they are, by comparison, uneventful and undramatic; at the same time, evening events are among the most significant in the poem and are associated with the beneficence of Eden now lost: rest, unfallen human love, a sympathetic universe, creation, and God's love for man.[31]

The restfulness of evening we have seen. Human love, a part of the magnificent evening in Book IV, is the primary event of Adam's first evening with Eve, yet even there all nature participates joyously:

> To the nuptial bower
> I led her blushing like the morn: all heav'n,
> And happy constellations on that hour
> Shed their selected influence; the earth
> Gave sign of gratulation, and each hill;
> Joyous the birds; fresh gales and gentle airs
> Whisper'd it to the woods, and from their wings
> Flung rose, flung odors from the spicy shrub,
> Disporting, till the amorous bird of night
> Sung spousal, and bid haste the ev'ning star
> On his hill top, to light the bridal lamp.   (VIII, 510–20)

Adam's remembrance of their first evening is perhaps forgivably self-centered; to his perception, the evening did seem to center on their wedded joys. The narrator's version of evening, as we have seen, is less man-centered. In fact, Adam himself recognizes a kind of interrelated harmony among all orders of life. Human love is not seen as separate from the rest of the natural world. All creation celebrates and even participates in the rites of man and woman. Love flows in a great circle, interanimating the world. The stars shed influence (the "in-flowing" seems particularly concrete and potent); the earth, in response, gives sign of gratulation. That sign becomes a sound echoed by the birds and in turn whispered to the woods by gales and airs. The woods and spicy shrubs, in cooperation with the birds, fling forth that joy as "odors." The circle closes as the nightingale sings, bidding the evening star to light the bridal lamp. As Milton emphasizes here and elsewhere, the world of Eden is not merely sympathetic, but a single whole, virtually a single body.[32] As Raphael explains:

> O Adam, one almighty is, from whom
> All things proceed, and up to him return,
>
> . . . .
>
> one first matter all,
> Indued with various forms, various degrees
> Of substance, and in things that live, of life.
> (V, 469–70, 472–74)

Milton's scale of nature or chain of being is a fluid continuum, ever flowing from body up to spirit:

> So from the root
> Springs lighter the green stalk, from thence the leaves
> More airy, last the bright consummate flower
> Spirits odorous breathes. (V, 479–82)

This radical unity of all things is a prominent feature of Milton's evening, where day shades imperceptibly into night, where "all things" are clad in the same sober livery and slink together to their beds, and the nightingale sings a love song for all creation.

Involved too in Adam's description of their evening nuptials is the very idea of creation: Eve as morning ("blushing like the morn") and evening as the time for love are here brought together, in evocation of the great "Biblical rhythm" of creation:[33] "Thus was the first day even and morn." The association of "evening and morning" with creation is secured by the sixfold repetition of the phrase in Book VII, the poem's central creation piece. It is evening too when the Son comes to walk in the garden, bringing both judgment and the offer of intercession. It is his mildness in judgment, and not his severity (as at the Last Judgment), that is stressed:

> Now was the sun in western cadence low
> From noon, and gentle airs due at thir hour
> To fan the earth now wak'd, and usher in
> The ev'ning cool, when he from wrath more cool

> Came the mild judge and intercessor both
> To sentence man: the voice of God they heard
> Now walking in the garden, by soft winds
> Brought to thir ears, while day declin'd.   (X, 92–99)

This is the last evening in Eden, gentle, cool, and soft—here more poignantly beautiful than ever because about to be lost—and as mild as the Son himself. Milton suggests a kind of association between them: both are "cool" (the Son is "more cool"). Syntax too establishes a link. Gentle airs "usher in / The ev'ning cool, when he . . . came." Momentarily we take the referent of "he" to be "evening," and then discover it to be the Son: "when he from wrath more cool / Came."

Evening, then, is throughout the poem directly associated with the beneficient creativeness in the universe, as expressed through creation itself, human love, and God's love for man. Indirectly, too, it becomes an epitome for paradise itself. Like Eden, evening represents both a delicate and precarious balance between day and night ("sufficient to have stood, though free to fall" [III, 99]), and at the same time a moving moment, never static (just as Eden offers not stasis and stultification,[34] but an opportunity for moral decision and gradual ascendance from body up to spirit).[35]

Twilight is an obviously useful symbol for a balance between countervailing elements. The idea of balance, as Fowler has pointed out, is central to *Paradise Lost*, where, in unfallen Eden, there are no seasons and an eternal equinox: day and night are always equal. He finds the "equinoctial theme" announced in a series of balance images, including the golden scales at the end of Book IV, as well as twilight itself:

> The sun was sunk, and after him the star
> Of Hesperus, whose office is to bring
> Twilight upon the earth, short arbiter
> Twixt day and night.   (IX, 48–51)

Twilight "maintains an even balance between light and darkness, but only briefly. So also the precarious stasis of prelapsarian life cannot long be sustained."[36] Fowler is surely right in stressing the importance of balance in the poem ("And earth self-balanced on her center hung"), and in seeing brief gray twilight as the image of that delicate balance. Twilight, or Hesperus (it is difficult to tell who is the arbiter), in a way acts as a kind of judge or arbitrator between day and night. Evening is perhaps an even-ing or leveling into balance and calm.[37] But there are some problems with this explanation.

By Fowler's own account, day and night in paradise are equal, so there is no need for an *arbiter*. For that matter, day and night in Eden are not really disputants. Like everything else, they harmoniously complement one another. And the point of day at which their powers are equal is in fact midnight, not twilight.[38] Hume, seeking a rational explanation, saw both dawn and dusk as times of indeterminate twilight. He thought Hesperus an arbiter "because when he follows the setting sun, he soon declares for the night, as when he precedes him [as Lucifer], he is on the side of day."[39] Hesperus as arbiter in Hume's view becomes simply a harbinger—at dawn forerunning day, at dusk forerunning night. But Milton may have intended yet more by the term "arbiter." Perhaps we as fallen readers are asked to think of Hesperus as an arbiter between opposing powers, and then (remembering Edenic harmony) to reject that meaning (a "fallen" meaning, and a measure of our moral distance from Eden) in favor of its original "unfallen" sense: witness, from *ad bitere*, "one who goes to see,"[40] as the "Moon sits Arbitress" over the belated peasant in I, 784. Hesperus (or twilight), then, does not judge between day and night. It simply stands witness *during the period between* ("'twixt") day and night, either as a protective presence or simply as a witness to the goodness of God's world.

That twilight period is in some respects not so much a balancing point as a process, not a stasis between day and night but a "grateful vicissitude" (VI, 8). Both words need close attention. Just as Eden itself is not really a stasis (*pace* Fowler), so evening, as we saw earlier, is always *in movement*. It does not "fall" suddenly but approaches gradually: "the sweet approach of ev'n or morn" (III, 42); "Now came still ev'ning on" (IV, 598); "sweet the coming on / Of grateful ev'ning mild" (IV, 646); "Ev'ning now approach'd" (V, 627); indeed, at its most sublime, evening can even "rise":

> And now on earth the seventh
> Ev'ning arose in Eden, for the sun
> Was set, and twilight from the east came on,
> Forerunning night.   (VII, 581–84, see also, V, 376)

The movement, the gradual change from light to dark, is itself "delectable," as Raphael says of evening in heaven (V, 629). Evening in Eden then becomes a kind of foretaste of heaven, where angels "Melodious

Hymns about the sovran Throne / Alternate all night long" (V, 655–56, recalling the nightingale who "all night long her amorous descant sung") and where, as Raphael later says,

> light and darkness in perpetual round
> Lodge and dislodge by turns, which makes through Heav'n
> Grateful vicissitude, like day and night;
> Light issues forth, and at the other door
> Obsequious darkness enters, till her hour
> To veil the heav'n, though darkness there might well
> Seem twilight here.   (VI, 6–12)

Vicissitude, in the seventeenth century, had already acquired some pejorative connotations.[41] Milton, however, insists that the vicissitude of evening, like the "ceaseless change" (V, 183) of all the unfallen world, is grateful,[42] that is, "pleasing," but also (in a universe throughout active and sympathetic) "thankful," and perhaps even "responsive" (as fertile soil is said to be grateful). Evening is not only a witness to God's goodness, but is grateful for it—thankful to God, but also pleasing to man, and something for which man himself should be grateful.[43] Before the Fall, Adam and Eve are indeed "grateful": in Eve's love song (IV, 639–56) and in the morning hymn (V, 153–208) they give thanks for Hesperus, "fairest of stars," for the moon, for "grateful evening mild." After the Fall (the original human act of ingratitude), evening itself changes. Twilight now becomes "disastrous," associated with the eclipse of the sun and with Satan (I, 597). Its light is now "dim," and (in Hume's word, p. 39) "doubtful." Evening is now not cool and mild, but dark and wet.

Whereas in unfallen Eden the "mists and exhalations" provide beauty or nourishment and praise God whether they are "rising or falling" (V, 185–91), after the Fall misty evenings are threatening:

> Thus Adam to himself lamented loud
> Through the still night, not now, as ere man fell,
> Wholesome and cool, and mild, but with black air
> Accompanied, with damps and dreadful gloom.   (X, 845–48)[44]

The nightingale's descant, accompanied by Silence, is now replaced by Adam's lament, accompanied by "black air." Here, as with the last evocation of evening in the poem (the dramatic time is noon; the evening scene is part of a simile), we are brought to the laboring world of the *Georgics:*

> The cherubim descended, as ev'ning mist
> Ris'n from a river o'er the marish glides,
> And gathers ground fast at the laborer's heel
> Homeward returning. (XII, 628–31)

It is only a step from this to the night in the fallen world of *Paradise Regained:*

> for now began
> Night with her sullen wing to double-shade
> The desert, fowls in their clay nests were couched;
> And now wild beasts came forth the woods to roam.
> (*PR* I, 499–502)

There is no mild evening; night falls rapidly, as in Virgil.[45] Instead of twilight's sober livery we have the far from protective sullen wing of night; instead of a calm and peaceful night, complement to day, a violent and stormy chaos, raised by Satan and the powers of darkness:

> Darkness now rose,
> As daylight sunk, and brought in louring night
> Her shadowy offspring unsubstantial both,
> Privation mere of light and absent day. (*PR* IV, 397–400)

The foul night yields only when the morning comes forth, with radiant finger to still the roar of thunder, chase the clouds, and lay the winds, as a white magician dispels "grisly spectres" with her magic wand. From this perspective the grateful evening mild seems more than ever a rich symbol of all that was lost.

University of California, Berkeley

NOTES

1. Charles Peake, ed., *Poetry of the Landscape and the Night: Two Eighteenth-Century Traditions* (London, 1967), p. 11.

2. I have used throughout the text in *Poems,* ed. J. Carey and A. Fowler (London, 1968). I have discussed the latter part of this passage (605–09) in "Milton's Moon," to appear in *Milton Studies,* IX, 1976.

3. 9th ed. (London, 1840), I, 306–07. Jonathan Richardson (father and son) agree: "Surely here is the most Inchanting Description of the Ev'ning that ever was made!" (*Explanatory Notes on Paradise Lost* [1734], p. 169).

4. For a partial list, see R. D. Havens, *The Influence of Milton on English Poetry* (Cambridge, Mass., 1922).

5. Reprint ed. (Folcroft Library Editions, 1971), p. 154.

6. "The Enthusiast" (1744), 200–02.

7. *Meaning in the Visual Arts* (Garden City, N.Y., 1955), pp. 300–01.

8.   Even now the house-tops yonder are smoking and longer shadows fall from the mountain-heights.

 Vesper gave the word to fold the flocks and tell their tale, as he set forth over an unwilling sky.

 Let us rise; the shade oft brings peril to singers. The juniper's shade brings peril; hurtful to the corn, too, is the shade. Get ye home, my full-fed goats—the Evening-star comes—get ye home!

This and future citations are to the Loeb Library edition, *Virgil*, ed. and trans. H. R. Fairclough, 2 vols. (London, 1916).

9. Panofsky, *Meaning in the Visual Arts*, p. 301.

10. "And straightway would they enter the fray and essay conflict, but ruddy Phoebus now laves his weary team in the Iberian flood, and, as day ebbs, brings back the night. Before the city they encamp and strengthen the ramparts."

11. See also XI, 182–83, 1, 210.

12. Night battles are special cases, fraught with extraordinary danger. Only once (*Georgics* III, 336–38) does Virgil describe evening as cool and refreshing. In *Aeneid* IV, 522–27, night is a time of stillness and sleep for all tired creatures, but not for Dido.

13. This and future citations are to *Spenser's Minor Poems*, ed. E. de Sélincourt (Oxford, 1910).

14. In the *Faerie Queene*, "noyous" night with its "sable" mantle is associated with evil and threats to man, and is contrasted with "joyous" day (1, xi, 49–51). In "Epithalamion," though the hours move slowly, night arrives suddenly (285–86).

15. *The Purple Island*, canto IV, st. 33, canto VI, st. 77, in *Poems*, ed. A. B. Grosart (1869), IV, 125–26, 194. In *The Locusts, or Apollyonists* (1627), night is thoroughly hostile: cloudy night whirls up the sky, bringing cold dew, night's "sable mantle," and deadly sleep (canto 1, sts. 5–7), ibid., II, 65–66. Milton may have remembered "sable mantle" along with "Night's black livery" (canto VIII, st. 5) from *The Purple Island*.

16. Notice how *long* it takes for night to fall in Eden in Book IV. At line 355 the sun is hastily declining, the stars that usher in evening arise; at line 540 the sun—nearing the horizon—appears to descend more slowly; at line 555 Uriel glides through the even on a sunbeam; at line 590 he returns now downward, for the sun has fallen beneath the horizon; at line 598 evening comes on; and at line 610, finally, the hour of night.

17. Compare "the gray-hooded Eev'n / Like a sad Votarist in Palmers Weed," *Comus*, 188–89.

18. Silent, with reference to the moon, means "not shining" (see *Samson Agonistes*, 87). Silence then appropriately appears when the moon is not yet shining.

19. *The State of Innocence: and Fall of Man* (London, 1745), p. 159.

20. "Hesperus, what more welcome fire than thou shines in the sky? for thou with thy flame confirmest the contracted espousals." Translation from Loeb Library edition, *Catullus, Tibullus, and Pervigilium Veneris* (Cambridge, Mass., 1956).

21. Contrast XI, 588, where Hesperus is "love's harbinger," and VIII, 519, where the evening star is bidden haste to light the bridal lamp.

22. Newton (9th ed., *Paradise Lost*) noted that Satan makes both Heaven and

the nightingale masculine here, though both are feminine elsewhere, "as the speech is addressed to Eve" (I, 352).

23. See H. Schultz, "Satan's Serenade," *PQ*, XXVII (1948), 17–26.

24. Herrick's epigram in fact deals with the *other* twilight, dawn, from the Latin *crepusculum*—"twilight" (dawn or dusk) (*Hesperides*, Holy Numbers No. 858).

25. See also "grateful vicissitude" (VI, 8) and "grateful truce" (VI, 407), both associated with evening.

26. IV, 185; IX, 582; XI, 276; V, 425, 630; II, 492.

27. Hume, *Annotations*, p. 100, commenting on III, 42.

28. Albert Cirillo, "Noon-Midnight and the Temporal Structure of *Paradise Lost*," *ELH*, XXIX (1962), 372–95.

29. See Fowler's notes in *Poems* to IV, 30; III, 616; and IX, 739. The sun at noon was associated with Christ the Sun of Righteousness.

30. "Noon-Midnight," p. 146.

31. The evening of the day of Christ's exaltation (V, 627), the first evening of the war (VI, 406), the evenings of Creation (VII), Adam's first evening with Eve (VIII, 518), the long evening I have been discussing (IV, 355–610), the following day when Raphael departs (VIII, 630), one week later, the evening before the Fall (IX, 48), and the evening after the Fall, when the Son comes (X, 92).

32. Compare V, 414–30, where the world is bound together in an alimentary cycle.

33. The phrase is Geoffrey Hartman's, in discussing another intimation of creation, the fall of Mulciber from "morn . . . to dewy eve" ("Milton's Counterplot," *ELH*, XXV [1958], 2).

34. Joseph Summers rightly emphasizes this aspect of Eden in *The Muse's Method* (Cambridge, Mass., 1962), chap. 3.

35. See V, 496 ff.

36. Note to IX, 50–51, in *Poems*.

37. Compare "The setting sun . . . *levell'd* his *ev'ning* rays" (*PL* IV, 540–43). L. S. Cox suspects a similar pun at *Samson Agonistes*, 1962 "Ev'ning dragon" (*MLN*, LXVI [1961], 583 n.).

38. See Fowler's long note in *Poems* to IV, 1013–15: "At midnight the powers of light and darkness are for a moment in equal balance. Then the *shades of night* begin to flee, and they continue to do so during the six hours that intervene before sunrise."

39. *Annotations*, p. 245.

40. Eighteenth-century editors, commenting on I, 784 (but not, curiously, IX, 50) knew this sense. Hume: "Arbiter most properly signifies a Looker on" (*Annotations*, p. 51); Heylin: "Witness, spectatress" (in Henry John Todd, *The Poetical Works of John Milton*, 3rd ed., 6 vols. [London, 1826], II, 98). Both Hume and Heylin cite Horace, *Epode* V, 49, "*arbitrae nox et Diana.*" See Christopher Ricks, *Milton's Grand Style* (Oxford, 1963), pp. 109–17, on "fallen" and "unfallen" meanings.

41. By Milton's time, vicissitude could be "impartial" or "dire." See *OED* and Johnson's *Dictionary*.

42. See Joseph Summers' chapter on "grateful vicissitude" in *The Muse's Method*.

43. "Grateful" is perhaps the most significant adjective applied to Eden. See Ricks' acute comments that, before the Fall, there would be no distinction between "pleasing" and "thankful": "Adam and Eve were thankful for what pleased them, and

being thankful is itself a pleasure," and "Certainly ingratitude is the great theme of the poem" (*Milton's Grand Style*, p. 113).

44. How changed from before, when Uriel comes "gliding through the even / on a sun-beam" (IV, 555–56). Nocturnal mist is associated with Satan, who "wrapt in mist / Of midnight vapor glide[s] obscure" (IX, 158–59).

45. Milton is probably echoing *Aeneid* VIII, 369: "*Non ruit et fuscis tellurem amplectitur alis*" ("Night rushes down, and clasps the earth with dusky wings").

LOVEMAKING IN MILTON'S PARADISE

Peter Lindenbaum

In *Paradise Lost,* Milton took the unusual stand of asserting that Adam and Eve engaged in sexual relations while still in Eden before the Fall, a stand which was, if not totally original with Milton, at least a departure from almost all treatments of his scriptural material by Christian poets, theologians, and biblical commentators before him. Any importance that the relative distinctiveness of such a stand implies is reinforced further by the enthusiastic outbursts of the poem's usually calm narrator when he touches on the subject of our first parents' nocturnal lovemaking (in Book IV) and on the related subject of the naked Eve's physical attractiveness. What amounts to an instance of Milton's personal emphasis in the poem, then, encourages the reader as well as Adam to view sexual love as the "sum" of prelapsarian bliss (VIII, 522); and when love of Eve proves to be the cause of Adam's fall, we are prompted to appreciate his decision as complex and difficult, even while we judge him mistaken in placing his love of Eve before obedience to God. The difficulty that Milton's own insistence upon prelapsarian sexual love works into Adam's decision is typical of the poet's presentation of prelapsarian life generally. Life in Milton's relatively difficult Eden is not so much significantly different from our postlapsarian existence as it is a pastoral image of our present complex life in small.

-

D ANIEL DEFOE seems to have been the first, and certainly not the last, of the critics of *Paradise Lost* to object to Milton's portrayal of Adam and Eve's prelapsarian lovemaking. His objection was not on the aesthetic grounds later raised by C. S. Lewis, but rather on those we might best call doctrinal or theological, and his objection (unlike Mr. Lewis') does have force or point. For since, as Defoe argued, barrenness is inconsistent with the state of perfection, Eve must have conceived at our first parents' initial act of intercourse in Eden.[1] But if their first in-

tercourse did in fact take place before the Fall, how could Adam and
Eve have passed the taint of original sin on to Cain? Defoe raised this
question in his *Review of the State of the British Nation* of March 29,
1712, merely, he claimed, as a "doubt" or "difficulty" in Milton's han-
dling of his story and not "to detract" from Milton, and he called upon
the learned author of the *Spectator* papers on *Paradise Lost,* or anyone
else for that matter, to resolve it for him. No solution proved to be forth-
coming, as indeed no solution is possible. For if one holds to the doctrine
of original sin, one has either to assume that God was guilty of inefficiency (when he commanded Adam and Eve to increase and multiply
and then failed to have them conceive a child upon any intercourse in
Eden) or simply to conclude that there was no sexual consummation
before the Fall. The difficulties attendant upon the first of these options
naturally enough helped push most Christian theologians and scriptural exegetes before Milton to the second position, that there was no
prelapsarian sexual union and that so "ungracious" a child as Cain
could only have been conceived after Adam and Eve had eaten of the
fruit. Milton, as Defoe pointed out, did not take the traditional stand on
this matter and even insisted on the fact that he was not taking it, and I
want in this essay to examine the significance of the stand Milton did
take and its implications for *Paradise Lost* as a whole.

I

Milton was not the first interpreter of the opening chapters of
Genesis to assume sexual intercourse between the unfallen Adam and
Eve. Many medieval and earlier Jewish exegetes, untrammeled by the
doctrine of original sin and hence with no need to have Adam transmit
that taint to Cain directly, had already imputed sexual union to Adam
and Eve in their innocent state. Even those rabbis who used their reading of Psalm xlix, verse 13, "Man tarrieth not overnight in his glory," as
a gloss on chapters ii and iii of Genesis, and who thus agreed with many
Christian commentators that Adam and Eve fell on the first day of their
creation, often made sexual intercourse one of our first parents' activities
in an hour-by-hour timetable of the events of their first day.[2] And Jacob
Cats, a Dutch diplomat and poet, whose poem in praise of marriage,
Trou-ringh, Milton may have read in the original Dutch or its Latin
translation, celebrated at length and with considerable vehemence the
sexual joys experienced by Adam and Eve while in Paradise (though

these joys seem to have been more appreciated by Cats' Adam than by his rather reluctant Eve).[3] There were, as well, Grotius' *Adamus Exul* and Vondel's *Adam in Ballingschap,* both of which plays deal with Milton's main subject, the Fall of Man, and both of which postulate, even if they do not greatly emphasize, sexual consummation before the Fall.[4] But if Milton's stand on prelapsarian sexual love was not original with him, it was certainly the position of a small minority, and the very prominence and emphasis Milton gave to the subject in *Paradise Lost* suggest that his stand reflects some particularly intense personal interest and belief and is not something he merely borrowed while reading earlier works in the hexameral tradition.[5] In *Paradise Lost* he was in fact very self-consciously assuming an extreme position in what he quite rightly understood to be a long-standing exegetical debate on the possible existence and nature of our first parents' sexual activity in Eden. The main outlines of that debate will help us to appreciate fully the distinctiveness of Milton's stand.

The debate was from its earliest stages clearly connected with attitudes towards sexual intercourse and marriage generally. At what is perhaps the opposite extreme from Milton was the fourth-century church father, St. Gregory of Nyssa.[6] Expressing the early Christian disapproval of conjugal union, Gregory put forward the argument that had Adam and Eve not fallen, they would have reproduced in a manner similar to that of the angels. In Gregory's view, as in that of other fathers such as St. John Chrysostom and St. John Damascene, prelapsarian life was a kind of angelic existence, and "whatever the mode of increase in the angelic nature is (unspeakable and inconceivable by human conjectures, except that it assuredly exists), it would have operated also in the case of men." While Gregory thus admitted that he no more than anyone else had any specific idea how angels or unfallen man might propagate, he was sure that it would be very different from "that animal and irrational mode" fallen man is forced to use.[7]

If Gregory of Nyssa could not even imagine the sexual act without its fallen manifestations of libidinousness and animal passion, Augustine could, and in Book XIV of *The City of God* he objected strongly to a view expressed by Gregory, among others, that God had created two sexes before the Fall with his eye on the manner of procreation to be used only *after* man first sinned. Such a view was plainly unacceptable, in Augustine's opinion, since it rendered God dependent upon man's sin to accomplish his ultimate plan for man and complete the requisite number of saints to fill the heavenly city.[8] Augustine was thus directly opposed to the argument that unfallen man would have reproduced the way angels do and asserted that God created two different sexes so that Adam and Eve might procreate specifically by means of sexual union, even without a fall from grace. Indeed, he argued elsewhere (and was followed by Aquinas in this) that were it not specifically procreation that God had in mind when he created Eve, he might more wisely have created a male companion as a helpmeet for Adam.[9] In Augustine's judgment, there *could* have been sexual union in the manner of fallen human beings even before the Fall, but with the important difference that in prelapsarian sexual love the generative organs would have been moved by the will, not excited by lust:

In such happy circumstances and general human well-being we should be far from suspecting that offspring could not have been begotten without the disease of lust, but those parts, like all the rest, would be set in motion at the command of the will; and without the seductive stimulus of passion, with calmness of mind and with no corrupting of the integrity of the body, the husband would lie upon the bosom of his wife. (Bk. XIV, chap. xxvi)

Contrary to what Gregory and others had implied, then, the sexual act was not in itself bad; what defiled it was fallen man's inability to procreate without being subject to lust and immoderate passion. Yet, for all his defense of the original purity of the sexual act itself, Augustine was quick to add that there was in fact no sexual intercourse before the Fall; his whole discussion was perforce being carried on in very theoretical and hypothetical terms. For, as he suggested in the *De Genesi ad Litteram*, either because Adam and Eve sinned soon after Eve's creation and were forthwith expelled from Eden or because they awaited God's specific command as to the time of their first act of intercourse, our first parents did not have the opportunity to participate in that passionless generation proper to their unfallen state.[10]

Augustine's argument had a great deal to recommend it, as it not only avoided the possible blasphemy of viewing God as dependent upon man's sin to accomplish his ends, but also neatly sidestepped the similar difficulties implicit in the idea of an unfruitful act of intercourse commanded by a God who wished to see man increase and multiply. It enabled Christians to hold to the doctrine of original sin and thus account for Cain's evil nature, and at the same time to accept even carnal sexuality with a gratefulness proper to man when approaching any of God's gifts. Augustine's logic proved in fact to be the most important and influential of the various patristic attempts to solve our question of prelapsarian sexual union. It was taken over outright by later theologians and commentators such as Aquinas, Peter Lombard, Peter Comestor, and the Renaissance Jesuit Benedictus Pererius,[11] and not only became what amounted to accepted doctrine of the Catholic church but was readily adopted by many Protestants also. Echoes of it are to be found, for instance, in Luther's assertion that Adam and Eve were virgin at their fall even though unfallen procreation would have been very pure and honorable work, and in the attack of the seventeenth-century Protestant convert, John Salkeld, on Gregory of Nyssa and St. John Damascene's view of an angelic prelapsarian Adam and Eve.[12] It would prove useful as well to all those Christian commentators who, by whatever reasoning, limited our first parents to less than a day in Paradise before their fall.[13]

Augustine can be said, then, to have effected a partial redemption of man's sexual organs—but only a partial one. Despite the argument that pure and unsinful sexual relations could have taken place in prelapsarian Eden (but did not), orthodox Catholicism continued to hold to what it understood to be St. Paul's, and indeed Augustine's own, distrust of postlapsarian conjugal love and thus to prefer celibacy over the married state. The opposition to celibacy as a necessarily better state, and particularly to a celibate clergy, was of course one of the main issues whereby early Protestant reformers differentiated themselves from the Catholicism they were attacking. Luther referred to those who deny there is any chastity in marriage and who prefer a celibate clergy as "the tools of Satan and the enemies of Christ." Calvin, in a similar polemical vein, looked upon the defamation of marriage and preference for celibacy as the particular "artifice of Satan" designed to confuse man and bring about his destruction.[14] Following their master's lead, a well-nigh endless number of sixteenth- and seventeenth-century Protestant preachers (many of them of distinctly Puritan learnings) were to accord marriage a dignity and respect totally new to the Christian tradition. St. Paul, whom no Protestant and least of all a Puritan would be likely to slight, may indeed have said that it was better to remain celibate as he was (1 Corinthians vii, 7) and have deprecated marriage in his "it is better to marry than to burn" (1 Corinthians vii, 9); still, the influential

Cambridge Puritan William Perkins could easily find other passages from Paul to justify the conclusion that though "marriage is of itselfe a thing indifferent, and the kingdome of God stands no more in it, then in meats and drinks . . . yet it is a state in it selfe, farre more excellent, then the condition of single life." [15]

But the many Protestant preachers who spoke and wrote on the subject of marriage were most concerned with presenting a practical code of conduct for life in a fallen world, and while they might pause to note that God ordained marriage in Paradise, they did not occuy themselves greatly with the theoretical question of whether there was sexual union before the Fall. And even when a poet who shares many of Milton's and the more adamant Protestants' beliefs does have time and cause to examine prelapsarian life in detail, he does not necessarily carry the Protestant enthusiasm over the joys and comforts of married life to the logical conclusion Milton did. The French Huguenot Du Bartas, in fact, though he did stop to present a delighted epithalamium at the point that Eve is presented to Adam, nonetheless backed away from the specific questions of whether and how Adam and Eve made love in Paradise. Proceeding much in the manner of Augustine, Du Bartas assumed that it was likely that God intended Adam and Eve to procreate in the way that fallen men do, though without the "tickling flames" that now surprise our "fond soule":

> Or, whether else as men ingender now,
> Sith Spouse-bed spot-less laws of God allow,
> If no excess command: sith else again
> The Lord had made the double sex in vain.[16]

DuBartas would venture such a statement, however, only in the form of a question and even prefaced the question (along with those of how long Adam and Eve remained in Paradise and whether they were virgin at their fall) with a warning to his muse that she should not attempt to deal with such unprofitable and unanswerable questions lest she prove "too busie-idle / And over-bold" (647–48) in treading such "too-curious" paths.

If distrust of sexual relations had led to the early Catholic disapproval of marriage generally and to the banning of sexual love from Paradise, the obverse of such an attitude not only praises marriage but reinstitutes its sexual consummation in Eden. Milton did precisely that and his particular contribution to this debate on prelapsarian sexual love was to bring the Protestant preachers' enthusiasm for marriage fully to bear on Adam and Eve's prelapsarian state. Far from considering speculation over our first parents' conjugal relations as "busie idleness," in *Paradise Lost* Milton portrayed prelapsarian sexual love with an explicitness approached by only one figure (Jacob Cats) in the Christian tradition before him.

II

Once Milton had determined in his own mind that there in fact was prelapsarian sexual love, he quite understandably made it an important part of Adam and Eve's Edenic life. In Du Bartas' view, Adam's "best and supreme delectation" in Eden was the frequent and direct communication he had there with God.[17] Milton's Adam would himself seem to hold to the same opinion after his fall, when he laments that what most afflicts him in leaving Paradise is being deprived of God's countenance (XI, 315–17); but before the Fall, while still experiencing all his joys, "the sum of earthly bliss" for him is the enjoyment, and specifically the sexual enjoyment, of Eve (VIII, 522).[18] Adam and Eve together, in their evening prayer, refer to their "mutual help and mutual love" as "the Crown of all our bliss" (IV, 728). And Satan even considers an embrace between Adam and Eve as Paradise in itself:

> Sight hateful, sight tormenting! thus these two
> Imparadis't in one another's arms
> The happier *Eden,* shall enjoy thir fill
> Of bliss on bliss, while I to Hell am thrust.   (IV, 505–08)

While such sentiments are probably to be expected from an Adam and Eve who are enjoying their mutual love and a Satan who is jealous of it, we cannot conclude from such evidence alone that the poet himself shared his characters' estimate of sexual love as the greatest of prelapsarian pleasures. Satan is hardly a figure whose words or opinions we can accept without careful examination, and one might argue that it is precisely because Adam puts too high an estimate on Eve and on his relationship with her that he falls—an act which Milton could not but censure. But we ought to be able to trust the poem's narrator, and when our guide through the poem also expresses abounding enthusiasm over the gift of prelapsarian sexual love, we have very good cause to consider both that Milton himself viewed that gift as the crown of Eden's blessings and that he wanted us to think so too.

The first time in the poem we see Adam and Eve retire for the night, the narrator breaks in with his famous and impassioned eulogy on wedded love. It is at this point that Milton most directly comments upon the earlier exegetical debate on prelapsarian sexual love, and it is here that the whole debate becomes not simply background material pointing to the relative originality of Milton's own stand but is worked into the very fabric of the poem itself.[19] I present the passage in full, because it is important that we be aware, among other things, of the sheer length of the outburst:

> into thir inmost bower
> Handed they went; and eas'd the putting off
> These troublesome disguises which wee wear,
> Straight side by side were laid, nor turn'd I ween
> *Adam* from his fair Spouse, nor *Eve* the Rites
> Mysterious of connubial Love refus'd:
> Whatever Hypocrites austerely talk
> Of purity and place and innocence,
> Defaming as impure what God declares
> Pure, and commands to some, leaves free to all.
> Our Maker bids increase, who bids abstain
> But our Destroyer, foe to God and Man?
> Hail wedded Love, mysterious Law, true source
> Of human offspring, sole propriety
> In Paradise of all things common else.
> By thee adulterous lust was driv'n from men
> Among the bestial herds to range, by thee
> Founded in Reason, Loyal, Just, and Pure,
> Relations dear, and all the Charities
> Of Father, Son, and Brother first were known.
> Far be it, that I should write thee sin or blame,
> Or think thee unbefitting holiest place,
> Perpetual Fountain of Domestic sweets,
> Whose bed is undefil'd and chaste pronounc't,
> Present, or past, as Saints and Patriarchs us'd.
> Here Love his golden shafts imploys, here lights
> His constant Lamp, and waves his purple wings,
> Reigns here and revels; not in the bought smile
> Of Harlots, loveless, joyless, unindear'd,
> Casual fruition, nor in Court Amours,
> Mixt Dance, or wanton Mask, or Midnight Ball,
> Or Serenate, which the starv'd Lover sings
> To his proud fair, best quitted with disdain.

> These lull'd by Nightingales imbracing slept,
> And on their naked limbs the flow'ry roof
> Show'r'd Roses, which the Morn repair'd. Sleep on,
> Blest pair; and O yet happiest if ye seek,
> No happier state, and know to know no more.   (IV, 738–75)

Milton was no mean polemicist himself, and the attack on the "hypocrites" who defame sexual union echoes both the vehemence and the words of Paul and, perhaps, Calvin or Luther. Paul's hypocrites of 1 Timothy, chapter iv were those ascetics who forbid marriage in a fallen world, whereas the whole context of Milton's use of the word and specifically his reference to "purity and place and innocence" plainly show that he also has in mind those who had ruled out even the possibility of sexual love in Paradise. Milton is clearly lumping together all opponents of sexual union, be it pre- or postlapsarian, and his "hypocrites" then would include Gregory of Nyssa as well as the Catholics of his own time who might still favor celibacy over married life. While to Milton and his Protestant audience, no term of abuse for a contemporary Catholic might seem too strong, that mantle of "hypocrite" does fall a bit heavily on Gregory and the other early church fathers who, while betraying an ascetic streak, were after all merely following what they understood to be the implications of the Gospels and St. Paul. Harsh as the term may be, it points up sharply the obvious strength of its speaker's feelings on an issue of evident importance to him.

The length of the outburst is of course another indication of the strong feeling behind it. Everything from the reference to hypocrites up to the description of the nightingales is, as eighteenth-century critics and editors such as Addison and Bishop Thomas Newton were wont to observe, very strictly speaking a digression from the straight narrative progress of the poem—though ultimately no more of a digression from the whole of the poem than the so-called digressions in "Lycidas." In a voice that seems indistinguishable from Milton's own (in view of Milton's distinctive stand on the very existence of prelapsarian sexual love), the narrator moves from a description of specifically prelapsarian wedded love to praise of wedded love in general. Because Adam and Eve's marriage, instituted by God in Paradise, was in the eyes of Milton and the Protestant apologists for marriage the example and prototype for all subsequent Christian marriages, this move or jump is not hard to understand. But by the time he is distinguishing postlapsarian wedded love

from prostitution, "Court Amours," and Petrarchan love, this narrator
has wandered well away from the ostensible main subject of this part of
Book IV—Adam and Eve in Paradise. Several scholars have pointed out
that it is not at all uncommon for expositors of Genesis to use Adam and
Eve's marriage in Paradise as an occasion to launch into extended praise
of marriage and an attack on all lustful and illicit relationships.[20] However, the fact that the digression here has precedents in no way softens
the impression that this outburst makes upon us as we read through the
poem. We seem to have come, in this extended and rhetorically heightened passage, upon a speaker who has struck upon a subject very dear to
his own heart and who cannot resist the temptation to rhapsodize on
that subject for a while. The whole passage is in fact only one of several
emotionally charged outbursts on the part of the narrator which have a
very significant effect upon our reading experience and interpretation of
events in the latter part of the poem. For, whether or not we remember
the outbursts specifically by the time we reach Adam's fall, they help to
predispose us towards understanding, though not necessarily condoning,
Adam's motives when he decides to disobey God's sole prohibition and
fall along with Eve. While we never lose consciousness of the fact that
Adam's acceptance of the fruit was a mistake which had disastrous effects for him and for all of us, these outbursts are greatly responsible for
bringing us to see that Adam did nonetheless have a difficult and meaningful decision to make, that he had something valuable and important
to lose in refusing the fruit.

   Another such outburst, much briefer but similarly interrupting the
poem's narrative action and attesting to the importance of prelapsarian
wedded love to the narrator, comes near the beginning of Book VIII.
Adam has just asked his question about celestial motions, implying in
effect that God has been inefficient in constructing a geocentric universe.
Milton has two different ways of telling us that Adam ought not to have
asked the question: one, of course, is Raphael's long answer telling
Adam that it is not for him, a mere human, to doubt the wisdom of
God's ways or logic; the other is having Eve wander off when Adam enters on such "studious thoughts abstruse" (VIII, 40). Milton implies that
in asking the question Adam is not paying enough attention to what
ought to interest him most—Eve and her beauty. Both right before and
after Eve moves off, we are told that she has such majesty, grace, and

beauty that those who saw her ought to wish her to stay (VIII, 43, 63). Yet Adam and Raphael continue to talk on their abstruse intellectual plane. Eve on her part prefers to have the discussion of such matters mixed in with a certain amount of immediate, less rarified and intellectualized, pleasure:

> Her Husband the Relater she preferr'd
> Before the Angel, and of him to ask
> Chose rather: hee, she knew, would intermix
> Grateful digressions, and solve high dispute
> With conjugal Caresses, from his Lip
> Not Words alone pleas'd her.   (VIII, 52–57)

Milton might at this point be having Eve adhere, insofar as her prelapsarian state allows for such a parallel, to St. Paul's instruction of 1 Corinthians xiv, 35, that women should ask their husbands questions at home rather than in church where it is shameful for a woman to speak. Paul, however, says nothing about interspersed kisses and conjugal caresses, and from these lines alone we might be tempted to doubt that Eve really cares about how the universe is organized. But the narrator of the poem has no such doubts. He has a moment before informed us that Eve is not uninterested in such matters—"Yet went she not, as not with such discourse / Delighted" (48–49)—and right after these lines intervenes with a highly charged rhetorical question which implies total approval of her desire to learn from Adam alone:

> O when meet now
> Such pairs, in Love and mutual Honor join'd? (VIII, 57–58)

The full force of this question runs somewhat counter to the earlier eulogy on wedded love, for it implies that one of the unfortunate results of the Fall has been the loss of true or ideal wedded love. But it does, in any case, direct our attention once again to a narrator to whom wedded love is very important.

Perhaps the most striking and revealing of the narrator's emotional outbursts—revealing in that it shows us a speaker very susceptible to Eve's charms and laboring under a great deal of stress as he writes—occurs in the middle of Book V. At the point that Eve is serving to Adam and Raphael that dinner which is in no danger of cooling, the narrator stops to consider her naked beauty, and breaks in with:

                                                         O innocence
                    Deserving Paradise! If ever, then,
                    Then had the Sons of God excuse to have been
                    Enamour'd at that sight; but in those hearts
                    Love unlibidinous reign'd, nor jealousy
                    Was understood, the injur'd Lover's Hell.   (V, 445–50)

A general distinction is being made in these lines between the love of
Adam and Eve (and that of Raphael also) and the libidinous love of the
Sons of God for the Daughters of Cain, this latter love to be described for
us in disparaging fullness much later on in the poem (XI, 573–92). The
scene here in Eden has to do though, not with the glittering enticements
of women anxious to catch men in an "amorous Net" (XI, 586), but with
Eve and with love that is pure, so pure that a third figure, the angel
Raphael, can look upon the naked Eve without either arousing Adam's
jealousy or becoming jealous of Adam himself. This scene in Eden, in
fact, presents such a special case that the narrator appears well on his
way towards assuring us and evidently himself also that it is all right to
become infatuated with feminine beauty, if that beauty belongs to someone as innocent and good as Eve. The rhetorical power of the repeated
and heavily stressed "then" in the clause "if ever, then, / Then had the
Sons of Gods excuse" builds up to the point that it expresses outright
the wish that one could allow oneself to become enamored. But still, that
clause carries within it its own contradiction: the word "excuse" implies
that becoming enamored at all, even of unfallen Eve, is a weakness or a
mistake, some lapse that must be pardoned. And "if ever," suggesting a
situation contrary to fact, implies by its very existence in this context its
opposite "never," and hence the idea that not even in Paradise and with
the sinless Eve does one have an excuse for becoming enamored; if the
words "if ever" had simply been left out, there would have been no such
implication. Though the narrator goes on and tries to make the qualitative distinction between the pure and good love of Adam and Eve and
the love of the Sons of God, the implication remains that becoming
enamored at all, whether by Adam or by the libidinous Sons of God, is
inexcusable and hence wrong.

       When we recall that the narrator moved into this passage as a result
of his enthusiasm for the innocent Eve's naked beauty, the main impression that we are left with after this brief but excited outburst in Book V
is that of a momentarily troubled and confused narrator, one who is con-

fused specifically by Eve. By this time in the poem, we no doubt can well sympathize with and understand this confusion. We too have witnessed, for instance, that moment when Eve

> with eyes
> Of conjugal attraction unreprov'd
> And meek surrender, half imbracing lean'd
> On our first Father, half her swelling Breast
> Naked met his under the flowing Gold
> Of her loose tresses hid.   (IV, 492–97)

Eve is indeed beautiful, and much of Milton's most effective and affecting writing has gone into the descriptions of her. We can understand, then, why the narrator himself might feel pulled in two different directions, towards, let us say, recognizing that passion must always be kept under the control of reason, and towards the recognition that Eve is, after all, very beautiful and ought to be cherished. And in the outburst in Book V, we find a narrator who momentarily betrays an intense personal awareness of just the feelings that Adam had to cope with when he had to choose between taking the fruit from Eve and living on in Eden without this particular Eve.

What is most remarkable about these outbursts, what in effect draws our attention to them so strongly, is that the narrator's voice in them is so different from his voice elsewhere in the poem, that voice which has angered the anti-Miltonists of this century. At other points in the poem, this narrator apparently shows no awareness at all either of Eve's beauty or of the effect that her beauty and love might have upon Adam. When Adam takes the fruit from Eve and receives death for his act, for instance, this same narrator sums up the action taking place in the vindictive and legalistic terms of "for such compliance bad / Such recompense best merits" (IX, 994–95) and four lines later describes Adam merely as "fondly overcome with Female charm" (IX, 999). With such a deprecatory formula as this last, the narrator would seem to be forgetting his own earlier excitement over that "Female charm." The fact that the narrator's voice is inconsistent is not in itself very damaging or even important, for the narrator is not a character as in a novel or a play; rather, he is in the poem primarily to direct and mold *our* consciousness as we read. And what becomes most significant about an outburst such as the one in Book V is simply that the feeling of confusion, the tension between what one feels one ought to do and what one would like to do, has been presented to us and has become part of our own experience as we proceed through the poem.

Were we to judge these emotional outbursts simply on the basis of the number of lines devoted to them in the poem, they might not appear of major importance. But their effect on a reader is considerable, especially if he has any awareness at all of the relative originality or distinctiveness of Milton's stand in the debate on the existence of prelapsarian sexual love (and the argumentative nature of the first of the outbursts, the eulogy on wedded love, suggests that Milton envisioned his readers as having at least some awareness of it). For not only are these passages a departure from the narrator's usual calm, they are also of course a reflection and extension of Milton's initial decision to endow Adam and Eve with the gift of prelapsarian sexual love. They compound and underline that original decision and provide what is evidently authorial endorsement of Adam's and Satan's enthusiasm for Eve and for marriage to her. These passages in effect tell us directly that marriage to Eve is something to be excited about, and it is in large part because of the emphasis they provide that even readers who are not Waldocks are likely to bristle at reductive summaries such as "fondly overcome with Female charm." While back in Book IV Adam himself referred to God's proclamation on the fruit of the Tree of Knowledge as "one easy prohibition"(IV, 433), these passages serve to show us how that prohibition could have become hard—hard enough to make Adam disobey it when forced to choose between his love of God and his love of Eve.

III

Both Milton's own stand on the very existence of prelapsarian sexual love and the emphasis given that subject by the narrator's excitement over it would appear to be preparing us for the particular moment in the poem when Adam must decide whether to accept the fruit from Eve and fall with her. It is at this point that the force of the emphasis on conjugal love as valuable and to be cherished comes into direct conflict with God's prohibition of the fruit of the Tree of Knowledge, and we would ordinarily expect a scene of considerable dramatic tension and excitement to do justice to a decision and moment of such significance. But, perhaps in order to prevent his audience's too easy identification with Adam when he makes his disastrous mistake and falls, Milton does two things which put some distance between Adam and ourselves at this important point: he has the lying Eve who offers the fruit appear far less attractive than anywhere else in the poem (she thus becomes someone whose offer we at least might resist accepting); and he reduces the dramatic tension and impact of the scene by having Adam quickly and incorrectly treat his decision as a foregone conclusion, a direct logical consequence of Eve's fall. Adam conceives of himself at his fall as the mere object of verbs, without an independent will ("And mee with thee hath ruin'd," "I feel / The link of Nature draw me" [IX, 906, 913–14]) and at no point in the inward speech following Eve's offer of the fruit does he pause and seriously consider not falling with her. Adam's decision is, in effect, made before we have a chance to argue it out for ourselves and hence place ourselves fully in his position.[21] While Adam's fall may be, then, the point in the poem at which Adam himself reacts most strongly to the feelings created in him by the gift of prelapsarian sexual love, it is not the point in the poem that *we* feel the effect of the poem's emphasis on that love most forcefully. That point comes earlier, at the end of Book VIII and the culmination of Adam's prelapsarian education by Raphael. It is at this earlier point that Adam most explicitly articulates, and hence lets us share, the feelings that Eve and his relationship with her arouse in him, and it is there that the whole treatment of prelapsarian sexual love is most likely to alter or influence our understanding of the poem's overall action and argument.

After Adam is "clear'd of doubt" on the organization of the universe, he agrees to descend to matters more "at hand" (VIII, 199) and to talk of his life in Eden. The term "at hand" is perhaps a slight joke on Milton's part at Adam's expense, for by this time in the poem, it can only refer to one thing for the reader: it is always Eve who is being "handed" into the bower or is seen walking "hand in hand" with Adam. Not surprisingly then, Adam's account of his own life narrows down quickly to the importance of Eve to him. And having been told by Raphael that he ought to joy in his fair Eve (VIII, 170–72), Adam proceeds to let slip the fact that the sum of his earthly bliss, the joy he experiences in Eve, is in fact passion:

> but here
> Far otherwise, transported I behold,
> Transported touch; here passion first I felt,
> Commotion strange, in all enjoyments else
> Superior and unmov'd, here only weak
> Against the charm of Beauty's powerful glance.   (VIII, 528–33)

Adam himself recognizes that there is something wrong in the strength
of this feeling and at first he incorrectly tries to blame Nature for it:

> Or Nature fail'd in mee, and left some part
> Not proof enough such Object to sustain,
> Or from my side subducting, took perhaps
> More than enough; at least on her bestow'd
> Too much of Ornament, in outward show
> Elaborate, of inward less exact.   (VIII, 534–39)

In the last two and one-half lines here Adam is committing much the
same error he did earlier in his question on the organization of the
universe: he is implicitly accusing God (through his handmaiden, Nature) of inefficiency, of putting more ornament or beauty than was strictly
necessary on the less important exterior Eve while not giving proportionate care to her more important inner faculties. Such a charge would
rightly bring down upon Adam a rebuke similar to that following his
earlier question on the heavens. But Adam goes on to a more complete
and less irreverent statement of the difficulty he experiences when dealing with Eve. He fully understands that he is the superior being, yet that
understanding does not help him much when he listens to what Eve has
to say:

> For well I understand in the prime end
> Of Nature her th' inferior, in the mind
> And inward Faculties, which most excel,
> In outward also her resembling less
> His Image who made both, and less expressing
> The character of that Dominion giv'n
> O'er other Creatures; yet when I approach
> Her loveliness, so absolute she seems
> And in herself complete, so well to know
> Her own, that what she wills to do or say,
> Seems wisest, virtuousest, discreetest, best;
> All higher knowledge in her presence falls
> Degraded, Wisdom in discourse with her
> Loses discount'nanc't, and like folly shows;
> Authority and Reason on her wait,
> As one intended first, not after made
> Occasionally; and to consummate all,
> Greatness of mind and nobleness thir seat
> Build in her loveliest, and create an awe
> About her, as a guard Angelic plac't.   (VIII, 540–59)

The number of harsh sibilants in a line like "Seems wisest, virtuousest, discreetest, best" may be expressing Milton's own disapproval of what Adam is saying here. But Adam himself is being very honest, and he is confessing to something which he too knows should not in theory be true. He knows he ought to be able to separate the value of what is being said from the person saying it, yet Eve's loveliness confuses him and makes it difficult for him to distinguish true wisdom from the mere show of it. What exactly Adam means by "loveliness" may not be totally clear, but it is evident from the last four lines of his account that he does not mean simply what Raphael is about to call her fair "outside." Her loveliness, for Adam, would appear to reside in the harmony of her whole being ("so absolute she seems / And in herself complete") and in the *combination* of her external beauty with inner virtues of nobility and greatness of mind.

Raphael's response to this troubled confession is, as Waldock noted in outrage, not completely to the point.[22] The angel directs himself mainly to the first part of what Adam had said—his confession of passion and the accusation against Nature—and berates Adam for hearkening only to Eve's outer appearance:

> Accuse not Nature, she hath done her part;
> Do thou but thine, and be not diffident
> Of Wisdom, she deserts thee not, if thou
> Dismiss not her, when most thou need'st her nigh,
> By attribúting overmuch to things
> Less excellent, as thou thyself perceiv'st.
> For what admir'st thou, what transports thee so,
> An outside? fair no doubt, and worthy well
> Thy cherishing, thy honoring, and thy love,
> Not thy subjection.   (VIII, 561–70)

Raphael insists, then, on accepting "loveliness" as only physical beauty. He goes on to tell Adam to have more self-esteem, to weigh Eve with himself and then "value" or judge (VIII, 570–73), advice which in view of the hierarchical scheme suggested in the formula "Hee for God only, shee for God in him" (IV, 299) is certainly sound enough. But Adam has said in his speech that he *has* weighed Eve with himself, and still he finds it difficult to determine whether what Eve says is wise or only seems so because it is she who is saying it; Raphael is thus reasserting doctrine which Adam has already acknowledged as true. And without providing any concrete help towards relieving the difficulty that persists even after Adam acknowledges Eve his intellectual inferior, Raphael reverts to an earlier part of Adam's speech, to the mention of sexual love as the "sum of earthly bliss" (VIII, 522). The angel proceeds into an attack which is particularly striking because it runs directly counter in spirit both to Milton's own unusual decision to grant Adam and Eve sexual love before the Fall and to the narrator's vehement defense of sexual love, back in Book IV, as proper and good for man even in Paradise:

> But if the sense of touch whereby mankind
> Is propagated seem such dear delight
> Beyond all other, think the same voutsaf't
> To Cattle and each Beast; which would not be
> To them made common and divulg'd, if aught
> Therein enjoy'd were worthy to subdue
> The Soul of Man, or passion in him move.   (VIII, 579–85)

Raphael does urge Adam to love what is higher and rational in Eve, and in the process makes a Neoplatonic distinction between sacred and profane love, or rational love and merely carnal passion:

> What higher in her society thou find'st
> Attractive, human, rational, love still;
> In loving thou dost well, in passion not,
> Wherein true Love consists not; Love refines
> The thoughts, and heart enlarges, hath his seat
> In Reason, and is judicious, is the scale
> By which to heav'nly Love thou may'st ascend,
> Not sunk in carnal pleasure, for which cause
> Among the Beasts no Mate for thee was found.   (VIII, 586–94)

This may be all very well and good in Neoplatonic theory, but Raphael is making sharp distinctions where Adam has just confessed he cannot make them. His love for Eve simply cannot be separated so easily into its rational and carnal aspects.

Adam has some cause to believe, then, that Raphael has oversimplified both what he has just said and his prelapsarian difficulties, and this is one of the reasons, I take it, that Milton has Adam only "half abash't" (VIII, 595) by Raphael's rebuke. The other possible reason would be that Adam is not sufficiently acknowledging the justice in Raphael's rebuke and the applicability of Raphael's remarks to him—that is, that he ought to be more abashed than he is. It would be very difficult and probably misguided to attempt to determine which of these interpretations is correct; most likely, both are. Raphael has not actually been contradicting the rest of the poem. Though the point of the narrator's eulogy to wedded love was to establish the body and that "sense of touch whereby mankind / Is propagated" as good and pure in themselves, in that eulogy the narrator referred to love, as Raphael in effect does here, as "Founded in Reason" (IV, 755). And no one has ever told Adam that there is no need for control in Paradise. Adam in fact implicitly accepts part of Raphael's rebuke as justified when he goes on to claim that he is only telling the angel what he feels inwardly as a result of Eve's loving words, actions, and compliance and is not therefore foiled (VIII, 600–08). Yet from the analysis of the conversation in Book VIII provided thus far, it should be clear that, as legitimate as Raphael's theories on the make-up of human nature may be, we cannot very easily accept Raphael simply as Milton's authoritative spokesman in the discussion.

What we have here in Book VIII is the kind of discussion or debate found frequently in Milton between two different kinds of beings, or even two human figures, who do not fully understand one another and are arguing on different levels—the kind of debate we witness, for instance, between Comus and the Lady. The two figures are putting forth arguments not completely related and are not successful in making themselves fully understood to each other. If Adam does not sufficiently apply Raphael's words to his own case, Raphael on his part does not comprehend and speak to the type of difficulty Adam is talking about. As far as the angel is concerned, man has reason and passions, and he must always keep reason uppermost and in firm control over the passions. Adam has learned what it means actually to *be* human, and his point is that ordinary human experience is not as simple as Raphael implies it should be, that even in prelapsarian Paradise, it is not easy to determine when the senses and passions are affecting reason and when they are not.

The turn that the discussion takes immediately after Raphael's rebuke of Adam helps to explain why the angel cannot fully comprehend Adam's very human difficulties in distinguishing between what his reason and what his senses tell him. Through the course of the poem there have been several suggestions, one of them rather sly, that Eve's particular attractiveness presents no great appeal to Raphael. The sly hint came at the angel's first entrance into Paradise, when the "undeckt" Eve was described as "Virtue-proof, no thought infirm / Alter'd her cheek" (V, 384–85); this description occurs just thirteen lines after Raphael himself has been called by the narrator an "Angelic Virtue" (V, 371). The phrase "Virtue-proof" on its primary level undoubtedly means that, as Merritt Y. Hughes says in his note to the line, Eve is proof against evil by her virtue; but there remains also the implication that Eve has little to fear from the "Angelic Virtue," Raphael, either because he is not interested in her nakedness or because she on her part does not feel much attraction towards him. Both of these possibilities prove subsequently to be true: as we have seen, Eve prefers to receive her information from Adam's lips rather than the angel's; and at the moment early in Book VIII when Eve wanders off to tend her garden and the narrator twice remarks that Eve had grace and beauty enough "that won who saw to wish her stay" (VIII, 43; see also 63), both Raphael and Adam fail either to notice that she is leaving or to beg her (as the narrator implies he at least would) to stay on with them as they talk. Raphael's deprecatory reference to Eve's fair "outside" and to that "sense of touch whereby mankind / Is propagated" here at the end of Book VIII merely makes more explicit an attitude of his which has only been suggested thus far. Raphael's rebuke betrays little appreciation of Eve's physical being and of human sexuality; and Adam responds with two final questions for his teacher which, given Adam's own feelings on those subjects, follow quite logically upon that rebuke: do angels love, and if so, how?

Raphael's answer is illuminating in several different ways:

> Let it suffice thee that thou know'st
> Us happy, and without Love no happiness.
> Whatever pure thou in the body enjoy'st
> (And pure thou wert created) we enjoy
> In eminence, and obstacle find none
> Of membrane, joint, or limb, exclusive bars:
> Easier than Air with Air, if Spirits embrace,
> Total they mix, Union of Pure with Pure
> Desiring; nor restrain'd conveyance need
> As Flesh to mix with Flesh, or Soul with Soul.   (VIII, 620–29)

The tone of these lines may well be difficult to grasp at first; it looks as if Raphael may be embarrassed or annoyed by the question, especially so since the answer is accompanied by "a smile that glow'd / Celestial rosy red" (VIII, 618–19). But, tempting as it may be to interpret that blush as a token of Raphael's embarrassment (or even repressed adult society's embarrassment at childhood's innocent and unrestricted interest and delight in sexuality), the narrator refers to the blush or glow as "Love's proper hue" (VIII, 619). Presumably then, the glow results from some fitting warmth or enthusiasm rather than shame, and Raphael is to be seen as basically pleased (though not without some hauteur) with the opportunity to talk about angelic love. The answer itself is, first of all, part of Milton's own overall emphasis on love in the poem: that even angels have some way of uniting to express their love, and a way that plainly has been modeled on human sexual embraces, reflects upon the goodness and propriety of sexual union for humans as well. But, at the very moment that Milton is having Raphael assert a type of similarity between angels and humans, that very similarity heightens or highlights the differences that remain between the two types of beings. Raphael's description of angelic love implies a nature for angels which is simpler than man's, because more uniform; angels can express their love through total union without having to rely upon or be distracted by limbs, flesh, or that sense of touch which Raphael spoke of so harshly. It is because Adam, even as an unfallen human being, has senses and a tangible, physical body that love presents more difficulties and dangers for him than for an unfallen angel. Because Raphael has no fleshly body, it is considerably easier for him to make that sharp distinction he insists upon between love that has its seat in reason and *carnal* pleasure. And the difficulty unfallen Adam experiences, both in distinguishing between what reason and what his senses and passion tell him and in trying to vindicate himself to Raphael, arises directly from his having been created by God as human, as a being of both spirit and flesh, with reason, passions, and a sense of touch.

Raphael had been sent by God to Adam to "advise him of his happy state" (V, 234) and to warn him of his danger; the angel's stay in Eden might have proved to be an education for him as well as Adam, had he been able to comprehend fully what Adam was trying to tell him in their discussion. But if Raphael has proved unable, in part simply because he is an angel, to grasp completely what Adam has to say about his human nature and the importance of Eve to him, we do not necessarily share the angel's point of view. If anything, we are by this point in the poem more likely to appreciate and hearken to Adam's words than to Raphael's. And we are so, not simply because we are fallen human beings with a natural penchant for sin, or merely because we too as human beings have been subject to the same conflict between reason and the passions or senses Adam speaks of (though undoubtedly such causes do contribute to our response), but rather in large part because of all the previous emphasis Milton himself has given to the subject of prelapsarian sexual love, first in his decision to endow our first parents with that love and then in his strategy of having his narrator stress the importance of that gift through rhetorically heightened passages of enthusiasm over it. Our sympathy with Adam at this important point in the poem is a reaction that Milton has gone out of his way to cultivate.

IV

The stated purpose of *Paradise Lost* is to justify the ways of God to man, and that justification hinges completely on Milton's ability to convince us that man alone is responsible for his Fall from grace, and God not at all so. Insofar as Milton's emphasis on prelapsarian sexual love brings us to appreciate Adam's reasons for accepting the fruit from Eve, it may well bring us also to object to the conditions God set upon Adam's life as unfair, and this whole emphasis on prelapsarian sexual love could easily work counter to Milton's overall purpose in the poem. Further, for Milton to choose the minority position of providing Adam and Eve with prelapsarian sexual love, and to insist upon that love as good, important, and the crown of Adam and Eve's prelapsarian bliss, and then to condemn Adam for succumbing to what in effect is the poet's own emphasis in the poem might also appear as patently unfair on the part of Milton, as well as his God. While I have assumed throughout the preceding discussion that the emphasis on prelapsarian sexual love in *Paradise Lost* is a consciously controlled and intended part of the poem's total meaning, the possibility does still exist that, as Waldock claimed, Milton was not at all times in full control of his material,[23] that this particular emphasis represents a personal and isolated interest that Milton could not resist indulging in to the point that it interfered with the meaning and intent of the poem as a whole. What militates against such a critical position is that the emphasis on prelapsarian sexual love does not necessarily bring us to condone Adam's decision to fall, as much as it brings us simply to see his decision at the point of his fall as complex and difficult. And insofar as this emphasis does that, it is in accord with a great deal else in the poem which points to the relatively complicated and difficult conditions of Adam and Eve's whole prelapsarian existence.

Criticism of *Paradise Lost* has, it appears, finally begun to free itself from preconceived notions of what Milton's Paradise ought to be like, notions derived not simply from other works in the hexameral tradition but of course also from that recurrent collective dream or mythic vision of a happy, carefree, womblike place from which we have all been expelled and to which we should like to return. That Milton was in Books IV–VIII portraying something other than a carefree, effortless existence has been recognized since the 1930s, though at first this recognition was itself clouded by the notion that Milton imposed fallen qualities upon prelapsarian Adam and Eve, and their life in Eden, to make the Fall itself dramatically acceptable and understandable.[24] The newer view of Milton's Paradise sees Adam and Eve's life there as encompassing growth and change and capable of allowing for complexity, difficulty, and even error in still specifically unfallen conditions. Since Ruth Mohl's 1949 study of the different possible meanings of and implications in the term "perfection" as used by Milton and theologians before him, a number of critics have been insisting that Adam and Eve's prelapsarian perfection was only relative and that their life in Eden was by no means static and easy, but rather involved a good deal of moral activity, educative growth or progress, and what borders upon good old-fashioned hard work.[25] It is with studies such as these, ironically perhaps, that a focus on the crown of Adam and Eve's prelapsarian bliss belongs. The sexual love that Milton granted our first parents in Eden, in fact, can even be seen as the culmination of all their prelapsarian difficulties as well as of their joys. For nowhere, as both the discussion on love in Book VIII and Adam's subsequent decision to accept the fruit tell us, is control in Paradise more necessary, important, or difficult for Adam (who is after all the most important human character in the poem) than over those passions which arise as a result of his love, and specifically his sexual love, of Eve.

Barbara Kiefer Lewalski, at the conclusion of her fine study of Adam and Eve's prelapsarian education through trial and error, observes that Milton undertook with his picture of a difficult Eden not only or even primarily to foreshadow the Fall but to redefine the terms of life in innocence.[26] Milton certainly has succeeded, as Lewalski suggests, in presenting a highly unusual and even unique picture of prelapsarian life, but I think we can say that his aim and achievement extended beyond that also. For, by making Adam's most important and notable difficulty arise out of a tension to which he as a human being is subject and Raphael as an angel is not, Milton is evidently concerned not merely with describing man in his unfallen state, but with distinguishing man from other types of beings, in this case angelic ones.[27] Milton is engaged, then, in defining man, in stating what it means to be human; and (as the narrator's and our own response to Eve's beauty might quickly suggest to us) the definition necessarily applies not simply to unfallen man but to man after the Fall as well. The whole emphasis on a difficult Eden and the insistence on the importance of prelapsarian sexual love which is an integral part of that emphasis in fact tend to undermine any hard and fast distinction one might seek to make between pre- and postlapsarian life; rather, such emphases point instead to the fact that in many respects, Milton's Eden is not qualitatively different from our postlapsarian existence.

This is not to say, however, that there are no differences at all between pre- and postlapsarian life in Milton's poem. Adam and Eve live in a harmony with the natural world around them—the flowers at Eve's approach "sprung / And toucht by her fair tendance gladlier grew" (VIII, 46–47)—a harmony we have since lost and can lay claim to only through the assertive fiction of pathetic fallacy. And in describing Paradise and Adam and Eve's life there, Milton has developed, as several critics have demonstrated, a type of "paradisal language," the effect of which is to remind us of the difference between our present life and conditions before the Fall.[28] The stream that runs through Paradise can be described, for example, as rolling "With mazy error under pendant shades" (IV, 239), and we understand that "error" in this instance carries only its original Latin force of "wandering at random" without its customary modern suggestion of a mistake or trespass. The word in fact means not even simply "wandering" but, as Christopher Ricks puts it, "wandering (not error)."[29] Since the stream never misleads man or contributes to his Fall in either the Genesis account or *Paradise Lost*, we must consciously exclude the tainted or "fallen" meaning of "error" from the context here. Milton plays in similar manner on a word like "wanton" when he uses it first with its usual suggestion of lasciviousness to describe the action of worshipers of the fallen angels (I, 414, 454) and then in a pure or innocent sense to describe Eve's disheveled hair (IV, 306) or the growth of the garden (V, 295). Every time we have to stop to distinguish which of several meanings or suggestions applies to the action in prelapsarian Eden and which must be excluded, we are being forced to acknowledge that there has, after all, been a change from an existence in which a word like "error" or "wanton" might have no pejorative connotations, to our own existence in which such words are inevitably associated with mistakes, transgression, and sin.

Milton's Paradise, then, is both like our present life and not like it, and the advantage of Milton's having portrayed it in such a way is that he can enforce upon our consciousness that there was a Fall which was important and disastrous for all mankind, and at the same time use the Edenic portions of his poem, not to indulge in dreams of what might have been or even to point to the wretchedness of man's present life by contrasting it with a better time, but to teach us about our present existence and by very direct means. When he does this last, Milton is treating his Paradise, if the anachronism will be allowed me, as a version of Empsonian pastoral: he is "putting the complex into the simple,"[30] presenting our complex life in small without establishing a qualitative difference between our present life and the simplified image epitomizing it. We may not wish to conclude as darkly as Empson does, that Milton wishes by this method to convey the idea that "the human creature is essentially out of place in the world and needed no fall in time to make him so."[31] Milton, wayfaring and warfaring Christian that he was, might well have exulted in the prospect of a human life that from the very beginning demanded control, concentration, and full moral engagement: such demands, like Edenic work, can be viewed as tokens of man's dignity rather than his misery. But Milton's choosing to portray a difficult Eden does mean that a statement such as Dr. Johnson's that since *Paradise Lost* "admits no human manners till the Fall, it can give little assistance to human conduct" is certainly wide of the mark.[32] On the contrary, that part of the poem dealing with Adam and Eve's life in Paradise, as Milton conceived it, is directly relevant to our present experience, and the education that Adam goes through in Books IV through VIII is our education as well as his. For what Adam learns, and what he learns most of all when his greatest prelapsarian blessing becomes his greatest source of worry and concern, is simply the particular joys, problems, and difficulties he experiences as a result of having been created specifically as a *human* being. The Edenic portions of *Paradise Lost* plainly need no apology, and the poem as a whole no special pleading, as it stands finally not simply as a justification of God's ways but also as a thoroughgoing statement of the human condition. And it is as a statement of what it means to be human that Milton's thoroughly Christian epic can continue to speak directly and forcefully to readers who themselves may no longer actively believe in the myth of the Fall and in the Christian doctrine that Milton chose to elucidate. The poem need not, then, presume upon, or be limited by, its audience's adherence to that Christian doctrine for its effectiveness.

Indiana University

NOTES

1. Defoe was evidently assuming that an act of intercourse in Paradise or any-where else is undertaken primarily for procreation and not simply as an expression of love, a perhaps conservative but by no means uncommon or unreasonable assumption. The Catholic church, with its preference for virginity and celibacy over the married state, tended since the time of Augustine to view marital intercourse in a fallen world as unsinful or excusable only if directed toward its natural end of pro-creation. The Church of England's *Book of Common Prayer* listed the three causes for which marriage was ordained as (1) the procreation of children, (2) a remedy against sin, and to avoid fornication, and (3) the mutual society, help, and comfort that one ought to have of the other; among Anglican writers and preachers of the sixteenth and seventeenth centuries, and among many of the more radical English Protestants as well, the most important of these ends was understood to be procreation. While Puritan preachers in the seventeenth century were to give greater and greater em-phasis in their discussions on marriage to the end listed third in the prayer book and thus to suggest that mutual help or companionship was the most important of the three ends, there was to be little writing before or even after Milton explicitly extol-ling the sexual act merely as an expression of love.

2. See, for instance, the Babylonian Talmud, *Sanhedrin*, 38b: "in the eighth [hour], they ascended to bed as two and descended as four" (*Sanhedrin*, trans. Jacob Shachter and H. Freeman [London, 1935], I, 242). The *Pir̄kê de Rabbi Eliezer* uses the same formula to refer to the intercourse of Adam and Eve but has that sexual union occur in the ninth hour of their first day. Most, but not all, Jewish sources assumed there was sexual consummation before the Fall: the *Midrash Rabbah*, the great com-pilation of rabbinic exegesis through the fifth century, has several passages revealing such an assumption (*Bereshith Rabbah*, chap. 18, par. 6; chap. 19, par. 3); and the eleventh-century commentator Rashi, with whose work Milton was probably familiar either directly or through the Hebrew lexicons of his day, argues that the tense of the verb—perfect having the force of pluperfect—in Genesis iv, 1 ("And the man *knew* his wife") shows that the conception of Cain took place before the expulsion from Eden narrated at the end of chapter iii (see *Pentateuch with . . . Rashi's Commentary*, trans. M. Rosenbaum and A. M. Silberman [New York, 1934], I, 17). The *Zohar*, however, suggests that Adam did not beget any offspring until he had sinned (60b–61a), and the *'Aboth D' Rabbi Nathan*, while presenting a timetable of man's first day similar to that provided in the *Sanhedrin* and *PRE*, gives no specific indication of intercourse having taken place before the Fall (17b).

3. For a summary of the passages of Cats' *Trou-ringh* ("The Marriage Ring")

relevant to *Paradise Lost* and a discussion of the possible connections between the two poets, see Geoffrey Bullough, "Milton and Cats," *Essays in English Literature . . . Presented to A. S. P. Woodhouse,* ed. Millar MacLure and F. W. Watts (Toronto, 1964), pp. 103–24.

4. For English translations of Grotius' Latin play and Vondel's Dutch adaptation, see Watson Kirkconnell, *The Celestial Cycle* (Toronto, 1952), pp. 96–220 and 434–79. Also worthy of notice in this context is Gervase Babington's comment on Genesis iv, 1 in his *Certaine Plaine, Briefe and Comfortable Notes upon Everie Chapter of Genesis* (London, 1592), fols. [22ᵛ]–[23ʳ] (misnumbered as 23ᵛ–22ʳ). The strongly Protestant Babington was anxious to prove that godly marriage was in every way holy and hence its physical consummation proper and fitting for Adam and Eve even in Paradise. He thus opposes those "wicked spirites" who have "snatched at" the observation that the first mention of intercourse between Adam and Eve occurs only after the account of the expulsion from Eden "and thereby sought to blemish godly marriage, saying it was then used, when paradise was lost and not before." Babington points out, using an example from 1 Samuel as evidence, that it was quite common for the Holy Spirit "to speake of that last which was done first, and of that before that was done after." And "so it may be heere very well, that Adam knew her before, although now spoken of, and not before, and so the Act of Mariage nothing impeached by this order of wordes." Babington would plainly have liked to have been able to assert that there was sexual intercourse before the Fall and is close to taking such a stand, but unfortunately his own (as it happens, mistaken) translation of Genesis iv, 1 as "*Afterward* Adam knew his wife" (emphasis added) would not allow him to do so.

5. Milton may well have read some or even all of the imaginative works and commentaries which granted Adam and Eve sexual union before the Fall, but none of them is likely to have been directly responsible for his taking the stand he did in *Paradise Lost.* Of them, only Cats' *Trou-ringh* gives anything like the emphasis Milton does to the first marriage and its physical consummation. If we wish to find the "source" for Milton's belief in and insistence upon prelapsarian sexual love, we are probably safest in looking no farther afield than the Puritan bias of Milton's own mind. For his stand on the very existence of prelapsarian sexual love can be seen as an extension of the definition of marriage generally that he put forward in his divorce tracts in the 1640s. In discussing Genesis ii, 18 in *The Doctrine and Discipline of Divorce,* Milton stated that "in Gods intention a meet and happy conversation is the chiefest and noblest end of marriage"; and later, in the *Tetrachordon,* he defined marriage as "*a divine institution joyning man and woman in a love fitly dispos'd to the helps and comforts of domestic life,*" there identifying the "final causes" of wedlock as "help and society in Religious, Civil, and Domestic conversation, which includes as an inferior end the fulfilling of natural desire, and specifical increase" (*Complete Prose Works,* ed. Don M. Wolfe et al. [New Haven, 1953–], II, 246, 612, 608). By relegating "increase" to the status of an "inferior end" and elevating the status of "conversation" (meaning companionship or society), Milton was, as John Halkett has recently pointed out, in effect making the marriage relationship itself the chief end or purpose of marriage and refusing to subordinate it to any further end or result, such as the procreation and rearing of children (see Halkett's *Milton and the Idea of Matrimony* [New Haven, 1970], p. 13). By not concerning himself, in *Paradise Lost,* with the question of how or when Cain was conceived, Milton was once again viewing the marriage relationship (and its sexual union which, in *Paradise Lost* if not in the *Tetrachordon,* epitomizes it) as a good or end in itself, capable of being discussed and considered in its own right without subordination to the further end of procreation.

6. Gregory and Milton could at least agree upon a literal rather than an allegorical interpretation of the opening chapters of Genesis; it might be argued that the allegorical reading of Philo Judaeus and Origen was further yet from Milton's stand, but it is difficult to consider together, even for purposes of contrast, writers who use such different terms. In the Platonic interpretation of Philo and Origen, Adam represented the mind or soul of man, and Eve, the senses. In this scheme, the very creation of Eve and recognition of her by Adam marked the beginning of man's Fall. With the Fall defined in this way, specifically prelapsarian sexual love would be an impossibility. See *De Opificio Mundi*, secs. xlvii–lix, in *Philo*, trans. F. H. Colson and G. H. Whitaker (New York, 1929), I, 106–33.

7. Gregory of Nyssa, "On the Making of Man," in *A Select Library of Nicene and Post-Nicene Fathers*, ed. Philip Schaff and Henry Wace, 2nd ser. (Grand Rapids, Michigan., n.d.), V, 407. Gregory's argument was based on Christ's statement recorded in Luke xx, 35–36 (and also Matthew xxii, 30), that at the resurrection from the dead, the resurrected will neither marry nor be given in marriage, will not be subject to death any more, and will be the *equal of the angels;* and the resurrection in Gregory's view, promised restoration of the fallen to their ancient unfallen state.

How removed Milton is from Gregory's view can be easily seen from the fact that Milton, like no writer before him, attributes to angels loving embraces markedly similar to human sexual embraces. When at the end of Book VIII Raphael describes how spirits embrace, he is talking about angelic love and not of angelic procreation, but the particular expression of love described there ("Total they mix, Union of Pure with Pure" etc. [626 ff.]) certainly reflects the human physical union that Gregory was so anxious to assert would not have been necessary for unfallen man. On Milton's originality in attributing embraces of affection to angels, see Robert H. West, *Milton and the Angels* (Athens, Georgia, 1955), p. 170.

8. Trans. Marcus Dods (New York, 1950), bk. XIV, chap. xxiii, p. 470. Augustine himself did not name Gregory of Nyssa explicity in chapter xxiii. Rather, it is from Aquinas and later commentators that we learn that Augustine's quarrel was specifically with Gregory (see *Summa Theologica*, I, §98, a. 2).

9. Augustine, *De Genesi ad Litteram*, bk. IX, chaps. iii–v, in *Patrologia Latina*, ed. J. P. Migne, XXXIV, cols. 395–96; Aquinas, *Summa Theologica*, I, §98, a. 2. In the view of St. Paul, of early Christian theologians generally, and of Milton, because Adam was created first and explicitly in God's own image, he (and all men after him) was closer to God and hence a more perfect being than Eve (and all women after her), created "occasionally" by God for man. While most Christian exegetes may not have gone as far as Milton in saying that Eve was created in Adam's image as opposed to God's, they still held to the belief that woman was inferior to man. Were it not for the need for procreation, the more perfect being would necessarily have been a more effective helper for Adam.

10. Bk. IX, chap. iv, cols. 395–96; *City of God*, bk. XIV, chap. xxvi, p. 475.

11. Aquinas, *Summa Theologica*, I, §98, a. 1–2; Lombard, *Sententiarum Libri Quatuor*, bk. II, chap. xx, in *Pat. Lat.*, CXCII, col. 692; Comestor, *Historia Scholastica: Genesis*, chaps. x, xxv, in *Pat. Lat.*, CXCVIII, cols. 1064, 1076; Pererius, *Commentariorum et Disputationum in Genesin* (Cologne, 1601), pp. 203, 227.

12. Martin Luther, *Works*, ed. Jaroslav Pelikan (St. Louis, 1958), I, 220, 237, 241; John Salkeld, *A Treatise of Paradise* (London, 1617), pp. 178–81.

13. There were many ways, several of them quite different from Augustine's, of arriving at this most common answer to the question of how long Adam and Eve

remained in Paradise, and later exegetes could always point to Augustine's argument as further evidence for their own conclusions. Christian as well as Hebrew commentators, for instance, looked to Psalm xlix for help in answering the question, and typological readings of the opening chapters of Genesis often assumed that since Christ was crucified at noon on the sixth day of the week, the ultimate cause of that act, Adam's fall, must have also occurred at noon on the sixth day, that is, the day of Adam and Eve's creation. For a summary of the various arguments used to prove Adam and Eve's stay in the garden was less than a day, see the sermon on Exodus xx, 11, of Milton's contemporary, John Lightfoot, *Works* (London, 1684), II, 1320–30.

14. Luther, *Works*, I, 135; John Calvin, *Commentaries on the First Book of Moses Called Genesis,* trans. John King (Edinburgh, 1847), I, 128–34.

15. *Christian Oeconomie,* trans. Thomas Pickering (London, 1609), p. 11.

16. *Du Bartas. His Divine Weekes and Workes,* trans. Joshuah Sylvester, Second Week, First Day, Part I, ll. 668–71, in *The Complete Works of Joshuah Sylvester,* ed. Alexander B. Grosart (New York, 1967), I, 105. The epithalamium for Adam and Eve's marriage is at First Week, Sixth Day, ll. 1062–91, ibid., I, 81.

17. Second Week, First Day, Part I, ll. 386–89; *Complete Works of Joshuah Sylvester,* I, 102.

18. Quotations from *Paradise Lost* are from Merritt Y. Hughes' Odyssey Press edition of the poem in *John Milton: Complete Poems and Major Prose* (New York, 1957).

19. For another, less overt reflection of the debate, see Adam's speech in Book X, when he lashes out at Eve with an attack which recalls Augustine's argument that but for the purpose of procreation a male companion would have been better for Adam and expresses the wish that Gregory of Nyssa's conception of an angelic prelapsarian Adam and Eve had been correct after all:

> O why did God,
> Creator wise, that peopl'd highest Heav'n
> With Spirits Masculine, create at last
> This novelty on Earth, this fair defect
> Of Nature, and not fill the World at once
> With Men as Angels without Feminine,
> Or find some other way to generate
> Mankind? (X, 888–95)

20. Sister Mary Irma Corcoran, *Milton's Paradise with Reference to the Hexameral Background* (Washington, D.C., 1945), p. 74; Arnold Williams, *The Common Expositor* (Chapel Hill, N.C., 1948), p. 88.

21. That Milton should reduce the dramatic impact of this scene does not mean that Adam has already fallen, that he is, as one group of critics would have it, "fallen before the Fall" (see n. 24, below); for it is precisely the mistake of looking upon his decision as already made, of *refusing* to engage himself fully in his decision, that is the failure of will which constitutes Adam's fall.

22. A. J. A. Waldock, *"Paradise Lost" and Its Critics* (Cambridge, Eng., 1947), pp. 43–44. Waldock was assuming, however, that Raphael was "obviously Milton's spokesman" (p. 42) in his answer to and rebuke of Adam.

23. Waldock, *"Paradise Lost" and Its Critics,* pp. 21, 25, 49–51.

24. See Basil Willey, *The Seventeenth Century Background* (London, 1934), p. 255; Waldock, *"Paradise Lost" and Its Critics,* p. 61; and E. M. W. Tillyard, *Studies in*

Milton (London, 1951), pp. 8–13. All three of these critics had Milton attribute fallen qualities to the unfallen Adam and Eve primarily for artistic reasons: Eve's fascination with her own reflection, her dream of Books IV and V, and Adam's confession in Book VIII that he is subject to passion are all viewed simply as anticipations of the Fall, designed only to make the Fall itself humanly convincing and dramatically plausible. Millicent Bell, in "The Fallacy of the Fall in *Paradise Lost*," *PMLA*, LXVIII (1953), 863–83, carried this reading to its logical conclusion and recognized that to consider Adam and Eve as fallen before the Fall was to make God, ultimately, responsible for the Fall, an implication she was willing to accept. She would have Milton giving the unfallen Adam and Eve fallen characteristics, then, as part of his belief that the Fall was a necessary and good act, the means whereby mankind could gain the requisite self-consciousness to direct itself toward redemption and the only Paradises Milton thought relevant to man in his present condition, each Christian's "paradise within" (XII, 587) and that "far happier place" into which Christ will welcome his elect at the world's dissolution (XII, 464). The poem becomes in this reading a divine comedy in which there is no real Fall and no meaningful Paradise lost but only one to be gained in the future.

25. See Ruth Mohl, "Milton and the Idea of Perfection," in *Studies in Spenser, Milton, and the Theory of Monarchy* (1949; reprint ed., New York, 1962), pp. 94–132; H. V. S. Ogden, "The Crisis of *Paradise Lost* Reconsidered," *PQ*, XXXVI (1957), 1–19; J. M. Evans, *"Paradise Lost" and the Genesis Tradition* (Oxford, 1968), pp. 242–71; Barbara Kiefer Lewalski, "Innocence and Experience in Milton's Eden," in *New Essays on "Paradise Lost,"* ed. Thomas Kranidas (Berkeley and Los Angeles, 1969), pp. 86–117; John S. Diekhoff, "Eve's Dream and the Paradox of Fallible Perfection," *Milton Quarterly*, IV (1970), 5–7; and Thomas H. Blackburn, " 'Uncloister'd Virtue': Adam and Eve in Milton's Paradise," *Milton Studies*, III, ed., James D. Simmonds (Pittsburgh, 1971) pp. 119–37. The studies focusing most thoroughly and convincingly on Eden's difficulties are those of Evans and Lewalski: Evans concentrates on the amount of physical labor our first parents had to perform to keep Milton's particularly exuberant garden under control; and Lewalski, on the pattern of trial and error by which Adam and Eve go about gradually improving themselves.

26. Lewalski, "Innocence and Experience," p. 116.

27. An angel's existence in Milton's poem is, admittedly, not necessarily easy either. Milton's angels are frequently sent off on useless errands, the logic of which they are not to question since the tasks are merely tests of their obedience. But because of the more complex nature of man's makeup, because man has both a spirit and a sense of touch, and the latter likely to confuse him even in his unfallen state, his very existence, in which his greatest blessing also constitutes his greatest problem, is seen as considerably more difficult than that of an unfallen angel like Raphael.

28. See Arnold Stein, *Answerable Style* (Minneapolis, 1953), pp. 66–67; Anne Davidson Ferry, *Milton's Epic Voice* (Cambridge, Mass., 1963), pp. 111–15; and especially Christopher Ricks, *Milton's Grand Style* (Oxford, 1963), pp. 109–17; and Stanley Eugene Fish, *Surprised by Sin* (New York, 1967), pp. 107–57.

29. Ricks, *Grand Style*, p. 110; see also Fish, *Surprised by Sin*, pp. 135–36.

30. William Empson, *Some Versions of Pastoral* (1935; reprint ed., New York, 1960), p. 23 and passim.

31. Ibid., p. 178.

32. Samuel Johnson, *Lives of the Poets*, ed. Arthur Waugh (New York, 1906), I, 126.